I0008897

The IDAR Method of Software Design

Mark A. Overton

The IDAR Method of Software Design
by Mark A. Overton

Copyright © 2014 Mark A. Overton.
All rights reserved.
Printed in the USA.

This book was set in Canberra FY and Linux Biolinum O using the LaTeX typesetting system, and was published by:

Mark A. Overton
1026 W. El Norte Pkwy #56
Escondido, CA 92026

Many of the designations used by manufacturers and sellers to distinguish their products are claimed as trademarks. Where those designations appear in this book, and the author was aware of a trademark claim, the designations have been printed in caps or initial caps.

While every precaution has been taken in the preparation of this book, the publisher and author assume no responsibility for errors or omissions, or for damages resulting from the use of the information contained in this book.

Artwork by David Wagner.

For more information, please visit http://idarmethod.com

Version: 430401

ISBN: 978-1496146144

Contents

All great truths begin as blasphemies.

— George Bernard Shaw

IDAR Quick-Reference

I   **Identify** each public method in an object
as either a command or a notice.
From its caller's viewpoint, a notice only
imports or exports needed information.

D   When graphing the calls to commands
among objects, the arrows must point **down**.
In this graph, an arrow connecting two boxes
means that code in the upper object (box)
calls one or more commands in the lower object.

A   A command or notice may, unknown to its callers,
aid its own object by performing part or all
of a previously commanded action.

R   Write a brief **role** for each object and
method that summarizes all services
it offers, avoiding any aspect of its
implementation (including aid). Callers
may rely on only what is stated in roles.

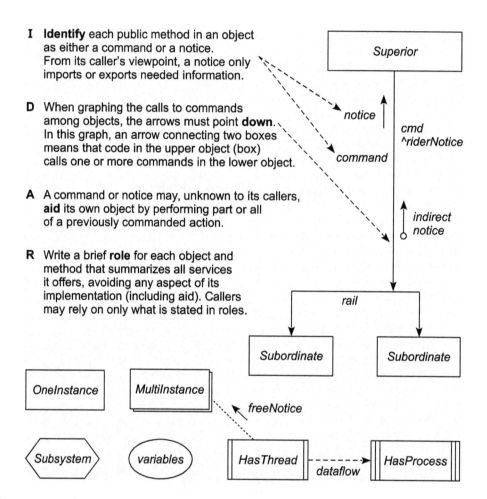

The Five-Step Design Process

1. Define the obvious objects at the top and bottom of the hierarchy.
2. Define the unobvious in-between objects using top-down, bottom-up, and white-box techniques.
3. Verify correctness of the design and its conformance to the four rules.
4. Improve and simplify the design (most designs are overcomplex).
5. Iterate until the design cannot be improved.

Part I

The IDAR Method:
Theory and Practice

Chapter 1

Introduction

— why is hierarchy a new way of thinking?

1.1 A Strange Problem

To design means to plan a structure. Because software has structure, it should be designed. If a program will contain only a few routines, you can often get away with coding it on the monitor without first designing it. But when software becomes larger than that, you need to design its structure before coding it, otherwise your program will devolve into disorganization. For nontrivial programs, design is important. And it's equally important that we be able to understand those designs.

But the software world has a strange problem: *The design of any substantial program is difficult or impossible to understand.* This problem is strange because one would not expect a mature profession that is over six decades old to have such a fundamental failing. Looking back in time, we see that our designs have always been expressed in the form of graphs. Flowcharts were employed in the 1950s, followed by call-graphs in the 1970s and 1980s, followed by several kinds of object-oriented graphs published in the years around 1990. Those were merged together, forming the Unified Modeling Language (UML) [27], which became the standard representation of designs. Sadly, UML diagrams fail to convey how software is intended to operate because UML is incompatible with how people understand organizations.

I'll verify these statements with some examples in the following sections, but first I'd like to mention the consequences of this problem of inscrutable designs. The worst consequence is that software tends to slide into messiness. Once a design has reached a certain size, the human mind is unable to fully understand it when expressed in UML, so its growth continues half blindly, resulting in disorganization, creating bugs and lengthening schedules. Designing in UML is better than coding on the monitor because you are forced to plan ahead, and you can see the interactions of objects. But our inability to understand the operation of a substantial design in UML means that most software is doomed to messiness, raising its cost and reducing its quality.

I am appalled at the situation we are in:

> *We have no effective way to portray how software operates!*

1.2   A Bold Claim

Let's make a bold claim about how a design is represented: *If a program is represented using an IDAR graph, you can quickly learn how it operates. But if it is represented using UML, it is difficult or impossible to discern how it operates.*

If you are designing new software that's too complex to hold in your mind, or are trying to learn the design of existing software, then the IDAR method will give you a great advantage—if this bold claim is true. We can verify this claim by comparing the same design represented both ways. To do so, it is necessary to provide you with synopses of both UML and IDAR graphs below.

Synopsis of UML Diagrams   UML defines several kinds of structural diagrams, but in the common ones, boxes denote classes or objects, and lines represent their associations or interactions, which are often method-calls. A line with no arrowheads indicates that both objects know about each other; an arrowhead means that only one object knows about the other. Decorations on lines indicate types of associations, but these are minor enhancements. At this point, you will understand the notations in the UML diagram in Figure 1.1 portraying an astrology application.

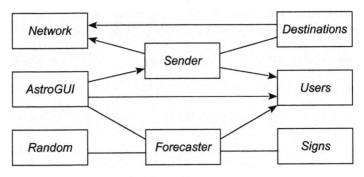

Figure 1.1: UML diagram of an astrology application

Synopsis of IDAR Graphs   Boxes denote objects, and they are always arranged like a corporate organizational chart, forming a command hierarchy. Command-lines with arrowheads connect superiors to subordinates. Short floating arrows are "notices" representing additional (noncommand) communications among objects. Commands and notices between objects are actually calls to methods in the destination-objects, and may be labeled with method-names by their arrows.

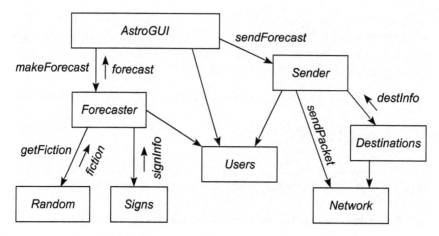

Figure 1.2: IDAR graph of the same astrology application

Figure 1.2 is the IDAR graph of the same design as in Figure 1.1, and each line in one graph corresponds to a line in the other. You can compare the two and decide for yourself which graph effectively communicates how this software operates.

In this IDAR graph, it's obvious that *AstroGUI* is the topmost controller object that commands *Forecaster* to *makeForecast* (a method-call), which in turn commands *Random* to *getFiction*, which returns its fiction in the *fiction* notice. Then *Forecaster* gives a forecast to *AstroGUI* via the *forecast* notice. *AstroGUI* also commands *Sender* to *sendForecast*, which in turn commands *Network* to *sendPacket*. It's obvious which objects are bottom-level specialized workers, and it's clear that *Forecaster* and *Sender* are middle managers. In an IDAR graph, the subordinates of a superior are its helpers, revealing how the superior's broader role was partitioned into the narrower roles of its subordinates, providing further insight into both how the superior operates and how the subordinates are used. Looking at this IDAR graph for less than a minute teaches you much about each object and how the design operates as a whole.

The UML diagram shows you none of these things. UML lacks the concepts of helping and subordinates, so it can be difficult or impossible to determine which of two interacting objects is helping the other. The UML diagram conceals how this program will operate because it conceals the underlying hierarchy. To understand how software operates, we human beings need to see a command hierarchy. That is an unchangeable part of human psychology (explored more on page 230), and is the reason that IDAR graphs communicate effectively and UML doesn't.

1.3   Naturally Messy

The absence of a command hierarchy is bad enough, but today's situation is even worse than that. UML allows any object in the program to interact with any other object in any way a developer desires. This absence of constraints on interactions among objects causes designs to become disorganized. A design in UML might start clean enough, as in Figure 1.3(a). But it's incomplete, and by the time all required objects have been defined and their interactions are drawn, the design resembles the spaghetti in Figure 1.3(b). Spaghetti is incomprehensible to humans, creating bugs. As an aside, this is a fragment of an actual design which has been fielded.

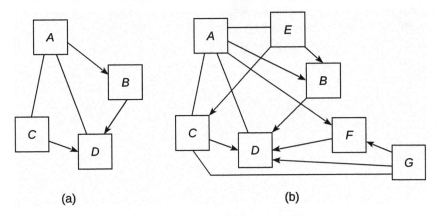

(a)   (b)

Figure 1.3: Evolution of spaghetti

The IDAR method imposes four rules on a design, which compose a system of reasonable constraints. The result is expressed as an IDAR graph. Such designs solve the problems described above as follows:

1. The four rules force objects to be organized as a command hierarchy, preventing designs from sliding into messiness. Fortunately, the rules don't excessively restrict communications and interactions among objects.

2. IDAR graphs reveal all interactions among objects, but you see them in the context of the surrounding hierarchy, giving you both a detailed view and a broad view concurrently, revealing how the software operates.

The IDAR method is more than a better way to design software. The repercussions of this method run deep, resulting in improvements to the principles and foundations of design, making designing easier, cleaner, and even enjoyable. Let's look at the root problem and its solution in more detail.

1.4 Hierarchy Discovered

The subroutine was invented back in the early 1950s, and represents one of the most important contributions to computer science. Edsger Dijkstra, a pioneer of computer science, had this to say about them:

> We should recognize the closed subroutine as one of the greatest
> software inventions. [6]

The power of the subroutine lay in the fact that one could create an operation using more detailed operations, which were usually statements in the programming language. But a subroutine could also call other subroutines, and thus build up an operation in multiple levels, forming operations having great capability.

Levels of Abstraction   Later, theoreticians in computer science realized that such a multilevel hierarchy of subroutines constitutes a hierarchy of abstractions, where a given level of abstraction is an operation (i.e., action or capability) assembled by operations that are more specialized. These levels of abstraction could be illustrated in a subroutine call-graph such as shown in Figure 1.4.

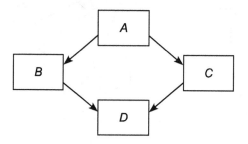

Figure 1.4: Call-graph of subroutines

Each rectangle is a subroutine, and subroutine calls proceed downward along the arrows. It's clear that subroutine *A*, for example, utilizes the services of subroutines *B* and *C*, and thus implements its level of abstraction with the assistance of the abstractions provided by the lower levels of *B* and *C*. In fact, subroutines not only permitted the use of abstractions, they almost required it. The subroutine, by its very nature, implements a higher level of abstraction than the operations it invokes. Recursion was rare enough that call-graphs proceeded only downward, forming a hierarchy of abstractions. These hierarchies of abstractions created and enforced by subroutine calls held sway for about four decades. "Procedure" is a synonym of "subroutine", so this style of design became known as "procedural design".

1.5   Hierarchy Lost

A well-designed object can do much more than a subroutine because it consists of multiple closely related subroutines (now called "methods") and data shared among them. Therefore, object-oriented programming (OOP) rapidly took over in the 1990s, supplanting designs based on subroutines. Unfortunately, something was lost in the revolution.

The UML diagram in Figure 1.5 portrays associations (method calls) among objects in a microwave oven. In UML, a method in an object may call any public method in any other accessible object, resulting in a network instead of a hierarchy. In their book, *Object Design*, Wirfs-Brock and McKean state that:

> *Object-oriented design is fundamentally different from procedural design.*
> *Objects are structured in a network and not a hierarchy.* [34]

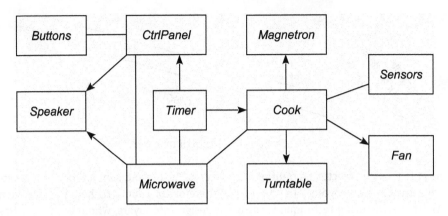

Figure 1.5: UML diagram of a microwave oven

Look again at Figures 1.1 and 1.5. They are clearly networks. But they portray no levels, and therefore do not represent hierarchies. The graphs are flat in the sense that no object appears to have greater capability or responsibility than any other. This is the great problem with today's OOP: Because all objects are equal, we are no longer compelled or even encouraged to create levels of abstraction.

However, it is certainly possible to create levels of abstraction with your objects. You can force yourself to arrange them into a hierarchy, and diagram it somehow. None of the UML diagrams can portray such levels because object-oriented design (surprisingly) does not possess the concept of levels of abstraction among objects. So UML will not help you. When it comes to designing a hierarchy of abstractions, today's state of the object-oriented art leaves you on your own.

In addition, the widely taught feature of inheritance cannot create a widely useful kind of hierarchy. It creates a hierarchy of categories because derived classes are required to be subcategories of their base classes. This same-category constraint means that the *Schedule* and *Valves* classes in a sprinkler timer, for example, cannot have a common base class, because they are unrelated. We want both of these classes to be under the *Executive* class, but inheritance forbids this unless we abuse it. Inheritance expresses "is-a-kind-of" relationships, and it's not true that a schedule is a kind of executive, or that a valve is a kind of executive. Thus, inheritance is of limited use. Section 6.6 (page 142) discusses this topic in more detail.

With no effective way to organize objects, many object-oriented designs end up resembling spaghetti. I have worked with much object-oriented code, and too much of it was a labyrinthine mess. The designers had no guiding principles on how to organize all that material. If we back up and look at this situation from a bird's-eye viewpoint, we see that today's OOP provides structure only at the bottom levels of software, leaving a chasm above that, as shown in Figure 1.6.

The lowest levels consist of statements in the programming language, methods (i.e., subroutines), and objects. And then a designer wanders around inside the chasm, groping for objects, until finally finishing the system.

UML provides a notation for the well known concept of subsystems, albeit with

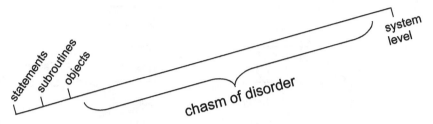

Figure 1.6: The chasm of disorder

no guidance for structuring multiple subsystems. As a result, subsystems form a network structure analogously to objects, and therefore provide little help to a designer. Another structuring technique is to slice a design into layers, where each layer has clearly defined responsibilities. Unfortunately, while this approach is well suited for operating systems and networking protocols, it is not broadly applicable elsewhere. (As an aside, refer to the Layer pattern in Section 7.1.4 on page 185.)

In practice, designers cross the chasm by defining some objects, and then half blindly defining some more objects, connecting them together with messages as seems appropriate, and repeating until the wide chasm has finally been bridged. The resulting "network structure" is often more accurately termed a "messy structure".

The core problem is that designers are given no guidance as to how to structure interactions and relationships among objects, so most of them do the best they can based on intuition, creating a tangle instead of a clean organization. Such disorder is difficult to implement and debug, causing delays and reducing quality.

I observe that many developers spend most of their time debugging their jumbled code. If you are a developer, think about what you spend most of your time doing. You probably spend an insignificant fraction of your time designing, a small fraction coding, and the bulk of your time goes into debugging. Improving the organization of code will shorten the longest bar in our schedules—debugging.

1.6   Hierarchy Restored

I was designing some software at home during a weekend in early April, 2013, and I remember deciding to have one object command another. Suddenly I stopped and excitedly said to myself, "What have I just done!?" I realized that I had designated some (but not all) methods as commands. The commands created ranks or levels among my objects, and the other noncommand methods (notices) could be used to convey information. I had created a hierarchy of abstractions implemented as a command hierarchy, and yet had retained the additional flexibility that OOP provides above a pure subroutine-based approach. I immediately realized that this was a significant discovery. It appears that nobody else has thought to divide methods into commands and notices like this. It was then that I realized that today's OOP lacks hierarchy, despite claims to the contrary. At that time, I only knew that the hierarchy created by command-methods cleaned up the messiness caused by today's OOP, yet without constraining designs unnecessarily. It was during a few months of much thought and experimenting with many trial designs that I came to understand the full impact and implications of this simple discovery. Formulating and refining the IDAR rules consumed yet more thought, effort, trials, and months.

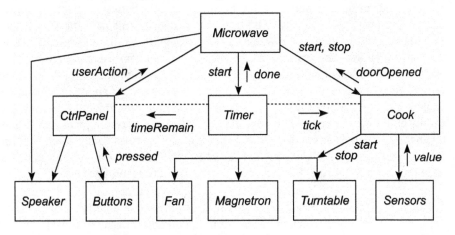

Figure 1.7: IDAR graph of a microwave oven

Figure 1.7 is the IDAR graph of a microwave oven, which is more complex than the astrology app. It must be noted that a dashed line with a floating arrow by it denotes a notice passed between two objects, neither of which commands the other. This example is the same design as the UML diagram in Figure 1.5, but now the levels of control are obvious. For example, it's clear that *Microwave* is the main controller object. The UML diagram concealed this important fact. You will correctly surmise that when *Sensors* tells *Cook* that the door is open, *Cook* will quickly command its subordinates to *stop*, and will send a *doorOpened* notice to *Microwave*, its boss, which will handle the consequences. None of this is apparent in the UML diagram.

The consequences of using such an object hierarchy are surprisingly extensive. Using a hierarchy based on commands and notices causes the fundamental thinking behind object-oriented design to change. Perhaps the biggest surprise is the number of benefits this method yields:

- Unlike a network structure, people easily understand a command hierarchy.
- Designs are nearly forced to use levels of abstraction, eliminating the usual disorganization in today's OOP, thus reducing bugginess.
- IDAR graphs are more informative than UML diagrams, making designs easier to remember and learn, helping both developers and maintainers.
- Subsystems can be defined naturally and easily under a hierarchy.
- Design becomes easier.

Design becomes easier because, compared with designing a network of objects, you can easily identify the top-level and bottom-level objects in a hierarchy and then define the missing objects between them. The top and bottom levels give you anchors and starting-points to work with.

1.7   Why "IDAR"?

Back in April, 2013, I only knew that I should *identify* the public methods in each class as commands or notices, and require that command-calls between objects be drawn pointing *down*. These are now a portion of the Identify rule, and the Down rule. Although these two rules did a wondrous job of cleaning up the messiness of OOP, they left loopholes. For example, a developer could make notices go anywhere and everywhere with no organization, turning the hierarchy into spaghetti. More rules were needed, but it was not obvious what rules would be strict enough to eliminate abuses and at the same time be lax enough to comfortably accommodate a great variety of designs. It required another ten months of brainstorming many ideas and testing them with a variety of designs before the missing rules finally emerged from the fog. They are the Aid and Role rules, and the need-to-know constraint which was added to the Identify rule. Here is a summary of the four resulting rules:

Identify	*Identify* every public method as a command or a notice. (A notice conveys information that an object needs to know.)
Down	Commands among objects must point *down* in the graph.
Aid	Public methods may covertly *aid* previously commanded actions.
Role	Every object and method has a *role* briefly describing its actions.

The acronym IDAR represents the words, "Identify, Down, Aid, Role", which are the four rules. The name IDAR thus serves as a mnemonic for these rules. For most developers, using commands, notices, and hierarchy in the form of IDAR graphs represents a new way of thinking about object-oriented design. It is different enough from present techniques that it justified the effort to write a book on the subject. So this is not yet another book on object-oriented design. Based on both trial designs and fielded designs, the new techniques described here produce designs that are cleaner, clearer, and simpler than the methods presently being taught.

1.8   The Third Foundation

A perspective of how the IDAR method fits into computer science will emphasize its importance. Computer science has the following three foundations:

Processor The first and lowest foundation is the processor (CPU). Developers must understand how it operates, starting with the concepts of memory, variables, sequential execution of instructions (and the corresponding statements in a high-level language), subroutines, and related topics.

Tools The second foundation consists of a wide variety of tools of the craft, such as the theory of computation, object-oriented programming, operating systems, algorithms and data-structures, programming languages, compilers, databases, graphics, networking, Internet, security, and more.

Organization Once developers have learned these two foundations, they are
ready to write code. Much code. A mass of code. It is here that we tumble into
the chasm of disorder. As mentioned earlier, the only ways to organize much
code are: (1) UML, which imposes no organization on a network structure, (2)
the concept of subsystems, which is too coarse, and (3) the suggestion to design
in layers, which is too restrictive. Lacking an effective discipline of organization,
the mass often becomes a mess.

This weak third foundation has been replaced with the IDAR method, which
is the only effective and broadly applicable way to organize a large quantity of
code, preventing the disorder seen in the chasm.

The fact that IDAR replaces the third foundation of computer science underscores
its great importance. The discussion of the chasm of disorder showed us the severity
of the problem of messiness arising from the weakness of the third foundation. IDAR
solves this severe problem, and solves it well, making it foundational.

1.9 The Goal

I am purely goal-driven. Unfortunately, that means I tend not to smell the flowers
along the way, focusing solely on what I'm trying to accomplish. Also, I am intensely
practical. I have a steel grip on what I call "practical reality". Corporations are like that.
At least the successful ones are. Therefore, this is their goal for software projects:

Fulfill the requirements in the
shortest possible schedule.

This book is written to help developers achieve that goal of fulfilling requirements
in the shortest schedule. This book cares nothing about traditions, the OOP-way, or
any other way. It is cold-blooded practical.

You might ask, "What about quality? That should also be factored in." The minimum level of quality should be specified in the requirements. A specification of level
of quality includes the number and level of annoyances, frequency and severity of
crashes, failure to meet real-time needs, security constraints, and any other areas of
interest to customers.

You might ask, "What about flexibility? We will be adding enhancements in the
future." This question falls under the topic of maintenance, and it also should be specified in the requirements. The requirements should anticipate likely enhancements
needed in the future. Beyond that, it's notoriously difficult to predict the future, so
the best we can do is make the software as clean and simple as possible. That maxi-
mizes its learnability, making maintenance easier. This use of the word "learnability"
perfectly describes a valuable trait of software.

Complexity and Schedule I have noticed that schedule is proportional to complexity, which should come as no surprise. So if a design is twice as complex, you can
expect it to take around twice as long to implement and debug, because you have
twice as much work to do. That seems obvious. So the goal above can be restated as:

Fulfill the requirements with the
simplest possible design.

This fact is the driving philosophy behind this book. Take it to heart. Although most developers and managers do not realize it, the software world has a serious problem with excess complexity. I shake my head in disbelief at the overcomplexity of most software I see. I discuss this painful problem of excess complexity more in Sections 6.2 and 9.3 (pages 137 and 248).

1.10   Who, When, Why

Who   This book is intended for students or software developers who know how to program. It is *not* necessary to know about object-oriented concepts because those are covered in Chapter 2. However, that chapter does not go into great detail nor does it have many examples of source-code because this book covers the topic of design, not implementation. You'll need to learn the fundamentals of both programming and programming languages elsewhere.

When   This is not a general book about the process of developing software. Although various agile techniques [19] blur and mix these, any piece of software consisting of multiple objects generally follows these phases:

1. Requirements analysis
2. High-level design (architecture)
3. Detailed design
4. Coding
5. Unit-test (and debugging)
6. System-test (and debugging)
7. Maintenance

This book only covers phases 2-3, high-level and detailed design. However, you also typically do some small-scale design in phase 7 (maintenance), and the IDAR method is suitable for that as well. Also, during phases 4-6, one sometimes needs to modify the design to accommodate unexpected needs or changes in requirements. All told, you will probably be using the IDAR method in all phases except phase 1 (requirements).

Why   It helps to remember that design is one of the shortest phases, but that it has a large effect on the later phases, especially debugging and maintenance. Software design has a large multiplier-effect: A small improvement in design can multiply into a large benefit later, in both quality and schedule. Unfortunately, the converse is also true, which I've seen several times over the years. A mistake in design causes much more damage later. Although I am not aware of specific studies on the topic, my observations indicate that the ratio of actual schedules for good-versus-bad design is 2x or even 3x. In general, well designed software is smaller than poor software, and is easier to debug, causing a multiplicative improvement in schedule (not to mention improved quality). I've seen messy projects where the designers were clearly lost in the chasm of disorder. In other cases, an aberration in the designer's personality caused him to overuse some aspect of design, and I discuss such "fanatics" in Section 9.3 on page 248. Heed the adage, "Design is the tail that wags the dog."

1.11 Overview of this Book

Chapters 3 through 5 form the heart of this book. Chapter 3 explains the four IDAR rules and the techniques for creating IDAR graphs in detail. You need to know whether your designs good or bad, so Chapter 4 on gauging goodness teaches you easy ways to assess the quality of your designs—by evaluating the criteria of clarity, cohesion, concealment, coupling, and need. Chapter 5 provides you with various methods of subdividing a program into a hierarchy of subsystems and objects. Interestingly, some of the same techniques used for object-level design also apply to method-level design within an object. This chapter describes both in detail, along with examples. These three chapters provide the tools that will make you an engineer instead of a sloppy hacker, because you will be able to reliably and systematically create good designs.

Chapter 6 reveals some swamps and traps to avoid, as well as good practices to adopt. This chapter stresses the importance of clarity and simplicity, and tells you how to achieve them. In fact, most chapters in this book remind you of the importance of maintaining simplicity, because excess complexity is common, appealing (to some people), and always harmful. Because designing with IDAR graphs is rather different from today's OOP, the design patterns that apply to IDAR graphs differ as well. Chapter 7 covers these interesting and useful new patterns, such as the Resourceful Boss and the Secretary.

The philosophical Chapter 8 on "Beyond Design" reveals some fascinating facts about why humans need a command hierarchy, the theory of OOP and design, the nature of engineering, and similar topics. Chapter 9 contains advice to managers, which includes instructions on how to think clearly. But even if you are not a manager, please take the time to read about fanatics in Section 9.3 on page 248.

Finally, Part II of this book explains the process used to design four substantial programs. These chapters have two goals: (1) to show how IDAR works in practice, and (2) to demonstrate that the IDAR method is well suited for a wide variety of designs. These are realistic applications, complete with mistakes made along the way.

1.12 Terse Style—Slow Down!

Nowadays, it appears that books about software are expected to be at least 500 pages, and they sometimes exceed 1000 pages. Unfortunately, the great verbal skill exhibited by their authors differs from most developers. The verbose writing style seen in most software books is not compatible with the kind of minds that read them. That was a polite way of saying that many developers get lost in the sea of words, wishing the author would communicate succinctly. I say that such authors "have words".

My writing is terse and direct. I write meat without fat. Like many developers, I do *not* have words. So slow down. Like many people, you are probably in the habit of skimming, and you cannot skim this book as you can with the bloated tomes. *Force* yourself to slow down, especially in Chapter 3. To read well, I suggest covering the unread portion of the page with a piece of paper that you slide down only after reading and understanding a line, forcing yourself to learn instead of skim.

1.13 Conventions

This book uses the following conventions for words and style:

- The word "class" refers to source-code.
- The word "object" refers to an instance of a class in memory at run-time, and to its behavior. "Object" is used most of the time.
- The word "subroutine" is used when it's not a member of a class, and "method" when it's a class-member.
- Constants are named with capitals and underscores as in MAX_DELAY_SEC.
- All other symbols follow this *camelCaseStyle*.
- Class names are capitalized as in *MiniReader*.
- Interface names are capitalized and suffixed with an "I" as in *DeviceI*.
- Type names are capitalized and suffixed with a "T" as in *SettingsT*.
- The names of instances (i.e., objects), variables, and class-members start with a lowercase letter as in *guideFrame* and *userHitStop*.
- An object that is the sole instance of its class, which is most objects, is named after its class (i.e., it is capitalized). Such a class should be declared to be `static`, making class and object identical. Static classes are described in Section 6.4 on page 138.

The snippets of code shown throughout this book are written in what I call "pidgin C++". It looks like C++ or Java, but some details are usually missing for the sake of clarity and brevity. I prefer to use structured English as pseudo-code, but when I did so, it looked so much like Ada that I was afraid that it would repel readers who are accustomed to using curly-brace languages. I am somewhat artistic, so I regard C and its ilk as the ugly ducklings of the language world. Languages resembling Pascal are more attractive, but since most readers of this book use C-like languages, I grumpily capitulated.

Some readers will criticize this book for its paucity of source-code. But this book is about design, and designs are expressed best in the form of diagrams and not code. Consequently, this book contains many diagrams and little code.

I use the pronouns "he", "his", and "him" in the gender-neutral sense, as I am aware that not all software developers are male. In fact, I encourage more women to enter this profession, as their representation is pitifully low.

Finally, I follow the logical British convention of *not* putting an ending comma or period inside a quotation unless it was present in the original text. Only if the ending period was in the original text will I write "quotation." Otherwise, I write "quotation". The only alteration of original text that I permit is the substitution of a comma for an ending period when the quotation occurs mid-sentence. This is a more truthful convention that removes an irritating dishonesty in today's American English syntax.

Chapter 2

The Basics of OOP

— let us start from the very beginning

This book describes a new method of object-oriented design which yields simpler designs (and thus shorter schedules) than traditional techniques. But you first need to know the fundamentals of OOP (Object-Oriented Programming), which this chapter will teach you. If you already understand the concepts of *class*, *object*, *message*, *method*, *inheritance*, and *polymorphism*, then you can skip this chapter. However, you might benefit from reading it anyway, as I present these concepts in a practical way that you have probably never seen before.

I will assume that you are familiar with the fundamentals of programming, which means that you already know about sequential execution of statements, as well as the concepts of variables and subroutines. Some words used in procedural (non-OOP) programming, such as "variable" and "subroutine", were changed in OOP. Table 2.1 shows the frustrating variety of synonyms used for several concepts.

Procedural	OOP	Other Synonyms	Count
variable, field	field	property, attribute, member	5
record	class	structure, tuple	4
subroutine	method	routine, procedure, function, subprogram	6
n/a	base	parent, superclass	3
n/a	derived	child, subclass, extended	4

Table 2.1: Too many synonyms

15

The first column of Table 2.1 lists the terms I have chosen to use for procedural programming, and the second column are my selected terms for OOP. Take careful note of these terms, as they are used throughout the remainder of this book. The rightmost column in the table is the number of terms for the same concept. A couple of concepts have five and six terms for them, which I regard as ridiculous. Yet we should not complain, as the multiple terms were created by people working independently of each other over a period of decades.

Speaking of having too many synonyms, I've noticed that we even have synonyms for ourselves:

- Programmer
- Computer scientist
- Software engineer
- Developer

The terms "programmer" and "developer" are equally popular as of this printing. However, "developer" often connotes bearing a broader responsibility which includes high-level design, whereas a "programmer" mostly writes code and seldom goes above low-level design. Since this book pertains to design, the term "developer" is more applicable to its readers and is consistently used throughout.

2.1   Hierarchy

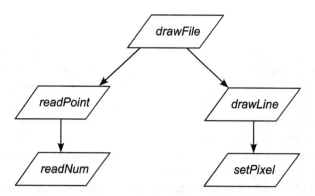

Figure 2.1: Hierarchy of subroutines

To start with, let's look at what happens when subroutines call other subroutines. Figure 2.1 shows a subroutine named *drawFile* which reads X and Y coordinates from a file, and draws lines to those points in a window. The *drawFile* subroutine calls *readPoint*, which in turn calls *readNum* (twice) to get the X- and Y-values of the next point. Likewise, *drawLine* calls *setPixel* many times to draw a line. In IDAR graphs, a subroutine (method) is represented by a parallelogram, so we'll use that notation in this discussion.

This graph represents a hierarchy of control, where each subroutine controls those under it. The graph also represents a hierarchy of abstractions, where "abstraction" is the traditional term referring to the synopsis of a capability or service. In practical terms, the graph is a hierarchy of services. The broadest (most general) services are at the top, and the most specialized services are at the bottom.

In this graph, drawing an entire file (the *drawFile* subroutine) is the broadest and most general service, and is thus located at the top of the graph. One level of service below it is reading a point and drawing a line (the *readPoint* and *drawLine* subroutines). These services are more specialized than the topmost service of drawing a file, and the topmost *drawFile* service uses these more specialized services to perform its chore. That's how levels of services work: A service above the bottom level is implemented as an assemblage of some subroutines under it, where each such subordinate subroutine contributes its piece to the chore being done by its caller.

2.2   Data-Structure

In the section above, we learned about the call-structure of subroutines, which is a hierarchy. Data also can have structure. For example, a *point* can consist of an aggregation of the fields *x*, *y*, and *color*. Such an aggregation of fields is called a "record" throughout this book and in some programming languages. It is called a "struct" in C and similar languages. A record is a data-structure, as illustrated in Figure 2.2.

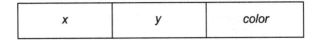

x	y	color

Figure 2.2: Data-structure of a point

The source-code below in C++ declares two points, *p1* and *p2*.

```
1   struct Point {
2       int   x;
3       int   y;
4       Color color;
5   };
6   Point p1, p2;
```

In case you haven't used them, the struct declaration lets you define a record containing some fields. In lines 1-5 of this example, we define a record (okay, a struct) consisting of three fields: *x*, *y*, and *color*. This struct is a new type called *Point* which you can use anywhere as if it were an ordinary type.

We use it in line 6 to declare two variables, *p1* and *p2*. Those variables are said to be *instances* of the type *Point*. The distinction between type and instances is important. The crucial difference is that a type does not consume any memory, but an instance resides in memory.

Type A type (in this case, *Point*) describes the structure of data, but does not allocate any variables in memory. You can think of a type as a cookie-cutter or a template: It describes a structure, but otherwise does nothing.

Instance An instance (in this case, *p1* or *p2*) is a variable in memory. Furthermore, that variable has some type which describes its contents. Every variable is an instance of some type, whether or not it's a record. In this example, we would say that *p1* is an instance of *Point*.

Instantiate When you create an instance of some type, we say that you are "instantiating" that type. The process of instantiating is called "instantiation". Instantiation can be done by declaring a statically allocated variable, as was done above in line 6. Or it can be done dynamically using the functions *malloc* or *new* in C and C++.

2.3   Classes and Objects

2.3.1   Containing a Method

Above, we saw that a record (or structure) contains some fields. A class is the same as a record in that it contains some fields. A class can be instantiated in the same manner as a record. But a class can also contain subroutines. As mentioned above, a subroutine is called a "method" in OOP.

What does it mean for a class to "contain" a method? It means less than you think. It only means that the *name* of the method is local to the class, in the same manner that the name of a field inside a record is local to that record. In the example of type *Point* above, the names of the fields *x*, *y*, and *color* are local to *Point*. You can do the same thing with names of methods. In that sense, we can say that a class contains methods in the same manner that it contains fields.

Finally, an object is an instance of a class, just as a variable is an instance of some type. The words "object" and "instance" can be used interchangeably, as they are the same thing. As with a record, so it is with a class: A class does not consume any memory, but an instance (object) does.

2.3.2   Members

All I have said is that a class is like a record, but it can also contain names of methods. At this point we need to define an important new term:

Member: A member of a class is any symbol defined in that class.

A class contains its members, which are fields, methods, constants, type-definitions, enumerations, and even nested classes in some languages. Here is a boring class declaration in C++:

```
1  class Boring {
2      void action();  // member method
3      int count;      // member field
4  };
5
6  Boring bore;  // declare an object of type Boring
```

Lines 1-4 are identical to a record declaration, except that the method *action* has been added. Line 6 declares an object (instance) named *bore* whose type is *Boring*.

Accessing fields

Suppose an object (such as *bore*) is an instance of a record or a class. How can you access its fields? You use the following dot-notation:

```
bore.count = 100;
```

You follow the object's name with a dot, followed by the name of the field you want. The asterisk-dot or right-arrow notation is used when you have a pointer to an object, as in this example:

```
Boring *pBore = &bore;
(*pBore).count = 123;
pBore->count = 0;
```

The right-arrow and asterisk-dot notations will be familiar if you've used pointers in C or C++. But you might not be familiar with how this syntax was extended to calling member-methods.

Calling syntax

How can you call a method that's a member of a class? For example, we have created the object *bore* which is an instance of the *Boring* class. This class contains a method named *action*. How can you call *action*? You use the same notations that you use for fields. Here are examples using *bore*:

To access a field	To call a method
bore.count	bore.action()
pBore->count	pBore->action()

It's important to note that any call to a member method has an instance associated with it. In this example, the calls to *action* shown above are associated with the instance *bore*.

Accessing members within a method

How can the code within a method access the fields inside its instance? When you call a method, the syntax of the call specifies which instance is associated with the call. The *action* method will probably want to access the field *count* in the instance *bore*. How can it access *count*?

Surprisingly, the fields in an object appear as ordinary variables inside a method. For example, the source-code for the method *action* might look like this in C++:

```
void Boring::action() {
    printf("%d", count);
    count = 1;
}
```

This method prints the value of the field *count*, and then sets it to 1. Remember that *count* is a member of the object, *bore*. Code inside a member method accesses a member field as if it were a file-local or global variable. While convenient, this also means that you cannot tell from reading the source-code whether a variable is a member or file-local or global. Organizations often use naming conventions to distinguish variables defined in these scopes. (A scope is an area in source-code.) Here is an example of a popular convention:

`count_` or `m_count`	a member in an object
`g_debugMode`	a global variable
`_decodeState`	a file-local variable
`numChars`	a method-local variable

2.3.3   Example: Point Class

We will look at an another example to make all this clearer. Suppose that you have defined the type *Point* from Figure 2.2. Furthermore, you want to be able perform the following operations on a point (which is an instance of *Point*):

set	set a pixel to a given value (*x,y,color*)
erase	set a pixel to the background color of the window
draw	physically draw the pixel in the window

This example illustrates the common situation where you have a group of subroutines that operate on some common data. It's convenient to put the subroutines and data into one class, as portrayed in Figure 2.3.

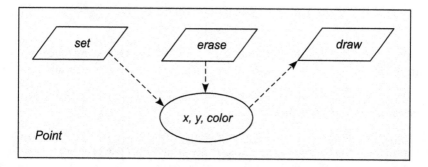

Figure 2.3: Point class

Data (variables and fields) are drawn surrounded by a circle or oval, and dataflows are drawn as dashed arrows. So this graph is saying that the fields (*x,y,value*) are written by *set* and *erase*, and read by *draw*. The large rectangle surrounding the entire graph represents a class or object. Everything inside the rectangle are members of the class, where a "member" refers to a field or method. In this example, the members of the class are *set, erase, draw, x, y, color*.

The source-code in C++ below declares this class *Point*:

```
1   class Point {
2      public:
3         void set (int newx, int newy, Color newcolor);
4         void erase ();
5         void draw ();
6      private:
7         int x, y;
8         Color color;
9   };
10
11  Point p1, p2;
12
13  void Point::set (int newx, int newy, Color newcolor) {
14     x = newx; y = newy;
15     color = newcolor;
16  }
17  void Point::erase () {
18     color = { 255, 255, 255 };
19  }
20  void Point::draw () {
21     pWindowArea->plot (x,y,color);
22  }
23
24  void main() {
25     p1.set (123, 456, RED);
26     p1.draw ();
27  }
```

Let's analyze this code piece by piece:

- Lines 1-9 declare the class *Point*.
- Lines 7-8 declare member fields *x*, *y*, and *color*, in the same manner as the struct declaration you saw above.
- Lines 3-5 declare member methods *set*, *erase* and *draw*.
- Lines 13-22 are the code for the three member methods.
- Line 11 declares variables *p1* and *p2*, which are instances of *Point*.
- Line 15 starts with color =. This field *color* is a member of the object specified when the method was called. Line 25 calls *set* with object *p1*, so *color* is the *color* field in *p1*.
- Lines 24-27 are a sample program that uses *p1*. Notice that the syntax for accessing the name of a method (e.g., p1.set) is the same dot notation that is used to access fields in records. Also, when going through a pointer as in line 21, you use the same right-arrow notation as you do with fields.

Here are the key points to remember:

- A class is identical to a record or struct, except that it also contains the names of methods.

- When calling methods, their names are used with the same syntax as you do for the fields within a record or struct (dot notation or right-arrow notation).
- When you call a method, the syntax of the call specifies which instance to use.
- Inside a method, the member fields of the instance are available as ordinary variables.

2.3.4   Public and Private

Lines 2 and 6 in the listing above introduce the concepts of public and private. Members that are declared private can only be accessed by member methods in the same class. In this example, that means that only the methods *set*, *erase*, and *draw* are able to access the private fields *x*, *y*, and *color*, because these methods are located within the class. Methods in other classes cannot access those fields. The fact that *x* is private means that the following line of code will cause a compiler-error if it's not located inside a method that's a member of this class:

```
objectName.x = 123;
```

In IDAR graphs, public members have an arrow pointing to them that originate outside the rectangle representing the object. Private members only have arrows to them originating from within the rectangle. This diagramming convention is illustrated in Figure 2.4. This diagram is identical to Figure 2.3, except for the additional arrows pointing to the public members.

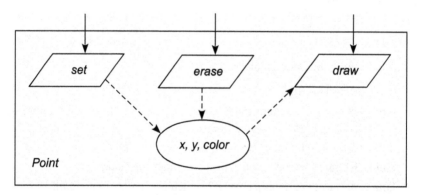

Figure 2.4: *Point* class, public and private members

Interface   You'll see the word "interface" quite a lot in discussion of OOP. The interface into a class or object is merely its public members. It's considered good practice to *not* put any fields in an interface. This means that an interface consists solely of methods. Actually, it can also include type-definitions and constants, but methods do the heavy lifting in any interface.

2.3.5   Constructors and Destructors

Section 6.4 on page 138 describes the static class, which is a simple way to implement a single-instance class. Most classes in designs only have one instance, so most classes should be static. But some classes need multiple instances, and when such a class is instantiated (creating an object), a constructor method is called. In addition, if you declare an instance of a class statically (not the same as a static class), its constructor will be called when your program is run, but before the main program starts. A constructor is an optional member-method, and if you supply it, you can use it to initialize the fields in the object or to allocate memory. In fact, a constructor can do anything you wish, but since it can be called prior to the main program, it's likely that many other objects have not been initialized, so I recommend not calling external methods in constructors. One exception is the Union pattern described in Section 7.1.5 on page 186.

When an object vanishes due to going out of scope or being deallocated, its destructor method is called. A destructor is optional, and its primary use is to deallocate memory that was allocated by a constructor or afterwards.

2.4   Thinking at the Object-Level

At this point, you are ready to step up to a higher level of abstraction in your thinking about classes and objects. We know that a class consists of some fields and some methods that access those fields. The traditional definition of an object says it consists of attributes (fields) and behaviors (methods). But we are still thinking in terms of the actions done by the individual methods. The change in thinking is this: Think of an object as being a worker that can provide a service. Think of the service offered by the object as a whole. Yes, it consists of fields and methods, but when designing at the object-level, you need to be thinking about what the entire object does.

Note that I'm using the word "object" instead of "class". Like a record, a class can do nothing until it has been instantiated (but remember to read about static classes on page 138). So the code performs its operations using instances (or objects). Therefore, our thinking is object-oriented and not class-oriented.

As an example, *Cooler* provides the capability of cooling a building. But when using the object, we must think of the individual methods it offers in its interface. Here is its class declaration in C++:

```
class Cooler {    // cools the building
    public:
        static bool setTemperature(int celsius);
        static bool setEnergySaving(bool enable);
        static bool turnOn();
        static bool turnOff();
};
```

Role   As part of object-level thinking, it's important to know the gist of what an object does. The "role" of an object is a brief description of the service it offers. In this case, the role is "cools the building." All methods in the interface should relate only to that role. Such a sharply focused role is said to have high cohesion. You'll learn more about such criteria for gauging the goodness of designs in Chapter 4.

2.5   Message-Passing

Now that you're thinking of objects as specialized workers who can only perform their roles, you might wonder how such workers communicate with each other. They do so by passing messages among each other. That is, an object *A* can send a message to object *B*. This is done by calling methods in interfaces. I hate to disappoint you, but message-passing is merely another name for calling methods. At the implementation-level, message-passing is merely method-calls.

But there's an important difference at the *conceptual* level. Ask yourself, "What does it mean when an object calls a method in another object?" It could mean that one object is commanding the other to do something. Or it could mean that one object is informing the other about an event that occurred. It might mean that one is telling the other about the results of a prior command. There are many possible meanings of a method-call. But they all have one thing in common: A method-call can be regarded as a message. Therefore, at the conceptual level, calling method *turnOn* in a *cooler* object can be regarded as sending the message "turn on" to *cooler*. And calling *packetArrived* in a *compress* object can be regarded as sending the message "a packet arrived" to *compress*.

Method-calls are simply the way that message-passing is implemented in most object-oriented languages. But it's not required to be done that way. It could be done using a message-queue in each object. At the conceptual level, there's no difference: A message is being passed.

Message-passing can be diagrammed. We use a rectangle to represent an object, and an arrow to represent a message. The name of the message (which is the name of the method) is a label next to the arrow. Figure 2.5 is an example of message-passing among several objects.

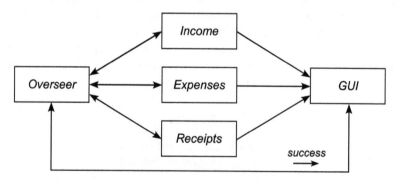

Figure 2.5: Message-passing (UML [27] communication diagram)

The diagram shows that in many cases, messages are passed in *both* directions between objects. Objects can have conversations with each other. One message from *Overseer* to *GUI* is labeled *success*. This tells us that (1) this message is a method located in the *GUI* object, (2) the method is named *success*, and that (3) it is called by code somewhere inside the *Overseer* object. It's reasonable to suppose that *Overseer* is informing *GUI* about the successful completion of a prior command (message).

2.6   Inheritance

In this section, you will learn about a feature that is present in most (but not all) object-oriented languages. If you have programmed only in C or BASIC, or have only written simple programs in other languages, then you have probably never encountered or used inheritance.

2.6.1   Additive Inheritance

There are two kinds of inheritance: additive and polymorphic. Additive inheritance allows you to add fields or methods to a class. You start with a class, which is called the "base class", and add members to it, resulting in what's called the "derived class". The concepts of base class and derived class are crucial, so let's discuss them in detail.

> **Base Class** This can be any class, and there is nothing unusual about it. Any of your classes can be used as a base class for inheritance. However, later in this chapter you'll learn about polymorphic methods, and they need a special declaration in the base class in some languages, including C++.

> **Derived Class** A special bit of syntax (shown below) tells the compiler that this class inherits from another class (the base class). Inheritance means that all of the public member fields and methods are available to the derived class. Some languages also have a protected category of members (in addition to public and private). Protected members are not available to users of an instance of a class; in that sense, they are private. But protected members are available to derived classes.

Inheritance in OOP is similar to a sole child who inherits all the possessions of his parents, and then adds his own possessions to them. A derived class inherits all public (and protected) members of its base class, and then adds more members declared within itself. The C++ code below declares a class called *Base*, which is used as a base class, and a derived class called *Derived*.

```
 1   class Base {
 2      public:
 3          void callMe();
 4      private:
 5          int  num;
 6   };
 7
 8   class Derived : public Base {
 9      public:
10          void doMore();
11   };
12
13   void Derived::doMore() {
14       callMe();    // fine
15       num = 1;     // ERROR!
16   }
```

Here is what this code is doing:

- Lines 1-6 declare an ordinary class, which we use as the base class.

- Line 8 says that *Derived* inherits from *Base*.

- Line 10 declares the member method *doMore* in *Derived*. At this point, the class *Derived* has the following members: *callMe, num*, and *doMore*. However, *doMore* cannot access *num* because it's private to its parent.

- Lines 13-16 are the implementation of the new method, *doMore*.

- Line 14 shows *doMore* calling the method *callMe* which it inherited from *Base*.

- Line 15 causes a compiler-error because code in a derived class is attempting to access a private member in the base class.

In Java, you declare inheritance as follows:

```
public class Derived extends Base { … }
```

The keyword extends is used in place of the ":" in C++, and the public specification is different. I prefer Java's syntax because it's clearer. Also note that Java's class declarations are not terminated with a semicolon. In C++, you must terminate each class declaration with a semicolon due to its historical relationship to the syntax of a struct in C. Java cheerfully discarded this syntactical anomaly.

As is true of subroutines, there are multiple terms for base and derived classes. As Table 2.1 showed, they are also called "parent class" and "child class", which is logical but uncommon for some reason. Additional names include "superclass" and "subclass", but they have the incorrect connotation that the subclass has fewer features than the superclass. The opposite is usually true. A derived class is also sometimes called an "extended" class, perhaps because Java uses the keyword extends when declaring a derived class. Does the fact that computer science has multiple names for many things annoy you? I use "base" and "derived" because these are the terms used in C++, and they have the correct connotations.

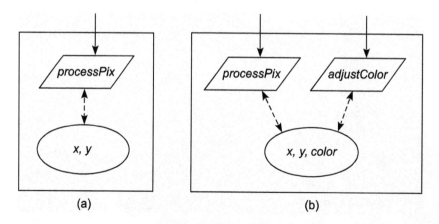

Figure 2.6: Additive inheritance

The diagrams in Figure 2.6 show a base class on the left (a), and a derived class on the right (b) that has an additional method and field. In this example, a pixel-processing object was enhanced to handle color.

It's worth emphasizing that when you define a derived class, you are actually defining a new type. Thus, you can declare variables (objects) using that type, assign one to another, pass them in parameters, and so on.

Composition

As the above example shows, additive inheritance is a way of adding a feature to an existing class. There is another way of adding a feature called "composition", which means that an object is composed of other object(s). To use composition, you will wrap a new class around an instance of the original class, and add your new feature. Figure 2.7 shows how this is done. The new wrapper class contains a *processPix* method that calls the original one, but the new one also works with color. The new class also has the *adjustColor* method, so the result of composition has the same interface as the derived class resulting from inheritance.

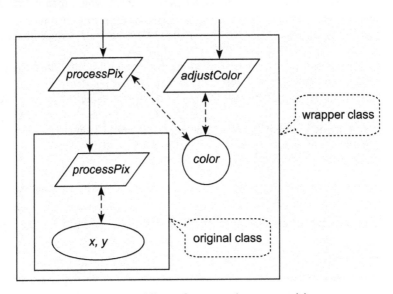

Figure 2.7: Adding a feature using composition

But composition can be more restrictive than inheritance. Looking again at Figure 2.7, we notice that it is not possible for the new *processPix* or *adjustColor* methods to access the fields *x* and *y*. This restriction occurs because *x* and *y* are private, so they can only be accessed by methods inside the base class. When using inheritance, these private fields can be declared as `protected` (in some languages), which makes them available to derived classes. This constraint on composition is both a problem and a blessing. It is a problem because some additional features cannot be implemented using composition (unless the original class is modified). It is a blessing because it forbids creating ugly interrelated connections between the two classes.

The main benefit of composition over additive inheritance is clarity. The source-code for composition makes it obvious that it is wrapping an object. But with additive inheritance, this relationship is concealed. You see a call to a method, look in the source-code for that class, and the method is not there. Where did it go? It's hidden in the base class, and you were looking in a derived class. Such concealing of design makes code harder to learn, and therefore makes maintenance slower, more frustrating, and more likely to introduce bugs. Avoid techniques that conceal design.

My advice is to use composition whenever possible due to its greater clarity. If composition is not possible, then you need to access `protected` members of a base class. Consider modifying the base class instead of inheriting from it to avoid the messy situation of two classes accessing the same fields that should be private.

2.6.2   Polymorphic Inheritance

The first kind of inheritance is additive. The second kind is polymorphic, which means *replacing* methods in the base class with different methods in a derived class. The OOP literature often refers to base methods as being *overridden* by derived methods. The word "polymorphic" comes from the Greek words "poly", which means "manifold", and "morphe", which means "form" or "shape". Hence, polymorphic means "multiple forms". The ability to replace one method with another means that the actual method that gets called depends on which class you instantiated.

The following rule about polymorphism is what makes it useful: *Any code expecting a pointer to an instance of a base class can be given a pointer to an instance of a derived class, and polymorphic methods in that derived class will be called instead of those in the base class, despite their being called using the base class pointer.*

That statement sounds confusing, but is worth careful study. The concept it is expressing is simple, but is difficult to say simply in English. Step-by-step, here is what it means:

1. Your code possesses a pointer which was declared to point to a base class.
2. That pointer actually points to a derived class (so somebody did a type-cast).
3. A method in the base class was declared to be polymorphic. Let's call it *poly*.
4. Both the base and derived classes contain a method named *poly*.
5. If you call *poly* using your base class pointer, you will call the *poly* located in the derived class. This is a replacement or override as described above.
6. But if *poly* had not been declared to be polymorphic, the above call would have called the *poly* method located in the base class.

As an example, suppose you are writing software that processes sound, and you want to output sound in one of two popular formats, MP3 or AAC. You want to call a *compress* method in a compressor object and have it perform the correct compression. Here's a way to do this using polymorphic inheritance:

1. Declare a base class named *Comp* containing a polymorphic method named *compress*. The code in *compress* will surprise you. It displays an error-message and kills the program! That's because this particular *compress* method should never be called. You'll soon see why.

2. Declare a derived class named *Mp3Comp* which inherits from *Comp*. It has a public *compress* method which compresses into the MP3 format.

3. Declare a derived class named *AacComp* which inherits from *Comp*. It has a public *compress* method which compresses into the Aac format.

4. Somewhere in the program, declare a pointer to an instance of *Comp*. Let's call it *pComp*. Note that this pointer is declared to point to the base class, and you can guess what we're going to set it to.

5. At run-time, make *pComp* point to an instance of *Mp3Comp* or *AacComp* (you must select one) as follows:

```
Mp3Comp mp3Comp;   // either file-local or some member field
AacComp aacComp;   // ditto
Comp*   pComp;
// ...more code...
if (we want to output an MP3 file) {
    pComp = &mp3Comp;
} else {
    pComp = &aacComp;
}
```

6. Anywhere the program wants to compress sound, it calls

```
pComp->compress(buffer);
```

which results in the correct *compress* method being called.

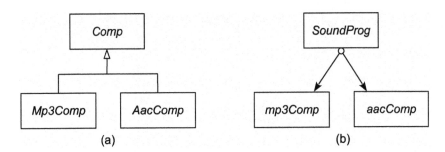

Figure 2.8: Polymorphic inheritance

Figure 2.8(a) shows the UML diagram [27] for this inheritance relationship. In UML, a hollow arrow signifies inheritance, and it points from a derived class to its base class. Figure 2.8(b) portrays the selection of MP3-versus-AAC described above, but using the IDAR graph notation. A bubble denotes indirection, meaning that a method-call is not done directly, but is instead selected at run-time by some technique. In our case, that technique is polymorphic inheritance, and the two choices are the objects *mp3Comp* or *aacComp*. This diagram is saying that *SoundProg*, representing the rest of the sound program, sends a message (which we know is *compress*) to either *mp3Comp* or *aacComp*, whichever was selected in step 5 above.

Notice that the class *Comp* is never instantiated. That's why its methods output error-messages; they should never be called. Some languages, including C++, allow you to declare such methods as abstract, meaning that there is no code for those methods. If a class has any abstract methods, then it cannot be instantiated. As a result, you *must* create a derived class which supplies the missing method(s). Such a supplied method is said to be "concrete". This feature of abstract methods allows an erroneous instantiation of the base class to be caught at compile-time, saving you the trouble of checking for this error at run-time.

You have already seen the C++ code above which selects an instance of either *Mp3Comp* or *AacComp*. The .h file containing the corresponding declarations of these classes is shown below:

```
1   class Comp {
2      public:
3           virtual void compress(Buf& data) = 0;  // abstract
4   };

5   class Mp3Comp : public Comp {
6      public:
7           virtual void compress(Buf& data);   // concrete
8   };

9   class Aa3Comp : public Comp {
10     public:
11          virtual void compress(Buf& data);   // concrete
12  };
```

File Mp3Comp.cpp:

```
1   void Mp3Comp::compress(Buf& data) {
2       // (code to perform compression into MP3 format)
3   }
```

File AacComp.cpp:

```
1   void AacComp::compress(Buf& data) {
2       // (code to perform compression into AAC format)
3   }
```

The following points are noteworthy about this source-code:

- Line 3 in the .h file declares *compress* to be (1) `virtual`, which means it can be overridden by derived classes, and (2) abstract by virtue of the `=0` which indicates that an actual method will not be supplied for this class.

- Lines 5 and 9 in the .h file indicate that these classes inherit from *Comp*.

- Lines 7 and 11 in the .h file declare *compress* without the `=0` at the end, so these methods are not abstract, and they therefore must be supplied in the class. These methods are concrete.

- Line 1 in both Mp3Comp.cpp and AacComp.cpp declare the *compress* method in the usual way. There is no indication here that these methods override one in the base class. Knowledge of inheritance is restricted to the `class` declarations in the .h file(s).

You can use polymorphic inheritance for some (or all) methods, and at the same time you can also add methods and fields to the derived class. Thus, a derived class can use *both* additive and polymorphic inheritance.

Finally, as you might have guessed, there are multiple words related to polymorphic inheritance. They are:

- "Virtual"—C++ uses the keyword `virtual` when denoting methods that are polymorphic. Note that in Java, *all* nonstatic methods are virtual.

- "Pure virtual"—This phrase refers to an abstract method. Because no code is supplied for such a method, that class cannot be instantiated.

- "Override"—A polymorphic method in a derived class is said to "override" the one supplied in its base class.

2.6.3 Uses of Inheritance

There are three primary uses of inheritance: adding features, selection, and specialization. There are also some problems caused by inheritance that developers should be aware of. These are discussed in Section 6.6 on page 142.

Adding Features

New features can be added to your class using additive inheritance. You've seen one example already: the pixel-processing class which we enhanced with color using a derived class. Other possibilities include working with later versions of hardware controlled by a class. If the newer hardware has a new feature, you can create a derived class and add the new feature to it.

As mentioned above, composition is usually superior to additive inheritance due to its greater clarity.

Selection

Developers often take advantage of the ability of polymorphic inheritance to select an instance of one of several derived classes. You've seen one example already with the sound-compressor classes.

Whenever you are faced with several ways of doing the same thing, this technique for selection might be applicable. You might need to compress/decompress or encrypt/decrypt data in multiple ways. Or you might need to support a device made by multiple manufacturers, such as HP, Canon, and Epson printers. Perhaps a circuit has undergone major revisions, and your software needs to support all versions. In such cases, the public methods (and the operations) are the same.

One way of handling such selection is the use of an abstract class (or "pure virtual class"), in which *no* method is supplied. All of its methods are abstract, so such a class contains no code! All code is supplied by the derived classes. At run-time, one of the derived classes is selected and used. Note that with this kind of selection, *all* methods come from one class. You are not using some methods from a base class and some from a derived class. Rather, you are selecting all the code in one of the derived classes. Such all-or-nothing selection can be done more clearly using the Dispatcher pattern (Section 7.1.3; page 183), avoiding inheritance and the obfuscation it brings.

Specialization (Is-A-Kind-Of)

This use of polymorphic inheritance is best illustrated with an example. Suppose your program processes financial data, and you need to pass blocks of such data around. You create a class for handling buffers called *Buf*. You also realize that there are two kinds of data passed in buffers: commands and information. You want to be sure that these two kinds of data are kept separate, so you create two derived classes called *CmdBuf* which holds command data, and *InfoBuf* which holds informational data. Each derived class knows the format of the data that's expected, so it (1) performs error-checks to be sure the data is valid, and (2) updates statistics (in another object) recording how much of each type of data has flowed through the buffers.

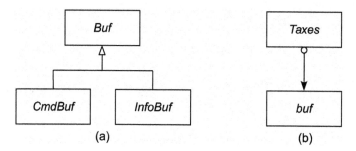

Figure 2.9: More examples of polymorphic inheritance

Figure 2.9(a) is a familiar UML diagram showing the inheritance relationships among these three classes. Figure 2.9(b) shows indirect messages between an object in the program (*Taxes* in this case) and a buffer object. Consider the following:

- A cmd-buffer is a kind of buffer.
- An info-buffer is a kind of buffer.

- A cmd-buffer is a specialized buffer.
- An info-buffer is a specialized buffer.

The phrase "is a kind of" is present in two of those statements. Each derived class implements a buffer which is a kind of general buffer. Notice that the alternate description of both uses the word "specialized". Each derived class implements a specialized kind of buffer, whereas their base class is a general buffer. The use of inheritance to implement such a specialized-to-general relationship between classes is called "specialization". Such a relationship is commonly called "is-a-kind-of" or "is-a" because one can say that "*A* is a kind of *B*."

2.7   Wrap-up

That was OOP in a nutshell. It was intended to be enough to allow you to understand the remainder of this book. It was not a complete discussion, as it failed to mention some common topics such as templates, and syntactic details of popular languages such as C++ and Java. This book is about a design technique which hinders messiness and is exceptionally understandable, so this explanation of OOP was only sufficient for that. Learning more about OOP in general and specific languages will mean buying more books.

2.8 Exercises

1. What is a field? Can it be public?

2. What is the difference between a type and an instance?

3. What is the difference between an instance and an object?

4. What is the difference between a class and a record?

5. A class contains fields, which are data. How can it also contain methods, which are code?

6. When you instantiate a class, you are instantiating:
   (a) The methods in the class.
   (b) The fields in the class.
   (c) Both.

7. Suppose several instances of a class were created, and that a member method accesses a member field declared in the class. How does that member method know which instance to access?

8. A class has only one method, and it is private. Can it be called?

9. How is message-passing between objects usually implemented?

10. What is the difference between additive and polymorphic inheritance?

11. Why is composition preferable to additive inheritance?

12. Suppose that you have declared a base class *Base* containing a method named *action*, and a derived class *Derived* also containing a method named *action*. Pointers *b* and *d* are both declared to point to an instance of *Base*. Pointer *b* points to an instance of *Base*, and pointer *d* points to an instance of *Derived* (via a type-cast).
    If *action* were not declared virtual, which *action* method(s) will be called by these two calls?: `b->action()`, `d->action()`.
    If *action* were declared virtual, which *action* method(s) will be called by these two calls?: `b->action()`, `d->action()`.

13. A buffer containing a command-ID along with associated data is given to an object. There are a variety of commands to be performed. Knowing that polymorphic inheritance can be used for selection, and that we need to select an object that implements each command, it was suggested that polymorphic inheritance be used. Discuss the feasibility of this idea.

14. You are designing a program for maintaining temperature in buildings, and you have two kinds of coolers available: compressor and swamp. Their basic operations are the same (*start* and *stop*), but they differ in some details. Write C++ class declarations for these starting with an abstract base class called *Cooler*.

Chapter 3

Core Concepts

— everything is a hierarchy

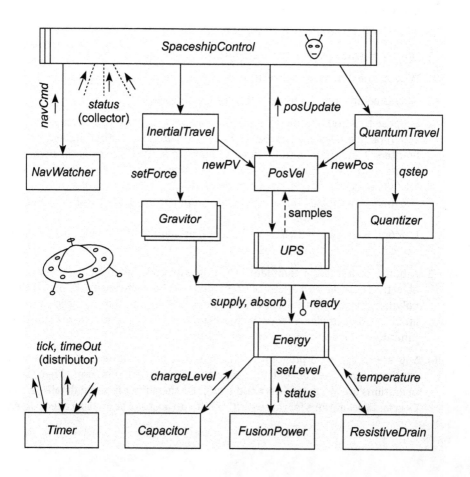

IDAR graphs portray the design of object-oriented software, and are the product of the IDAR design method. This method consists of four memorable rules along with an accompanying design-process covered in Chapter 5. Components of IDAR graphs and the four rules are inseparably intertwined, and both are described thoroughly in this chapter. Consequently, this is the core chapter of this book, so I suggest reading it carefully. An IDAR graph reveals the following primary aspects of a design:

1. The objects that exist in the software

2. How they communicate and interact with each other

3. Their hierarchy of services (i.e., their command hierarchy)

These are the three things that you need to know when designing new software or learning the structure of existing software. The third item above, hierarchy of services, is absent in traditional OOP. As mentioned in the Introduction in Section 1.6 (page 8), IDAR graphs enable designers of object-oriented software to think in terms of a service hierarchy. Prior to IDAR graphs, the best that could be done was to show the communications and associations among objects as an unstructured and often spaghetti-like diagram. Inheritance is often thought to produce a widely useful kind of hierarchy, but it fails for the reasons given in Section 6.6 on page 142. Without the ability to represent a service hierarchy, software is difficult to understand and tends to be disorganized, both of which produce more bugs.

A hierarchy of services is also a hierarchy of capabilities or detail. Objects in the upper levels have broad capabilities and know little detail. The objects at the lower levels provide services that are more specialized, representing the details of how the higher layers perform their chores. Theoreticians refer to this layering of services as an "abstraction hierarchy", and it is expressed as a command hierarchy in an IDAR graph. Section 8.1 (page 230) probes more deeply into why people need this kind of hierarchy in designs.

3.1 Applicability

Which levels of design is an IDAR graph appropriate for? The graphs that developers use to portray commonly encountered levels of software are listed below:

1. Graph of network of computers

2. Graph of network of processors

3. Graph of system showing subsystems

4. Graph of subsystem showing objects

5. Graph of objects showing methods

6. Pseudo-code of methods showing their logic

An IDAR graph is best for levels 3-5, and perhaps level 2 (network of processors). Thus, it is useful for what is commonly called high-level design (or architecture) and detailed design. It is not suitable for level 1 (network of computers) because, for the sake of reliability, most networks are not structured as command hierarchies.

3.2   Overview

This chapter describes IDAR graphs in complete detail. To help you keep the overall picture in mind when reading all of that material, we will begin with an overview. I will concurrently present the four rules governing IDAR graphs, which are: Identify, Down, Aid, and Role, forming the acronym IDAR. These rules are defined below:

Identify   Identify each public method in an object as either a command or a notice. From its caller's viewpoint, a notice only imports or exports needed information.

Down   When graphing the calls to commands among objects, the arrows must point down. In this graph, an arrow connecting two boxes means that code in the upper object (box) calls one or more commands in the lower object.

Aid   A command or notice may, unknown to its callers, aid its object by performing part or all of a previously commanded action.

Role   Write a brief role for each object and method that summarizes all services it offers, avoiding any aspect of its implementation (including aid). Callers may rely on only what is stated in roles.

In this book, "class" refers to source-code and "object" refers to an instance of a class in memory at run-time. A class and its object(s) have the same role, so regarding their actions, the words "class" and "object" are interchangeable.

A box represents an object, which is an instance of a class. It can also represent a class having *no* instances, which is a subroutine library. A stack of boxes represents multiple instances of the same class. If an object contains a thread or process, it is said to be "active"; draw double or triple vertical lines on the sides of its box.

Because they point down, calls to commands among objects cannot form a cycle in the graph, but instead define a hierarchy of superiors and subordinates.

Draw a call to a notice as a short floating arrow paralleling a command-arrow. If there is no command-arrow, draw a dashed line connecting the two boxes (with no arrowhead), and then draw the arrow for the notice paralleling that dashed line, as illustrated by the *priceChange* notice in Figure 3.1.

Figure 3.1 is an example of an IDAR graph for a simple system used to trade stocks. Table 3.1 explains the commands and notices used in the graph. The "C/N" column indicates whether the method is a command or a notice.

The *Stocks* object maintains a list of relevant stocks for *Brains*. When the price of a stock goes outside the limits prescribed in the *watch* command, *MarketWatch* calls the *brokeLimit* notice in *Brains*, which it needs in order to *makeMoney*. Then *Brains* might call the *buy* or *sell* commands in *NetBroker*. This broker reports the results of a transaction in the *result* notice, and gives a *priceChange* notice to *MarketWatch*.

Enclosure   The dotted enclosure in Figure 3.1 indicates that the source-code of the classes for both *MarketWatch* and *NetBroker* is contained in file market.cpp. Such an enclosure is helpful when a file contains multiple classes (which is encouraged).

Object-level and Method-Level   There are two kinds of IDAR graphs. Above, you read about object-level graphs that portray the command hierarchy and interactions

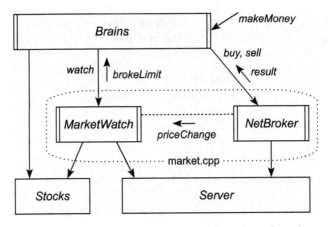

Figure 3.1: A design for computerized trading of stocks

Caller-Object	Method	Callee-Object	C/N	Role of Method
(not shown)	*makeMoney*	*Brains*	C	Profit on stocks
Brains	*watch*	*MarketWatch*	C	Watch list of stocks
MarketWatch	*brokeLimit*	*Brains*	N	Stock exceeded limits
Brains	*buy, sell*	*NetBroker*	C	Buy/sell this stock
NetBroker	*result*	*Brains*	N	Result of buy/sell
NetBroker	*priceChange*	*MarketWatch*	N	Stock price changed

Table 3.1: Commands and notices used in the stock-trading program

among the objects in your design. But inside an object, another kind of IDAR graph can be used to show the calls among your public and private methods. When people refer to an "IDAR graph", they are usually referring to an object-level graph. But don't neglect method-level design, which is frequently called "detailed design". This chapter shows you how to create both kinds of IDAR graphs.

Superiors and Subordinates   By definition, a superior commands its subordinates. IDAR graphs portray this relationship at the object-level, and also at the method-level where superiors *call* their subordinates.

In essence, an IDAR graph portrays a hierarchy of commanding objects (superiors and subordinates), with ancillary communications shown with notice-arrows. The four rules are the centerpiece of the IDAR method, so they should be memorized. This overview omitted important details and features of IDAR graphs, which are described in the remainder of this chapter. Also, Section 9.1 on page 243 presents a different summary of IDAR graphs intended for nontechnical people.

3.2.1   CD-Player

Knowing that many people learn best by example, let's begin this detailed presentation of IDAR graphs with Figure 3.2 which depicts a fragment of the design of a portable CD-player of the kind that was popular before MP3 players and smartphones took over the market. It has a simple display for showing the tracks on the CD, buttons for selecting a track, playing and stopping, and little else.

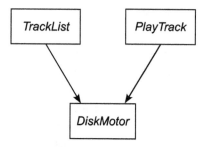

Figure 3.2: Commanding objects in a CD-player

After reading the overview, you know that this IDAR graph is telling us that the *DiskMotor* object is commanded by both the *TrackList* and *PlayTrack* objects. As I describe the various features of IDAR graphs, they will be added to the graph of this CD-player, which will serve as a running example.

3.3   Boxes

Boxes represent objects, not classes. Paradoxically, they are usually labeled with the names of classes, as explained by the following table:

Item	Drawn As	Name in Box
Object is sole instance of a class	Single box	Class
Noninstantiated (subroutine library)	Single box	Class
Few objects from the same class	Single box for each	Object
Few objects from the same class	Stacked boxes	Objects
Many objects from the same class	Stacked boxes	Class
Implementations of an interface	Stacked boxes	Interface

3.3.1   A Box Depicts an Object

If a class will produce a small, fixed number of named instances (objects), you can draw a box for each instance, as shown in Figure 3.3(a). This example is for a milling machine having x- and y-motors to move its table, so there are two instances of the *Motor* class, named *xmotor* and *ymotor*.

I have observed that most classes have exactly one instance. In our example CD-player, *all* classes have only one instance. Figure 3.3(b) shows this common case. You should make such a single-instance class static to avoid the additional complexity of managing and passing around an instance. Static classes are discussed in Section 6.4 on page 138. A static class and its object are identical, so the box represents both. Note that the name in the box is that of the class (and thus is capitalized) because the instance of a static class is neither separate nor named.

Figure 3.3: Boxes for individual instances of a class

Some classes have *no* instances because they contain only methods and no fields, such as a *Math* class. Such a class is a subroutine library and need not be instantiated, making it similar to a static class. In this situation, a box represents the class.

3.3.2 A Stack of Boxes Depicts Multiple Instances

If a class will produce multiple instances, the stack-of-boxes notation in Figure 3.4 is used to represent all of the objects. If the number of objects is small and fixed, their names can be placed within the stack, as portrayed in Figure 3.4(a), consuming less space than drawing a separate box for each instance as we did in Figure 3.3(a).

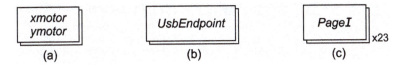

Figure 3.4: Boxes for multiple instances of a class

It is usually not practical to list all instances in a box, so the stack representing the multiple instances is labeled with the name of their class, as shown in Figure 3.4(b). You would need to do this for a *UsbEndpoint* class for example, because you don't know how many USB endpoints will exist.

3.3.3 A Stack of Boxes Depicts an Interface

A stack of boxes is also used when several classes implement the same interface. The stack of boxes still represents some number of objects, but in this case they are instances of different (but closely related) classes. The stack is labeled with the name of the interface. Figure 3.4(c) shows this use of stacked boxes. The "x23" by the side of this stack indicates that there are 23 classes and instances. The x-notation is optional (but recommended) for any stacked box.

Java and C# support interfaces directly using the `interface` keyword, but in C++ the inheritance mechanism must be used.

3.3.4 More About Boxes

Even though boxes represent objects, they are usually labeled with class names, as the two most common situations—single instance and numerous instances—preclude labeling with object names. But this oft-usage of class names makes an IDAR graph appear to be a hierarchy of classes. It's not. It's a hierarchy of objects.

Inheritance relationships among classes may be portrayed with a separate UML class diagram, allowing the IDAR graph to focus on interactions among objects.

An object often contains other objects. For example, a medicine object is likely to contain an object for each chemical used in the medicine. The private fields in many objects are themselves objects (as contrasted with simple variables and records). In such cases, you might be tempted to draw boxes inside a box. Don't. Instead, draw such boxes separately in the usual manner. Containment relationships are termed "composition", and are discussed later in this chapter on page 68.

With that background in mind, it's time to thoroughly learn the four rules that form the heart of the IDAR design method.

3.4   The Identify Rule

This rule tells you to designate all of the public methods in your objects as commands and notices, where notices must satisfy a criterion. In the overview in Section 3.2, the Identify rule was defined as follows:

> *Identify each public method in an object as either a command or a notice. From its caller's viewpoint, a notice only imports or exports needed information.*

For example, suppose an object has the role "resizes a photo", which is a common operation in smartphones. Only a command is allowed to commence a resize operation because resizing involves more than conveying information. A notice may only convey information needed for resizing. For example, a *twoPoints* notice would tell the object the coordinates of the user's two fingers.

The Identify rule only considers the actions of notices as viewed by its callers in other objects. But inside your object, invisible to outsiders, both commands and notices may secretly perform additional actions to help fulfill your object's responsibilities. Such covert aid is discussed later on page 48 under the Aid rule.

3.4.1   Commands

A command is a public method in an object. And as the word "command" suggests, calling a command means that you are ordering its object to perform (or at least start performing) the action described in the command's role, similar to a boss commanding an employee. In most cases, the command performs that action completely. But in some designs, the command returns without finishing its job (i.e., it's nonblocking), leaving the unfinished portion to be done by something else inside the object, such as an internal thread or covert aid.

The names of most of your commands will be verbs or verb phrases because a superior (anthropomorphically) speaks that verb when it is commanding your object. For example, a superior might say, "restore frame", which becomes the *restoreFrame* command. The name should use the imperative (commanding) mood in language. More examples of commands are *encrypt, send, moveMotor* and *commitWithdrawl*. Notices must be informative, so their wording tends not to be imperative.

Also, when a program is run (or a process is started), the operating system calls an entry-point method which is usually named *main*. By running such a main method, often called the "main program", the user is commanding that object (and the entire program) to do its job. Therefore, a main method is identified as a command.

Object-level Thinking of Commands

Here's an important change in your thinking:

> *From*   A method calling a command.
> Example: "A method in *TrackList* calls *DiskMotor.run*."
>
> *To*   An object commanding another object.
> Example: "*TrackList* commands *DiskMotor*."

That is, we don't say that one method calls another, though that is what happens. We are thinking at the object-level by saying that one object commands another. When designing an IDAR graph, try to stay at the object-level of thinking. You will need to think of individual methods (the commands), but even with those, you can think in terms of one object sending that command to another. A command is a method, so how can we "send" a command?

Senses of "Command"

This book uses the word "command" in the following ways, each representing a way of thinking about a call to a command-method. Below, *A* and *B* are objects:

Noun: "*A* sends a command to *B*"—In this usage of "command", the method-call represents an edict sent from one object to another, and is object-level thinking.

Noun: "*A* calls a command in *B*"—In this case, "command" refers to a method identified as a command, and is method-level thinking.

Verb: "*A* commands *B*"—This usage refers to the act of commanding an object, and is object-level thinking.

In this book, you can determine the intended sense of "command" by its context. The following is a contrived (yet true) sentence that uses "command" in all three ways: "To command an object, you must send a command by calling a command."

Drawing Commands

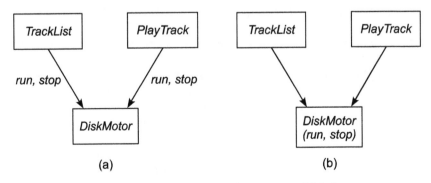

Figure 3.5: CD-player showing command-labels

A command is drawn as an arrow connecting two boxes. Obviously, these represent commands at the object-level because individual methods are not shown in IDAR graphs, except as labels. Stated precisely, an arrow from object *A* to *B* means that the code in *A* calls one or more commands in *B*.

Figure 3.5(a) shows the commands *run* and *stop* that are inside the *DiskMotor* object as labels next to the command-arrows. Figure 3.5(b) illustrates an alternate way of showing commands by listing them in parentheses within the box. These are *not* parameters, but are names of methods identified as commands.

Indirect Commands

Commands can be called indirectly through pointers (a.k.a. addresses or references), or via intermediate software discussed more on page 72. Sending a command using a hard-coded target-name is regarded as direct. Otherwise, it is regarded as indirect. Also known as "dynamic binding", indirection allows the command that's called to be selected or changed at run-time. An indirect command is depicted by a small bubble placed on the tail of its command-arrow, opposite the arrowhead.

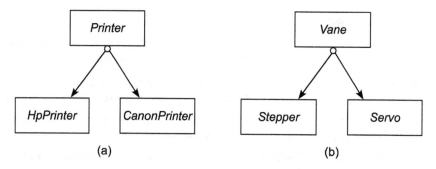

Figure 3.6: Indirect commands

Figure 3.6(a) portrays a *Printer* object which can print a document using an HP or Canon printer. Internally, *Printer* uses a pointer to select a command in either *HpPrinter* or *CanonPrinter* as appropriate, and calls that command to send data to the printer. Figure 3.6(b) is the same graph, but with different labels. A *Vane* object can move an air vane by commanding one of two kinds of motors—a stepper motor, or a closed-loop servo motor. The appropriate *move* command is selected using a pointer.

In both cases above, indirection is used to select one of two alternatives. In IDAR graphs, such exclusive selection is depicted by having the command-arrows emanate from the same bubble.

Polymorphic inheritance is a way to implement indirect commands in these situations where multiple objects perform the same functions in different ways. There can be an "is-a-kind-of" relationship in such cases. For example, a stepper motor is a kind of motor, and a servo motor is a kind of motor. You would derive classes *Stepper* and *Servo* from a base class called *Motor*.

Avoid indirect commands. That also means you should avoid inheritance. Any indirect call to a command, including polymorphic inheritance, makes software more difficult to learn because the source-code doesn't tell you the specific method which will be called. Inheritance causes other problems as well, described in Section 6.6 on page 142, which also provides alternatives to inheritance. The Dispatcher pattern is a good alternative to inheritance and indirect commands, and is described in Section 7.1.3 on page 183. "Is-a-kind-of" relationships are seldom prominent in software, and the troubles with inheritance usually cause it to do more harm than good. The strong historical emphasis on inheritance was a serious mistake as explained in Section 8.9 on page 241. So-called "mixin" classes also use indirection, and they can usually be replaced with ordinary subordinates.

3.4.2 Notices

In our CD-player, when the motor has spun up to its correct speed, *DiskMotor* needs to notify *PlayTrack* of that fact so that its action of playing can progress. Figure 3.7 shows this change incorporated into the design. The short floating arrow labeled "slew" denotes a call to a notice-method located in *PlayTrack*.

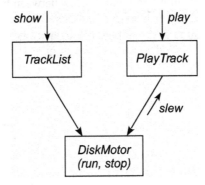

Figure 3.7: CD-player with a notice

Notices are needed because objects interact with each other in more ways than downward commands. Subordinates often need to talk to their superiors. Objects under the same superior will often converse with each other. An object may need to receive notifications from several other objects that are far away in the hierarchy. All such noncommand interactions are performed by the public methods that you have identified as notices.

For a public method to qualify as a notice, (1) it may only convey information into or out of its object (except for any covert aid), and (2) it must satisfy the need-to-know constraint.

Need-to-Know Constraint The Identify rule imposes the following need-to-know constraint on notices: "... a notice only imports or exports needed information." The key is the word "needed". Briefly, the need-to-know constraint is this: *An object receiving information from a notice must need to know it in order to do its job,* similar to a worker telling a coworker something he needs to know. We can elaborate on this constraint by noting that an action initiated by a command consists of one or more steps. The command's method-call may perform any number of these steps, including none of them. After that call returns, any unfinished steps must be done by other methods inside the object. We can now precisely state the need-to-know constraint: *One or more steps of a command's action must need the information obtained by a notice, even if such steps are performed after the command-call has returned.* Therefore, the information supplied by a notice is not required to be used by a command, although it often is. It may be used by any method that assists a commanded action. This constraint also causes pass-through notices (termed "tramp notices") to be forbidden. An exception is the case of isolation described in Section 4.2.4 on page 100.

Also, any notice can be re-identified as a command because a command is allowed to convey information. However, a notice enjoys an advantage over a command: It is not confined to the hierarchy, as any object may call a notice in any other object, giving notices greater flexibility. Therefore, if a method qualifies as a notice, I suggest identifying it as a notice. A possible exception to this bias in favor of notices is a method that is called only by superiors of its object.

Drawing Notices   Draw a call to a notice using a short floating arrow pointing in the direction of the call, paralleling a command-arrow between two objects, as illustrated by the *slew* notice in Figure 3.7 and the *tuneDone* notice in Figure 3.8. Label the notice-arrow with the name of the notice. If the notice exports data, suffix its name with a caret ("^") as exemplified by the *getStatus* notice in Figure 3.8.

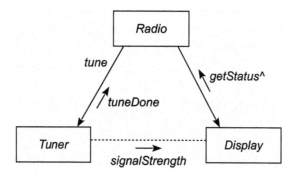

Figure 3.8: Free and bound notices

Free Notices vs. Bound Notices

A notice between two objects is termed a "free notice" if neither object commands the other; otherwise, it is a "bound notice" because it is bound to a command-line. In the *Radio* object, *tuneDone* is a bound notice. For a free notice, first draw a dashed line between the objects that has no arrowhead. This dashed dummy line indicates that a message is passed between the objects, and that it's not a command. Then draw the notice's floating arrow paralleling that dashed line, as illustrated by the *signalStrength* notice in Figure 3.8. I encourage you to read some important discussion about free notices in Section 6.11.2 starting on page 155.

Importing Information (Import-style Notices)

The caller of an import-style notice gives information to the callee object. In the case of our CD-player in Figure 3.7, the *DiskMotor* object calls the *slew* notice in *PlayTrack* to tell it that the motor has reached its desired speed, which is called "slewing" or the "slew speed", and which *PlayTrack* needs to know for playing a track. Import-style notices are the most common, and are typically used for:

Setting inputs Notices can store information in an object to be used by a subsequently called command. An example is *setFont* which is used by the *drawText* command in a *TextWindow* object.

Dataflows Import-style notices are used by consumers of buffers in dataflows. An example would be *freshData* which gives its object a new buffer to consume.

Response from a server A common example would be a remote database. Such a notice would include any data retrieved by the server, or it could indicate a time-out or other error. Examples are *statusOfQuery* and *resultsOfWrite*.

Events A wide variety of events can occur, such as keyboard-presses, mouse-clicks, screen-touches, clock-ticks, data available at an I/O socket or device (such as an arriving Ethernet packet), a DMA-completion, and many others. The notice-methods corresponding to these events could be *kbPress*, *mouseWasClicked*, *touchStart*, *clockTicked*, *enetBufAvail*, and *dmaIsDone*. If an object that you are designing needs to know about such an external event, you should include a notice for it called by the object that handles that event.

State/status changes A notice can announce a change of state, such as *active* or *dead*. And on page 236 of *Object Thinking* [32], David West adds, "We are not looking for *dead* so much as 'I'm dying, gasp, gasp ... the butler did it' written in blood with the object's last exhalation. Or, less colorfully stated, *failing*."

The completion and results of a prior command When the action started by a previously called command finishes, its object can call a notice in another object indicating that it's done and optionally providing results and associated data. In a multithreaded system, another thread often performs commanded actions, and such a done-notice is often called from that internal thread. Examples are *moveIsDone*, *packetWasSent*, and *resultOfMeasurement*.

Progress of some activity If a time-consuming action is in progress, its object may call a notice to report percentage done, passing a milestone, or completion of a chore. For example, a notice in a GUI can update a progress-bar, or the progress of a CPU-intensive chore may be monitored to predict when it will finish. Examples include *kbytesCopied*, *percentDone*, *filesReadSoFar*, *didPost*, and *writesAreDone*.

Exporting Information (Export-style Notices)

A notice may return information (to its caller) that is related to the role of the object containing the notice. Such export-style notices are often used for:

Getting results A command may leave its results in private fields in the object, which are fetched later by notices.

Dataflows Export-style notices can be used by producers of buffers in dataflows. Such a notice might be named *iNeedAnotherBuf*, and its caller is requesting another buffer from the producer.

Resource requests An object could call a bound notice named *iNeedMemory* (in its superior), requesting memory needed to perform a commanded action. This is the Resourceful Boss pattern described in Section 7.1.2 on page 180.

Status queries A notice such as *getStatus* would return the status of its object.

Progress queries A notice named *getPercentDone* could be called several times per second to update a progress-bar for a slow operation.

Object-level Thinking of Notices

Earlier, I stated that you should think at the higher level of objects commanding objects. The same is true of notices. You should not think of a method within one object calling a notice (method) within another object. This is method-level thinking, which is appropriate when designing the methods within objects. But when designing at the object-level as we are, you should think in terms of objects commanding and notifying other objects. In the CD-player, we say that "*DiskMotor* notifies *PlayTrack*." This ability to think at the object-level for both commands and notices is an important feature of the IDAR method.

Like the word "command", the words "notice" and "notify" are used in multiple ways. If object *A* calls a notice-method in object *B*, then we say that:

- "*A* notifies *B*" (stressing interactions of objects)
- "*A* sends a notice to *B*" (stressing messages between objects)
- "*A* calls a notice in *B*" (stressing methods in objects)

The following contrived (yet true) sentence uses the words "notice" and "notify" in all three ways: "To notify an object, you must send a notice by calling a notice."

As an aside, I considered other names for "notice". It provides information, so an obvious name is "informer", which has undesirable connotations. It helps its object, suggesting "helper" or "help", but saying "object *A* sent help to object *B*" sounds odd. Another possible name is "event", but some notices are not events, such as results of prior commands, progress reports, and sensor readings. So "notice" it shall be.

Order of Calls

A notice which helps a commanded action by supplying information may be called before, during, or after the call to the command. Let's label these events as follows:

C = the call to the command
R = the return of the command
N = the call to the notice

Here are the three possible orders of these events, and how information supplied by an import-style notice can help in each of these cases:

N-C-R Because the notice is called before the command, the notice must store its information in fields in the object. The subsequently called command, or its following activity, is required to use that information. For example, a *start-Cooking* command in a microwave oven needs to know the cooking-time which is provided by a prior *userSetTime* notice.

C-N-R A command waits (blocks) until the notice is called that provides it with the information it needs. Such a notice usually reports the occurrence of an event. As an example, the *heat* command in a furnace-controller object will (1) command the *GasValve* to open, (2) wait for the *hotEnough* notice from the *Thermometer*, (3) command *Blower* to run, and (4) return. This C-N-R case can occur in a single-threaded design via an upward notice called by a command.

C-R-N The notice is called after the command has returned. If the command has finished its duty, the (export-style) notice will fetch its results. If it didn't finish, the (import-style) notice is probably reporting an event which will allow the object to perform one or more of the unfinished steps. As an example, the *heat* command in the furnace above could return after opening the valve, leaving step 3 (starting the blower) to be done when the *hotEnough* notice is called.

3.4.3 Nonmethod Commands and Notices

Besides calling methods, the following are some other ways that objects can send commands and notices to each other:

Message-Queue An object could contain a message-queue (mailbox) to which messages are added by other objects. Each such message must be identified as a command or a notice.

Semaphore Sometimes an object will contain a semaphore which other objects post (increment) in order to signal the object. This signal must be identified as a command or a notice.

Messages An object might receive inter-process or inter-thread messages by some technique other than those mentioned above, such as a signal, socket, or pipe, and these must be identified as commands or notices.

Field An object can contain a public field accessible to other objects. Reading or writing such a field can be either a notice or command, based on whether doing so is in the object's role. Also, see getters and setters on page 70.

All discussion in this book applies to every possible interaction between objects, and each must be identified as a command or a notice. This book usually assumes that method-calls are used, because they are the most common.

3.5 The Down Rule

In the overview in Section 3.2, the Down rule was defined as follows:

> *When graphing the calls to commands among objects, the arrows must point down. In this graph, an arrow connecting two boxes means that code in the upper object calls one or more commands in the lower object.*

This rule can be stated simply: Commands go down in the graph.

Hierarchy

This simple rule has an important consequence: Your design is forced to consist of a hierarchy containing no cycles. Technically, an IDAR graph is a DAG, which stands for "directed acyclic graph". But most people don't know what a DAG is, so I use the synonym "hierarchy" instead.

Some New Terms

I defined the terms "superior" and "subordinate" earlier. This book also uses "boss" as a synonym of "superior", and "worker" as a synonym of "subordinate".

High-Level and Low-Level The hierarchy in an IDAR graph resulting from the Down rule suggests two more useful definitions:

> Objects around the top of the graph are called "high-level".
> Objects around the bottom are called "low-level".

As you'll see in Chapter 5, which describes the process of design, you will treat high-level and low-level objects differently. Low-level objects tend to either interact with external devices or contain specialized algorithms or data. High-level objects tend to be similar to managers in that they plan, command, and coordinate the actions of low-level objects.

Multiple Superiors

You might have noticed something unusual about the hierarchy shown in Figure 3.7: The *DiskMotor* object has *two* superiors, which are *TrackList* and *PlayTrack*. We are not accustomed to this situation because in human institutions, the workers almost always have exactly *one* boss. But there are a few exceptions. A secretary working for a large department in a corporation accepts chores from several managers. A private figure skating coach works for several parents, teaching their children to ice skate. In IDAR graphs, objects commonly have multiple superiors.

3.6   The Aid Rule

In the overview in Section 3.2, the Aid rule was defined as follows:

> *A command or notice may, unknown to its callers, aid its object by
> performing part or all of a previously commanded action.*

After a command has been called, any public method (notice or command) in its object may secretly perform any of the duties of that command, regardless of the method's role. Covertly aiding an object like this is almost always done by a notice due to this common sequence of events:

1. A command is called and does not finish its duties. The command might or might not have returned (i.e., the call may be nonblocking or blocking).
2. Later, a notice is called, usually announcing an event the object was waiting for, allowing it to proceed with those unfinished duties.

3. Because the object now has some work to do and the CPU is currently executing inside the object in the notice, the notice itself does some or all of that work on behalf of the command, aiding both the command and the object.

From its caller's viewpoint, a notice only conveys information. Any additional actions done by the notice are regarded as covert aid because the notice's caller is unaware of them. Such actions are usually the object's reaction to the information.

For example, in our CD-player, suppose the CD has spun-up and the *slew* notice has been called to tell *PlayTrack* that "the motor is up to usable speed." The object's reaction to this news will be to command *LaserMotor* to *move* the laser to the track to be played. Instead of having a separate internal thread command *LaserMotor*, the *PlayTrack* object has the *slew* notice do this, as portrayed in Figure 3.9. From the viewpoint of its caller, the *slew* notice only conveys a fact about motor-speed, but internally, that notice also covertly aids its object (*PlayTrack*) by performing part of the play-operation that was started by a previous call to the *play* command.

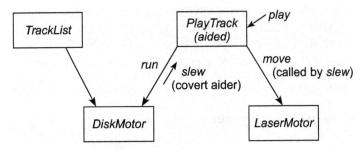

Figure 3.9: CD-player illustrating aid

The Aid rule imposes the following constraints on aid:

Previous Command A public method (a command or usually a notice) may aid only a previously commanded activity within its object. You must be able to specify which command initiated the activity being aided.

Covert Although the caller of a public method is allowed to know that aid is likely to occur and that method-returns might be delayed due to such aid, the caller must not know any details about the aid. Aid is covert.

Covert aid is a way to allocate CPU-time. When a public method is called, the CPU is executing your code, and you can use that opportunity to secretly perform pending actions. Thus, you use a call to your public method as a way to allocate (or steal) CPU-time to do other work that is not in the method's role.

Some final remarks: Your aid-arrangement is an important facet of your design, so document aid-actions in each method's header-comments. A notice that provides aid performs an action, so your first impulse may be to mis-identify it as a command that performs that action. You can read more about this common mistake in Section 6.9 on page 150. The Role rule, described next, covers the actions of a public method as seen by an observer located *outside* the object. The Aid rule covers the additional (covert) actions of a public method as seen by an observer located *inside* the object.

3.7   The Role Rule

Roles are the core of your design, making them very important. So I will carefully explain what a role is and the characteristics of a good one.

3.7.1   What It Does, and Not How

A role is a concise sentence or phrase describing the actions that an object or method can perform for its callers. Together, these actions compose the service offered to callers. "Actions of a role" and "role's actions" are phrases used in this book that refer to the actions covered by a role.

A role is written from the viewpoint of a caller, so it reveals *what is done, but not how it is done*. A role must not reveal any aspect of the inner workings (implementation) of its object or method. Related concepts that are well known include:

Abstraction: The traditional term for "role" used by theoreticians.
Information Hiding: Concealing internal design-decisions from external agents.
Black Box: Visible actions performed by concealed mechanics.
Encapsulation: A boundary separating outer behavior from inner apparatus.
Separation of Concerns: Designing modules around concerns (areas or matters).

You should memorize this sentence: "A role must state *what* is done and not *how*."

3.7.2   Creating Good Roles

Clarity, cohesion, and concealment are the main criteria for gauging the quality of a role. They are described in detail in Section 4.1, starting on page 79, so only a synopsis is provided below:

Clarity After reading a role, do you know what its actions are, or are you still wondering? Clarity indicates how well a role communicates its actions. A clear role tells you plainly what the object or method does. An unclear role leaves you unsure. The action in the role "sets speed" is clear, but "system utilities" is unclear because this role provides no clue as to what its actions are.

Cohesion How closely related or associated are the actions of the role? That is its cohesion. Highly cohesive actions are tightly related. This subjective measure often (but not always) correlates with how much code and data the actions will have in common after they are implemented. For example, "manages calendar" has high cohesion because it only has one action. "Sends and receives messages" has good cohesion because its actions are complementary. "BCD math library" has medium cohesion because all of its actions operate on BCD numbers, but are otherwise unrelated. "Computes pace and paints glyphs" has no cohesion because its two actions have nothing in common that would associate them with each other.

Concealment How well does the role conceal the implementation (inner workings) of the object or method? That is its concealment. The role "returns first item in the linked list" has no concealment because it describes how the method operates. But "returns newest client-ID" has high concealment because it gives no clue about how its action is implemented.

Here are four types of roles, along with their typical quality levels:

Vacuous A role such as "processes X" or "handles X" (where X is a noun) has good cohesion and concealment, but tells you almost nothing, giving it poor clarity. Avoid such roles whenever possible.

Trait-Based Instead of stating its actions explicitly, a trait-based role specifies a trait that all of its actions possess. For example, all actions covered by the role "fast operations" have the trait of being fast, and all actions of the role "safety services" relate to safety. The actions implicit in the role "initializes this object" have the shared trait of being performed at the same time. For such roles, concealment is good, cohesion varies (but is often poor), and clarity is often poor to medium because actions are specified implicitly instead of explicitly.

Managerial A role containing a verb like "manages" or "controls" indicates that something is managed. Its clarity depends on how obvious its actions are. "Controls valve" is clear, but "manages car" probably isn't because you aren't sure what managing a car entails. Concealment for managerial roles is high, and their cohesion is high because managing is their sole action.

Common A common role explicitly identifies one or more actions, using a verb for each. Clarity is that of the role's least-clear action. Its cohesion is based on its number of verbs (actions) and how related they are. Having one verb is ideal, two can be good, and three or more is suspect because cohesion will probably be poor. Concealment depends entirely on whether the verbs describe *what* is done rather than *how* it is done.

Dividing On a related topic, every superior has a broad (general) role that you will divide into pieces, each piece being a narrower (more specialized) role for a subordinate, as portrayed in Figure 3.10. You cannot design well until you become adept at such partitioning of roles. Section 5.4 on page 117 provides a step-by-step procedure for creating such a hierarchy of roles.

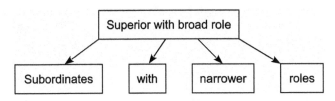

Figure 3.10: Dividing a broad role

3.7.3   The Role Rule

In the overview in Section 3.2, the Role rule was defined as follows:

> *Write a brief role for each object and method that summarizes all services it offers, avoiding any aspect of its implementation (including aid). Callers may rely on only what is stated in roles.*

Your object or method must do all that it claims to do. For example, the role of the *PlayTrack* object in our exemplary CD-player is "plays a specified track on the CD." If it (understandably) refused to play a track containing rap or metalcore, it would be performing less than its stated role, despite how strongly we agree with its taste in music. Also, extra actions that are not in the role are forbidden, except for covert aid. This requirement eliminates the common problem of unexpected side-effects.

After defining the commands in an object, recheck all roles and callers to verify that (1) the commands cover all aspects of the object's role, (2) the commands do nothing extra, and (3) callers don't rely on anything not stated in the roles. After a command completes its chore, a common mistake is to have it command an unrelated (out-of-role) follow-up action in another object. This mistake is called "temporal chaining", and is described in Section 6.8 on page 147. If starting that follow-up action is not in the command's role, don't do it.

As mentioned earlier, a command need not finish the duties described in its role. A command is only required to initiate or start doing its duties, and its method-call may return without finishing them (i.e., the call may be nonblocking), leaving the undone portion to be performed by any mixture of other methods or threads or covert aid.

Notices also have roles, and because notices are informative, their roles must have the form "tells the object that X" (import-style) or "returns X to the caller" (export-style), where X is some information. Examples are "tells the object that lifting is done" and "returns status of lifting to the caller." In addition, if a block of data (i.e., a buffer) accompanies a notice, its role will contain a phrase similar to "gives a new buffer to the called/calling object." If you prefer to think of an object as a person, the role for an import-style notice becomes "tells me that X."

Effects of Aid on Roles A role may not state what specific aid is provided. The Aid rule governs covert actions, and the Role rule governs overt actions. Unfortunately, covert aid leaks into the overt realm a little, affecting roles in two ways:

- Roles should mention that aid can delay method-returns. If timing is a concern, roles should state the frequency and longest duration of these delays.

- Surprisingly, providing aid can be the purpose of a notice, and its role would be "this notice tells the object that it may administer aid in this call." Such a role is acceptable because it reveals no details about the aid.

3.7.4 Cross-Cutting Concerns

There are areas of activities which must be done by many objects, but which don't fall under their roles. By far the most common area is debugging. Most code outputs debug messages by commanding a debug-object which filters such messages. But the roles for methods do not state that they may output debug messages, so such activity means objects are performing more actions than their roles allow. Activities such as outputting debug messages, logging events, monitoring health, updating statistics, and ensuring security are necessary in the system, and are known as "cross-cutting concerns" in the literature because they are other areas that cut across many objects. The program is designed around its "core concerns", but these cross-cutting concerns must somehow be accommodated. This is an area of active research, but two good ways of addressing them that conform to the IDAR rules are:

- Implement these activities in objects which are commanded by the rest of the system. Example objects include *Debug*, *Logging*, and *RunTimeStats*.
- Employ the Union pattern (see page 186) which creates a two-level shadow-hierarchy that can send cross-cutting commands to any and all objects.

These two techniques handle most cross-cutting concerns elegantly and without resorting to hidden side-effects as is often encouraged in the literature. The Role rule makes a sensible exception for such activities. Objects and methods may do them (or command them) without mentioning them in their roles.

3.8 The Rules Form a Team

To see how the four rules complement and interact with each other, we must first make a clearer distinction between overt and covert actions:

Overt The overt actions of both commands and notices are those which their callers are aware of. These actions are stated in roles, and you can regard them as the exterior view of an object or method.

Covert These actions of commands and notices are concealed from their callers. They are part of an object's internal implementation, helping the object do its job. Only the code inside the object knows where these actions are done.

Rule	Methods	Constraint On Methods	Constraint On Callers
Identify	Notices	Convey needed info.	—
Down	Commands	—	Calls go down in graph
Aid	Both	May aid prev. com. action	Ignorant of any aid (covert)
Role	Both	Exactly fulfill their roles	Rely only on roles (overt)

Table 3.2: Constraints imposed by the four rules

Table 3.2 shows the constraints that each of the four rules imposes on public methods (that is, commands and notices), and on their callers. Study this table, paying particular attention to the constraints imposed on methods versus their callers.

Curiously, the actions of a command are constrained only by its object's role; a command is otherwise free to do anything you wish. But calls to it are constrained by the Down rule to only proceeding downward in the graph. On the other hand, a notice has no constraint on its callers; it can be called from anywhere you wish. But it is constrained by the Identify rule to only conveying needed information. Part of the strength and versatility of the IDAR rules arise from this ability to choose between flexible actions or flexible callers. But you cannot have both, which is why the IDAR rules prevent messiness.

IDAR is based on dividing actions into categories based on function and visibility. Actions are divided by function into commands and notices, yielding the choice between flexible actions or callers. This division assumes that objects' interactions are either imperative or informative. You can read more about this philosophical topic in Section 8.7 on page 238.

Actions are divided by visibility into overt and covert. This division of actions into known-to-caller versus hidden-from-caller represents another strength of the IDAR method because it permits your public methods to do more than their official duties as stated in their roles, providing additional options for structuring implementation-related activities inside an object. This division assumes that a caller cares only about what an object does from an external perspective, and not how it does it internally.

As you can see, the IDAR rules are well-thought-out, versatile, and elegant. When designing with them, their constraints don't feel constraining.

3.9   More About Notices

3.9.1   Indirect Notices

Perhaps you realized that *TrackList* in the CD-player also needs to contain a *slew* notice called from *DiskMotor*. But doing so is a problem for *DiskMotor* because when it's time to send the notice, *DiskMotor* needs to call one of two *slew* notices—one in *TrackList* and one in *PlayTrack*. How can it know which one of these it should call?

Bubble Denotes Indirection   Calls to notices (as well as commands) can be direct or indirect. You can have each superior pass the subordinate a pointer (address) to its *slew* notice as a parameter in a command. Later, the subordinate calls the notice indirectly via that pointer. Such indirection is depicted by a bubble (circle) on the tail of the notice's arrow, as it is for commands as you read earlier. Figure 3.11 shows this change incorporated into the design of the CD-player.

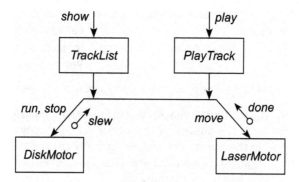

Figure 3.11: CD-player with indirect notices

Rails   The horizontal line, called a "rail", indicates that both *TrackList* and *PlayTrack* command *DiskMotor* and *LaserMotor*, and that the *slew* and *done* notices are present in both of those superiors. Rails are discussed in detail on page 66.

Unfortunately, an indirect method-call, such as this *slew* notice, makes learning code more difficult because determining which method will be called requires more effort. A way to avoid this indirection is to pass a flag into *DiskMotor* telling it which superior commanded it. That approach works, but it hard-codes knowledge of all superiors into the code for *DiskMotor*, which reduces flexibility and increases risk in the likely situation of adding another superior later. It also creates more dependencies in *DiskMotor*, making its code more difficult to use in another product. Your decision in a case like this requires that you make a compromise.

```
class DiskMotor {
    public:
    typedef void (*NoticePtrT)(void);
    static void run (int speed, NoticePtrT slewNotice);
    static void stop (NoticePtrT stoppedNotice);
    // other declarations
};
```

Assuming that we chose to use indirection, we pass a pointer to the notice to be called later, as shown in the code-listing above. In this C++ *DiskMotor* class, the *run* command accepts the slewNotice parameter, which is a pointer to a notice-method which tells the superior that the motor has reached its slew speed. Also, the *stop* command accepts the stoppedNotice pointer; it points to a notice which will inform the superior that the motor has come to a complete stop.

As with commands, sending a notice using a hard-coded target-name is regarded as direct. Otherwise, it is regarded as indirect. Several techniques are available for sending both direct and indirect notices, and passing a method-address as described above is only one of them. These techniques are described in Section 6.11.3 starting on page 160.

3.9.2 Rider Notices

Earlier, you learned about bound notices that follow command lines, and free notices that don't. Both bound and free notices can be indirect. There is one more common kind of notice: The method-return of a command can be regarded as a notice. When you call a command, whether it's blocking or nonblocking, it will eventually return, and information can ride on that method-return back to the caller in several ways, such as a function-value. Such returned information is called a "rider notice".

A rider notice is *not* drawn as a separate arrow, but instead is depicted as a label by the corresponding command-arrow prefixed with a caret ("^"). Two examples are shown in Figure 3.12.

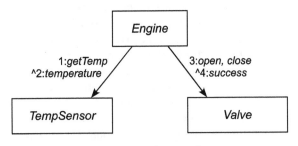

Figure 3.12: Rider notices

Riding on Method-Returns   In Figure 3.12, the *Engine* object commands *TempSensor* to read a temperature by calling its *getTemp* command. The result is returned as a function-value when the command returns. You can think of this returned value as a notice that is riding on a method-return. Also, *Engine* commands the *Valve* to open or close, and the return-value of this method-call indicates success or failure. In general, a command can supply information at return-time, which is a rider notice, in any of three ways:

- The command can return information in its function-value, as was used in the examples of *TempSensor* and *Valve*.

- The command can change its parameters. In C++, this is done using pointers or references.

- The method-return itself is often regarded as a notice that says, "I finished the action you commanded, sir!"

If one or more of these techniques is used to communicate information from a command back to its caller, then the method-return is a rider notice. One consequence of this definition is that any function that computes and returns a value can be regarded as a command to perform the computation followed by a rider notice containing the result.

Rider notices enjoy several advantages over bound and free notices:

- A subordinate can easily have multiple superiors. This is the most important advantage because it makes objects more flexible and reusable.

- Objects are simpler because they contain fewer methods.

- Programs are more efficient due to having fewer calls.

- Rider notices reduce dependencies (couplings) among classes. A notice using a method-call causes the caller to be dependent on the callee's existence and interface, reducing reusability and modifiability.

Employ rider notices whenever you can. The advantages listed above make them superior to bound and free notices consisting of separate methods and calls.

A notice can return a rider notice. Such an export-style notice was discussed earlier. If an import-style notice also returns information, it is both import-style and export-style, and is labeled on the graph with its name, followed by a caret, followed by the name of its returned data, as seen in Figure 3.21 on page 65. In this example, the label on the pair of notices is *iNeedData^hereItIs*, indicating that the called notice is *iNeedData*, and that it returns the rider notice, *hereItIs*.

It is possible to have a rider *command*. This occurs when a subordinate calls a bound notice in a superior, and then that superior responds with a command that rides on the notice's method-return. This situation is uncommon enough that there is no special notation for it. A designer would represent both the notice and the following rider command in the ordinary manner (i.e., with separate arrows), except that the command label would be prefixed with a caret.

Here is the general rule regarding carets: The name of a method precedes a caret, and the rider notice or rider command it returns follows the caret.

Sequence Numbers   You might have noticed that the commands and notices for the engine in Figure 3.12 were prefixed with sequence numbers. In many cases, showing the sequence of messages in this manner helps portray the design more clearly. In this example, the events shown in Table 3.3 cause the valve to be opened.

No.	Message	Description
1	*getTemp*	Read engine temperature (command)
2	*temperature*	Temperature reading (rider notice)
3	*open*	Open valve (command)
4	*success*	Confirmation that valve is open (rider notice)

Table 3.3: Sequence of messages

I prefer to use sequence numbers in an IDAR graph instead of drawing a separate sequence diagram in UML because the labels make interactions among objects clearer. People learn designs fastest when structure and behavior are combined, as they are in IDAR graphs embellished with sequence numbers, because folks can see the structure in action. UML separates structure and behavior because it employs several different kinds of diagrams for both, forcing people to remember one diagram while examining another, hampering learning.

3.9.3   An Example of Notices

Figures 3.9 and 3.11 show a common use of bound notices: A subordinate tells a superior about the progress, completion, or results of a prior command. In addition, free notices are used to transfer information between objects that don't command each other, such as the *percentDone* notice sent to the GUI (Graphical User Interface) in the flight-reservation program shown in Figure 3.13. The GUI uses this notice to update a progress-bar. The notice sent by *Reservations* is indirect because it has multiple superiors, but the *olSearchIsDone* notice sent by *Offloader* is direct because it has only one superior (*Searcher*). The *flightInfo* notice is a rider because it's carried back by the method-return of the *findFlight* command.

The class declaration for *Searcher* is given below in C++:

```
class Searcher {
   public:
   // Commands:  (called by my superiors)
      static bool addSearchSpec (int itemNum, int itemValue);
      static bool search ();
      static int  getResults (SearchResultsT& resultList);

   // Notices:  (called by my subordinates)
      static void dbActionIsDone (DbResultT& dbResult);
      static void olSearchIsDone (SearchResultsT& resultList);
};
```

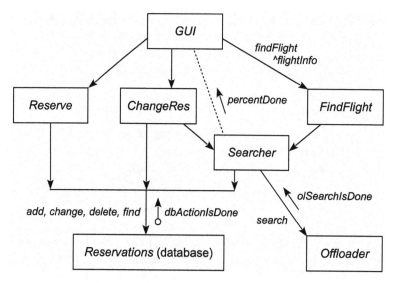

Figure 3.13: Flight-reservation program

3.10   Subsystems

A subsystem is a portion of the program that performs a well-defined job and has few dependencies on the rest of the program. Such independence is achieved by imposing the following requirements on a subsystem:

- It must consist of a hierarchy. That is, it is a DAG. It is a sub-hierarchy within the main hierarchy of the program.
- It must have one subsystem-manager at the top of its hierarchy. This "subman", as it's termed, has the same name as the subsystem it controls.
- Objects outside a subsystem may only know about its subman. Thus, all commands (except the rare rider commands) and directly called notices originating outside a subsystem must be directed to its subman. In other words, a subman is the interface into its subsystem.

A subsystem can contain as few as two objects: the subman and its subordinate. The source-code of subsystems often contain around six to ten classes, although there is no limit to their number.

I recommend that the source-code for a subsystem be placed in only one file, even if it will contain over 5000 lines of code. Doing so has two advantages: (1) the code is easier to browse and learn because it's together and not scattered among multiple files, and (2) the names of classes and objects under the subman will be file-local instead of global. If you must have multiple files, I suggest placing the subsystem's internal objects (but not its subman) into a namespace devoted to the subsystem.

I stated that objects may not be nested in the graph, one inside of another. Likewise, subsystems may not be nested. There is a sense that a subman owns all objects and subsystems internal to it, but they are not nested. But in source-code, you may nest classes and/or namespaces within a subman when convenient.

3.10.1 Drawing Subsystems

If a design commands (i.e., uses) a subsystem, then the entire subsystem is depicted by a single elongated hexagon, labeled with the name of the subsystem. In the example given in Figure 3.14, *Airlines*, *Hotels*, and *CarRental* are subsystems. These are also the names of their subman objects. Figure 10.5 on page 282 shows another example of using a subsystem.

The design of each subsystem is given in a separate graph. Each such subsystem graph is drawn as follows:

- Its subman is drawn as an elongated hexagon at the top of the graph.
- The hierarchy under the subman is drawn in the usual manner.
- External subordinates (objects and subsystems) are drawn to document their existence and interactions, but they are drawn with dashed lines to indicate that they are not part of the subsystem.

Let's look at a graph to make this verbiage clearer. Figure 3.15 shows the MAC layer in a digital radio. This design is used as an example of the design process in Chapter 5, and is presented in Section 5.5 on page 124. The *MAC* object at the top is the subman for this subsystem. Note that *PHY*, which is an external subsystem, is drawn dashed. It was included in this graph to show what external objects and subsystems are commanded by this subsystem. The *PHY* is a dependency because the *MAC* subsystem contains direct calls into the *PHY*. Keep the number of dependencies as low as possible; refer to the CR Metric in Section 4.4.3 on page 106.

While the use of direct commands to external objects is acceptable in a subsystem, it is usually poor practice for a subsystem to have direct calls to external notices in a superior, as doing so hard-codes knowledge of a broad swath of the design into the subsystem. Such direct bound notice-calls also restrict the subsystem to be usable only by its one superior, making it difficult to add a second superior. Use rider or indirect notices instead. For example, the *PHY* uses indirection for its *slotStart* and *slotDone* notices, making it independent of its superior, the *MAC*.

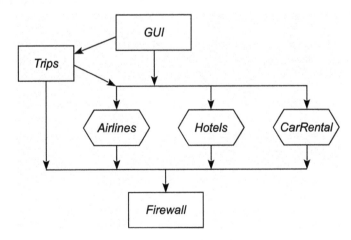

Figure 3.14: Commanding subsystems

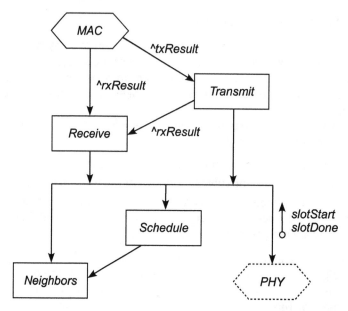

Figure 3.15: MAC subsystem of a digital radio

You can provide a subsystem with pointers to all of its required external notices and subordinates. Consequently, the subsystem will have *no* dependencies. This is the Component pattern described in Section 7.5.2 on page 216, utilizing dependency injection [9]. A component is more portable than a typical subsystem, albeit at a cost of severely reduced learnability due to indirect commands.

3.10.2   Sending Notices to a Subsystem

Objects inside a subsystem may call commands in objects located outside the subsystem. But external objects are unaware of internal objects, so how can external objects send notices to objects inside a subsystem? There are two ways:

Route notices through the subman. With this arrangement, the subman object contains all notices needed by external objects. Those notices merely forward their calls to notices in the appropriate objects within the subsystem.

Use indirect notices. A subsystem can provide external objects with pointers to notices so they can send notices into the subsystem. The exemplary *MAC* subsystem receives indirect notices from the *PHY*, which means the *MAC* previously supplied their pointers to the *PHY*.

The first method has the advantage of avoiding indirect calls, making the structure of the code easier to learn. Unfortunately, it adds dependencies and boosts complexity by adding relay-notices to the subman. The second (indirect) method reduces dependencies at a cost of also reducing learnability. You will need to weigh this trade-off between learnability and independence.

3.11 Method-Level Design

You have learned several rules and techniques for portraying designs at the object-level using IDAR graphs. Such graphs are called "object-level IDAR graphs". As mentioned earlier, there is a different kind of IDAR graph, called a "method-level IDAR graph", which can show the calls among methods *inside* of an object, and even their accesses to fields. For brevity, the phrase "IDAR graph" denotes an object-level IDAR graph, which is the most common kind.

I have noticed that the graphs of internal method-calls in most objects is shallow, usually being no more than two levels. In these common cases, method-level design is trivial or nearly so, and is not worthwhile. A method-level graph is helpful only when you have chains of three or more method-calls, or non-trivial dataflows.

To draw a method-level IDAR graph, first draw a large box or hexagon representing the object itself. All of the methods and fields must fit inside, so draw it as large as necessary to contain everything. When drawing on paper, the box or hexagon will usually cover the entire sheet.

3.11.1 Methods

Inside the large box or hexagon, each method is drawn as a parallelogram which is labeled with its name. Each public method has an arrow pointing to it starting from outside the large box, representing external calls to it. Each is labeled with a "C" or "N" to indicate whether it's a command or a notice. Figure 3.16 is an example.

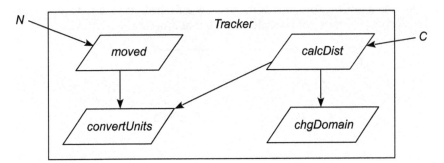

Figure 3.16: Public and private methods within an object

After drawing a parallelogram for each method, you can draw arrows among them representing their calls. An arrow is drawn from caller to callee. Developers prefer that such arrows point downward, but they are not required to do so. The result is a subroutine call-graph similar to Figure 1.4. In Figure 3.16, *moved* calls *convertUnits*, and *calcDist* calls both *convertUnits* and *chgDomain*.

An indirect call is depicted by a small bubble (circle) on the tail of its call-arrow, as is done with indirect commands and notices in object-level IDAR graphs. Also, following the drawing conventions for subsystems, external objects and methods are drawn with dashed lines. These show that such objects and methods are accessed by your methods, but that they are outside of your object.

The IDAR rules do not apply to method-level design, except for the Role rule. Write a role for every private method (your public methods already have roles).

You will notice that a method-level IDAR graph closely resembles an object-level IDAR graph. Both kinds of graphs share the concept of commanding, because when one method calls another, you can view the caller as commanding the callee. Also, as you proceed down its hierarchy, an object-level IDAR graph smoothly transitions into a method call-graph, without an abrupt change, and we take advantage of that fact when designing the methods inside an object. This smooth transition allows us to employ a similar design-process at the method-level as is used at the object-level. This continuum from object-level to method-level unifies two historically opposing design-approaches. I discuss this topic in Section 8.4 on page 235.

The process of design using the IDAR method is covered in detail in Chapter 5, and includes techniques for designing at both the object-level and method-level.

3.11.2   Fields

Fields are drawn as circles or ovals, labeled with their names. Movements of data between methods and fields are depicted by dashed arrows. If a method writes to a field, the arrow points to the field. If it reads the field, the arrow points to the method. If a method both reads and writes a field, then both arrowheads are drawn. If the access is indirect, the usual bubble is placed on the method (or object) performing the access, as illustrated in Figure 3.27(c) on page 71.

Usually only the most important data-movements are shown between methods and fields, such as messages entering and leaving a message-queue, or data entering and leaving a buffer. You don't want to draw a dashed arrow for *every* field-access because doing so clutters the graph so much that it becomes unreadable.

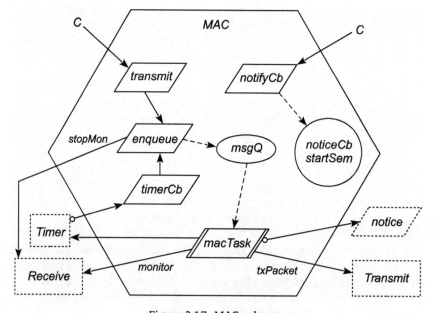

Figure 3.17: MAC subman

An example of a method-level design is shown in Figure 3.17. The steps used to design this example are given in Section 5.6 (page 128). The most prominent feature of this example is the large hexagon denoting the *MAC* subman. All objects and methods outside that hexagon are drawn dashed, because they are external and are present only to show what the subman interacts with. The *transmit* and *notifyCb* methods are public, so they are the only methods which other objects may call directly. Both are commands, although notices are obviously permissible in a subman. The most important data-movements in this design are the flow of messages from the private *enqueue* method to *msgQ*, and then from *msgQ* to *macTask* which processes the messages. This example follows the common Inbox pattern (page 207), which funnels all events into a message-queue which is read by one thread (*macTask*). The doubled side-lines indicate that *macTask* is a thread, as you'll learn next.

3.12 More Features of IDAR Graphs

At a minimum, IDAR graphs portray the command hierarchy among objects, along with their notices, and subsystems. However, these graphs can portray much additional useful information, such as threading, dataflows, popular objects (utilities), and hardware. You saw that rails are a convenient graphing feature similar to organizational charts used in corporations, and they greatly reduce clutter.

3.12.1 Threads, Processes, and ISRs

In the CD-player, we want *TrackList* and *PlayTrack* to run in their own threads so they won't block calls from their superiors. Also, *DiskMotor* and *LaserMotor* contain interrupt service routines (ISRs), which ought to be denoted on the graph somehow.

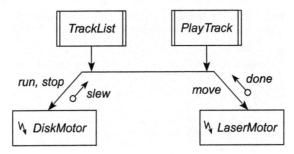

Figure 3.18: CD-player with threads and ISRs

Figure 3.18 shows these changes. Two of the objects now have doubled vertical lines. This double-line notation was taken from UML, and indicates that the object is "active", meaning it contains a thread. In our case, both *TrackList* and *PlayTrack* contain threads. To minimize deadlocks, timing-holes, and contention problems, you should keep the number of threads in your design to a minimum.

Figure 3.19 shows how we depict active objects containing a thread, process, or an ISR. An object containing a thread is shown in Figure 3.19(a). If the object is a subman, small vertical lines are added inside the left and right corners of its hexagon as shown in Figure 3.19(b). An object containing an ISR can be depicted with a lightning-bolt, as in Figure 3.19(c). If a subman (or object) contains or runs as a heavyweight process, it is drawn with *two* additional vertical lines, as illustrated in Figure 3.19(d). Such a process is often an executable file.

Figure 3.19: Active objects with a thread, ISR, or process

Within a method-level IDAR graph, if a method is a thread or process, its parallelogram is drawn with doubled or tripled vertical lines, as shown in Figure 3.17.

If an object contains a thread or process, then usually at least one of its methods, public or private, runs forever in a loop. Such a loop typically waits for mail to appear in a mailbox (following the Inbox pattern), or for a semaphore to be posted, and then performs an action.

If you are planning to have processes interact with each other, consider replacing those processes with threads. Inter-process communication is clumsy and thus complicates your code. As the byline of Chapter 6 states, "Complexity is the enemy." Avoid processes.

Objects in embedded systems often have direct access to interrupts. You can perform brief processing chores in an ISR, which often eliminates the need for a thread in an object. You are encouraged to take full advantage of ISRs because, by eliminating threads, they eliminate some (but not all) potential timing troubles. ISRs are common in embedded software, and are almost unheard-of everywhere else.

In the CD-player, *DiskMotor* does not have its own thread, and yet it needs to call a *slew* notice when it's at slew speed. How can it call *slew* when it has no thread? The call to *slew* is made from its ISR. In Figure 3.18, the lightning-bolts in *DiskMotor* and *LaserMotor* indicate that they contain ISRs. Be careful when calling methods (such as *slew*) outside your object from an ISR, because such methods must be fast and must not block. In the header comments of your source-code, you should document which methods are expected to be called from an ISR.

Threading Model   An exceptionally useful feature of an IDAR graph is that it reveals the threading model, which is the threads that objects run under. For example, in Figure 3.20, you can see that *Sub1* and *Sub2* run under *ThreadA*, and that *Sub3* and *Sub4* run under *ThreadB*. Also, *Contend* can run under either thread, warning you to check for resource contention in *Contend*. In addition to commands, you can also see which threads notices will be called from. In UML, little of this is clear.

3.12.2   Dataflows

A dataflow between two objects is drawn as a dashed arrow pointing in the direction of flow. Showing such dataflows helps developers to learn your design. To make them more distinct from free notices, draw dataflows using a coarser dash-pattern or in a different color. Most dataflows occur between successive stages (objects or subsystems) which are under a common superior, as depicted in Figure 3.21.

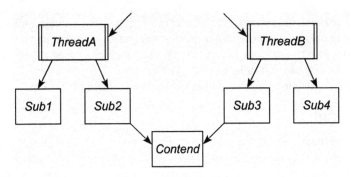

Figure 3.20: An IDAR graph shows the threading model

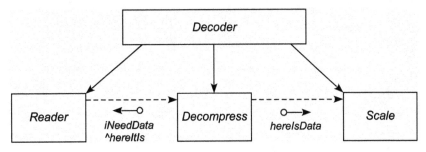

Figure 3.21: Example of dataflows (coarser dash-pattern than free notices)

Data is usually conveyed by notices, such as *iNeedData, hereItIs*, and *hereIsData* in Figure 3.21. This particular graph illustrates both the pull- and push-models found in several dataflow design patterns. In addition, dataflows occurring in the vertical dataflow pattern can be conveyed by commands. These and other dataflow patterns are described in detail in Section 7.3 starting on page 198.

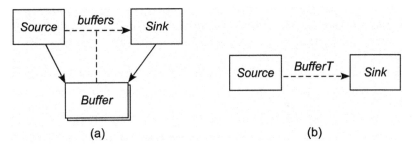

Figure 3.22: Dataflow of instances of a class or record

Figure 3.22 portrays a dataflow consisting of instances of a class or record. IDAR graphs usually do not indicate what type of data is flowing because it's usually obvious. But if you wish to show the type, draw another dashed line to the class for the type, as exemplified by Figure 3.22(a). This notation separates code, which is in the stacked boxes for *Buffer*, from its data in the dataflow. If a dataflow has a type that is not a class, you can label the dataflow with its type as shown in Figure 3.22(b).

A dataflow usually consists of buffers transferred between objects, but a simple dataflow can also be implemented by having the source-object write to a file and the destination-object read from it. A dataflow could even consist of a write and then a read from a big global variable, as portrayed in Figure 3.27(a) on page 71. A dataflow is depicted as a dashed arrow regardless of the mechanism of transfer.

3.12.3   Rails

Designs often have one or more superiors commanding the same subordinate(s). Such an arrangement is drawn using a horizontal line and short vertical connectors similar to its analogous use in a corporate organizational chart, as portrayed in Figure 3.23. The horizontal line is called a "rail".

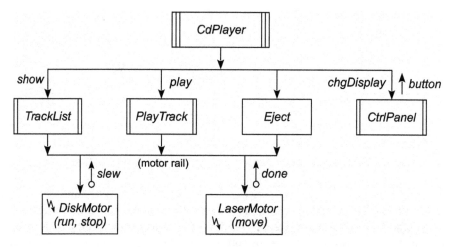

Figure 3.23: CD-player, final version

In the design shown in Figure 3.23, three objects (*TrackList*, *PlayTrack* and *Eject*) command the same two subordinates (*DiskMotor* and *LaserMotor*). To avoid drawing a mess of crossing lines, they are grouped along a rail, which I labeled the "motor rail" in this IDAR graph. A command passing through this rail is directed to one of the two motors. Likewise, a notice sent from a motor into the rail is allowed to be directed to any of the superiors above the rail.

The new *CdPlayer* object at the top controls the entire CD-player. The extra line-pairs on both sides indicate that *CdPlayer* is a process, which is the usual case for a topmost object in a program. The top-level object in GUI-based designs is the GUI itself, but in most other designs, I name that topmost object after the role of the program. I could have drawn four lines below it to its four subordinates, but instead I chose to portray them as a rail because it's more attractive than four long lines.

Stated precisely, a rail indicates that each superior above the rail commands some or all of the subordinates under it. For most rails, every superior commands *all* subordinates under the rail, although this is not required to be so. A rail can also show that a subordinate sends indirect notices to multiple superiors, or that multiple subordinates send the same notice to a superior. Rails are often labeled when all of its subordinates are in the same general category or have some common trait. For example, the "motor rail" above is so named because all subordinates control motors.

There are three purposes of a rail: (1) to eliminate crossing lines when multiple superiors command multiple subordinates, (2) to funnel notices sent from multiple subordinates and/or sent to multiple superiors, and (3) to beautify the graph when one superior has multiple subordinates or one subordinate has multiple superiors, such as was done above with the rail under *CdPlayer*.

On occasion, several subordinates serve as helpers or tools for several superiors, and the specific subordinates commanded by each superior are haphazard and unimportant. In this situation, grouping the subordinates under one rail gives rise to the Layer pattern described in Section 7.1.4 on page 185.

One sometimes needs to graph free notices with multiple sources funneling into one destination, or with one source fanning out to multiple destinations. These can be grouped through a dashed rail that is independent of the command hierarchy, as portrayed in Figure 7.12 on page 192.

Electrical engineers use the term "rail" to refer to a main conductor that routes power. The analogy with routing commands and notices is close enough that it is appropriate to use the term for this feature of software design.

3.12.4   Branches

If a superior has many subordinates, then drawing those subordinates in a wide row may consume too much space on the graph. Likewise, a row of many superiors over one subordinate may be too wide. As Figure 3.24 shows, branches are a technique that reduces width in both of these situations.

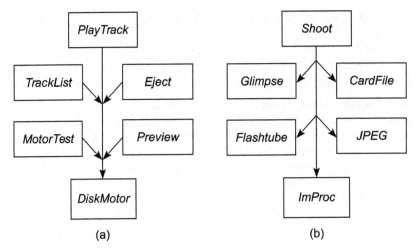

Figure 3.24: Branches

Figure 3.24(a) shows how a hypothetical row of five superiors in our CD-player could be packed into a small area. The vertical central line serves the same purpose as a rail. Figure 3.24(b) is an excerpt from the digital camera in Chapter 12, and portrays the opposite situation of five subordinates under one superior.

3.12.5   Popular, Collector and Distributor Objects

Popular Objects   Most nontrivial programs contain at least one lower-level object which is commanded in many places. In pre-OOP days, such objects were often called "utilities". Roles of popular objects include I/O, communications, various conversions and manipulations, and mathematical functions. In addition, some objects implement cross-cutting concerns described earlier, such as debug-output, and these tend to be called in many places, making them popular.

Drawing all the commands to popular objects would turn an IDAR graph into a mess, and would not tell the reader anything that he doesn't already know. A reader assumes that many objects command such utilities, so there's no point in drawing lines to them in a graph. However, I recommend including such objects somewhere in an IDAR graph to document their existence. A popular object is depicted with several short unconnected command lines, which is a graphical way of saying that many objects command it. Figure 3.25(a) illustrates this graphical convention. You can see examples of its use in the applications in Part II of this book.

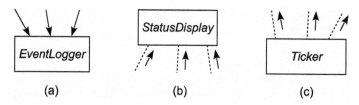

Figure 3.25: Popular, collector, and distributor objects

Collector Objects   These are similar to popular objects, but notices (instead of commands) are sent to such an object from many places. Thus, a collector object collects notices, and is depicted in Figure 3.25(b). Collector objects are often GUIs, event loggers, and collectors of statistics or performance data. The Collector pattern is centered around collector objects, and is presented in Section 7.2.1 on page 188.

Distributor Objects   These are the opposite of collector objects in that they send notices to many places. Such an object might listen to messages from some kind of input, and then broadcast them as notices. Or, like the *Ticker* seen in Figure 3.25(c), it may disperse time-based "tick" notices to whomever needs them. The Distributor pattern is centered around distributor objects, and is presented in Section 7.2.2 on page 190.

A distributor object may send notices directly or indirectly. Direct notices create unrelated compile-time dependencies in the distributor object, and indirect notices make software harder to learn because, when looking at a call in source-code, you don't know what method will be called. Your design of a distributor object thus faces a trade-off between independence and learnability.

3.12.6   Composition

Developers often consider one object to be composed of other objects. We might say that an object "possesses" or "has" or "contains" others. We would be tempted to represent such composition by nesting boxes in an IDAR graph, where a large outer box would possess the boxes (objects) drawn inside of it. This temptation is especially strong for subsystems because all objects under a subman are possessed by it. However, objects are never nested in IDAR graphs. That is, you never draw a box inside a box or hexagon. IDAR graphs express composition in the following ways which are subtle and blend well with the command hierarchy:

Subsystem A subman possesses all objects under it, clearly showing composition. If some object possesses a hierarchy of subordinates, consider promoting it to a subman to make the possession obvious.

Sole Superior A common way to determine composition is to (1) observe that a subordinate has only one superior, and then (2) assess whether the subordinate could ever acquire a second superior in the future. Having a sole superior with no chance of acquiring another suggests that the subordinate is an intrinsic piece of its superior, and is thus part of the composition of the superior.

Enclosure If the classes are in the same source-file, which should be true of all small subsystems, a dotted file-enclosure (see page 36) surrounding the relevant objects would express their tight affiliation. As above, a bit of common sense tells you whether subordinates are pieces of their superior.

For example, the *TempSensor* and *Valve* objects shown in Figure 3.12 on page 55 have one superior—*Engine*. Common sense says that they will never have another superior because they are pieces of an engine, making you conclude that *Engine* is composed of those subordinates. This example required two sentences to explain. But in practice, you will determine composition quickly by common sense when you examine an IDAR graph. When creating your graph, do not let the question of composition distract you, as it's less important than defining your objects well.

3.12.7   Lollipop Labels

Crossing lines can make an IDAR graph unsightly and more difficult to read. If you find that you are unable to avoid crossing lines even when using rails, you can use lollipop labels to eliminate the crossings, as shown in Figure 3.26.

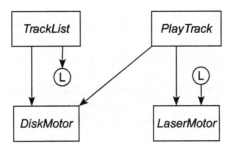

Figure 3.26: Lollipop labels

To keep the lollipops small, you should put only one letter in them. In Figure 3.26, the lollipop "L" labels the *LaserMotor* object, which is commanded by *TrackList*. Also,

I don't suggest using more than three kinds of these labels (three different letters) in one graph. Even the most complex designs in Part II of this book only needed *one* kind of lollipop, so three should be sufficient.

3.13   Common Issues in Software

Initialization must always be done, and it's often troublesome in a complex system. The IDAR hierarchy enables you to employ a simple and elegant technique for both initialization and shut down. It is described in Section 6.5 on page 141.

The following sections describe additional issues that commonly occur in software, and how they are addressed in IDAR graphs.

3.13.1   Data-Storage Objects

An object's role can be to hold data without changing it. Chapter 5 refers to these as data-storage objects, and examples include stacks, queues, trees, and databases. A notice transfers data, but that's also part of the role of a data-storage object, so are its data-transfer methods commands or notices?

In addition, objects commonly employ setters and getters, which are one-line methods that write and read private fields in their objects, thus encapsulating (hiding) those fields. Such methods are also known by the pretentious synonyms, "mutators" and "accessors". Are they commands or notices?

Here is a reasonable criterion: If methods exist to both import and export the same data, and that data is not changed or filtered, then those methods must be identified as commands because they directly fulfill their object's role.

Such commands include the *push* and *pull* methods in a queue or stack, the *insert*, *delete*, and *find* methods in a tree or list, and so on. But if the data is changed or filtered (for example, encrypted or subsampled), then the object's role is more than mere storage and transfer. Its data-transfer methods convey information needed by a command, and thus may be identified as notices.

Suppose you created a *Preferences* object whose role is "stores user's preferences." Its setters/getters are commands because its data is both imported and exported without being changed.

3.13.2   Global Variables

A global variable is drawn as a standalone circle or oval in an object-level IDAR graph. It does not appear inside of an object (box). Figure 3.27(a) is an example of drawing a global variable. We know that we should avoid using globals, but Section 4.2.1 on page 91 lists some situations where they are appropriate.

A popular way to hide global variables is to put them in a data-storage object and access them with setters and getters. A simple way to prevent this is to follow this exclusive-or rule: A field may have a setter or getter, *but not both*. This rule forces setters to supply data to commands and getters to fetch results of commands, making both become import-style and export-style notices, respectively. But some globals such as *Preferences* cannot be avoided, so don't apply this rule strictly.

3.13.3 Passing a Chunk of Data

Often, one object will write to a chunk of data that is too large for parameters, and another will read it. Figure 3.27 shows three ways of sharing it.

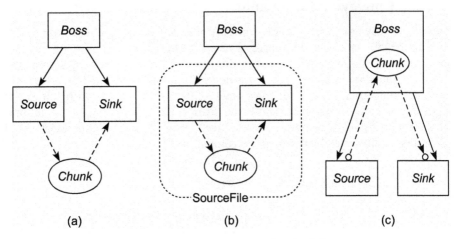

(a)   (b)   (c)

Figure 3.27: Ways to pass a chunk of data

The most popular way to share such a chunk, but not the most desirable, is to make it a global variable, as shown in Figure 3.27(a). The *Source* object writes to it, and *Sink* reads it. Such "common coupling", as it's called, is poorish.

A better way is illustrated in Figure 3.27(b). The chunk, *Source* and *Sink* objects are all placed in the same file of source-code. The chunk is declared as file-local, and is thus out of the global namespace. Sharing data this way is called "filewide coupling". Its problem is that the *Source* and/or *Sink* objects might actually be multiple objects or even subsystems, so they are often too large for one source-file.

A good technique is depicted in Figure 3.27(c). The chunk is located in a mutual superior, which gives pointers to its subordinates so they can access the chunk. Some designs place the chunk in the *Source* object, which returns a pointer to it in a notice.

Also, refer to the similar tidbit-problem described in Section 6.12 on page 163.

3.13.4 An Object with No Commands?

We sometimes encounter an object that is never commanded to perform its role. Such an object is initialized in one of several ways, and it will then perform its actions in response to notices or dataflows. To do its job, the object may be spawned as a separate thread or process, or it might covertly do its job in notices. In any case, the object has no command ordering it to perform its role, and thus operates independently with no superior. Does IDAR allow such a design?

Such objects often have a *conceptual* superior. A spawned object is commanded to perform its role by virtue of being spawned, which can be represented as an indirect command (with a bubble on its arrow) labeled "spawn" or "create thread" or similar, originating at the spawning object. However, some top-level objects might truly have no conceptual superior, like little kings. In this case, the IDAR graph will have multiple topmost objects (which could be submans), and they or their subordinate hierarchies will interact with each other as equals using notices and/or dataflows. Such an arrangement is acceptable in an IDAR graph, albeit uncommon.

3.13.5   Conveying Commands

Commands may be conveyed by intermediary objects. For example, when commands and notices are sent between processes or processors, they are not direct method-calls, but must be sent indirectly with the assistance of the operating system and often intermediate software. When drawing such messages, always use a bubble to indicate indirection, and do *not* show any intermediate software. Such software is merely a conveyor of messages and is thus part of the infrastructure, and not part of the core design. Rather, draw arrows directly from senders to *final* recipients of messages, as illustrated by the *saveKeys* command in Figure 3.28.

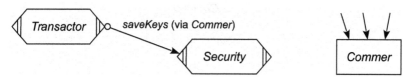

Figure 3.28: Messages between processes are indirect

The *saveKeys* command is actually sent to *Commer*, a popular object which forwards it to *Security*. But this command is drawn directly to its final recipient, which is *Security*. It's helpful to document the intermediary by the command label, as shown by the "via *Commer*" remark in Figure 3.28. In general, objects that convey messages should be drawn separately on the graph as popular objects, except for well-known intermediary software such as CORBA or DCOM (which should still be documented in parenthetical notes by labels for commands and notices). However, if an intermediate object serves as a front (interface) for only *one* object, then it is a proxy or adapter and not part of the infrastructure, so messages to/from it are drawn.

3.13.6   Imperative Notices

A notice sent from a subordinate to its boss may tell the boss that it needs to do something. The boss will then do it, making the notice similar to a command. Such an "imperative notice", as it's called, is allowable in three situations:

Relaying commands sent by a higher boss Suppose your mailman delivered a court-summons to you. The mailman has not commanded you to appear before the court; the court commanded you. The mailman merely notified you that "the court sent you this letter." Similarly, a subordinate may forward (relay) a command from a higher boss to its boss in a notice. In Figure 3.29(a), *BiggerBoss* is above *Boss*, giving it the right to have its commands relayed to *Boss* in the *cmd* notice via the subordinate *Relay* object. The role of such a notice is "tells me that a higher boss wants me to X," where X is an action. But unlike infrastructure software described above, an object such as *Relay* that conveys a command in a notice always appears in an IDAR graph.

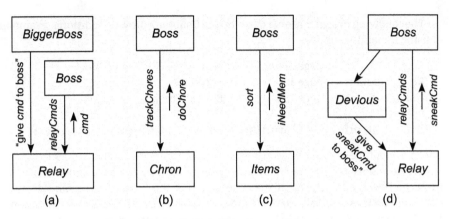

Figure 3.29: Imperative notices

Echoing commands sent by the boss A secretary may tell her boss to attend a meeting. Though she appears to be commanding him, she isn't because he told her to notify him of his scheduled activities. Similarly, a notice may echo a command to the subordinate's boss, originating from that boss. In Figure 3.29(b), the boss gives *Chron* some chores to be tracked, which *Chron* dutifully parrots back at the appropriate times in the *doChore* notice. The role of that notice is "tells me that I should now X," where X is a chore.

Requesting help in fulfilling a command A worker in a shop may tell his boss to locate a tool. Though he appears to be commanding his boss, he isn't because his boss previously told him to repair a machine, and the tool is needed for that job. Similarly, a notice may request assistance or a resource the subordinate needs in order to fulfill a prior (or perhaps future) command. For example, in order to perform the *sort* in Figure 3.29(c), *Items* requested some required memory via the imperative *iNeedMem* notice. Such help-needed notices often request information, memory, access to something, or references (pointers) to other objects needed to fulfill a command. They can even request maintenance or repair. In any case, the role of such a notice is "tells me that the caller needs X in order to function," where X is assistance or a resource, like a shop-worker requesting a needed tool.

Figures 3.29(a-b) also include the commands *relayCmds* and *trackChores*, which are sent from the boss and which grant the subordinate permission to relay or echo commands in imperative notices. Such "permissive commands", as they are termed, are not required, but are helpful because they make your design clearer.

From the point of view of their callers, imperative notices satisfy the Identify rule by exporting information (that tells the boss something needs to be done). But such a notice is in a semantic gray-area as it causes the boss to perform the stated action, encouraging a dishonest developer to have a subordinate command its boss. But his sneaky notice will not qualify as relaying a command from a higher boss, or echoing a command from its boss, or requesting help to fulfill a command. It therefore should have been identified as a command, which would then violate the Down rule.

The following design patterns described in Chapter 7 provide additional examples of using imperative notices:

Boss	page 177	Watcher	page 192
Resourceful Boss	page 180	Secretary	page 195
Union	page 186	Shared Thread	page 211

3.13.7   Laundering Commands and the Imaginary-Arrow Test

Another loophole created by imperative notices is shown in Figure 3.29(d). A dishonest developer is using *Relay* to convey commands to the *Boss* which originated from the *Devious* object, which is a subordinate of the *Boss*. Thus, a subordinate is commanding its superior, violating the Down rule. This situation is what Page-Jones calls "inversion of authority" [22] wherein "a subordinate gives orders to its boss." The *Relay* object is laundering commands by concealing their source (*Devious*) in a manner similar to how organized crime launders money to hide its source.

The solution is to apply this test: *Draw an imaginary command-arrow from the originator of each command to its ultimate recipient, and verify that it points down.*

This imaginary-arrow test is actually a generalization of the Down rule. In the example of Figure 3.29(d), we would have seen that such an imaginary arrow would point upward from *Devious* to *Boss*, exposing the violation. Don't forget to apply the imaginary-arrow test to commands arriving from an outside source such as a communication channel, ensuring that originator(s) of commands have greater authority than their destination(s).

3.14   Summary

This chapter showed you how to create IDAR graphs, which are based on four rules for designing object-oriented software, concisely stated as follows:

Identify Identify every public method as a command or a notice. A notice may only convey needed information (in either direction).

Down Command-arrows must point down in the graph.

Aid Public methods may covertly aid previously commanded activity.

Role Briefly describe what each object and method does, excluding any covert aid. Callers may only rely on what is stated in roles.

These rules cause a design to consist of a command hierarchy, which is also a service hierarchy, with high-level objects having broad control and little knowledge of details, and low-level objects having narrow control and deep knowledge of their specialties. Notices provide the extra flexibility needed to accommodate the various kinds of communications required among objects.

In addition to these things, you learned about many features of IDAR graphs, including rider notices, subsystems, threads, dataflows, and method-level design. These features clearly reveal the salient aspects of a design, allowing the design to be learned quickly and making it easier to identify bugs early-on.

3.14.1 Checklists and Tables

For each object:

- Did you write a clear, brief role for the object?
- Does the object's role exactly cover all actions done by all commands?
- Have all public methods been identified as commands and notices?
- Have accesses to public fields been identified as commands and notices?
- Does every method have a role?
- Does the action of every method exactly cover its role?
- Does every notice convey needed information?
- Is each method's covert aid documented (outside of their roles)?
- If the object is active, is it drawn with double/triple vertical lines?

For each IDAR graph:

- Do all commands go down?
- Do free notices parallel dashed lines?
- Are rider notices used as much as possible?
- Do most roles have high clarity, cohesion, and concealment?
- Are popular objects (utilities) included on the graph?
- Are dataflows included on the graph?
- Is each subsystem shown as a separate graph?
- For each subsystem: Do external objects hard-code calls only to its subman?
- For each subsystem: Are all notices sent to external objects indirect or riders?

Summary of definitions:

Term	Definition
Command	May perform any action (must go down in the graph)
High-level	At or near the top of the IDAR graph
Indirect call	Calling a method through a pointer (incl. polymorphism)
Lollipop labels	Circles with letters used to avoid crossing lines
Low-level	At or near the bottom of the IDAR graph
Notice	Must convey needed information in either direction
Notice, bound	A notice paralleling a command-arrow
Notice, free	A notice not paralleling a command-arrow
Notice, rider	A notice that rides on a command's method-return
Popular object	Has too many callers to be diagrammed
Rail	Horizontal line funneling or distributing calls
Role	Summary of the service provided by an object or method
Subman	Manager of a subsystem
Subordinate	Commanded by a superior
Subsystem	A separate hierarchy commanded by the program
Superior	Commands a lower-level object (subordinate)

Summary of drawing-rules:

Item	Depiction in an IDAR Graph
Command	Downward arrow (usually labeled)
Contains ISR	Lightning-bolt
Contains process	Two extra vertical lines on each side
Contains thread	Extra vertical line on each side
Dataflow	Coarse dashed arrow (also for field-accesses)
External to subsystem	Dashed box or hexagon
Field	Circle or oval
File-enclosure	Dotted line around objects in a file
Indirection	Bubble on beginning of call-arrow
Method	Parallelogram
Method-call	Arrow from caller to callee
Multiple instances	Stacked boxes (labeled with class name)
Notice, bound	Short floating arrow paralleling a command-line
Notice, export-style	As above, but suffix name with caret
Notice, free	Short floating arrow paralleling a dashed line
Notice, rider	Datum-name prefixed with caret by command-line
Object	Box
Popular object	Unconnected command-arrows touching box
Subman	Elongated hexagon
Subsystem (using)	Elongated hexagon

3.15   Exercises

1. What does a box usually represent?

2. In what situations should you use the stacked-box notation?

3. What is the Identify rule?

4. What is an important rule regarding the direction of arrows for commands?

5. In terms of their abilities and constraints, what is the difference between a command and a notice?

6. Describe these kinds of notices: import-style, export-style, rider, bound, and free.

7. What are some advantages of rider notices over bound and free notices?

8. Two applications communicate with each other using *Intercom* objects in each. In one application, the *Intercom* object sends arriving messages as notices to its boss. The notices usually contain commands for the boss, so this design was rejected in a design-review on the grounds that a subordinate is commanding its boss. Do you agree with this rejection? Why or why not?

9. The role for a *Legal* object is "verifies that a purchase is legal, and if so, notifies both parties by email that they can proceed." Discuss whether and why this role is good or poor.

10. In the example CD-player, suppose the *PlayTrack* object receives a *nextTrack* or *prevTrack* notice from the *ControlPanel* object when the "Next track" or "Previous track" button is pushed by the listener. These notices cause *PlayTrack* to skip to the next or previous track. List two problems with these notices.

11. A superior commands a subordinate to query a remote database. Describe two ways that the result of the query can be communicated back to the superior.

12. What do triple vertical lines in a box signify?

13. In a design, a notice transfers a buffer of data and decompresses it. A reviewer complained that this notice is illegal because it does more than convey needed information, violating the Identify rule. What do you think?

14. What is the main problem with using indirect commands?

15. Why must all commands and hard-coded notice-calls made by objects outside a subsystem be directed to its subman?

16. An object inside a subsystem (not its subman) gives the address of one of its notices to an external object, which uses it to indirectly call notices inside the subsystem, bypassing the subman. Is this method of supplying pointers and sending indirect notices permissible? Why or why not?

17. When is a parallelogram permitted in an IDAR graph?

18. When is a box permitted inside the large box of a method-level IDAR graph?

19. In a method-level IDAR graph, what would a lightning-bolt within a parallelogram signify?

20. What is the Role rule?

21. Why is writing roles for objects important?

22. In Figure 3.17 on page 62, *macTask* has double lines on its sides. What do these double lines signify?

23. When a command completes in a subordinate, it needs to send a notice to one of several superiors. Which technique for sending notices would you recommend if the command is allowed to block? Which would you recommend if the command must not block?

24. The Role rule prescribes actions that a public method may do. The Aid rule also prescribes actions the method may do. How do these actions differ?

25. The role of the object *ProcessTimecards* is "reads all timecards and updates databases for employees and payroll." It calls a command named *getEmployeeSkills* located in an object named *EmployeeInfo*. Is this good or poor design, and why?

26. What is an imperative notice?

27. In what three situations is an imperative notice allowed?

Chapter 4

Gauging Goodness

— cling to painful truth

_____

This chapter helps you when you are in the midst of creating a design. How can you determine whether your design is good or bad? If you've been designing software for years, then you have probably developed an instinct for what is good. But instincts are fallible and vary too much among people. Fortunately, there are several well-defined criteria for gauging the quality of designs, so we don't need to rely on unreliable instincts. These criteria are listed in this table:

The quality of	is gauged by
Roles	Clarity, Cohesion, Concealment
Couplings	Scopes, Promise, Indirect, Extent, Dataflows (SPIED)
Hierarchy	Need

These are almost the only criteria available for gauging design-quality that are practical, understandable, and assessable mentally, making them useful during the design process. A good role will have high *clarity*, *cohesion*, and *concealment*. Five criteria will help you to define good *couplings* (interactions) between objects and methods. The *need* criterion measures the quality of your hierarchy; that is, how well subordinates assist their superiors. Knowing these criteria will improve your ability to create clean designs because they measure the most important aspects of cleanliness.

Based on his investigations of software quality, Larry Constantine unveiled the concepts of *cohesion* and *coupling* in the late 1960s as part of Structured Design [37] (also termed Composite Design), which in turn was publicized by Glenford Myers, Wayne Stevens, Ed Yourdon, and Meilir Page-Jones.

4.1 Quality of Roles

Clarity, cohesion, and concealment allow you to gauge the quality of the role of an object or method. All three can be subjectively graded as "high", "medium", "low", or "none", giving you four levels with little mental effort. In Section 3.7.2 on page 50, I provided a synopsis of these for all four types of roles. This section discusses these subjects in more detail. Material from that synopsis is repeated here for the sake of continuity. Also, most roles state their actions explicitly with verbs, but a few state them implicitly via a shared trait, as explained later on page 81. So for most roles, you can replace "action" with "verb" in the discussion below.

4.1.1 Clarity

The clarity of a role is its effectiveness in communicating the actions offered by an object or method. For example, "posts a deposit" is clear, but "slow operations" is not. Here is a good test of the clarity of your role: Pretend that you are somebody who knows what your system should do, but is not familiar with your design. Read the role from that fresh viewpoint. If it conveys sufficient understanding of its service, the role is clear. But if he must ask further questions about the service (actions) that is offered by the object or method, the role is unclear (vague).

4.1.2 Cohesion

Cohesion is the degree that the actions of a role are related or associated with each other. By convention, a role having only one action (which should be most of them) is regarded as having high cohesion. Complementary actions such as lock/unlock are highly related and thus have high cohesion. Clarity must be decent before you can assess cohesion. In a broad sense, cohesion measures how much knowledge the actions have in common, which usually translates into shared code and/or data. But not always. The actions in the role "monitors program-health and logs any health-problems" are *monitors* and *logs*, which will probably share little code or data. But these two actions are related by cause-and-effect and their association with health, giving them decent cohesion. Here are more examples of gauging cohesion:

- "Waits for a given event, or waits for any event in an event-list." These very similar wait-actions are obviously highly related and thus have high cohesion.

- "Rotates or stretches an image." These two operations are related in that they both affect an image, and both are matrix transforms, so their cohesion is medium to high.

- "Monitors and maintains pH-level." Maintaining pH requires monitoring it, so these actions are related both by need and by being associated with pH, giving them medium cohesion.

- "Arms alarm and starts polling entry-sensors." These two actions of an object for a burglar alarm are only weakly related, and thus have low cohesion.

- "Changes font color and dash-pattern of lines." These two actions have almost nothing in common, and thus they have almost no cohesion.

4.1.3 Concealment

Concealment is the degree that a role conceals the inner workings of its object or method. A role should state *what* is done, but not *how*, thus concealing the implementation. Roles can be polluted with bits of implementation by revealing:

Internal Code A role saying "it does X, Y, and Z", perhaps adding "repeatedly", is describing the sequence of actions to be performed, perhaps in a loop, instead of their composite effect.

Internal Data The poor role of a *getRequest* method might say "pops the request-queue," revealing that requests are stored in a queue. A good role would be "returns the oldest request," which hides the internal data-structure.

Aid is part of implementation, so keep the particulars of it out of your roles. For example, the role of a notice might be, "cancels dialog and frees associated memory." That command-like role actually describes the aid which that notice provides. (Section 6.9 on page 150 discusses this trap of confusing aid with commands.) This role should be, "tells the object that Cancel was clicked (aid will delay method-return)." The details of its aid should be documented in the method's header-comments, not in its role.

Couplings A role may not refer to another object or method because couplings of some code to other code is an aspect of implementation. "Manages packet-traffic" is fine because a role may state that an object manages something that is not code, but a role with a phrase like "tells *Fizz* to start fizzing" has poor concealment because it reveals that your object controls another. But here is an exception: It can be permissible to mention a well known object in a role, such as "adds a new medical record to *PatientDatabase*" or "transfers funds between accounts and notifies *Security* of any security violations."

Location A role mentioning "high level" or "low level" is describing an object's location in the hierarchy, instead of what it does.

The solution to such mistakes is to think solely in terms of the service provided to callers, which is *what* is done rather than *how* it is done.

4.1.4 Four Types of Roles

To help you quickly assess the clarity, cohesion, and concealment of a prospective role, I have divided roles into the following four categories, listed in order of generally increasing clarity: vacuous, trait-based, managerial, and common.

Vacuous Roles

The two verbs "processes" and "handles" are so broad and vague that they are almost meaningless. They merely indicate that an unspecified number of unspecified actions are done. These void verbs are used in the following ways:

- When working with data, these verbs mean "performs actions on". For example, the role "processes statistics" means actions are done on statistics, but says nothing about what those actions are.

- When working with events, these verbs mean "performs actions in response to." For example, "processes a time-out" and "handles mouse-move" both say that some unspecified actions are done in response to an event.

- "Handles" is also used when performing actions in a state of a state-machine. A typical example would be "handles the waiting state".

- "Handles" can be used in the sense of managing, as in "handles selections". In this case, the verb is not vacuous as "manages selections" was the intended meaning, putting such a role in the managerial category discussed below.

These verbs are mostly applicable to methods, but they can also apply to objects. For example, a *SensorProcessor* object would have the role "processes sensor-data."

Vacuous roles have high cohesion merely because they contain only one verb. They have good concealment because they communicate almost nothing, but they usually have little or no clarity for the same reason.

When you find yourself using one of these vacuous verbs, the first test is to replace "handles" with "manages" to see if you are actually referring to managing. If you are not, then your role essentially says "I do something", which has no clarity. Try hard to find an alternative wording that is clearer. Failing that, try to change the design. In some situations, such as a general message-handler, it is not possible to avoid such a vacuous verb, but its presence tells you to make the attempt.

Trait-Based Roles

A trait-based role specifies a trait that all of its actions possess. Examples of such roles are "secrecy services" and "start-up operations." You can reword such a role as "all of its actions X," where X is a verb phrase that states the trait contained in the role. The two above examples would be "all of its actions relate to secrecy" and "all of its actions are done at startup-time." The role thus identifies actions implicitly (by their shared trait) instead of explicitly.

Only 14% of the objects' roles in the applications in Part II of this book are trait-based, but a higher percentage of *methods* will be trait-based due to the need to initialize, set-up and tear-down, as these common operations share the trait of time.

In addition, if the role has a verb, it's vague and is usually one of these: "initializes", "sets-up", "tears-down", "prepares", "offers", "provides", "performs", or "implements". Table 4.1 shows some trait-based roles and their corresponding verb phrases.

Concealment for trait-based roles is good. Their clarity is usually poor, but improving as traits become more narrow because folks have a good idea of what actions are needed by specialized traits. If clarity is sufficient to assess cohesion, you will probably find that cohesion is mediocre at best. For example, "logging services" has a narrow purpose (logging things) and thus good clarity, but it probably has mediocre cohesion because some of its actions will be unrelated except that they pertain to logging. "Common utilities" has a broad purpose because the shared trait is high popularity, so you don't know what it does, giving it no clarity and unknown cohesion. If clarity is poor enough that you can't assess cohesion, then the role is poor. But having a "common utilities" object with a poor role is better than having many tiny objects with good roles because perceived system-complexity will be lower.

Trait-Based Role	All of its actions... (shared trait)
BCD math library	perform BCD math
Common utilities	are needed by many objects
Offers GPS services	use data from the GPS-chip
Hardware abstraction layer (HAL)	control hardware (devices)
Services for administrators	are only for administrators
Secrecy services	relate to secrecy
Performs tests	test something
Provides training features	relate to training
Offers cryptographic services	relate to cryptography
Initializes this object (temporal)	are done at start-up time
Prepares for display of list (temporal)	are done before displaying list
Clean-up after filtering (temporal)	are done after filtering

Table 4.1: Sample trait-based roles and their verb phrases

You see from Table 4.1 that a trait can be anything imaginable. For example, a GPS unit provides a device with its position and the current time by receiving signals from GPS satellites. Suppose we define a *GpsServices* object containing two commands, *getTime* and *getPosition*. Time and position are unrelated, but these two commands obtain their information from the same source, which is their shared trait, so they were tossed together, yielding low cohesion.

Trait-based designs with low cohesion can vex maintainers. For example, a later version of the device containing the GPS unit might also get its time from WWV, which are shortwave radio stations operated by the US government. "GpsServices" is now a misnomer, but maintainers can't split it or change its name because too many other objects have references in their source-code to the name "GpsServices".

Also, methods or objects that funnel commands or messages have trait-based roles. One example is the *ioctl* system-call in Unix/Linux. Its role is "I/O services", so its actions share the trait of being related to I/O. Another example is this method in a command-interpreter:

```
void CmdInt::doCommand (int cmdNum, ByteArray params);
```

A method such as this one accepts a wide variety of commands funneled into it from some source, such as a script or I/O port. When commands arrive in a stream, you are forced to perform them with a method like this whose role is "performs incoming commands." The shared trait is membership in the interpreter's command-set.

Temporal Roles These roles contain verbs like "initialize", "set-up" and "tear-down", which are vague actions done at a common point in time, which is their shared trait. For example, "set-up" consists of several unspecified actions done before an upcoming event or action. But like other trait-based roles, these don't tell you what specific actions are done, giving these roles poor clarity. Table 4.2 lists some common points in time, along with vague commands that are frequently used in them.

Initialization is an important subset of temporal roles because it is always needed. Many objects contain an *initialize* or *configure* command that is called during start-up, and its role is "initializes this object." Despite its poor clarity, initialization must

Point in Time	Vague Commands
Program start-up	*initialize*
Before an operation or event	*setup, prepare, configure*
After an operation or event	*cleanup, finish*
Program shut-down	*teardown, shutdown*

Table 4.2: Common times and corresponding commands

be done, so such commands cannot be avoided. An orderly way to initialize and shut down is described in Section 6.5 on page 141.

Problems   There are two problems with trait-based roles: (1) They tell you why actions were grouped together instead of what those actions are, usually resulting in poor clarity, and (2) such an object often has low cohesion, making it likely to be split in maintenance. If its name is littered around the rest of the system, the split will require much effort. We saw this problem above when attempting to split *GpsServices*. On the other hand, a trait-based role can be tolerably *good* if, due to its decent cohesion, all of its actions are at least somewhat related, making you confident that the class will never need to be split.

Some trait-based roles can become managerial or common (both described next) by rewording them. For example, "health services" can be changed to "monitors and maintains system-health", a common role with two related actions that isn't bad. Also, "hardware abstraction layer" has medium clarity, and can be changed to "manages all devices" which still has medium clarity. Hence, rewording a trait-based role will not necessarily improve it.

Managerial Roles

The following words are used in managerial roles: "manages", "controls", "governs", "maintains", "executive", "oversees", "supervises", and any synonyms of these that I might have overlooked. All of these indicate that something is being managed. Above, you saw that "handles" can also be managerial.

What can be managed? Anything that your object's superior must be aware of. This is usually (1) your object's own data, such as a schedule, or (2) an external entity such as data or a device, or something in its environment such as temperature. But it's essential that superiors know about what's being managed.

Warning: Managing subordinates is *not* a valid reason to use a managerial word in your object's role or name, as it will result in no concealment. A role should describe a service being offered, not how it is implemented, and the presence or absence of subordinates is an aspect of implementation which must be concealed. A managerial word may only apply to things that your object's superiors will know about.

A class that manages its own data and permits the creation of multiple instances follows traditional OOP. For example, the role of a *Stack* class would be "manages a stack," and all of its commands (such as *push* and *pop*) share that purpose.

What activities are involved in managing? Your ease of answering that question is your assessment of the clarity of such a role. For example, you have a fair idea of what "manages traffic" or "manages track-list" comprises, but "manages weather" has poor clarity due to the vagueness of what managing the weather comprises. The clarity of managerial roles generally ranges from medium to high.

The cohesion of a managerial role is high because it contains only one action: managing. Concealment for a managerial role is usually high because such a role does not state how it manages its responsibility.

Finally, the verb "monitors" in a role means that your code watches the actions of others. But what does it do in response? If it handles failures, or can cause those others to start or stop, then the monitor is actually a manager. But if the monitor only passively collects information about an activity without affecting it, then it is an observer and not a manager. Therefore, the verb "monitors" is ambiguous, so I suggest replacing it with either "manages" or "observes".

Common Roles

Common roles are so named because they are the most common kind. A common role identifies its action(s) using verbs, and does not qualify as being one of the other types of roles. The clarity of such a role is that of its *least* clear verb. Table 4.3 contains examples of common roles.

Matches symptoms with diseases.	Reminds users about events.
Lays off people.	Starts or stops a motor.
Focuses the lens.	Prints on a printer.
Encrypts and decrypts data.	Validates fields in a record.

Table 4.3: Some common roles

You should use managerial and common roles as much as possible. Don't confuse common roles, which are desirable, with common coupling (discussed later), which is undesirable. I must warn you that roles with verbs such as "initialize", "set-up", "configure", "tear-down", and so on, are not regarded as common. Rather, they are temporal and were discussed above under trait-based roles.

Concealment for a common role can vary widely, based solely on whether its verbs are describing *what* is done versus *how* it is done.

Assessing cohesion requires that a role have at least decent clarity, and most common roles have high clarity. The cohesion of a common role is a function of both its number of verbs (i.e., its number of actions) and how related they are:

1. Having only one verb in a role is ideal. It will have high cohesion because it performs only one action. It satisfies what is called the "Single Responsibility Principle". Note that though the role has only one verb, an object may have multiple commands which together perform the action of that one verb. For example, the role "reminds users about events" in an *Events* object may contain these commands: *create*, *cancel*, *changeTime*, *register*, and *deregister*.

2. Two verbs can be complementary, such as enable/disable, encrypt/decrypt, open/close, encode/decode, lock/unlock, raise/lower, read/write, and so on. The cohesion of such a dual is usually high because duals are usually tightly related, and their implementations often share a substantial amount of code

and/or data. But if the two verbs are not complementary, the resulting cohesion is usually no better than medium, and can even be "none", depending on how unrelated the two actions are.

3. A role with three or more verbs is a list of actions that will probably have low cohesion. And, as mentioned above, a two-verb role that is not complementary can have low cohesion. In such cases, you should attempt to raise the level of abstraction of the role. This topic is discussed next.

Raising a Role's Level of Abstraction

Below are examples showing why the cohesion of a list of actions usually will not be good. After these, I show how these roles can be improved.

1. "Adds or deletes events from schedule, and notifies user of upcoming events in the schedule." Notifying a user is not related to adding events, but both of these actions access the schedule, giving this role mediocre cohesion.

2. "Connects or disconnects a socket, and sends or receives data through the socket." This role mixes connection-control with data-transfer, giving it two weakly related actions and thus mediocre cohesion.

3. "Scans document, compresses pixels, dials phone number, and sends pixels through the modem." This list of unrelated actions has no cohesion.

The cohesion of a multi-verb role will improve by raising its level of abstraction. Find one verb that summarizes the role's actions. That verb might need to be managerial. Here are the results for the examples above:

1. The three actions in this role can be summarized as "manages schedule."

2. The four actions in this role can be summarized as "manages socket."

3. The four actions in this role can be summarized as "sends a fax."

All of these higher level roles have high cohesion and concealment, while keeping good clarity. If you are unable to replace a list-like role with a higher abstraction (i.e., one verb that summarizes it), then your object or method lacks a single overarching purpose, and you should attempt to improve the design. However, sometimes you must choose between (1) sharing some code between two mostly unrelated actions, yielding poorish cohesion, and (2) separating them to achieve high cohesion. Also, you might need to combine them to improve performance. For example, if you are computing information from a stream of data, then the intermediate values in those computations might allow you to compute statistics faster, causing you to combine both computations into one role, despite its worse cohesion.

Table 4.4 shows the number of verbs in the roles of the objects in the example applications in Part II of this book. I confess that three of my objects have three verbs in their roles, but the great majority have only one verb, with a fair number having two verbs. These numbers are typical of well-designed programs, except for the Drawing Application: It has many roles of the form "stores and paints an X." These have two verbs, and perhaps could be reworded as "manages an X."

| | Number of Verbs | | |
Application	1	2	3
Pen plotter	7	5	1
VDL subsystem	11	1	1
Drawing Application	15	13	1
Digital Camera	28	3	
Heating/Cooling System	11	2	

Table 4.4: Number of verbs in applications

4.1.5   Remarks About Quality of Roles

The four types of roles are summarized in Table 4.5. Its "Clarity", "Cohesion", and "Concealment" columns show typical values, but keep in mind that exceptions are possible. The "% Objs" column is the percentage of objects (not methods) having each type of role in the example applications in Part II of this book.

Type of Role	Clarity	Cohesion	Concealment	% Objs
Vacuous	None	High	High	0
Trait-based	Low	Low to Med	High	14
Managerial	Med to High	High	High	14
Common	High	Med to High	Varies	72

Table 4.5: The four types of roles

The four types of roles were presented as though they were mutually exclusive, but they're not. It is possible (but rare) to have mixtures of them. For example, "handles queued buffers and starts conversion" is both vacuous and common, and "manages operator's dialog and provides features for operators" is both managerial and trait-based. For such mixed-type roles, you should (1) regard clarity to be the least clear part of the role, (2) evaluate cohesion over all parts of the role, and (3) regard concealment to be the least concealing part of the role.

Beware of any side-effect, which will ruin cohesion. Such an unrelated action adds an unrelated verb to the object or method's role, causing its cohesion to plunge. But remember that cross-cutting concerns (Section 3.7.4 on page 52) need not appear in a role, and thus will not hurt clarity or cohesion.

The roles of notices are interesting because notices can convey information in either direction. Import-style notices have roles of the form "tells its object that X," where X is some information. Export-style notices are similar, saying "tells its caller that X." Such roles have high clarity and cohesion because they contain one clear verb, "tells". Such roles also have high concealment because they reveal no inner workings, such as aid. But delayed method-returns due to aid should be mentioned in a parenthetical note in the role, like this: "tells its object that a new buffer is available (note: return may be delayed due to covert aid)." Such a parenthetical remark must not reveal any aspect of the nature of the aid that the notice provides, but serves only as a warning that the call might not return immediately.

4.2 Quality of Couplings

A coupling is any interaction between two methods, and by extension, any interaction between two objects. Somebody learning your code will spend much of his time learning its couplings, making it crucial that you define them well. A coupling can be as straightforward as one method calling the other. Or they might be coupled through a shared variable: One method writes to it and the other reads it.

Chain of Couplings   When one is learning how code works, he will often follow a chain of couplings that are part of a chore of interest. He might see that one method calls another, which in turn writes to a buffer, which in turn is read by some other method which computes something and hands that to another method, and so on. Furthermore, one often must start with a result and follow couplings *backwards* to locate its cause. Because folks learn code by following such chains of couplings forwards and backwards, you need to design your software to make such chains easy to follow in either direction. "Easy to follow" means that a minimum of searching the source code is needed in order to locate the two methods involved in a coupling. We can summarize your goal as:

Make it easy to locate both sides of each coupling.

SPIED: Five Principles of Good Coupling

Many kinds of couplings are available to you. But some are much easier to follow than others, having good visibility of what happens on both sides. My list of good and bad kinds of coupling contains 15 items, which is too many to be useful when designing. An examination of the common traits underlying good and bad coupling reveals five principles (or criteria) of good coupling which form the acronym SPIED:

Scopes principle:	Minimize scopes of shared variables.
Promise principle:	Don't rely on a flimsy promise.
Indirection principle:	Minimize indirection.
Extent principle:	Minimize extent of coupling.
Dataflows principle:	Draw the dataflows.

Each of these principles is elaborated in the following sections, along with the 15 kinds of coupling they apply to. I suggest learning these five principles well enough that they become part of your intuition of what is good versus poor.

4.2.1   Scopes Principle: Minimize Scopes of Shared Variables

Somebody following your code might see where you write to a variable. Now he needs to find the method that reads it. Or, he sees where you read a variable, and needs to find the method that writes to it. How quickly can he find it?

The smaller the scope of a variable, the more quickly one can find the methods that access it. Therefore, to make chains of coupling easier to follow, your variables need to have the smallest possible scopes. Each such scope is a form of coupling described below.

Parameter Coupling

A parameter in a method has the smallest possible scope, as it is only known to the caller(s) and callee. Due to its great visibility, such a coupling is effortless to follow. As will be pointed out in the Extent principle below, you can have too many parameters, forcing you to pass in (or pass back) the data in other ways.

Parameter coupling was called "data coupling" in the days of Structured Design. But I realized that many kinds of coupling between methods are based on mechanisms of transferring data, so the name "data coupling" is ambiguous. I prefer the more precise term "parameter coupling".

Field Coupling

When methods within an object exchange information using their object's private member fields, they are employing field coupling. Figure 4.1 portrays two methods that share a field named *memberVariable*. In it, *method1* writes to the field and *method2* reads it. This form of coupling is popular and generally acceptable. But if a class is large, the scope of its fields is also large, making it more difficult to follow couplings, motivating you to either split the class or minimize field coupling within the class.

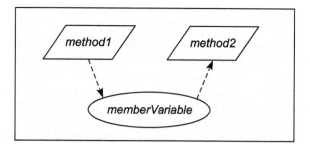

Figure 4.1: Field coupling within an object

Also, the Extent principle below warns you not to accumulate excessive couplings by profligately adding fields, so its advice is to be stingy with fields.

Filewide Coupling

Filewide coupling occurs when two methods or objects access the same variable located in the same source-file. The variable is not global, nor is it a member of either class. It is local to the source-file. For such coupling to be possible, the source-code for both methods must be located in the same file as the variable.

Common practice places the code for each class in its own file, in which case the scopes of filewide and field coupling are the same.

But you will often have several classes that are both small and closely related. Usually they are subordinates of a larger superior. In this situation, I encourage you to put all of these classes (subordinates and their superior) in the same file in order to make it easier to follow couplings among them. Doing so also has the benefit of permitting filewide coupling among those classes.

Stamp Coupling

Stamp coupling occurs when the address of a record (i.e., structure) is passed among methods, but not all the data within the record is used by each method. Figure 4.2 portrays this situation, where the address of the record is first fetched by *start*, and is then passed as a parameter to *method1*, *method2* and *method3*.

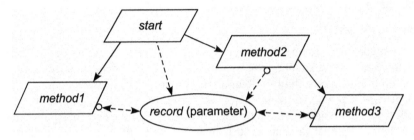

Figure 4.2: Stamp coupling

The word "stamp" hearkens back to the day in which ink was applied to a physical stamp to create a form on a piece of paper. Every possible field was present, but folks would only fill in the applicable items on the form, leaving many blank.

This kind of coupling often occurs due to laziness, as it's easier to put all the data that several methods need into one record and pass it around, than it is to think about what data each method needs and then thoughtfully organize the design to minimize the resulting coupling.

At its worst, stamp coupling is a form of global variables. Developers who are prevented from having globals, perhaps due to coding standards, instead put all the globals into one record and pass it all over the place. Such stamp coupling offers no advantage over global variables, and it has all the disadvantages of globals, which are (1) couplings are hard to follow because learning where or when a particular variable is written or read is difficult, (2) it encourages sloppy communication among methods, (3) it hinders reuse, and (4) it creates more dependencies among methods.

If you find that a record is partly accessed everywhere and fully accessed nowhere, take the time to examine each field in the record. Identify where each is used. Think about alternative designs that coalesce accesses to within one object, which will allow a field in the record to become a field in an object, creating field coupling. Also, try to create groups of fields in the record, where each group becomes a subrecord within the record. Passing such a subrecord into a method is parameter coupling, and it reveals exactly what data is being transferred and used.

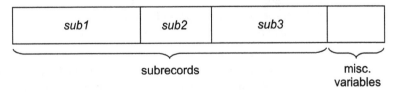

Figure 4.3: Avoiding stamp coupling by dividing a record into subrecords

One situation that causes stamp coupling is having a large operation that occurs in stages, requiring several method calls to compute and write all the data in the record. In this case, a subrecord can be created for each stage. The subrecord is read or written as a whole by the method corresponding to a stage, and other data from the main record can be passed in separately to that method as individual parameters. Figure 4.3 shows a large record divided into three subrecords, with some remaining fields that are suitable for parameters.

Common Coupling

Common coupling occurs when you use a global variable. One method writes to it, and another reads it, coupling the two methods and their objects. A global serves as a common area, hence the term "common". Figure 4.4(a) is an example of a global variable which is written by one object, and read by another. Figure 4.4(b) shows a public field in an object accessed by another object. A public field in a public object is equivalent to a global variable, so such an access is a form of common coupling.

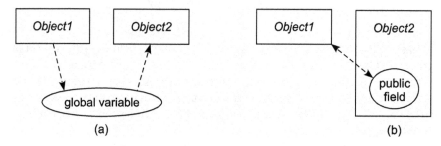

Figure 4.4: A typical global variable (a), and a public field (b)

Despite the popularity of global variables, everyone knows that they should be avoided. But why? Here are some problems they cause:

- Code is difficult to learn and difficult to remember because finding out where a particular variable is written or read is difficult, making chains of coupling hard to follow. A learner of the code, which might be you after a few months when you've forgotten what you did, must search the files for references to a global, and examine each one. If you are fortunate, a smart editor with tags is available to ease finding references. At worst, you must do a brute-force text-search through all source-files to learn about each global variable. As you can imagine, this process is slow and error-prone.

- Globals encourage sloppy communication among methods because it's effort-less to add another global variable, write to it here, read from it there, and then you don't need to go through the effort of figuring out the proper way to pass it as parameters. Good design is difficult, and globals are a lazy way out.

- Global variables hinder reuse because they are additional dependencies in a method or object. Reusing code can be like grabbing and pulling out a clump of spaghetti with your hand. There will be many stringers hanging down that you'll need to deal with. The linker will output a list of undefined externals, and

you will be forced to fix each one. Each such missing global requires research-
ing where the global was accessed and why, and figuring out another way to
accomplish its duty. This is miserable work.

- Another problem with the additional dependencies mentioned above is that
changing the type of a global variable can cause side-effects in various places,
making maintenance difficult.

Before adding a global variable, identify the methods and objects that will access
it, and try to change the design so that the global variable becomes local to an object
or file, representing the more-desirable field or filewide coupling, respectively.

After having said all that against their use, there are some valid uses of global
variables, all of which are system-wide in some way. Either they are values needed in
many places in the system, or they are values which are set in many places.

Constants Constants and conditional-compilation flags that are needed by many
objects are commonly made global.

Configuration At startup-time, programs often set variables to configuration values read from .rc-files, .ini-files, registry-entries, or command-line parameters.
Such variables are then never changed, so they behave like constants, and in
fact are used for the same purposes as constants.

Statistics You can collect statistics from various places in the program by making
the statistics variables global. They are incremented throughout the program.

We avoid common coupling due to the low visibility of the accessing methods.
But if you have only a few globals, you can put them on your IDAR graph, along with
the dataflows to and from them. Their presence on the graph makes such couplings
visible enough to be acceptable. An example of such an acceptable global is Figure 13.6
on page 344, which is one of the example applications in Part II of this book.

Public fields create common coupling, but such coupling of fields can be less severe
than global variables. In my opinion, it is acceptable to allow outside objects to only
write a field or to only read it, *but not both*. This rule allows public fields to be used
for transferring data to and from a data-processing command in the object.

Definition Coupling

A definition creates a symbol representing a constant, record type, enumeration,
string, etc. When a class uses a definition, there is a compile-time coupling between
the class and the definition. Definition coupling often occurs when a definition is
needed on both sides of some other kind of coupling. If a definition is primarily
intended for calling methods in one class, it should be defined in that class. Otherwise,
the definition has a broader use, and it should be located where developers can quickly
find it when following couplings, such as in a system-wide file. But during development of a large project, such a file will change often, potentially wasting everyone's
time with unneeded recompilations. In this case, the definitions are best put in files
with narrower scope, such as one file within each subsystem, relegating the system-
wide file to holding definitions of items passed between subsystems. An alternative
is to break up the monolithic system-wide file into multiple system-wide files.

4.2.2   Promise Principle: Don't Rely on a Flimsy Promise

Frail Coupling

When two objects or methods interact, one has a need and the other fulfills it. Let's name these two parties the "needer" and the "fulfiller". Normally, a fulfiller is aware of a needer's need, and has agreed to fulfill it. We can say that the fulfiller has made a promise to fulfill the need. But what might happen if that promise is weak or missing? This situation can occur when there is only a verbal agreement between developers, with nothing documented, or when the developer of the needer observed some happenstance behavior in the fulfiller, and decided to rely on it. Reliance on such a flimsy protocol or unpromised behavior is hazardous because an innocent change in the fulfiller can break the needer. Such reliance on the unreliable is termed "frail coupling". For example, you might carelessly

- assume that operations were done in a specific order. For example, your code could rely on initialization being done in a certain order. Maintenance might change this order, causing an obscure breakage.

- rely on an unpromised trait in incoming data. Perhaps you relied on packets' ID-numbers incrementing sequentially, or on a datum being located at a hard-coded offset in a packet. In the future, when somebody changes that hidden trait, your object will fail.

- rely on an object or data being left in a certain state. An apparently-safe change that affects its leftover state will cause your code to fail.

- assume that shared data is valid at a certain time. A small and reasonable change in the writer could break your reader.

- rely on a side-effect. Even if it is stated in a role, such a secondary aspect of operation could change in maintenance, causing failures.

- store a value in the unused bits in some output-data. Even if the writer of that code promised that those bits would remain unused in the future, such a verbal promise may be forgotten in a year when he moves to another project.

- assume that an output-buffer (that you did not create) is large enough. When maintenance adds more output, it could overflow.

- assume that a particular identifier is the last item in an enumeration. When somebody adds a new item later, your code will fail.

- create an enumerated list in one place, and a parallel list of array-values somewhere else. An innocent change in either list will break code.

- rely on other objects to free memory that you allocated. Freeing memory is likely to be overlooked in a few cases, creating memory-leaks.

In every case above, code relied on an unreliable trait of other code. Each trait was unreliable because it was promised weakly or not at all, making the trait likely to change, especially during maintenance when the coupling has been forgotten.

Frail coupling is worse than common coupling because it is both less visible and more fragile. You can find all instances of common coupling involving a variable by examining all references to it in a smart editor. Sadly, there is no similar procedure for detecting frail coupling. A labor-intensive way to identify frail coupling in your object or method is to find and examine the assumptions its code makes about its inputs or environment. If any such assumption is an aspect of behavior or data that is unpromised or subject to change, that assumption is an example of frail coupling.

Frail coupling occurs too often, especially the kinds involving buffer sizes, parallel lists, and freeing memory. People appear to create such frail couplings with little regard to their vulnerability to innocuous changes. One way to avoid some kinds of frail coupling is to conceal the unpromised aspects of your code and data from their users. If an unreliable trait is required, you should do whatever it takes to make it a reliable promise in the fulfiller.

Priority Coupling

Priority coupling is a form of frail coupling, but it involves the priorities of threads. It's exceptionally poor because its symptoms can be intermittent, and thus very difficult to debug. When two threads rely on their relative priorities to operate correctly, they are coupled by priority. One thread does not know that it is fulfilling a timing-requirement in the other thread, nor does anything else in the system, making a thread vulnerable. For example, suppose an application sends a message to a group of destinations over an Ethernet connection in this loop:

```
for (i=0; i<largeNumber; i++) {
    UDP::sendMsg (message, dest.ipAddr[i], dest.port[i]);
}
```

This loop looks fine. It simply sends *message* to some destinations. What could go wrong? Did you notice that this loop sends many messages at full processor-speed? If the Ethernet thread were to block, these messages would overflow the buffers in the IP-stack. (The Ethernet thread and IP-stack are the multi-level networking code inside the operating system.) But when you test your code, it works fine. The reason it works is that in your system, the Ethernet thread has a higher priority than your application. So each call to *sendMsg* causes the Ethernet thread to wake up and run (pausing your thread), and send the message, before your loop can run again.

But suppose an occasionally-run maintenance-chore blocks the Ethernet thread just when your loop runs. Then it will overflow the IP-stack's buffers. This failure might occur only once every few days; how will you debug that?

One solution to such stealthy coupling is to put a small time-delay in the loop:

```
for (i=0; i<largeNumber; i++) {
    UDP::sendMsg (message, dest.ipAddr[i], dest.port[i]);
    nanosleep (&millisecond, NULL);
}
```

That Posix *nanosleep* method causes the calling thread to sleep for the given time, and we are using it to delay the thread by one millisecond to give the message time to work its way out of the system. Another technique is to wait for a notice from the operating system telling you that the message has been physically sent.

Inversion Test   A good test for multithreaded systems is to invert the priorities of all threads. That is, turn them all around so the lowest priority becomes the highest, and vice versa. This inversion will cause the system to run slower, and a high frequency event may need to be slowed down. But the program should still run correctly. If it does not, there is priority coupling in there somewhere. Eliminate it, lest it cause a production-halt due to customers reporting occasional crashes.

Here is another kind of priority coupling:

```
1  startTransfer (&doneSemaphore);
2  doneSemaphore.clear ();
3  doneSemaphore.wait ();
```

The *startTransfer* method starts a data-transfer in another thread, which releases the given semaphore when it is done. This code clears the semaphore to be safe (a good practice), and then waits for it to be released when the transfer is done. The problem is that if the transfer-thread has higher priority than the code above, then the code will execute in this incorrect order:

- *startTransfer* will cause an immediate switch to the transfer-thread.
- The transfer will finish and release the semaphore before *clear* was called.
- The *clear* will clobber the release, causing the *wait* to wait forever.

But if the app-thread had a higher priority than the transfer-thread, this code would run fine. Hence, we have a case of priority coupling. The solution is to clear the semaphore *before* it could possibly be released, which means clearing it before the call to *startTransfer*. The fix is to swap lines 1 and 2 above.

As you can see from these examples, priority coupling can be sneaky, and even simple, innocent-looking code can exhibit it. Fortunately, the inversion test reveals priority coupling immediately. I suggest performing this test in any project that uses multiple threads in order to eliminate common causes of intermittent failures.

Content Coupling

This pathological form of frail coupling occurs when one method accesses the instructions inside another method apart from calling it, or surreptitiously accesses the data within another object. Modern high-level languages make it difficult to engage in this vile form of software-immorality, but some hackers might take on the challenge. For example, you might notice that the instructions at some address form a bit-pattern that you want, so you hard-code the address of those instructions in another method. Or using assembler language, you can jump into the midst of a method. Obviously, content coupling makes maintenance a nightmare because the accessed code (the fulfiller) has made no promise to not change its bits.

But there are two situations where content coupling is useful. First, you sometimes need to write dummy data to buffers or to a file, often for testing or measuring performance. On systems with little memory, internal code or data is a handy source of such dummy data, eliminating allocation of scarce memory.

The second situation is the generation of pseudo-random keys for encryption. Such keys are formed from random numbers, which are hard to find in a computer.

One technique used in conjunction with others is to exclusive-or the contents of memory with the keys, making the keys more random. A method using such a key would be content coupled to other items in memory.

With the exception of these two special situations of procuring dummy data and of "generating entropy" as it's called in the cryptographic world, content coupling is never used—for good reason.

4.2.3 Indirection Principle: Minimize Indirection

This principle of good coupling is probably violated more than any other, so take extra care to avoid the forms of indirection described below. All indirection should be kept to a minimum because such accesses are difficult to follow. Both code and data can be accessed indirectly, and the most common cases are covered below.

Indirect Calls Through a Pointer

All forms of indirect calls use a pointer to the method being called. Calling methods indirectly is highly language-dependent, so depending on your language, the pointer can be accessed using a method-pointer in C and C++, a virtual method (polymorphism), a delegate in C# or Python, or an interface in Java.

Calling a virtual method in an object causes the compiler to call the method using a pointer, even if the method has not been overridden. In Java, all methods are virtual (overridable). In C++, you must use the `virtual` keyword to make a method virtual.

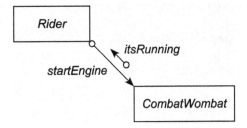

Figure 4.5: Indirect-call coupling

Figure 4.5 is an example of indirect method-calls (also termed "dynamic binding") for both a command and a notice. The arrow representing the indirect call always has a small circle (bubble) on its tail.

As mentioned on pages 42 and 54, you should use direct calls whenever possible, because indirect calls are harder for a person to follow. The problem is that somebody reading the code cannot immediately tell what method will be called. In an editor, a person will right-click on the call, then click on "Go to definition," and if the call is not direct, this click will *not* take him to the method being called. The person then is forced to search around to determine what will actually be called. Following such a coupling backwards is equally difficult because a person must (1) determine where and when some method-pointer is set to the method of interest, and then (2) determine where calls are made using that pointer. Except for a few cases involving notices, indirect calls should be avoided because following them is too time-consuming.

Indirect Calls Through an Instance

This form of indirection is a defect in most object-oriented languages. It hides the called method by concealing its class, as shown in this C++ example:

```
schInstance->getSpan(firstItem, finalItem);
```

Where is getSpan located? One can only find out by searching for the declaration of schInstance, and noting its class. When following a chain of couplings, finding such called classes wastes some time. However, a static class has no instance, so a call directly specifies the class with this clear syntax:

```
Schedule::getSpan(firstItem, finalItem);
```

Where is getSpan located? It's obviously in class Schedule, so one immediately knows where to look for that method.

The first syntax conceals the location and the second syntax reveals it, removing a step of syntactic indirection, making this very popular form of coupling faster to follow. In addition to this gain in visibility, static classes offer several more advantages. Please refer to Section 6.4 on page 138 for a detailed discussion of static classes.

Indirect Addressing of Messages

Method calls are one form of message passing. Other forms include inter-thread, inter-process, and networking system calls for transferring messages. All messages have a source and a destination, and you should avoid indirection for both, aiding those who are following such couplings. For example, suppose an inter-process pipe requires that both sides (source and destination) register for indirect notices. A pipe-ID symbol should be passed into the call that sends a message. The receiving notice should be passed that pipe-ID in a parameter, and it will validate that value using the same symbol. Using a pipe-ID symbol in the pipe's interface makes it easy for somebody following couplings to find both sides by searching for that symbol.

Indirect Actions Through Control Coupling

Control coupling occurs when a parameter changes the behavior of its method. Thus, the behavior is specified indirectly, via the parameter. Such coupling can occur with any parameter type, but is often seen with boolean flags. There are several kinds of control coupling, with selection coupling being the worst. In every case, the action of a method becomes less clear, making it more difficult to follow a coupling.

Selection A parameter can select which operation to perform. When you see a parameter named something like *commandNum* or *requestNum*, the method probably exhibits selection control coupling. Selection control coupling is unavoidable when messages are arriving from an I/O port or have been funneled for some other reason. If funneling is not needed, consider splitting such a method into multiple methods, one for each selectable operation.

Alteration A parameter can alter internal operation. An example would be a *skim* flag telling your *playAudioFile* method to quickly skim the audio, continuously playing brief fragments as it races through the audio file.

Addition A similar form of coupling is a flag telling a method to perform another action in addition to its usual action. Several functions offered by the standard C library and Unix/Linux have a `flags` parameter which causes alteration and/or addition control coupling. For example, this parameter in the open function can be set to O_CREAT [sic], which will cause open to create a new file if necessary, which is addition control coupling.

Hybrid Having a parameter perform multiple duties based on number ranges makes it a hybrid. For example, *frequency* in a radio could also determine AM or FM based on its sign. Hybrid control coupling is tolerable when the sign of a parameter determines its meaning. Something similar to hybrid control coupling is often seen in return-values of methods, where sign is used to indicate success or failure. I suggest avoiding hybrid control coupling that's any more complex than this as it's an invitation to make mistakes.

Description A mild form of control coupling is a parameter which describes some condition about another parameter. An example is the flag *badZipCode* which tells the method that the passed-in ZIP-code is invalid. Description control coupling is probably harmless, as it merely informs the method about the state of a parameter, but does not directly tell the method to do anything differently.

Control coupling can also occur in notices. Again, description coupling in notices is harmless. Selection control coupling is acceptable if the selector-parameter is merely an event-number or similar. In this case, the caller of the notice is not commanding one of several actions, but rather is informing the object that one of several possible events has occurred.

Indirect Data-Access

The problem with accessing variables indirectly is that it is difficult to determine (1) which variable will be accessed, and (2) what other methods will access that variable. Thus, couplings are harder to follow in either direction. The following discussion covers common uses of pointers to data.

A pointer to a variable can be passed into two objects so that one can write it and the other can read it. This is a poor solution to the tidbit problem described in Section 6.12 on page 163 because the coupling between objects is concealed, making it hard to detect and even harder to follow. Try to use something more visible, such as field coupling. Even common coupling is better than passing pointers into objects.

For a pointer that can point to one of several variables, do not conceal the code that selects the variable that it will point to. That is, put the selector-code near the method(s) that uses the pointer. A developer following the coupling can more easily determine what the pointer could point to.

On a related topic, in C and C++, developers often pass a pointer as a parameter to a method which will return a value using that pointer. This situation is equivalent to passing a parameter by reference, and such a coupling is easy to follow.

If you are transferring only a small amount of data, consider copying it instead of passing a pointer to it. But for large buffers and records, you are forced to use indirection because copying such data would be too burdensome. This situation is actually a dataflow, which is covered by the Dataflows principle described later.

4.2.4   Extent Principle: Minimize Extent of Coupling

This principle tells you to minimize the number of couplings in your design. Some specific ways to do this are to minimize the number of

- variables shared or transferred between methods and objects,
- layers in your design, especially thin layers that do little,
- links in each chain of couplings.

Each of these points is amplified below.

Minimize Shared/Transferred Variables

Shared Fields   Methods in the same class can interact with each other by sharing fields in their object, which is field coupling. While field coupling is acceptable, it can be overdone. If an object has too many fields, and several methods are writing and reading them, then this situation can be similar to that of global variables. In fact, it might surprise you that all of the disadvantages of common coupling (described page 90) are also true of field coupling. From the point of view of the methods in an object, fields are identical to globals. They are a way of sharing information among methods. They have all the disadvantages of globals, *but not as severely.* For example, to find all accesses to a field, you only need to search the methods in the class, and not all the methods in the program. Therefore, due the narrower scope of fields, couplings employing shared fields are easier to follow than those using global variables. Knowing that fields have a cost (albeit lower than globals), I suggest that you be stingy with them, keeping them to a minimum by thinking hard about alternatives before adding a field.

Parameters   Due to their great visibility, it's best to pass information in parameters. But each parameter is a separate coupling, so having many parameters represents an increased extent of coupling. When a parameter-list becomes too long, here are some things to try:

- Redesign the organization (interfaces) of class(es) to avoid having to pass so much information into one method.
- If some parameters seldom change across many calls to the method, consider making them member fields set with setter methods.
- Pass a record into the method instead of many parameters.

Minimize Layers

A layer is regarded as one or more objects that together form a foundation upon which the higher level software relies. A layer is helpful when it provides a useful service, but often layers are defined that do little. Such a layer increases extent of coupling by lengthening all chains of coupling that pass through the layer. Due to a defect in their personalities, some people enjoy defining such do-little layers; they are "abstraction fanatics" revealed in Section 9.3.2 on page 249. Obviously, you want your objects and layers to do something substantial (refer to the Meaty rule on page 152).

Tramp Coupling

The colorfully named tramp coupling is an inspiration of Meilir Page-Jones [24]. In IDAR graphs, tramp coupling can appear in three forms: data, commands, and notices. A tramp has the effect of adding an empty layer at some spot in your design, lengthening a chain of couplings. But this problem is minor enough that you can ignore the presence of some tramp coupling. However, it should cause you to re-examine your design to see whether you can eliminate the tramp without making the design worse somewhere else.

Tramp Data

This form of tramp coupling looks like parameter coupling, but the called method does not use the parameter. Instead, the parameter is passed on down in another call to another method. The data is merely passing through the software neighborhood like a tramp or bum, doing nothing. Figure 4.6(a) shows this situation. The parameter *mode* in the call to *create* is not used by *create*. Rather, it uselessly passes on through into the call to *draw* where it is needed. The call to *create* is an example of tramp coupling, and the call to *draw* is an example of parameter coupling.

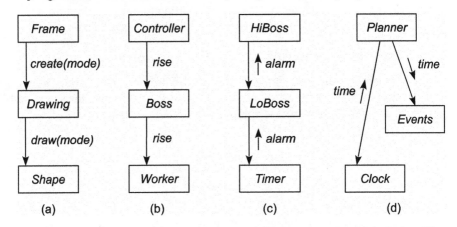

Figure 4.6: Tramp data (a), tramp command (b), tramp notice (c), isolation (d)

Additional problems with tramp data are that it reduces performance slightly, and it creates a dependency on the tramp's type in the methods that pass the tramp along.

Tramp Commands

A command is a tramp if it forwards its entire responsibility to another command down the hierarchy. In the example shown in Figure 4.6(b), a controller for a fixture on an assembly line sends a *rise* command to make a table rise. The *Worker* needs this command, but to avoid hard-coding knowledge of the lower-level design into the controller, it sends the *rise* command to *Boss*, by calling its *rise* command. It in turn calls *Worker.rise*. The *rise* method in *Boss* is a tramp because it did nothing except forward its command down the chain. It reminds me of bureaucrats in the Chinese government during chairman Mao's rule who learned to survive by forwarding the slogans on down and doing little else.

Tramp Notices (and Isolation)

Unlike tramp data and commands, tramp notices are forbidden. A notice is required to convey information needed by the callee or caller object, which a tramp notice fails to do, violating the Identify rule. The *alarm* notice in *LoBoss* in Figure 4.6(c) is an example of a forbidden tramp notice because *LoBoss* does not need its information.

However, tramp notices are permitted in the case of isolation. Suppose a superior wishes to isolate some or all of its subordinates (and their subordinates) from other objects. That isolated hierarchy is commanded only by the superior. Isolation also means that outside objects are ignorant of that hierarchy, and objects in the hierarchy are ignorant of outside objects. Therefore, all direct incoming and outgoing notice-calls to/from the hierarchy must pass through the superior, becoming tramps in the superior. Such tramps do not violate the Identify rule because the superior would have needed those notices if it had implemented the hierarchy's roles inside itself (becoming a monolithic object). Figure 4.6(d) illustrates this situation. We isolated *Events*, placing it under the control of *Planner*, forcing the *time* notice from *Clock* to be routed through a tramp in *Planner*. Submans often contain tramp notices because they isolate their entire subordinate hierarchies, as do the head objects of several design patterns such as Adapter and Façade. In addition to tramp notices, an isolated hierarchy might also need to employ tramp commands in its superior.

4.2.5   Dataflows Principle: Draw the Dataflows

To reveal couplings consisting of transfers of bulk data, you should draw dataflows passing between objects or subsystems. You should also include dataflows of records entering and leaving a data-storage object, as illustrated in Figure 4.7.

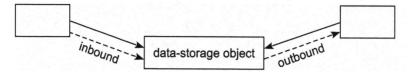

Figure 4.7: Dataflow to and from a data-storage object

Yes, the dashed dataflow lines parallel command lines, making them appear to be redundant. But the dataflow lines are useful because they reveal both sides of indirect data couplings that would otherwise be concealed.

When a dataflow connects two subsystems, you should graph it in *three* places: the main IDAR graph, and in both subsystem graphs.

The Indirection principle tells you to avoid indirection, but dataflows force you to do otherwise. Drawing dataflows on your IDAR graphs reveals these couplings despite their use of indirection.

4.2.6   Remarks About Coupling

Bandwidth   Another aspect of coupling is the quantity of data that is transferred per second, which is the *bandwidth* of an interface. High bandwidth interfaces are often sensitive to brief interruptions, and such software might fail if the garbage-collector or some other "CPU-hog" decides to run while data is being transferred. Also, high bandwidth interfaces themselves tend to boost CPU-usage, which can make response sluggish and reduce battery-life on portable devices.

It's important to make a distinction between data that is *copied* versus data that is moved merely by changing pointers. Bandwidth refers to amount of data copied. This immediately suggests a method of reducing bandwidth: Transfer data using pointers to buffers instead of copying the buffers themselves.

Prudence tells us to minimize the number of methods and objects involved in high bandwidth traffic. Identify high bandwidth interfaces, and if possible, devise some means of reducing their bandwidth. For example, if only a portion of the data will be used, filter out the unused data at its source, reducing the bandwidth of the downstream interfaces.

Although you can create a metric by assigning numeric scores to the principles or kinds of coupling described in this chapter, I think it's better to make them part of your intuition instead. In light of their importance, I will repeat the five principles of good coupling here. Do you remember what the SPIED acronym stands for?

Scopes Minimize scopes of shared variables. Parameter and field coupling are the best. Common coupling is the worst.

Promise Don't rely on a flimsy promise, which is frail coupling.

Indirection Minimize indirect accesses to code or data. Such indirection uses pointers, virtual methods, or parameters that specify actions.

Extent Minimize extent of coupling, which is the number of couplings.

Dataflows Draw the dataflows, including those to/from data-storage objects.

4.3 Quality of Hierarchy — Need

The *need* criterion is new to software design because a role hierarchy is new to OOP. *Need* is a gauge of how well you extracted narrow roles from broad roles. When roles have been defined properly, each subordinate assists each superior with services it needs. Thus, the degree of such need is a measure of the quality of your hierarchy. Here is the formal definition of this criterion:

> *Need is the extent that a superior needs services*
> *provided by a subordinate.*

Need should be high. A superior should rely on at least some services offered by each subordinate. However, cross-cutting concerns are an exception: A superior may command a cross-cutting subordinate without needing any service from it.

There are several ways that people can try to cheat the hierarchy, most of which result in a superior having little or no need for its subordinate. Additional symptoms include violating the Role rule and defining dishonest roles. Here are some signs that a superior has little need for its subordinate:

- The subordinate does not assist the superior.
  To assess assistance, the superior's role must be honest, reflecting the chore that it will actually do. Absence of assistance might indicate that the superior is commanding actions outside of its role (side-effects), violating the Role rule.

- The subordinate's actions are not covered by the superior's role.

  When a superior finishes its chore, a common mistake is to have it command the next chore that needs to be done, though doing so violates the Role rule. Such temporal chaining is described in Section 6.8 on page 147.

- Swapping both objects, and redefining their notices and commands as needed, yields an acceptable design.

  If moving the superior under its subordinate results in an acceptable design, you need to carefully examine the honesty of the roles of both.

- Removing the subordinate does little or no harm to the superior (i.e., it can still fulfill its role).

  For example, you might make a message router a high-level object because it commands subordinates to *processMsg*. But removing a subordinate won't harm such a superior, as it will merely discard messages sent to a nonexistent object. Such a router should be a low-level distributor object (refer to the Distributor pattern in Section 7.2.2 on page 190). However, if the superior also receives essential assistance from subordinates, then such a design would be acceptable because its routing capability would not be the main item in its role.

- Reversal of assistance: The superior assists a subordinate, and that subordinate provides little or no assistance to the superior (instead of vice versa).

  The message-router object mentioned above is a good example of this reversal: It assists its subordinates by relaying messages to them. But those subordinates don't assist their superior.

  More generally, if a designer notices that data flows from one object to the other, he can mistakenly make the IDAR graph similar to a dataflow diagram, with the superior sending data downward. It is likely that the superior is assistive and should be under the subordinate and not over it. Or perhaps both objects should be under a common superior, with the data passed in horizontal notices. If such assistance is the primary chore of the superior's code, with no other commands telling subordinates to do their chores, the design should be changed. In order to pretend to be a manager, the superior might contain managerial commands, but it will relay them to the subordinate which will do most of the work, making them tramps in the superior. The swapping test above will often expose reversal of assistance.

  In good designs, assistance will be bidirectional when a superior helps a subordinate perform a command, and that command in turn helps the superior. For an example of this, refer to the Resourceful Boss pattern in Section 7.1.2 on page 180. But you should suspect a reversal if most assistance is downward.

- A superior whose code will be narrow has a vague grandiose name and role.

  The above message-router could be named *SysController*, even though it mostly relays messages to subordinates. An honest name for it is *MsgRouter*, which is clearly narrower and lower level. Section 4.1.4 (page 83) states that managerial words like "manager" and "controller" should be avoided in some cases. Their use can be vague. Vagueness reduces clarity by concealing an object's actions.

- When pretending that the two objects are people, their roles would not make sense in a corporation.

  For example, suppose a *TimeMaster* object were to send a *wakeUp* command to a subordinate. In a corporation, this would be like observing that the secretary commands the vice president to wake up after a meeting. Realizing that the secretary controls the VP, you make her the CEO of the company, with the VP reporting to her. Though she might feel honored, having a secretary be the CEO of a company is preposterous. The *wakeUp* command between objects should be re-identified as an imperative notice that echoes a command originating with the boss (refer to Section 3.13.6 on page 72).

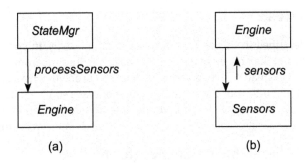

Figure 4.8: Example of low need (a), and high need (b)

Let's look at an example of a superior with little need for its subordinate, and how to improve it. Figure 4.8(a) shows a *StateMgr* whose role is "manages engine-state", and *Engine* whose role is "controls the engine". *StateMgr* monitors all sensors, which is the state of the engine (hence the role of managing its state), and sends their values to *Engine* in the *processSensors* command 100 times per second. *Engine* uses these sensor values to control throttle position, air-fuel mixture ratio, and other things, as well as slowing down or stopping if temperature becomes too high. Let's evaluate this design in terms of the signs listed above.

- Not assisting: The superior reads sensors, and its subordinate does not help it do that. *Engine* does not assist *StateMgr*.

- Swapping is acceptable: After swapping these objects, the sensor monitor would send sensor values to *Engine* in notices, which is a good design.

- Removing subordinate: If the *Engine* object were gone, *StateMgr* could still monitor sensors. So removing *Engine* has only a minor effect on *StateMgr*.

- Reversal of assistance: *StateMgr* assists *Engine* by giving it sensor values, while *Engine* does not assist *StateMgr*.

- Vague grandiose name: *StateMgr* mainly reads sensors. Calling it a "manager" is vague and deceptive, as is the word "state" in its role and name.

- Roles in a corporation: This design is similar to making a secretary CEO over the VP because she has a better view of the company than he does because she periodically tells him the status of parts of the company.

This design has many signs that the superior does not need its subordinate. The corrected design is shown in Figure 4.8(b). The *Engine* object's role is still "controls the engine", but *StateMgr* is no longer falsely called a manager, but is now *Sensors* because its role is "reads sensors and reports them to my superior". In this improved design, *Engine* needs its subordinate (*Sensors*) because it needs sensor values in order to control the engine.

The key to creating a good hierarchy is for every superior to need assistance from its subordinates, even if that help is only a small portion of their available services. If a design avoids the sneaky tricks described above, has honest roles and obeys the Role rule, all subordinates will be needed to help fulfill their superiors' roles.

4.4   Metrics

The metrics described in this section can be computed easily, in your head, making them useful during the process of designing. You can write a program (tool) that reads source-code and evaluates these metrics for you. The problem with such a tool is you can only use it when it's no longer useful. The tool reads source-code, which means you have already created the design and implemented it. By then, it is probably too late to change the design. That is why I regard *post facto* metrics as impractical.

4.4.1   HD—Hierarchical Distance (for Notices)

Can we measure the distance across the hierarchy that a notice travels? Doing so would give us a badness metric, because the farther a notice travels, the more unrelated the objects become that are communicating using the notice. I'll propose that a useful metric for this distance is the number of command-arrow hops needed to travel from the sender of a notice to its receiver. Let's call this metric HD, which is the Hierarchical Distance covered by the notice. I define it precisely as follows:

> *The HD metric for a notice is the minimum number of hops (transitions) across command-arrows required to travel between the sending and the receiving objects, without passing through subordinates of both.*

Let's clarify this definition with a graph. Each notice in Figure 4.9 is named "hdx", where x is its HD metric.

- *hd1* is a bound notice paralleling a command-arrow between a subordinate and its superior. All bound notices have an HD value of 1.

- *hd2* is called a "peer-to-peer" notice because the sender and receiver have a mutual superior (boss), making them peers.

- *hd2v* is an upward notice (it could also go downward) that bypasses one boss. When counting the hops, we had to travel through a subordinate (*Obj2*) of the receiving object (*Obj1*). But we did not travel through subordinates of *both* the sender and receiver (*Obj3* and *Obj1*), so this HD value of 2 is valid.

- *hd3* is a communication between two objects that are becoming rather far apart, thus having little relationship to each other.

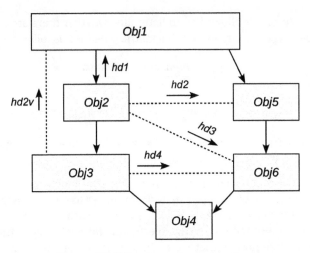

Figure 4.9: HD values of some notices

- *hd4* is sent from *Obj3* to *Obj6*, which are far from each other in the hierarchy. Passing through a subordinate of one object is permissible, but the definition forbids passing through subordinates of both sender and receiver because having a mutual (or closely related) subordinate usually does not imply that two objects are closely related. Therefore, we could not pass through *Obj4* which would have produced an HD value of 2 instead of 4.

You should examine any free notice that was removed by being routed through the hierarchy (possibly in violation of the Identify rule). The HD of such a notice is the number of method-calls from sender to receiver.

In general, the larger HD becomes, the less related the receiver is to the sender of the notice. Thus, a large HD (3 or higher) suggests that the receiver is unrelated to the sender, representing an unrelated dependency if the notice is direct.

As an example of how the HD metric can be useful, consider the notices for handling the current-limitation in the digital camera in Figure 6.11 on page 157. Those notices have an HD of 4. Such a large HD correctly suggests that these are unrelated dependencies in the senders.

A "distant" notice is one having an HD of 3 or higher. Making it indirect would reduce learnability, which is worse than the irritating unrelated dependency. If you can't remove it some other way, leave it alone. Collector and distributor objects are exceptions; distant notices involving them are acceptable.

4.4.2   FNR—Free Notice Ratio

Most substantial designs have some free notices because objects sometimes need to communicate with each other apart from the command hierarchy. Most commonly, peers working under the same superior need to exchange data with each other, like coworkers on a software-development team. But in a poor design, objects have too many of these couplings (interactions) among themselves, resulting in too many free notices. The FNR metric allows you to determine whether there are too many non-command couplings in your design. This metric is defined as follows:

$$FNR = \frac{number\ of\ free\ notices}{number\ of\ classes}$$

The number of free notices must be computed according to these rules:

- If multiple free notices parallel the same dashed line, they count as only one free notice. We are actually counting the number of free paths.

- Any free notice can be removed by replacing it with multiple notices that parallel command lines in the hierarchy, from sender to receiver. But keep in mind that in many cases, a tramp notice is illegal. Such removal merely conceals noncommand couplings among objects, and does not remove those couplings. Therefore, free notices that were removed in this manner must be added to the total. Thus, the numerator is actually the number of call-based inter-object couplings that do not follow command lines.

- Do *not* count free notices sent by distributor objects, or sent to collector objects. Such well known funnels of free notices are not scattered interactions among objects, and thus do not contribute to messiness.

There is no hard-and-fast limit for this metric, but you should consider alternate designs if your FNR exceeds 0.4. A value over 0.5 is strong evidence that too much communication among objects occurs outside of command lines. However, if your design makes heavy use of dataflows (which are usually handled with free notices), or has some unusual reason for needing many free notices, then a high FNR is to be expected. So don't use 0.4 or 0.5 as a firm pass/fail threshold because you also need to account for the nature of your program.

The environmental chamber on page 164 has an FNR of 0.33 (4 free notices and 12 classes). This program is an example of what a well-designed program with a larger-than-usual FNR looks like.

4.4.3   CR—Class-Ratio (for Subsystems)

A subsystem that only utilizes one external class is probably more modular than one that relies on several external classes. The Class Ratio metric (CR) measures the *lack* of modularity of a subsystem, and is defined as follows:

$$CR = \frac{number\ of\ external\ classes}{number\ of\ internal\ classes}$$

Note that I used the word "classes" instead of "objects". Multiple instances of a class are counted only once, which means that we are counting classes. The internal classes consist of the subman and all classes that are part of the subsystem. Each external class represents a dependency—a class on which the subsystem depends. Minimize these. Here are the metrics for the subsystems found in this book:

Subsystem	Page	External	Internal	CR Metric
MAC	60	1	5	.20
Fax	116	3	8	.38
VDL	289	4	13	.31
Items	311	1	11	.09

Smaller values of this metric are better. I consider a value of .4 to be borderline, and anything above .5 to be unacceptable. I've found that typical values are around .2 to .3. If a subsystem has a poor (large) CR metric, investigate whether the lower level classes it uses are fine grained. For example, there may be numerous utility classes available in a system, and a subsystem might need several of these before it can do useful work. In such a system, you will need to use higher thresholds of acceptability than my suggested values above.

4.4.4   Fan-Out, Fan-In, and Direct Dependencies

The concepts of *fan-out* and *fan-in* were created as part of Structured Design in the 1960s, and are related to coupling. Figure 4.10 shows how these are defined.

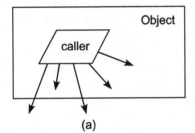
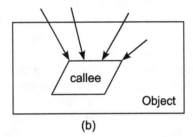

Figure 4.10: Fan-out (a), and fan-in (b)

Fan-out   Fan-out is the number of different methods that are called by a method or object. Calling one method from multiple places from within the same method or object counts as only one call. Therefore, we count the number of *unique* callees. Also, each different method-address fetched is considered to be a call, even though any calls made using that address occur elsewhere. Figure 4.10(a) shows a method with a fan-out of five. If a method has both many lines of code and a low fan-out, then it is a monolith that might need to be split. On the other hand, a method having few lines and a high fan-out consists mostly of method calls, and it's possible that one or more methods it calls should be merged into the calling method. A high fan-out also makes reuse of the method more difficult due to the need to either reuse the methods it calls or somehow remove those calls.

Fan-in   Fan-in is the number of unique callers that a method has. For indirect calls, you should count the number of places the address of the method is fetched, in addition to the actual calls. Figure 4.10(b) shows a method with a fan-in of four. Any popular method will have a high fan-in. Having a high fan-in is generally good, as it means that the method or object is being used much in the program. But if a method has a fan-in of only one, then it has only one caller. If that caller is small, then it's likely that the callee should be merged into its caller. A chain of methods with low fan-in is a sign that the design was divided into too many levels (a common mistake), and should be flattened by merging some levels together.

Direct Dependencies   A measure of coupling similar to fan-out is the number of classes upon which your class depends. On the IDAR graph, count the number of objects which your object commands or notifies, and add classes supplying definitions. This sum can suggest that your class is too large or too small, or that roles in your design were poorly divided into sub-roles, causing excessive coupling.

4.4.5   LOC—Lines of Code

A good metric is the number of lines of code in a class, commonly called LOC. Folks disagree on the precise definition of LOC, but I prefer to count only executable statements (that generate CPU-instructions), thus excluding blank lines, comments, block boundaries, and declarations. If LOC is under 50 or so, the class may be too small, and you should consider merging it into another. If the class has only one superior, the class can be merged into its superior, adding to its private methods and fields. If LOC is over 500, and especially if it's over 1000, you should attempt to extract a new class from that large class, creating a superior-subordinate pair. Section 5.4.2, starting on page 118, provides some techniques for doing this subdivision.

The same reasoning applies to methods, but with smaller numbers. A very small method having only one caller probably should be merged into its caller, unless there's a good chance that it will acquire another caller in the future. A method exceeding around 150 executable lines may be worth splitting. As a rule, I suggest that you have around 25 executable lines in each method, where "around" is broadly interpreted. Getters and setters will have one line in each, and a method with a large number of repetitive cases or steps may exceed 150 executable lines and still be acceptable.

Either mistake of being too large or too small makes code harder to learn and understand. This topic of sizes is explored more in Section 6.10 on page 151, which culminates with the Meaty rule.

An objection to the LOC metric is that it cannot be computed until the code is written, and by then, it's difficult to change the design. But splitting a class or merging a class into its sole superior is a minor change in design and often not a terribly time-consuming change in code, making LOC reasonably useful.

4.5   Summary

The truths that this chapter taught you may be painful, but removing shortcomings in your designs now will save your organization from more pain later. Below are the primary criteria and metrics described in this chapter:

- The quality of a role is gauged by its *clarity, cohesion,* and *concealment*. Clarity is the plainness of the actions expressed by a role; cohesion is their relatedness; and concealment is how well inner workings are hidden. A role can usually be regarded as vacuous, trait-based, managerial, or common. Managerial and common roles are best.

- *Coupling* is an interaction between two methods. Make the SPIED principles of good coupling part of your intuition. They are: Minimize *scopes* of shared variables; don't rely on a flimsy *promise*; avoid *indirection*; minimize *extent* of coupling; draw the *dataflows*.

- *Need* gauges the quality of your hierarchy by assessing the degree that each superior needs each of its subordinates. A low need means that the hierarchy is incorrect because a subordinate is not providing a service that contributes to the role of its superior.

- Metrics: For free notices, the HD metric tells you how related or unrelated the dependencies are among objects, and FNR indicates whether noncommand communications (couplings) among objects are excessive. LOC tells you whether your classes or methods are too large or small.

Other aspects of designs are more difficult to gauge because they are more subjective. They are discussed in Chapter 6 (starting on page 136), which covers Good and Bad Practices.

4.6 Exercises

1. What are the three criteria for gauging the goodness of a role? (one word each)
2. Describe each of those three criteria.
3. In a few words each, describe the four types of roles.
4. What is coupling?
5. Briefly describe the SPIED principles.
6. What is the *need* criterion?
7. A processor has a small fast memory and a large slow memory. An object called *HighSpeed* contains the methods and data that will be placed in fast memory. What type of role, clarity and cohesion does *HighSpeed* have?
8. An object called *Helpers* contains helpful methods such as *squareRoot*, *intToAscii*, *zeroMem*, *debugPrint*, and others. What type of role, clarity and cohesion does *Helpers* have?
9. A *Robot* object controls robots on an assembly line. Its role is "perform the initialization, calibration, and health-monitoring of a robot, as well as running a script which causes it to make the required motions on the assembly line." What type of role, clarity and cohesion does *Robot* have? How could this role be improved?
10. When a serious error is detected, an *emergencyShutdown* method is called which turns off motors and other high-power devices, closes open files, closes I/O connectors, and halts the program. What type of role, clarity and cohesion is this description?

11. A class *Employee* contains methods that can query and change information about a specific employee, such as name, address, salary, etc. Its role is "manage employee data." What type of role, clarity and cohesion does *Employee* have?

12. The role of the method *employeeInfo* is "given an employee-number as a parameter, returns a record containing information about that employee." What type of role, clarity and cohesion does *employeeInfo* have?

13. The role for *ItemMgr* is "allocates and frees several kinds of items, such as memory, files, pipes, queues and semaphores." What type of role, clarity and cohesion does *ItemMgr* have?

14. A command has this role: "computes a discounted price, computes and adds sales tax, and computes and adds shipping cost based on the selected shipper". What type of role, clarity and cohesion does this command have?

15. The records in a data-storage object have a key field which is matched with the key in incoming messages. The matching record is then fetched, and both record and message are processed further. The IDAR graph has arrows for commands and notices to all of these objects, and dashed arrows for the flow of messages. Which principle of good coupling is being violated?

16. Given that people will follow chains of coupling in your code, what is your goal?

17. A project adopted the policy of putting all variables accessed by two or more objects in the same system-wide file, making them easy to locate. Which principle of good coupling does this policy violate?

18. A developer on your project put an *Interposer* object between every pair of communicating objects in his design. These interposers merely pass their calls through, unchanged, but are present in case any interfaces change. Which principle of good coupling does this approach violate?

19. What form of coupling do the interposers exhibit?

20. When testing your audio noise removal object, you noticed that the noise only consists of single-sample spikes, so you changed your code to only employ a spike-removal algorithm. Which principle of good coupling does this violate?

21. *Checksum* has a *copyBuffer* command which copies a passed-in buffer to a holding buffer inside the object, and a *calc* command that computes the checksum of the holding buffer. What kind of coupling do *copyBuffer* and *calc* exhibit?

22. A developer made all methods in his classes `virtual` to allow them to be overriden, in case somebody wanted to do so. Which principle of good coupling does this decision violate?

23. A bright team invented the *consorter* architecture in which you first registered desired actions (that is, methods) with other objects. Then, as the program was running, when you wrote a value to such an object, all its registered actions were called (in order of registration) and were passed the value. In essence, each object in this architecture was an energetic variable because writing to it caused actions to occur. Which principle of good coupling does the consorter violate? Believe it or not, this architecture was fielded and promoted within a large company.

Chapter 5

How to Design

— design is the tail that wags the dog

<hr>

Good design is essential because small changes in design can have large effects on quality and schedule. That is why I bylined this chapter, "Design is the tail that wags the dog." Along with Chapter 3 (on core concepts), this chapter is key to knowing how to design a hierarchy of objects. You might have been honored with the privilege of designing an entire program, or perhaps a new subsystem. Often, you'll find that you need to enhance a portion of existing software. When doing this, you often find that the software is a mess, or that enhancing it will turn it into a mess. In such cases, I suggest that you refactor that portion. I have refactored subsystems with great results, so I recommend it highly. In addition to producing better software, such a redesign will give you pride in your work. The ugly alternative is for such chores to merely make monstrous messes more muddled.

But when starting your design, you will probably experience the infamous writer's block that novelists are reputed to face when staring at a blank sheet of paper. Where do you start? In the Peanuts comic strip, Snoopy solved this problem by always starting his novel with, "It was a dark and stormy night" [28], and hoping the rest of his novel would pour forth in a spontaneous flood of creativity. But real life usually does not work that way. This chapter gives you a step-by-step process for defining the objects in your design, which is the most difficult part of designing.

To narrow the search for objects, I first present the two kinds of objects you'll need to look for: verbs and nouns. Then I provide a procedure for finding and organizing the objects in your hierarchy. After that comes a five-step procedure for designing and perfecting. It's not as easy as following a cookbook. You'll need to do some hard thinking, but these procedures and suggestions will identify some objects for you, and help you to find the rest.

5.1   Requirements Document

Hold on; this section does *not* say what you expect. You expected it to tell you to carefully document what the software is supposed to do. That's true. You must have a requirements document describing what the program should do, because without it, you don't know what to design. The document doesn't need to be complete or rock-stable, but it needs to have enough so you can proceed with design without having to redo much of it later when some major requirement changes or is added. For a large system, the document should contain ample diagrams and user stories, and should not resemble a thick novel containing only text.

The surprise in this section is that it addresses a couple of the major causes of *failure* of projects. You would expect that most failures are due to incompetence. Not so! Few of the failures I've seen in my career have been due to incompetence. I have observed that there are two primary causes of failure:

Fanatics These are otherwise intelligent developers who have a fetish for some aspect of software, and overuse it badly, which makes software overcomplex, which in turn breaks the project's schedule. Those missed deadlines risk the entire project. I devoted Section 9.3 starting on page 248 to fanatics.

Wrong Product The other major cause of failure of projects is implementing the wrong thing. I have seen some large chunks of software be discarded because the requirements document was written by people who were out of touch with the actual users. Because they were not talking with them, they were guessing what those users wanted. We often guess wrong.

Similar to the wrong product, the phenomenon of "creeping featurism" periodically adds features to the product, causing the entire design-coding-debugging process to thrash, with the ultimate result of lengthening schedule and reducing quality. Somebody needs to talk with customers about what's important and what's not, and then cut out wasteful features with sharp scissors.

Talk With Your Users An important lesson I have learned from experience is: Talk with your users! Having a few users join the development team on-site is worthwhile, with their offices mixed among the developers' offices. Also, it seems that most users of applications and embedded software have the following simple requirements:

Just work, and don't hassle me.

That's an important lesson to learn, and one that is often violated. Talk with your users, and learn well what they actually need. Then write simplicity, reliability, and sufficient performance into your requirements document.

5.2   Nouns and Verbs

Historically, OOP has encouraged (and even required) developers to name objects with nouns. The traditional procedure for finding objects is to (1) force somebody to write a requirements document, (2) read the requirements document and underline its nouns, yielding a list of prospective objects, and (3) winnow the list down to the best objects and use those in the design. Verbs become methods in the final noun objects. This technique of finding objects works well much of the time, but sometimes you will find that a verb object is more appropriate. To put these two types of objects in perspective, out of all the objects defined in the example applications in Part II of this book, 86% are nouns and 14% are verbs. In the VDL subsystem of the pen plotter, almost a third of the objects are verbs. Nouns are clearly dominant, but there are enough verb objects around that they should not be neglected.

The first step in overcoming a case of writer's block—perhaps we should call it "programmer's block"—is knowing that you don't need to conjure up objects out of nothingness like a writer facing a blank sheet of paper. You only need to consider the two kinds of objects, verbs and nouns, with several subtypes of noun objects.

5.2.1 Verb Objects

The name of such an object is a verb, and it performs one action: its verb. That object neither represents nor is named after a thing capable of performing its action. Rather, it is named after the action itself. That action dominates its role. A verb object has the following traits:

- It has one primary command, which has the same role as the object.
- That primary command and the object have the same name, or at least the same root name. Multithreaded systems can be an exception, as the primary command may be named *start* or *run* if it's nonblocking.
- Any other commands in the object play supportive roles such as setting modes, transferring data, preparing for a call to the primary command, or cleaning up after it has been called.

In practice, a verb object may contain multiple primary commands. They will have minor differences, such as being nonblocking versus blocking or exchanging data in different ways. But each must fulfill its object's role.

Examples of verb objects are shown in Table 5.1. *Compose*, *Shoot*, and *Review* were taken from the digital camera presented in Chapter 12.

Object	Pri. Command	Role of Both
Compose	*compose*	Lets user compose a picture in the camera
Shoot	*shoot*	Takes a picture
Review	*review*	Lets user review pictures in the camera
Search	*search*	Searches for a pattern in the image-data
Mix	*mix*	Mixes a chemical into the solution
Stretch	*stretch*	Linearly stretches a shape
Compress	*compress*	Compresses a block of bytes

Table 5.1: Verb objects and primary commands, with their roles

You can find verb objects in the requirements document in the same manner as you would for noun objects. For example, the phrase "the packet is encrypted and sent" contains the verb "encrypted", suggesting that you create an *Encrypt* object.

5.2.2   Noun Objects

There are a variety of types of noun objects, many of which are listed below. Out of all these, only agent nouns explicitly tell you what the object does.

Data The name, role, and commands of a data object are focused on the data it contains and perhaps manipulates. Examples include *IdarGraph*, *Histogram*, *ElectricalSchematic*, and *Schedule*. To its superiors, such an object appears to hold data, but in fact the data could be stored in the object's subordinates, which would be a concealed aspect of its implementation.

Data-Storage This common subset of data objects stores data for subsequent retrieval, with little or no alteration of the data. Such objects can consist of merely a few closely related fields, a data-structure, a file, a relational database, a remote file-system, or a server of some kind. Examples include *Settings*, *Books*, *UndoList*, *MsgQueue*, and *Stack*. Unfortunately, you might be tempted to use a data-storage object as a place to conceal global variables to be accessed with getters and setters. Try to eliminate such globals by surrounding them with methods that do more than mere gets and sets. As mentioned in Section 3.13.1 on page 70, a simple rule to eliminate such dishonest globals is to never have both a setter and getter for the same field.

Agent Nouns You can suffix a verb with "er" or "or", changing it into a noun. For example, the verb "slice" becomes the noun "slicer", and a *Slicer* object chops a large message into smaller pieces (slices) suitable for transmission. Grammarians call such nouns "agent nouns" because they are names of agents that perform actions. Agent nouns commonly seen in software include "encoder", "decoder", "printer", and "scanner".

If your agent-noun object has one primary command with accompanying supportive commands, you probably should name it after the corresponding verb instead, unless that verb is also a noun (such as "slice"), making it ambiguous. Unambiguous verbs are clearer than agent nouns, so use them when possible. For example, compare *Shoot* with *Shooter*: *Shoot* is stronger.

Result Nouns Nouns that describe the results of an object's action, which I call "result nouns", are similar to agent nouns. Most of these words end with the "tion" suffix. For example, the result noun "decimation" comes from the verb "decimate", and its agent noun is "decimator". I suggest using the corresponding agent nouns instead, as they tend to be clearer than result nouns. Also, use the corresponding verb if the object has a primary operation.

Categorical Nouns This noun is the name of a category (which is a trait) which the object is responsible for, so all of its commands relate to that category. For example, *SecurityServices* contains commands related to security, *Health* contains commands related to the health of the system, *GuiUtilities* contains commands to embellish a GUI in various ways, and so on. Categorical nouns result in trait-based roles, which tend to have poor clarity. Managerial and common roles are preferable, but sometimes a trait-based role can't be avoided.

Concrete Nouns Such an object uses, monitors, or controls a physical substance, thing, or device that is tangible, being made out of matter. It is often an electronic or mechanical device, but can be any physical thing. The object should be named after the material thing it's responsible for. Examples include *Door, Sand, Water, Valve,* and *Camera.* One commonly encounters these objects in embedded software, such as inside a printer, and less frequently in applications running on general purpose computers. Each physical device usually needs a concrete object to monitor or control it, and such objects tend to be at or near the bottom of IDAR graphs.

Metaphors This kind of object is named after a physical thing which performs an analogous function. Except in GUIs, metaphoric object names are uncommon, but here are some examples:

Hose	Transfers data between two objects
Tank	Contains unused memory
Glue	Holds characters together in text
Handle	Can be held for moving an item
Button	Can be "pressed" with the mouse
Guard	Prevents unauthorized access

With the exceptions of agent nouns and result nouns, we assume that the designer meant "noun operations" or "manager of noun" or "controller of noun". For example, the object *Schedule* means "manager of schedule". Also, Section 4.1.4 on page 83 notes that the name of a boss should not contain a managerial word such as "manager" or "controller" unless it manages something that its superiors know about.

5.2.3   An Example

After reading all the paragraphs above, you are probably longing for an example to help make it all real to you. The example of a fax subsystem in Figure 5.1 contains a variety of objects, which are listed in Table 5.2.

Object	Type	Role
Fax	Noun (result)	Send/receives faxes (manager of subsystem)
Receive	Verb	Receives a fax
Send	Verb	Sends a fax
SpeedDials	Noun (data)	Stores speed-dial numbers in NVM
Connect	Verb	Establishes and breaks phone-connections
Negotiate	Verb	Negotiates resolution+mode with other fax
Modem	Noun (concrete)	Controls IC to modulate/demodulate bits
IP	Noun (categorical)	Image Processing (compression and scaling)
Printer	Noun (agent)	Prints pages (external subsystem)
Scanner	Noun (agent)	Scans pages (external subsystem)
Pipe	Noun (metaphor)	Transports buffers from source to sink

Table 5.2: Objects in a fax subsystem

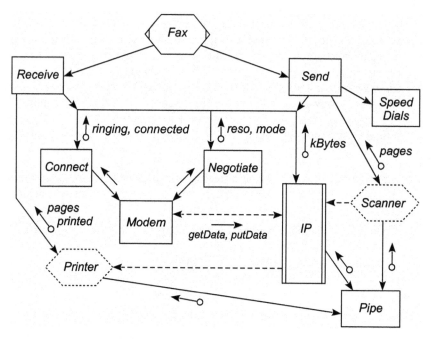

Figure 5.1: Fax subsystem (*IP* is Image Processing)

The roles of all objects are brief, which is a sign of high cohesion, indicating that the design is good. But this example has an unusually large percentage of verb objects; noun objects are usually more dominant.

5.3   Services are the Goal

The various types of objects described above have one thing in common: They provide services. When finding objects for your design, you should focus on only one goal: finding services. An object provides a service. Section 3.7.2 stresses that roles are to describe services, and it also presents a list (on page 80) of common ways that roles are polluted by mixing aspects of implementation into them. Those mistakes are: revealing details of any aid; revealing internal data-structure; referring to neighboring code; speaking of the object as being at some "level"; and describing a repetition or sequence of actions instead of stating their result.

The rest of this chapter discusses how to find services. But you will notice that it actually discusses how to find what are called "objects" (not "services") because being object-oriented means using the term "object". But the word "object" was a poor choice because it encourages you to only consider noun objects, neglecting verb objects. The word "service" is ideal as it focuses your mind on your goal of creating a hierarchy of services. Service-Based Design (SBD), described in Section 8.2 on page 232, is superior to traditional object-oriented design because it doesn't overlook the verb objects that traditional OOP misses. Services are a superset of objects. As you are finding so-called "objects", keep in mind that you are actually looking for services.

5.4   Designing in Five Steps

Unlike writing a novel, identifying the objects in your design can be done partly in a step-by-step fashion, which is described below in detail. While following this process, always keep your goal in mind: Define services.

Except for white-box techniques discussed on page 121, take care to think in terms of *what* each object does, and not *how* it will do it. When considering a prospective object, ensure that its role only specifies the service it provides without reference to its internal structure, internal algorithms, subordinates, or to any other objects in the neighborhood, except perhaps well known objects.

If you are creating the top-level design of a medium-size system, your graph will contain several subsystems, and for a large system, that top-level graph is likely to consist mostly of subsystems.

During the process of design, you will scribble several trial designs onto pieces of paper. Even if you enjoy doing everything on your computer, initial software design is best done on paper, so be sure to have some scratch-paper handy.

5.4.1   Step 1: Define Obvious Objects

Start with the easiest objects first, which are those at the top and bottom of the graph, as illustrated in Figure 5.2. These can usually be identified quickly. With those in place, it's easier to find the unobvious objects that will be between them.

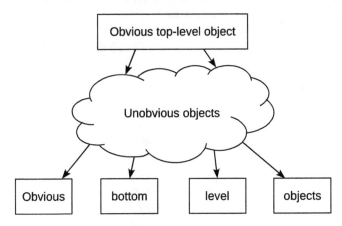

Figure 5.2: Obvious and unobvious objects

Top Object   This is usually the easiest of all to identify, simply because you have no choice—you *must* have a top object in your hierarchy. If you are designing a subsystem, you will need a subman object which interfaces to its superiors. Draw a hexagon at the top of a sheet of paper, and label it with the name of your subsystem. If you're fortunate enough to be designing an entire program, you'll need some kind of main controller at the top. If your program is GUI-based, then the GUI itself will often (but not always) be that main controller. If so, draw a box or hexagon for that. Otherwise, draw a main controller object at the top whose name is an abbreviation of the role of the entire program. This role might be broad enough to give the main controller poor cohesion or clarity. Unfortunately, you usually have little or no control over your program's role.

Bottom Objects   The bottom-level objects in the graph are the next easiest. It's not hard to identify what data needs to stay around in data-storage objects, so draw those. All items outside your program that it interacts with will probably need bottom-level objects to monitor, control, and communicate with them. These include physical things which your program uses, which are your concrete objects.

If you are designing a subsystem, it will probably command objects and/or subsystems that are outside your subsystem. Draw such external items with dashed lines at the bottom of your IDAR graph. From your point of view, they are bottom-level objects under your command.

If your design is at a medium or high level in a substantial system, then it's likely that some bottom-level objects will be submans—managers of subsystems. The fax design shown in Figure 5.1 is an example of a medium-level subsystem, and its bottom levels include two subsystems—*Printer* and *Scanner*.

5.4.2   Step 2: Define Unobvious Objects

Now that you have the top- and bottom-level objects identified and anchoring your IDAR graph, it's time to fill in the gap between them. This is usually done in three ways concurrently: top-down, bottom-up, and white-box. I know that sounds disorganized, but it works well, and all three are discussed below.

During this process of defining objects, don't forget to consider verb objects. These perform one action (which the object is named after) with supportive commands. You don't want to overlook such helpful workers.

Top-Down Design

When defining objects top-down, you will select an existing object on the graph that is too large to be implemented directly, starting with the topmost controller. The role of this "large object", as we'll call it, will remain unchanged, but this object will be hollowed-out as you delegate its responsibilities into its new subordinates which you need to define. These subordinate services will help the large object perform its role, so the large object will manage these subordinate activities instead of perform them.

But first you should ask yourself whether your large object is suitable as is. If an implementation of the object will be a comfortable size, then there is no reason to subdivide it. Let's assume that the object's role is still too broad to be implemented directly with a reasonable size. Therefore, portions of the object's activities need to be delegated to subordinate objects with narrower roles. In fact, if you are designing at a high level, you will be defining subordinate subsystems instead of mere objects.

Before parceling its responsibilities into subordinates, you should document what the large object will do, in more detail than its role. You will typically write a few paragraphs completely describing the service to be offered. I suggest that you put this requirements document at the beginning of the source-code of the object, making this information readily available to maintainers. Instead of writing this document yourself, it is acceptable to refer to a portion of another broader document. Based on this document, here are some ways to extract candidate subordinate objects from your large object:

Data The document may mention some data that the large object maintains or uses. If this data can be managed by nontrivial methods having good clarity and coupling, then they can be made a subordinate data object.

Interaction Nouns Your large object might interact with some items. "Interact" means that it uses, affects, controls, monitors, or changes those items, which are nouns. Those nouns are likely to represent good subordinate objects.

An example is the main controller object in the home heating/cooling system described in Chapter 13 on page 333. This object monitors the main control panel, controls the power switches, and monitors and changes the temperature of the house. Hence, its subordinate objects are *MainPanel*, *PowerSwitches*, and *House*. As a second example, the requirements document for the drawing program described in Chapter 11 on page 294 states that it manipulates items in a view area within the window. These nouns suggest that subordinate objects *View* and *Items* would help relieve the burden on the *GUI* object.

Other Interactions Think of what databases, servers, devices, processes/threads your large object will need to command, or transfer information to/from. All such communications can be wrapped in objects. Also, your large object may need to send or receive specific kinds of data or messages. Sending a general message often requires a number of lines of code, and you typically only need to use a few kinds of messages. Such specialized accesses can be encased in subordinate objects to avoid repeating tedious code.

Agent Nouns I mentioned earlier that an "agent noun" is created from a verb by appending "er" or "or" onto it. It is the name of a thing (an agent) which performs the given operation. For example, the agent noun "sender" performs the operation of sending. In the requirements, an agent noun is a suggestion to create an object named after this noun, and containing the given operation as its primary command.

Operations If the large object is responsible for several distinct operations, then each would be a candidate as a subordinate (often verb-type) object. Go through every operation described in the requirements. This is often a fruitful source of objects. An exemplary *Dishwasher* object could delegate its responsibilities to *Wash*, *Rinse*, and *Dry* objects, which it will manage. As a second example, assume that a digital camera has a *Shoot* object. Its description states that it focuses the lens and determines the exposure, suggesting that subordinate objects named *Focus* and *Exposure* would be helpful. If there are a large number of operations, you may be able to group them within subordinate objects, although their roles might be trait-based with poor clarity.

Parallel Operations If the large object requires that multiple operations be active concurrently, consider making each such activity a subordinate object.

Categories Try to think of categories for the various operations the large object must perform. Each category can be an object, or a subsystem at the higher levels. Such an object faces the danger of being trait-based and unclear. But it can have good clarity if the trait is well-defined and not too common. For example, a *Health* subsystem can monitor and control the health of the system, and is an umbrella covering a variety of operations, including some run-time tests and performance measurements.

States or Modes If the large object will have several states or modes, each can be a subordinate object. Unfortunately, a role of "handles state X" is vacuous and is likely to have poor clarity due to the ill-defined operations in it. Examples of state-based objects include *Idle*, *Inputting*, and *Converting*. Also, in the digital camera whose design is described in Chapter 12 on page 314, we created high-level objects based on the camera's modes, which are: menu, compose, shoot, and review.

Time Consider whether the large object's actions can be divided by time. If an operation has distinct phases or states over time, each can be a subordinate object. But be warned that this approach can yield unclear roles. If an object is named something like *PostProcess*, then the defining feature of its operation is temporal—it runs *after* some event. Try to find a better alternative.

Common Items After you have defined several objects, think of any operations, data, or interactions with other items that they have in common. Think of some service that would make life easier for two or more existing objects.

Some of the above techniques will define a command that would be the only member in a new object. Instead of defining such a simplistic object, let the command be a private method in its superior. The IDAR method smoothly transitions from object-level into method-level design, so after designing at the object-level, some of your method-level work will already be done.

Bottom-Up Design

In the bottom-up approach, you are given the bottom-level objects defined in Step 1, and you want to build greater services using them.

Needed Services Think of lower-level services that higher-level objects are going to need, such as interacting with something, monitoring, logging, moving data in or out, presenting data, transforming data, or error-recovery. Define objects for them that command the bottom-level objects.

Combining Think of which objects will be used together during the operation of the program. They will be companions either in time or by passing information among themselves. Also, consider which objects are closely related to each other. You can define a manager object over such a group of objects to create a higher level of service.

Adding a Feature You can create an object which adds a useful feature to a lower level object. For example, the new object could queue requests for services of one or more lower objects as a method of thread-bridging. A new object could transfer data to/from a file or server, commanding a lower object that can only accept buffers. A new object could add security (such as encryption or verification) or reliable transport to a lower object.

White-Box Design

A so-called "white box" allows you to see what's inside an object, to see how it works. I believe "clear box" would be a clearer term. In contrast, top-down and bottom-up described above are black-box design techniques. There are two kinds of white-box techniques: data and code.

Data Data that the large object must remember will be its fields. If you can think of some data that a set of methods can operate on, then you can define a new subordinate object. An example is the pen plotter in Chapter 10 on page 271, in which we maintain the x-y coordinate of the pen. But there are also some operations done on coordinates, such as scaling them, so the data and their operations compose the *Coord* object.

Write down names (or actual declarations) of fields the large object will need. Then, examine each group of tightly related fields and try to define commands and notices that use them. If the fields store data for later retrieval, you may be able to create a data-storage object. If the fields are involved with an operation, you may be able to create a noun or verb object.

I have used this technique after implementing an object and discovering that it was uncomfortably large. Its fields were already declared in its source-code, so reading them and considering subordinate objects consumed little time.

Code Write pseudo-code (i.e., structured English) for all the methods in your large object, or at least for the capabilities you plan to implement soon. You need not include all details, but the pseudo-code should express all of the object's actions in a high-level manner. Extract subordinate objects in the following ways:

Operations on Data You may notice that several methods or sections of pseudo-code are centered around a few fields, suggesting that they should be separated as a new object.

Sections Pseudocode often consists of a sequence of sections or steps, and each such section could be a verb-type object.

Similar Code Similar sections of pseudo-code present in multiple places can be moved into a separate object (or a private method).

Cases A `case` or `switch` statement that selects one of several operations accessing the same data could be moved into a new subordinate object, along with that data. Each method can implement one such operation.

Block Statements Examine block statements such as `if`, `for`, and `while`. Each of these can demark an operation suitable as a subordinate object.

Services While pondering and writing the pseudo-code, you will think of auxiliary services that are needed, as well as some chores and operations contributing to the object's role. All of these are candidate objects.

Some of these approaches, such as extracting sections, can yield objects having high (and thus poor) coupling, so take extra care to maintain low coupling.

While sketching your trial versions of IDAR graphs, take the extra time to draw and label the important commands and notices, ensuring that commands always go down and that notices only supply needed information (plus any covert aid). Once your graph becomes a complete hierarchy, your job becomes easier because you will have a complete design to work with. At that point, you can verify that it's correct.

5.4.3   Step 3: Verify Correctness

This step consists of rereading the requirements, hand-executing the design to ensure that it meets those requirements, and ensuring that all error-cases and debugging-needs are covered.

Pretend to be the CPU, and hand-execute every operation from beginning to end on the IDAR graph. Think about every command and every notice involved in the operation. Also try to think of all conditions and modes that can cause interactions with other objects. You'll be surprised at the number of oversights such hand-execution reveals.

Hand-execution requires that you reread the requirements. You will probably find a number of details that were omitted, a few of which might have a major effect on the design. Read each statement, and verify that the design satisfies it. Do this by following every operation through the design by hand.

An important part of requirements is handling the numerous error-cases. Think of everything that can go wrong, and hand-check how they are handled in your design. Often, over half the code involves dealing with error-cases, yet we often neglect error-handling in designs. In some situations, designing software around error-handling instead of core operations results in the best design.

You must debug your code, so don't forget to design for debugging. Be sure your design includes facilities to monitor or log the data and events that occur at important spots in the program. Debugging is much easier if you have good visibility into all areas of the software, which is provided by software called "instrumentation". A good debugging system also allows you to enable such instrumentation in selected areas at run-time and not only at compile-time.

The main features in the requirements should be implemented well in your design. Delaying features that you plan to add later is fine, but recheck to be sure that they can be implemented within your architecture. A few minutes of thought about this now can save days of redesigning and recoding later. If you are using an agile process, as I believe you should be, then you will not be designing everything now. Think about how those missing features will interact with your design to be sure you have accommodated their needs.

While you are checking these things, you should also check that your design satisfies the four rules of IDAR graphs. Can you recite those rules from memory? Every public method must be a command or notice, and all commands must go down in the graph. Notices may provide covert aid internally; however, from their callers' point of view, they may only convey information needed by recipient objects. Actions of both methods and objects must exactly fulfill their roles, forcing you to read and verify the fulfillment of all roles. While not hard rules, check your use of the good practices described in Chapter 6.

5.4.4 Step 4: Improve and Simplify

Stop! You will probably fail this step. Most designs are overcomplex for what they do, and yours will also fail unless you attack your design in this step. Overcomplexity is such a serious problem that I devoted Section 6.2 on page 137 to this topic. Attack your design by questioning every decision and trade-off you made. Write down and review the roles of your objects and methods. For each object, ask yourself:

- How good are the clarity, cohesion, and concealment of the object's role?
- Have I minimized the extent of coupling to other objects, and maximized the visibility of that coupling? Recheck compliance to the SPIED principles.
- Does every superior have a strong need for its subordinates?
- How straightforward is the design? For example, the operation "transmits data over radio waves" could lead you to create a *RadioWaves* object containing a *transmit* command. Such thinking is contorted, leading to excessive complexity. A *Transmit* object would be a more straightforward design.
- Will a direct free notice travel far (large HD metric) to a noncollector object? Distant notices to a collector object are fine, but other direct free notices deserve attention because they create dependencies in the callers that perhaps ought not to be there. Check them, and ask whether you really want those caller-objects to know about their callee-objects.
- Is the object too large or too small? See Section 6.10 on page 151 for a discussion about appropriate sizes.

Simplify! Initial designs are usually too complex because we humans are unable to think of optimal designs on the first attempt. Simplify by asking yourself:

- Can one or more do-little objects be merged into others without overburdening the resulting larger objects? Tiny objects are common; remove them.
- Can multiple processes or threads be combined?
- Can some or all processes be replaced with threads?
- Can a notice be replaced with a rider notice?
- Can a direct free notice be removed?
- Can an indirection be removed?
- Can inheritance or templates be eliminated? Removing these often results in a great improvement in both simplicity and understandability.
- Can a layer (perhaps over your operating system) be removed?
- Can a communication-framework (such as CORBA or DCOM) be replaced with Posix-calls or an intermediary object?
- Can a complex data-structure be simplified?

5.4.5 Step 5: Iterate

At this point, you have probably thought of a few changes you'd like to make, so go back to Step 1 or 2 and scribble some more.

That's the process of design that I believe works best for both new designs and for refactoring. Three or four iterations through this process will usually yield a good design, unless you are facing an unusually difficult problem. And perhaps you could do all this on your computer instead of on paper, but I've never tried it.

If you are creating a lower-level design, it's possible that you subdivided objects too much in parts of your design. As a result, some of your objects will be too small. I've noticed that this is a common tendency in object-oriented design. Look again at your objects, and estimate how much code will be in each. If there's not much, and the object has only one superior, then it probably should be absorbed into its superior as additional private methods and data. There is a trade-off between number of objects and sizes of those objects, and you should keep a proper balance between these two. On the one hand, you should avoid creating many objects that do little because the objects together will form a complex design-structure. Yet you should also avoid creating bloated objects that do too much. This topic of size-versus-structure is discussed in detail in Section 6.10 on page 151.

5.5 An Example of the Process

I'll illustrate this design process with the real-life problem of a MAC-layer for a digital radio. Any gadget you own that is wireless contains a MAC-layer, such as a router, printer, earphones, laptop, and of course, your cell phone. All such devices contain radios, and a radio contains the layers shown in Table 5.3, listed from top layer to bottom layer. Software implements a portion of the PHY-layer, and all layers above the PHY are purely software. The design of a simple PHY was shown in Chapter 1.

Layer	Description
Protocol	Data-transfer protocol
Networking	Maintains a network of devices
MAC	Transmits/receives a packet to nearby radios
PHY	Converts bits to/from analog signals
Analog electronics	Filters and amplifies analog signals
Antenna	Converts signals to/from radio-waves

Table 5.3: Layers in a digital radio

5.5.1 MAC Requirements

Role of the MAC Subsystem

The role of the MAC is "transmit a packet to a specified in-range radio, or receive a packet sent to this radio from another in-range radio."

Detailed Description

The following requirements for the MAC-layer explain not only what the MAC-layer does (which is its role), but they also describe the over-the-air protocol. You need to know that protocol in order to design the MAC-layer.

The MAC subman has only two important public methods. The first is the *transmit* method which commands it to transmit a packet to another radio. The other is the *notifyCb* method which commands it to send a notice to its superior whenever this radio receives a packet or finishes a transmission. By the way, in the radio world, "rx" is the abbreviation for "receive" and "tx" for "transmit".

To send a packet of data, two radios first communicate over a control-frequency to agree on a time and frequency for the transmission. Several working frequencies are available for data-transfers, but there is only one control-frequency. Whenever any radio is idle, it constantly listens to transmissions from other radios on the control-frequency, and updates (1) its internal neighbor-list, which contains radios it has heard from recently, and (2) its schedule, which keeps track of times and frequencies of all transmissions planned by all radios that it can hear (i.e., the in-range radios). Also, every radio transmits a "hello" message on the control-frequency if it hasn't transmitted for some other reason in the last few minutes; the purpose of these transmissions is to prevent other radios from deleting this radio from their neighbor-lists due to absence of receptions from it.

When a radio wishes to transmit a packet, it first checks the neighbor-list to be sure that it has heard from the target-radio in the last few minutes, thus ensuring that it's still in-range. Then it finds a free time-frequency-duration (TFD) in its schedule, and sends an RTS (Request To Send) message on the control-frequency, proposing that TFD for the data-transmission. The frequency in a TFD is always one of the working frequencies. The sender then waits for a CTS (Clear To Send) from the target-radio on the control-frequency, which approves the transmission or proposes an alternate TFD. The data transmission is done at the agreed-upon TFD, and the sender then waits for an ACK (acknowledgement) from the target-radio sent on the *working* frequency. If one of the above waits times-out, the sender retries up to a retry-limit.

5.5.2   Initial Objects

The requirements document above omits some details, such as how retries are to be done when partway through the protocol. But for an object-level design such as ours, such details don't matter.

Step 1 above tells us to start with obvious objects, the first of which is the top-level one. That would be the subman for this MAC-layer subsystem. That one was easy.

Next are the bottom-level objects. Obviously, this MAC-layer needs to communicate with the PHY-layer, so we'll need a subman object for the PHY. Data-storage objects tend to be bottom-level, so let's read the document and look for them. We see that a radio needs to maintain a neighbor-list and a schedule. Let's call those objects *Neighbors* and *Schedule*. Drawing these objects gives us the graph in Figure 5.3 containing only the obvious objects—those on the top and bottom.

5.5.3   Rough Design

Step 2 is to define the unobvious objects, and I remember that at this point, I did not know what unobvious objects to put in the gap between the top and bottom levels, perhaps because they are unobvious. So I took the advice on page 119, which describes techniques for top-down design, and looked at the main operations that

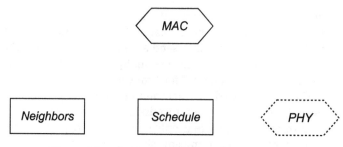

Figure 5.3: MAC-layer—top and bottom objects

the MAC needed to do. Those main operations are transmit and receive, so I scribbled down *Transmit* and *Receive* objects. Connecting them with command lines gave the rough design in Figure 5.4.

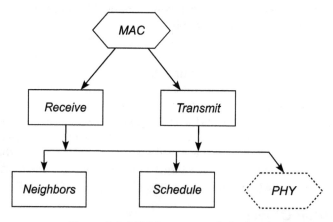

Figure 5.4: MAC-layer—rough design

5.5.4 Polishing the Design

Step 3 is to verify correctness and conformance to the IDAR rules.

A rule-check shows that there are no violations of the IDAR rules in this design. All public methods were identified as commands and notices (in fact, it has no notices). All commands go down. Every object and method has a role.

After thinking about this graph some, and rereading the requirements, I realized that all the details of the protocol—RTS, waiting for the ACK, doing the transmission, and waiting for the final ACK—could be done in *one* method inside the *Transmit* object. There will be some private methods (not objects) within *Transmit* to handle repetitive detail, but at the object-level, I realized that I was done with transmission.

Likewise, the *Receive* object could contain a method which plowed through the details of the receive protocol. So I was done with receive as well. At the object-level, it's hard to imagine the design being any simpler than this. At the same time, the internals of the objects will not be overcomplex.

But carefully stepping through all operations of the MAC made me realize that the commands were incomplete. During a transmit-sequence, *Transmit* needs to command *Receive* to receive the CTS and ACK messages, and update the *Schedule* and *Neighbors* if other transmissions happened to arrive while waiting for those. During a receive-sequence, *Receive* does *not* need to command *Transmit* to send the CTS and ACK messages, as it can command the *PHY* directly to perform such simple transmissions. Also, *Schedule* should update *Neighbors* when the schedule is updated. These changes led to the final graph in Figure 5.5.

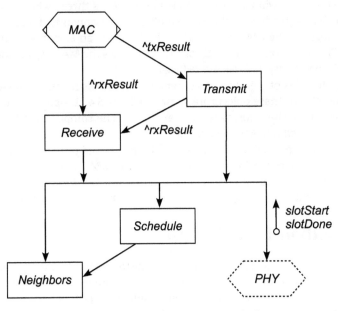

Figure 5.5: MAC-layer—polished design

Object	Role
MAC (subman)	Transmit a packet to a specified in-range radio, or receive a packet sent to this radio from any in-range radio
Receive	Receive any packet sent to this radio from an in-range radio
Transmit	Transmit a packet to a specified in-range radio
Schedule	Maintain transmission schedule of all in-range radios
Neighbors	Holds list of all in-range radios and their characteristics
PHY	Transmits or receives at a specified time and frequency

Table 5.4: Objects in the MAC subsystem

Step 4 in this design process is to improve and simplify. I am a strong believer in KISS, which stands for "Keep It Simple, Stupid." An important technique for doing so is minimizing the number of threads. I could have put a thread in both *Receive* and *Transmit*, and in fact that was my original plan. But multiple threads would have caused problems with contention and races, all of which vanish when only one

thread is employed. I saw that by carefully defining object interfaces, I could fulfill the
requirements of the MAC using only one thread, denoted by the vertical bars in the
hexagon for *MAC*. This simple threading arrangement guarantees mutual exclusion
between transmissions and receptions, and it also ensures that the request-queue in
MAC is only serviced when the radio is not busy. But remember the requirement
that the radio be constantly listening when it's doing nothing else? That means the
thread will be blocked within the *Receive* object, so that when a request arrives at the
MAC object, a check will need to be made in the *caller's* thread whether to interrupt
the listen that is pending in the *Receive* object. Consequently, there will be some
nontrivial logic in the *MAC* object, which is shown as an example of method-level
design in Figure 5.9. Yes, having only one thread makes the *MAC* object more complex,
but overall complexity and risk are reduced.

Listing the roles of objects in documentation is always helpful, and requires little
effort. The roles of these objects are shown in Table 5.4. Despite the complexity of
the protocol, all of these roles are short and clear. The complexity is hidden mostly
within the *Transmit* and *Receive* objects.

I included the most important notices in this graph. Did you notice that the notices
sent by *Transmit* and *Receive* are riders? Because the *MAC* object has the only thread
in this subsystem, its subordinates block until their actions are done, allowing their
notices to be sent to their superior (*MAC*) in the simplest way possible.

5.6   Method-Level Design

The earlier sections in this chapter show you how to design a hierarchy of objects (and
subsystems). At this point in the design process, you are ready to design the methods
within your objects. The various methods inside an object will call each other, and
you need to know how to design those methods and calls.

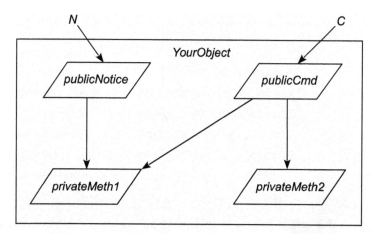

Figure 5.6: Public and private items within an object

The calls among public and private methods within an object form a hierarchy,
with public methods being heads at the top of the hierarchy. To say it simply, you

will have a multi-headed hierarchy. Figure 5.6 illustrates an object having two public methods and two private methods. Public methods are shown with a call-arrow entering from outside the object; private methods are only called from within the object. A similar graph is presented in Chapter 3.

Most importantly, such a call-hierarchy is similar to an object-hierarchy that only uses rider notices. This similarity causes the process of designing methods to be similar to the process you learned for designing a hierarchy of objects.

Data   But there is one major difference: data. An object contains data, and you need to design that data. When designing your hierarchy of objects, you didn't need to think much about data, aside from defining your data objects. But inside an object, you need to define the data-structure(s) *before* designing the hierarchy of method-calls. Methods operate on data, and the structure of data affects the definitions of methods. So design your data-structures first.

5.6.1   Continue the Same Process

As a reminder, a method is denoted by a parallelogram, and a method-call is denoted by an arrow from caller to callee, as shown in Figure 5.6. A method-call is similar to a command in that the caller is commanding the callee to perform its function, so we use the same diagramming notation for both.

To design a hierarchy of methods, you can continue the same design process that was described in Section 5.4 on page 117, pretending to identify ever smaller objects, each of which is ever more specialized. Continue this process until you can conceive of no more objects and are tempted to start writing pseudo-code. Each tiny object produced by this process only contains one or two methods, and those become private methods within your object.

To be more specific, we can follow the applicable steps in our five-step design process, but apply it to one object as described below. The advice given below is similar to that in Section 5.4 because delegating responsibilities at low levels is intrinsically no different than at higher levels.

5.6.2   Obvious Methods

In an object, you can find obvious methods in a manner that's analogous to the ways of finding obvious objects described in Section 5.4.1 on page 117. These are the top- and bottom-level methods.

Top Methods

The top-level methods are already known: They are simply all the public methods of the object, both commands and notices. Draw parallelograms along the top of a sheet of paper for each public method. All additional methods you identify will be private to the object.

Bottom Methods

Unlike a subsystem or program, not all of the bottom-level methods in an object are always obvious; some can be unobvious. As if to compensate, the top-level methods are already known. Bottom-level methods frequently communicate with or interact with other objects or the operating system, so writing a list of your object's interactions with the outside world will identify some of its bottom-level methods. Bottom-level methods are often needed to:

- Execute CPU-intensive algorithms.
- Parse or fill buffers.
- Bridge between threads.
- Adapt or "wrap" methods in other objects.
- Control external devices.
- Send messages over a port.
- Communicate with an external service.
- Update state-machines.

You might be able to think of a few bottom-level utilities needed within the object. If the object commands subordinates, you might find it handy to create adapter methods (using the Adapter pattern described in Section 7.5.3 on page 217) to make those calls more convenient in some way. For example, you might want to add the ability to block your thread until the subordinate has called your notice method indicating an operation is done.

5.6.3   Unobvious Methods

The techniques for finding unobvious methods parallel those for unobvious objects described in Section 5.4.2 on page 118. You can find methods top-down, bottom-up, or by using the white-box technique.

Top-Down

Assistants   For each method, think of some sub-operation that would assist the method in performing its chore. Look at what the duties of the method are, as specified in its role. Also, document its role in the method's header in the source-code, so it won't get lost.

Operations   If a method implements several operations, you can define subordinate methods to perform each operation, called using a `case` or `switch` statement. Your method has become a dispatcher, dispatching commands to their command-handler methods. The Dispatcher is a design pattern described in Section 7.1.3 on page 183.

States   If a method will have several states, each can be a subordinate method, called in a dispatcher-like manner using a `case` or `switch` statement.

Time   If a method does its work in several steps or stages or phases over a period of time, then each such step might be a separate method. But be careful that the clarity of these methods is good, as this technique of subdividing can easily produce methods with unclear roles.

Bottom-Up

Look at the commands in subordinate objects available to you, and at any bottom-level methods you defined. Consider how they could be used together to provide useful services within the object.

White-Box

Scribble some pseudo-code for the method, detailed enough that you could write code based on it. Its verbs suggest subordinate methods. Also, try to divide the pseudo-code into sections, where each section has good clarity, cohesion, concealment, and coupling. Each such section can become a subordinate method. The contents of a large `if` or `else` section could become a method. The contents of a loop can be delegated to a method, but be careful of performance-critical innermost loops.

Look over the data within the object, and try defining methods which access and/or process it. Consider defining a method for each operation performed on or transforming the data. In fact, if you can define a set of methods which *only* access or transform the data, and the amount of code in those methods is substantial, then they (and the data) can be made a separate, subordinate object.

5.6.4   An Example of Method-level Design

For our example, let's design the MAC subman in the MAC-layer shown in Figure 5.5. First we'll draw the public methods in the object, and external objects and methods that they work with.

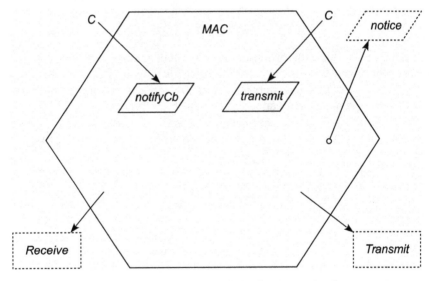

Figure 5.7: MAC Subman—external communications

Figure 5.7 is the starting-point. The huge hexagon represents the entire *MAC* subman object. Remember that methods are drawn as parallelograms, and fields are drawn as ovals or circles.

Now we'll think about private members in the MAC object. The superior of *MAC* will call *MAC.transmit* to transmit packets, and it doesn't want those calls to block, so we need a thread. Let's call it *macTask*, which is a member method. Furthermore, MAC's superior might want to queue transmissions, so we need a message-queue between *MAC.transmit* and *macTask*. Let's call it *msgQ*, which is a field. By the way, this object is following the Inbox pattern described in Section 7.4.1 on page 207. Figure 5.8 shows our progress in this method-level design.

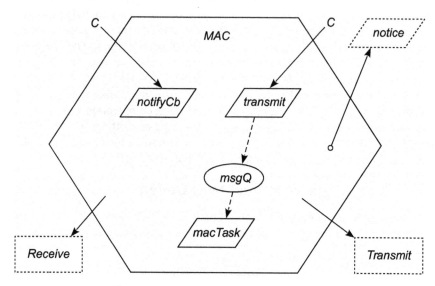

Figure 5.8: MAC Subman—partial design

Let's think through the operation of each public method, and add any missing pieces. *MAC.notifyCb* saves the pointer to the superior's notice-method; let's call it *noticeCb*. Also, *macTask* first waits for that call to *notifyCb*, so *notifyCb* also needs to post to a semaphore, which is another field called *startSem*.

MAC.transmit puts its message in *msgQ*. However, the thread is usually monitoring a receive instead of waiting on *msgQ*. So any receive that is monitoring the control-frequency needs to be stopped by calling *Receive.stop*.

We forgot that after a few minutes, the radio should transmit a "hello" message if it hasn't transmitted anything else during that time, so we need a timer that is reset upon transmit. The timer object will be external to the *MAC* object, and will indirectly call a private callback method (notice) within it, which we will name *timerCb*. If the timer times-out, it calls *timerCb*, which must put a message in *msgQ* and call *Receive.stop* to cause the thread to process items in *msgQ*.

Now we have two methods calling *Receive.stop*, so let's make the stopping of monitoring be another private method. But thinking about this a little more, we notice that both *transmit* and *timerCb* need to (1) stop the receive-monitoring, and (2) add a message to *msgQ*. So let's add a method which does both of these, named *enqueue*, whose role is "add a message to the queue and ensure that *macTask* quickly fetches it by stopping any monitoring." This combining of the two responsibilities "stop monitoring" and "add message" reduces the cohesion of *enqueue*, but its role will still have tolerable cohesion and good clarity, so I'll tolerate it.

The next step in design is to recheck conformance to requirements, and consider improvements and simplifications. Because this is a real-time design, we must be careful about which methods block, and ensure that their threads won't be needed for other purposes while blocked. The risky part in our design is having *macTask* block on both the *Receive* object and the *msgQ*, but it appears that we always call *Receive.stop* after putting something in the *msgQ*, so this design should operate correctly. The alternative is to add a second thread dedicated to waiting for a reception, boosting complexity and possibly adding race-conditions. Let's leave the design alone.

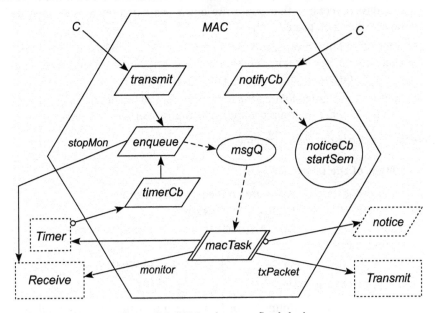

Figure 5.9: MAC subman—final design

Figure 5.9 shows this final design. We have defined three private methods (*macTask*, *enqueue* and *timerCb*), and several fields. The public method *noticeCb* does not call anything, and it would appear questionable drawn alone, so I added a data-flow from it to the fields to show that it sets fields.

I showed only the most important data-flows, primarily the messages to and from the message queue. If the data-flows for all accesses to all fields were to be drawn, the diagram would be so cluttered with unimportant data-flows that it would be incomprehensible, so they are omitted.

5.7 Summary

The key points in this chapter that you should remember are:

- To avoid wasting your time implementing the wrong thing, ensure that your requirements document specifies what the customer needs. Talk to your users and specify simplicity and reliability, avoiding creeping featurism.
- To avoid overlooking suitable objects, keep potential verb objects in mind, as well as the usual noun objects.
- Look for services, and don't allow the word "object" to lull you into overlooking verb objects. When you have a choice, a verb is clearer than a noun.

- The obvious objects are the controller at the top and those at the bottom.
- Find unobvious objects using top-down, bottom-up, and white-box tactics. In the top-down approach, you should write a requirements document for a high level object, and use several techniques to isolate candidate objects from it. Bottom-up design combines objects, or adds useful features over them. White-box design requires that you write down fields or pseudo-code, and define objects based on pieces of them.
- A few iterations through the five-step process will usually yield a good design. Evaluate clarity, cohesion, concealment, coupling, and need, and try to improve them. You must simplify. And again I say, simplify.
- Method-level design follows the same process as object-level design, albeit with changes in what the topmost and bottommost methods will be.

Here is a concise list of topics to remember:

Five Steps of the Design Process

1–Obvious Objects	These are on the top and bottom
2–Unobvious Objects	These are in between
3–Verify	Ensure correctness and conformance to rules
4–Improve/Simplify	Find weaknesses, and simplify, simplify
5–Iterate	Repeat until you are proud of the design

Finding Objects Top-Down

Interaction Nouns	Nouns in doc for things interacting with your object
Other Interactions	Various things (not in doc) your object interacts with
Agent Nouns	Nouns which are doers of actions (such as *Developer*)
Operations	Actions your object must perform
Categories	Group operations into categories
States or Modes	These are phases, such as *Idle* and *Converting*
Time	Dividing actions by time
Parallel Operations	Each operation can be an object

Finding Objects Bottom-Up

Needed Services	Lower-level services that higher-level objects will need
Combining	Using multiple objects to assist a higher-level object
Adding a Feature	Adding a useful feature to a lower-level object

Finding Objects Using White-Box

Data	Defining objects around fields for a large object
Code	Defining objects from pseudo-code and data

You may be impatient to rush through the design-stage with its five-step process, so you can start the actual programming. But remember that a small mistake in design can cause much damage later. That is why design is the tail that wags the dog. Force yourself to slow down and do a good job of designing.

5.8   Exercises

1. What are the two kinds of objects that you should keep in mind when creating a new design?

2. What are two sources of obvious objects for a new design?

3. What are some ways of finding unobvious objects?

4. What are the five steps of the design process?

5. A simpler MAC only uses one frequency for everything, and uses CSMA (carrier sense multiple access), which simply means, "Listen before talking." The radio listens briefly, and if the frequency is quiet, transmits its packet and waits for an ACK. CSMA is much simpler. How would the MAC-design change?

6. A laser printer receives commands via its USB port containing the pixels to be printed on a new page. Pages can be queued for printing. The printer uses the paper-picking mechanism (which works with the paper-tray) to move the picker into the pick-position. The same main motor used for paper-pick also rotates the drum. When the drum is at the correct position, the pixels begin to be sent to an LED-array which exposes the drum. The paper passes through the fuser, which melts the toner onto the paper. When the paper is out of the fuser and has been ejected, the main motor stops. The fuser is heated under processor-control to keep it at the desired temperature. A control panel has a power LED, ready LED indicating the fuser is at the correct temperature, and buttons for turning power on/off and ejecting a page. What are the bottom-level objects needed in the internal software of this printer?

7. What top-level object is needed in this printer?

8. What threads will be needed in this printer? To answer this question, you'll need to carefully think about what operations need to occur concurrently, and what threads should not block.

9. Add objects that will be needed in between the bottom-level and top-level objects, and draw an IDAR graph for this printer, with the important notices and dataflows shown and labeled. Don't forgot to note (with double vertical lines) which objects contain threads.

10. You are writing a program that creates wills, and its *BuildAssets* object is responsible for displaying the owner's assets in a form on the screen, and letting the user add, delete, or modify items in that list of assets. The program records the name, description, and value of each asset. The code for *BuildAssets* would be too large, so it needs subordinate objects. What subordinate objects would you define, and what would be their roles?

Chapter 6

Good and Bad Practices

— complexity is the enemy

Chapter 4 on Gauging Goodness disclosed several well-defined criteria for grading how good or bad a design may be. Clarity, cohesion, concealment, and need can be graded as high, medium, low, or none, and the many forms of coupling can be graded by their conformance to the five SPIED principles of good coupling. But this chapter describes a number of practices that are more heuristic, so providing such gradings for them is not possible due to their greater subjectivity. But I have observed that the good practices tend to yield good designs, and the bad practices lead to bad designs.

This chapter discusses a variety of topics, including learnability, simplicity, instantiability, inheritance, unrelated dependencies, temporal chaining, aspects of notices, coding style, the relationship between size and complexity, unit testing, and others. Awareness of these will make you a better developer.

6.1   Learnability

"Learnability" is my term for how quickly software can be learned. It's a good measure of the cost of maintenance, because maintainers spend much of their time learning the structure of code. Here are some factors affecting learnability:

- Conformance to the SPIED principles of good coupling. These five principles result in couplings that are easy to follow and thus easy to learn.
- Clarity of coding-style. I discuss this controversial topic starting on page 166.
- Avoidance of side-effects, which means following the Role rule.
- Simplicity or complexity of design, which is a major factor in learnability. It's important enough that the next section is devoted to it.

6.2 Complexity and Simplicity

The aphorism in the subhead of this chapter is, "Complexity is the enemy." I wrote that wholeheartedly. I strongly dislike and even hate unnecessary complexity, as my extensive experience has made me sorely aware of its high cost. I've seen too much thoughtless complexity in my career. What is thoughtless complexity?

Simplicity Requires Effort Decades ago, I began noticing that creating complex designs requires little thought, effort, or (gasp) competence. I also saw that creating a simple design required much more effort, creativity, and competence. I observed that few people put the effort into creating simplicity, or even knew that simplifying designs was both possible and desirable. Therefore, I was (and still am) frustrated that most designs were overcomplex for what they accomplished. Ease of producing complexity and difficulty of designing simplicity are the opposite of what one would expect of a designer, so I expressed this counterintuitive observation in the following paradoxical proverb:

It's easy to create complexity, and hard to create simplicity.

Simplicity is an Innate Ability Another unobvious fact that I've observed is that the ability to create simplicity seems to be an innate gift in certain developers. Likewise, the tendency toward excess complexity seems to be an innate defect in some other developers. Surprisingly, this defect is seen most often among top performers. I discuss this observation further in Section 9.3.6 on page 255. While everyone can improve his designs by taking the suggestions provided in this chapter, those with the gift of simplicity will always produce simpler designs, and thus they will always be more competent in design than others. This is a fact that managers badly need to know. Managers: Find out who on your team has the gift of simplicity, and have them design the architecture. Also have them review the detailed designs created by other team members. Your schedule and your bosses will thank you.

Step 4 of the five-step design-process on page 123 contains a list of suggestions for simplifying a design. The remainder of this section consists of some guidelines that will help reduce complexity. Some of this material duplicates content elsewhere in this book, so these descriptions are kept brief.

Persistence In light of the proverb above, don't accept your first acceptable design! Once you have a decent design, dream up ways to simplify it. Persist until the design is minimal. Bill Gates had something to say about this; see Section 9.3.6 on page 255.

Inheritance By the time you're done reading this book, you will be weary of my harping on the costs of inheritance. Inheritance usually has a higher cost than alternate techniques. Use them. Section 6.6 starting on page 142 discusses the problems with inheritance, and its alternatives.

Overweight Designers often use heavy techniques when light ones would suffice. For example, only use multiple threads when one thread won't suffice. Only use a process when a thread won't suffice. Only use middleware such as CORBA or DCOM if no lighter alternative (such as Ethernet messages) will suffice.

Instantiability   Make all classes static, except those that need multiple instances. Such classes (described below) simplify code. Doing otherwise is overweight.

Too Many Levels   Creating too many levels of abstraction, each doing little, is a common failing in designs. Developers who often fail in this manner are "abstraction fanatics", and are described in more detail in Section 9.3 on page 248. If you look at source-code and notice that one or more layers does little real work, it probably means that there are too many layers, like an overgrown bureaucracy. Just as a good company will cut out useless layers of management, you will need to merge and refactor these layers so that each does a substantial amount of work.

Gut-Feel Test   Here's a test you can apply to help decide if your design is simple enough: *If it seems overcomplex for what it does, it probably is.* This gut-feel test tells you to stand back from the details and ask yourself what the design is trying to accomplish. Then subjectively gauge whether its complexity is appropriate for the intrinsic complexity of the problem. I remember one project had a subsystem for maintaining a log. As usual, the design was overcomplex, and one developer remarked, "All it's doing is writing to a file." That subsystem failed the gut-feel test.

6.3   Refactoring

Refactoring consists mostly of shuffling around existing code to conform to a better design. I have refactored subsystems, and got wonderful results. This work proceeds quickly because you don't need to re-code and re-debug everything. The algorithms are already present and working. It's mostly cutting and pasting, with a whole lot of renaming and changing interfaces. Given its speed and good results, I recommend refactoring. I suggest reading [8], which is the landmark book on this subject.

Unfortunately, refactoring scares managers. They think that you are rewriting everything, which will take a long time and invalidate all past testing. A manager has a strong motivation to play it safe and have you simply hack the mess to make it work. That is understandable. A manager is punished for failure and taking unnecessary risks, and refactoring software is risk without benefit from a manager's point of view. I suspect the only way you will be given permission to refactor is if you show that it's necessary for adding a newly required feature. Even then, it's a difficult sales-job.

So instead of a large refactoring effort to clean up a large mess, I recommend that you perform what is called "micro-refactoring". Whenever you make a little change, you also clean up the small area around your change. Over time, such incremental cleansings add up to a substantial cleansing, causing code to gradually become cleaner instead of messier as usually occurs.

6.4   Static Classes

In typical software designs, most classes have only one instance. A class provides a service, and you usually only need to have one instance of that service. As a result, it is wasteful to go through all the mechanics that is required of classes that can produce multiple instances. Perhaps because they were taught to do so, most people habitually make all of their classes instantiable, enabling them to produce multiple unneeded instances. Such a class has a higher cost than static classes (described below) because:

- Each call is harder to follow because you can see its instance in the source code but not what class it belongs to, forcing you to search for its class. A static class clearly specifies the class in the call, eliminating the search. This topic is discussed more in Section 4.2.3 on page 96.

- It must be instantiated or its instance declared somewhere. Then that instance must somehow be made available to all objects that need it. This is often done by passing instance-pointers to those objects in their constructors or set-up calls. A static class has no instance, eliminating all that complexity.

- To make matters worse, when only one instance is required, developers often use the Singleton pattern (see [10]), adding code to enforce the creation of only one instance, boosting cost even more by adding more complexity to the class.

- Public and private items are mingled together in the same class declaration, revealing its private items to everyone, decreasing the security of the class. A static class conceals its private items, making it more secure.

- Each method-call is passed an instance-pointer in a hidden parameter, causing the compiler to emit instructions to load that pointer, making the code a little larger and every call a little slower than a static class.

These five kinds of cost can be eliminated simply by making the class static. The following is true of a static class:

- It cannot (or should not) be instantiated.
- All of its methods are "class methods" (declared `static` in C++, Java, and C#).
- Its fields are statically allocated. This is easily done in C++ by making them local to the implementation-file, instead of being members of the class.
- Because the class is not instantiated, no constructor or destructor is needed. But C# thoughtfully provides you with a "static constructor" in which you can initialize your static fields or join the union (see the Union pattern in Section 7.1.5 on page 186).

In essence, a static class is a namespace for public methods, with private items properly hidden to improve security. Here's how to declare a static class:

C++ Inside the class declaration, declare every method to be `static`. Or you can create a `namespace`. Do not declare any private items in the class. Instead, make them `static` (i.e., local to file) in the .cpp file.

Java Declare all public methods as `public static`. Declare all fields and other methods as `private static`. Do not declare the class itself to be `static` as that will not do what you expect.

C# Both the class itself and all of its members (both methods and fields) must be declared to be `static`.

For an example in C++, let's design a *Stat* class that keeps some statistics on events occurring in the program. Its chief methods are *addEvent* and *getNumEvents*, along with some secondary members. Its code is shown below:

File stat.h:

```
1   class Stat {
2      public:
3          static void addEvent();
4          static int  getNumEvents();
5          // and other methods
6   };
```

File stat.cpp:

```
1   #include "stat.h"
2   static int numEvents = 0;   // member field is a file-local var
3
4   void Stat::addEvent() {
5      numEvents++;
6   }
7   int Stat::getNumEvents() {
8      return numEvents;
9   }
10  // and other methods
```

File eventer.cpp:

```
1   // some code that handles an event
2   Stat::addEvent();
3   // more code
```

Here are some noteworthy points about this source-code:

- In lines 3-4 of file stat.h, every member method is declared to be `static`. This is how you tell the compiler that a method is not to be associated with instances.

- The header file stat.h contains no field declarations because the class is never instantiated. Any such fields would never exist in memory unless they also were declared `static`. You could declare `static` fields, but you would need to duplicate those declarations in stat.cpp—an annoyance in C++.

- In line 2 of file stat.cpp, a variable is declared which is local to that file. Because you will not have any fields in the class declaration, you must put them in the .cpp file instead. They should be statically allocated and file-local. They are ordinary, local-to-file variables. I suggest keeping them together so that in the unlikely event that the class will need multiple instances, the variables can be easily moved into the class declaration in the .h file.

- In line 2 of file eventer.cpp, the call to *addEvent* specifies the class instead of an instance. This was done because more than one class might have an *addEvent* method, so the class containing the desired *addEvent* needed to be specified.

The naming convention used in this book specifies that a class name shall start with a capital letter and that an object name shall start with a lowercase letter. But for a static class such as *Stat*, the class and its resulting object become identical, so it's appropriate to use a capital letter to denote both.

Theorists might argue that a static class is not a class at all, but it doesn't matter: For single-instance usage, a static class has lower cost during coding, debugging, and maintenance. Also, you might hear the argument that you lose flexibility with a static class because it will be harder to create multiple instances in the future. You must correctly assess whether you wish to pay the cost of increased complexity now to get an unlikely benefit in the future. In fact, most classes are so unlikely to ever need multiple instances that you can say YAGNI—You Aren't Gonna Need It. YAGNI is a wise rule used in Extreme Programming [15].

If your class will realistically have only one instance, you should make it static in order to simplify your code, eliminating those five costs and improving robustness.

6.5 Initialization and Shutdown

In a complex system, the order of initialization of objects is important because, as part of their initialization, some objects utilize the services of their subordinates, so those subordinates must be initialized beforehand. Consequently, you will need to initialize your objects in a bottom-up order, and shut them down in a top-down order. The hierarchy in an IDAR graph enables you to easily perform this orderly initialization and shutdown.

The following is a simple and effective method of initializing a complex system. Every object that needs to be initialized must (1) have its own *initCount* variable (which is 0 upon object-creation), and (2) have an *initialize* command which performs the following steps in this order:

1. Increment *initCount*. If its new value is 1 (i.e., it was 0), then this is the first call to *initialize*, so perform the next two steps (else skip them).

2. Call the *initialize* command in every subordinate (if any).

3. Perform the object's initialization, commanding its subordinates as needed.

This order ensures that subordinates can be commanded during step 3, the object's own initialization. Over the entire hierarchy, this algorithm causes objects to initialize starting at the bottom and proceeding upward.

However, a subordinate with multiple superiors will receive redundant *initialize* commands, because every superior will command it to initialize. So each object must ignore the redundant commands by incrementing and checking its internal *initCount* variable, which counts the number of times that *initialize* was called. This variable is a counter and not a flag to ensure that *shutdown* will work correctly.

This approach is also suitable for a multi-phase start-up. For example, if objects need to be commanded to start after they have been initialized, you can employ *start* commands that operate like *initialize* above, except that each object will use its own *startCount* variable instead of *initCount*.

Shutdown will operate analogously, but in a different order, like this:

1. Decrement *initCount*. If its new value is 0, then this is the final call to *shutdown*, so perform the next two steps (else skip them).
2. Perform the object's shutdown, commanding its subordinates as needed.
3. Call the *shutdown* command in every subordinate (if any).

This algorithm works because it causes the object to shut down only after the last of its superiors has commanded it to shut down. Therefore, this object is operative for all of its superiors during the process of shutting down. Over the entire hierarchy, this algorithm causes objects to shut down starting at the top and proceeding downward.

These two algorithms assume that (1) every call to *shutdown* has a corresponding call to *initialize*, and (2) *initialize* and *shutdown* will not be called by multiple threads. If you must call these commands from multiple threads, you will need to protect them with mutex (mutual exclusion) semaphores.

6.6   Inheritance

Traditional OOP stresses inheritance to the point where one would think that it is the foundation of OOP, and that all good designs should utilize inheritance. In fact, some people believe that inheritance is the sole means of creating a hierarchy. For example, *Object-Oriented Programming Using C++* states that, "Hierarchy is captured through inheritance" [25]. None of this is true.

Inheritance creates a hierarchy of *categories*, not of *abstractions*. When graphed as a tree or a UML class diagram, the most general kind of item is at the top, with the more specialized classes under it. Such a taxonomy can only represent one kind of category, so it is not a substitute for a command hierarchy where objects from a variety of categories need to work under a common superior. For example, an IDAR graph of a partial design of a sprinkler timer is shown in Figure 6.1.

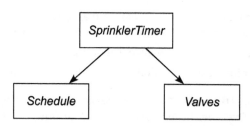

Figure 6.1: Sprinkler timer

The question to ask is: How can this design be represented using inheritance? A schedule class should not inherit from a valve class, and a valve class should not inherit from a schedule class because they are unrelated and thus cannot be placed in the same category of any kind. Also, the *SprinklerTimer* class should not inherit from schedule or valve classes. There are no is-a-kind-of relationships among any of these three classes, so having one inherit from another would not be appropriate. We must conclude that an inheritance hierarchy is more limited than an abstraction hierarchy, and in fact is *too* limited because it cannot represent a general design, not even one as simple as this sprinkler timer.

For the reasons explained below, inheritance actually *increases* the cost of software, and it also reduces security.

Excess Complexity   I have seen overcomplex software where developers strained themselves trying to divine is-a-kind-of relationships in the problem, no matter how tenuous, and then (here's the mistake) based their design around these relationships. But the design almost always can be structured in other simpler ways. Most usage of inheritance increases complexity.

The coolness-factor of inheritance can worsen matters. Kids fresh out of college want to use the cool things they learned in college, and inheritance is high on the list. Using inheritance is cool because it's interesting and more complex.

Maintenance   There are a couple of aspects of inheritance that boost cost during maintenance. Both arise from the fact that inheritance makes code harder to learn. First, people learn code by following method-calls. They'll right-click on a call, and click "go to definition" and expect to be taken to the method that will be called. But with inheritance, they don't know what will be called, so they are forced to search for derived classes, select the most likely, and hope the method wasn't overridden elsewhere. What should take two seconds takes minutes. In addition, when trying to follow a call, the target-method might not be implemented in the current derived class; it might be in some base class. Then a maintainer is forced to search through each level of the class hierarchy until the method is found.

Second, when common methods in the base class are changed, maintainers are likely to overlook a piece of code hidden in one of the derived classes, introducing an obscure bug. This is known as the "fragile base-class problem".

Scattering   Both problems described above are caused by the tendency of inheritance to scatter related code around in various places. That is a serious problem. When looking at a method call, it's not clear which methods might be called (as mentioned above). Then, related methods themselves are dispersed among the base class and various derived classes. Both structure and code are scattered. When changing code, some piece of scattered code is likely to be overlooked, creating a bug. On page 471 of his popular book on software engineering [30], Sommerville has this to say about inheritance:

> *The problem with inheritance in object-oriented programming is that the code associated with an object is not all in one place. This makes it more difficult to understand the behaviour of the object. Hence, it is more likely that programming errors will be missed.*

Inheritance incurs a substantial cost due to its scattering effect.

Reduced Security   Polymorphic inheritance is implemented by a compiler using pointers to methods. In C++, declaring a method to be `virtual` makes it polymorphic. All such method-pointers are a security-risk because an attacker can overwrite them to make them point to the attacker's shell code instead, and thus execute an exploit. In fact, the situation is worse than that. In C++, every object that has any virtual methods contains a hidden pointer called `vptr`, which points to a table of method-pointers known as the "virtual table", as shown in Figure 6.2.

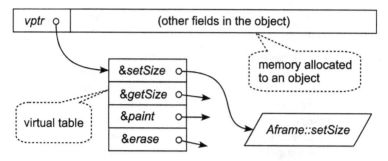

Figure 6.2: Pointers associated with a virtual table in C++

We see that the object itself contains a pointer, and the table to which it points contains a pointer to every virtual method. An attacker only needs to overwrite *any* of these pointers to allow arbitrary code to be executed. Having an object contain a pointer to a table of pointers (a chain of two pointers) makes it doubly vulnerable. If many objects contain a pointer to a table of pointers, then the software is becoming inexcusably risky.

The vptr pointer is written by the object's constructor, so it is essential that this constructor be called before any virtual methods are called. This is why you must call a "placement new" in C++ when type-casting freshly allocated memory to a pointer to a class containing any virtual methods. The chance of improper construction can only increase security risk.

Polymorphic inheritance is risky due to having many pointers in known locations which an attacker can exploit. For more information on the interesting topic of security risks in both C and C++, I suggest reading *Secure Coding in C and C++* [29].

Alternatives   The alternatives to inheritance listed below usually have lower cost.

If-Then-Else Use an if-then-else in a method instead of overriding it to change its behavior. The operation of the method becomes obvious, reducing hours (cost) spent learning. If you use an override, somebody is likely to see the original method, study and modify it on the assumption that it's the correct method. When he discovers it's the wrong method and that another is being used, you can imagine his anger—at you. Overrides raise cost.

Enhance the Class If you want to add some methods to a class, add them to that class instead of inheriting from it. Adding methods makes the source-code clearly show (1) what methods are present, and (2) their interactions with each other. Adding code in a derived class conceals the locations of methods and their interactions, and exacerbates the scattering problem.

Dispatcher Object If there are multiple implementations of the same interface, you can write a dispatcher object whose methods consist solely of case or switch statements which call methods in the selected objects. This structure is faster to learn (lower cost) because all choices are clearly shown in each switch statement. You can learn about the Dispatcher pattern in Section 7.1.3 on page 183. Note that this advice directly opposes the popular belief that "if you have multiple `switch` statements with the same labels, you should be using inheritance." Wrong. Inheritance scatters selection-logic around, obscuring the fact that selection is even occurring, much less what the choices are. That raises cost of maintenance, while not reducing cost of initial design and coding. Inheritance obfuscates, but a dispatcher object provides great clarity.

On the other hand, an appropriate use of inheritance would be in a GUI because the behavior of objects often needs to change due to the addition of specialized features in specialized kinds of objects. But GUIs represent only a small fraction of all software, so inheritance should be uncommon.

Thinking   Inheritance has been taught so well that it has become a way of thinking. When designing, folks are in the habit of first looking for is-a-kind-of relationships in the problem. As mentioned in Section 3.4.1 on page 42, such relationships are uncommon in practice, so basing a design on tenuous is-a-kind-of relationships will yield a worse design, as experience shows. As a consequence, if the first thing you do is look for is-a-kind-of relationships, you have already failed. If you are in the habit of thinking in terms of inheritance, remember that real life is not arranged that way. Try to break that habit by thinking in terms of a command hierarchy of services instead. Almost all software is modeled better as a hierarchy of services than as a hierarchy of categories.

6.7   Unrelated Dependencies

In the source-code of your class, a dependency is a reference to another class. If code in that class does not help your class do its job, the reference is an *unrelated* dependency. It could be a call to a command or notice that doesn't help your class fulfill its role. Or it could be as simple as using a symbol-definition or type-definition in another class whose services you don't need.

An unrelated dependency in the code for your class will hinder porting or reuse of the class. The more such linkages your class has to the outside world, the more difficult it will be to use your class in a different environment. A bit of good news is that most classes will never be ported to another environment, so unrelated dependencies per se are usually only an irritation and not a problem.

However, an unrelated dependency can be a symptom of an underlying problem in the design. Below, I discuss several kinds of unrelated dependencies, starting with the least harmful, progressing to the worst.

Cross-Cutting Concern

As described in Section 3.7.4 on page 52, a cross-cutting concern is a secondary aspect of the program that affects multiple objects. Examples of these include:

- Some collector objects
- Gathering system-statistics
- Debug-output calls
- Logging events
- Monitoring system-health
- Enforcing security-policies

You cannot avoid having an unrelated dependency on a cross-cutting object. Cross-cutting activities must be performed, and that means sending commands or free notices to the appropriate objects. Also, such dependencies don't create tangles because they funnel into only a few locations—the objects implementing the cross-cutting concerns. Dependencies on cross-cutting objects are acceptable.

Definition

Using a definition from an unrelated class is nearly harmless because you are not calling code in that class. However, when you are forced to refer to an unrelated class to obtain a definition, you should ask yourself whether definitions can be organized better.

For example, if object *Caller* calls object *Callee* and not vice versa, and it passes data to *Callee* of a type that's not used elsewhere, then that type should be defined in class *Callee*. If it were defined in *Caller*, then class *Callee* would be forced to have an unrelated dependency on *Caller* in order to obtain the definition of the type.

If a definition is shared among three or more classes, I suggest placing it in a folder named "Common" or "Shared" containing widely needed definitions. Keeping such definitions out of classes eliminates unrelated dependencies on those classes.

Notice

There are several kinds of notices to consider. First, indirect notices do not add dependencies, much less unrelated dependencies, so they are not a problem, except that they reduce learnability. The remaining discussion assumes that notices are direct.

An export-style notice means your object is procuring data it needs from another, so the dependency is related to your object's role and thus is acceptable. The remaining discussion assumes that notices are direct and import-style.

An upward bound notice is sent from a subordinate to its superior. But such a notice is poorly related to the subordinate's role. For example, in Figure 6.5, *Motor* calls the *done* notice located in *Scanner*. But to move the motor, *Motor* needs no services offered by *Scanner*, making the notice unrelated to *Motor*. However, subordinates often must communicate with their superiors, so such notices are acceptable. But, if it's likely that your subordinate will be used in a different environment or with multiple superiors, you'll need to make such bound notices indirect or riders in order to avoid hard-coding environmental knowledge into the subordinate.

That leaves free notices. Calling an import-style free notice means that you are giving data to another object and expecting nothing in return, like giving alms. That was kind of you. But the resulting dependency is unrelated to your object's role.

The HD metric measures the badness of a free notice (page 104). A peer-to-peer notice has an HD of 2, which is acceptable because two subordinates under the same superior are likely to be somewhat related to each other, so the dependency will not be entirely unrelated. However, a free notice with an HD of 3 is questionable, and 4 or higher certainly should be scrutinized. But making such a notice indirect reduces learnability, and routing the notice through the hierarchy conceals the communication, both of which are probably worse than the unrelated dependency. In general, I recommend that you retain a directly called free notice, unless you can remove it by some clean technique, such as modifying the surrounding hierarchy as illustrated in the example of a digital camera in Section 6.11.2 on page 156.

Command

Unless it is for a cross-cutting concern, an unrelated command is a serious matter because it means that your object is commanding an action that is outside its role, violating both the Role rule and the *need* criterion. For example, Figure 6.3(a) shows a fragment of the design of a 3D printer. *Printer* commands *PlasticPump* to start pumping molten plastic out of the nozzle. But *PlasticPump* realizes that the plastic is too cold (and thus too hard), so it commands *Heater* to heat the plastic, and then it starts the pump.

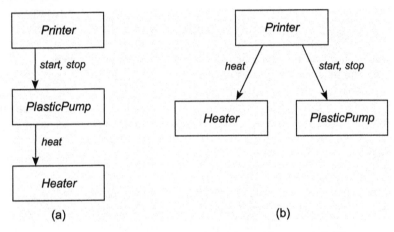

Figure 6.3: Unrelated command (a), and its removal (b)

But the role of *PlasticPump* is "pumps plastic", which says nothing about heating it. So *Heater* is an unrelated dependency in *PlasticPump*, and it reveals a violation of the Role rule. A good solution is to make *Heater* and *PlasticPump* peers under *Printer*, as portrayed in Figure 6.3(b).

The next section describes a more common error which still involves calling an unrelated command.

6.8   Temporal Chaining

One frequent mistake is what I call "temporal chaining", which occurs in a multi-step procedure. After an object finishes its step, it (wrongly) commands the next step to start. The result is a design where each object chains to the next. Such an architecture reminds me of Rube Goldberg machines in which each mechanical contrivance starts the next. For example, the ball rolls along and knocks over a lamp, which pulls a string, which opens a door, which releases the cat, which... and the list goes on. Temporal chaining is like that. In an IDAR graph, temporal chaining reveals itself as an unrelated dependency in the form of a command.

One example is shown in Figure 6.4. This is a fragment of the design of an all-in-one printer, showing the software for the scanner on top of the printer. The scanner

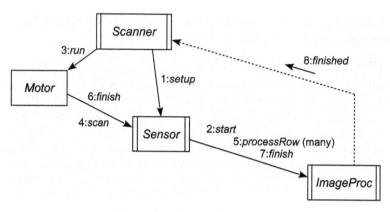

Figure 6.4: Temporal chaining

has a sensor-bar that is moved across the scanner-glass by a motor. As the motor is moving, the sensor-bar captures rows of pixels, which are processed by *ImageProc* (image processing). The sequence numbers show that a job is started when *Scanner* commands *Sensor* to *setup* and *Motor* to *run*. *Scanner* then waits for a *finished* notice indicating the scan-job is done. To remove gear backlash and to accommodate the distance needed for acceleration, the motor is always commanded to start moving a little *before* the position at which scanning will start. In this design, both *Motor* and *Sensor* are guilty of temporal chaining:

Motor When the motor has reached the scan-start position, *Motor* needs to do something to cause the scan to start, so it commands *Sensor* to *scan*. Also, when the motor's movement has finished, *Motor* commands *Sensor* to *finish*.

Sensor When *setup* in *Sensor* is done, it commands *ImageProc* to *start*. Also, when *Sensor* has finished, it commands *ImageProc* to *finish*.

In the cases above, when an object finished its step, it commanded another object to do the next step. Do you see any weaknesses with this design?

I see the following problems with it, and I have experienced all of these problems with software that I have ported and maintained. Those miserable experiences have given me a strong dislike of temporal chaining.

Poor error-handling What happens if there's an error in *Sensor*? Will it command *Motor* to stop? But it can't, as that would create a cycle of commands. What if there's an error in *ImageProc*? How are *Motor* and *Sensor* to be told to quit? In designs done this traditional way, there is often no nearby controller object to fix a broken chain. So the objects in the chain must fix themselves. The problem with this approach is that error-recovery is dispersed among all objects in the chain, instead of being centralized in a superior. With so many objects involved, error-cases are likely to be overlooked, making the program unreliable.

Difficult to maintain All three subordinate objects control some part of their environment. So all four objects contain some control-code, causing control-code to be dispersed instead of centralized. If a maintainer needs to make a change, he is likely to introduce a bug due to the difficulty in learning where all the relevant code is located and what it all does.

Violates the Role rule If this design had followed the Role rule, such unrelated commands could not have been included in the design, and thus temporal chaining could not have occurred. The role of *Motor* says nothing about capturing pixels with the sensor, so the Role rule forbids *Motor* from commanding *Sensor*. The Role rule prevents temporal chaining.

Violates the need criterion In this design, *Motor* has a dependency on *Sensor*, but to perform its role of moving, the motor doesn't need the sensor. *Sensor* has a dependency on *ImageProc*, but to perform its role of exposing pixel-rows, the sensor doesn't need image processing. The *need* criterion prevents temporal chaining.

A chain of three or more links such as this example is easy to spot: The IDAR graph looks like a chain. Even if the chained objects are arranged vertically, the graph will still resemble a chain instead of an organizational chart as expected.

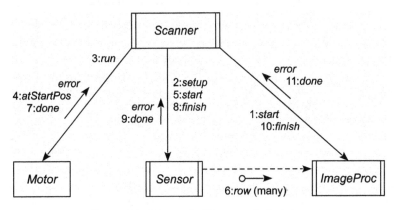

Figure 6.5: Removal of temporal chaining

Figure 6.5 shows how this example can be fixed by having the controller object do all the controlling and error-handling. This approach is the Boss pattern described in Section 7.1.1 on page 177.

Don't be daunted by the many messages shown in this IDAR graph. The essence of this design is that each subordinate does what it's told and sends a notice back to its superior, *Scanner*. The one exception is that *Sensor* sends many *row* notices to *ImageProc*. As an aside, the unrelated dependency for this dataflow between them has been removed because that notice is indirect. *Scanner* gets the address of the *row* notice from *ImageProc*, and passes it to *Sensor* in its *setup* command.

If an error occurs anywhere, a subordinate merely reports it to its superior, which is responsible for all clean-up. Thus, all control and error-handling are centralized in one place, making this code easier to learn and maintain than when it was scattered among all these objects.

6.9   Confusing Aid with Commands

You can easily define a command that should be a notice that provides covert aid.
This mistake is a form of temporal chaining described above. For example, in the CD-
player of Chapter 3, *PlayTrack* commands *LaserMotor* to *move* the laser. When the
move is done, *PlayTrack* should start playing immediately, so you could naively have
LaserMotor command *PlayTrack* to *playNow*, as illustrated in Figure 6.6(a).

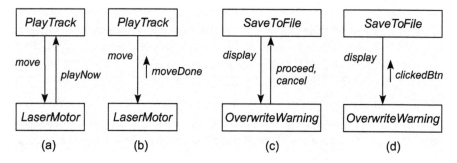

Figure 6.6: Confusing aid with a command

But this is not a legal IDAR graph because the subordinate is commanding its
superior, violating the Down rule. *LaserMotor* should be ignorant of what surrounding objects can do, so it should not command another object to do a chore that is not
in its own role, violating the Role rule. Therefore, it should not know what should
happen after its move is done. Also, *PlayTrack* should not make the *playNow* method
public because it represents an implementation-dependent way that the operation of
playing was divided into steps. Instead, *LaserMotor* should send a *moveDone* notice
to *PlayTrack* telling it the move is done, and let that *moveDone* notice do whatever
it wishes, constrained by the Aid rule. Figure 6.6(b) shows this fixed design. Interestingly, the executable code for the incorrect and correct approaches is identical. In
Figure 6.6(b), we merely renamed a method and re-identified it as a notice.

This is an easy mistake to make because the *moveDone* notice starts playing, so it's
natural to name it after its action, causing you to define it as a *playNow* command. In
this case, the method actually imports information about the occurrence of an event,
and playing is the object's internal (covert) reaction to that information.

A second example is a *SaveToFile* object which commands *OverwriteWarning* to
display a warning message with buttons for OK and Cancel. After the user clicks a
button, *OverwriteWarning* commands *SaveToFile* to either *proceed* or *cancel*, as seen
in Figure 6.6(c). These commands to its superior are named after their actions, which
is natural, but wrong, because those internal actions should not be revealed to the
world. Those commands should be replaced with a *clickedBtn* notice (Figure 6.6(d))
that aids its *SaveToFile* object with appropriate covert actions.

In general, if your object performs a job consisting of multiple steps, and each
step requires a call to a public method in your object, then it's likely that the first
such method will be a command initiating the job, and the following methods will
be notices informing the object about relevant events enabling it to make progress
on the job. The events could be mouse-clicks, screen-touches, data available, or

many other things. The action done in each step should be hidden, as it is part of implementation—how the job was divided into steps.

A "yes" to any of the following questions about a command indicates that it probably should be a notice that provides covert aid to its object:

- Does calling this command tempt you to violate the Down rule?
- Is this command called when an event occurs or data arrives?
- Does the action done by this command represent the object's reaction to an event or to the arrival of data?
- Is this command's action part of an active job in the object?
- Will this command's caller be exceeding its own role by causing a follow-on action? That is, is this command's action outside its caller's role?

6.10   Size Versus Structure

Some developers are not aware that there is a trade-off between method-size and overall complexity. Here are two extremes to avoid:

Bloated Methods, Few Calls If you make methods very large, they become difficult to understand because their logic spans several screenfuls on the monitor, forcing a learner to scroll up and down a great deal while trying to keep the hidden portions in mind. Such scrolling and reliance on memory is why large methods are a form of increased complexity to be avoided. On the other hand, using large methods means that there are relatively few calls among methods, so their call-structure is easy to learn and remember.

Tiny Methods, Elaborate Calls If methods are tiny, they are effortless to learn due to their small size and simplicity. On the other hand, there will be many calls among them, forming a large call-tree which will be difficult to learn and keep in mind. This extreme is the sign of an abstraction fanatic, described in detail in Section 9.3.2 on page 249.

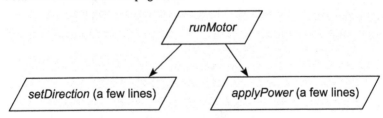

Figure 6.7: Small methods with a fan-in of one

I will focus on the mistake of creating tiny methods because it is the most common. Figure 6.7 illustrates this situation. The methods *setDirection* and *applyPower* are both tiny, each containing only a few lines of code. And, each has only *one* caller. Having small methods with a fan-in of one is the clue that the call-structure was over-designed by subdividing methods too much. By the way, do you remember what fan-in is? It's described in Section 4.4.4 on page 107.

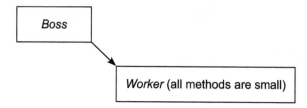

Figure 6.8: Tiny object with fan-in of one

The mistake of tiny methods also commonly occurs at the object level, creating tiny objects. Figure 6.8 illustrates this situation. All of the methods (public and private) in the *Worker* object are small. Therefore, the object itself is trivial or close to it. If it only has one boss (as shown), then you should consider merging such an object into its boss, as private methods within the boss. Having small objects with a fan-in of one suggests that objects were subdivided too much.

An example of this common mistake of making objects too small is given in [11]. This article is an empirical study of a system called "WebCSC", and it provides the following statistics about this system:

> WebCSC comprised over 7,439 classes and approximately 266K lines of code (LOC).

LOC only counts executable lines of code, and ignores declarations and comments. If you use a compact coding style in a C-like language as recommended on page 166, LOC will be about 0.45 times the number of source lines. Doing the division of the WebCSC numbers tells us that each class contains only 36 executable lines of code. That is too small. And that's the average; half of the classes are smaller! Most of these classes consist of a few small methods. Those methods need to be larger, and the classes combined into fewer and larger ones with a coarser granularity.

Trade-off   When methods or classes become too small, the call-structure surrounding them becomes more complex, raising overall complexity. When methods or classes are too large, their complexity raises overall complexity. This is the trade-off between size and structure. Figure 6.9 illustrates how complexity increases when methods or classes are too small or too large.

The values of lines of code on the X-axis are rough estimates based on experience. Overlarge methods are uncommon. As mentioned above, the most common mistake I see is methods being too small. I recommend that methods doing the core work contain 12-80 lines of executable code; straying outside of this range probably means that overall complexity is rising. But remember that support methods such as getters and setters are expected to be much smaller than the core methods. I suspect that being overlarge is not as severe a mistake as oversmall. When too small, elaborate call-structure and the many interconnections among objects are more difficult to remember than the contents of an overlarge method.

Meaty Rule   The need to avoid small classes gives rise to the Meaty rule, which states that, "All classes must do something substantial. A class having under 50 executable

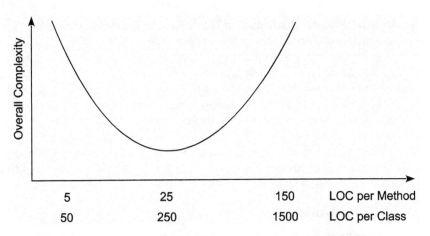

Figure 6.9: Too small or too big increases overall complexity

lines is suspect." In a recent project that employed the IDAR method, 11 new classes ranged from about 90 to 400 executable lines. They were meaty but not bulky.

Objects that merely change interfaces (which include some design patterns) are exceptions to the Meaty rule because heavy work is not expected of them. Also, having some tiny methods is harmless and common. For example, if a class uses a queue of incoming messages (i.e., the Inbox pattern on page 207), then most of its public methods will consist of only about five lines of code which create a message and put it into the queue. Getters and setters are even smaller, typically containing only one line of code each. But if the class's workhorse methods are also small, then your class is small, and you should consider merging it into another.

6.11   Notices

The Identify rule specifies that a notice must convey needed information to an object, and the Aid rule allows it to covertly aid a previously called command. These rules still leave great liberty for notices. They can be sent in any direction and to any objects needing information, near or far. As you can imagine, there are some good and bad practices associated with notices.

To achieve greatest learnability and reusability, notices should travel as short a distance as possible. And for the same reasons, we prefer that they travel vertically, to an object in the same chain of command (up or down) as the sender of the notice. In other words, free notices should be avoided. The list below ranks the desirability of destinations of a notice, starting with the most desirable destination:

1. Rider notice to boss
2. Subordinate
3. Boss
4. Peer (under same boss)
5. Long distance to a collector object
6. Higher boss or lower subordinate
7. Long distance to a noncollector object

The underlying principle is that notices should be sent to nearby objects, because sending them to objects farther away encodes excessive knowledge of the surrounding design into the senders of notices. The HD metric (page 104) is a useful measure of the travel distance of a notice. The goal is to keep objects as parochial as possible, and hence as ignorant of their surroundings as possible, in order to minimize scattered unrelated dependencies in the design.

As mentioned on page 146, exceptions to this parochiality guideline include collector objects. These are popular destinations of notices, and are often a GUI or the proxy for a GUI. Objects implementing cross-cutting concerns are also exceptions, such as a *Statistics* object which will receive notices (or commands) from many other objects. A possible exception would be the topmost object in the IDAR graph, which should usually be named after the program itself. Such an object is well known, and thus dependencies on it can be tolerated.

6.11.1   Rider Notices

As described in Section 3.9.2 on page 55, when a command returns, it can carry a rider notice back to its caller. You are encouraged to use rider notices as much as possible due to their advantages, which are reprinted below:

- Greater simplicity
- Greater efficiency
- Easily handles multiple superiors
- Reduced dependencies due to the absence of direct calls
- Improved reusability due to those reduced dependencies
- Elimination of cycles of dependencies

Polling   Notices are commonly used to report events from a subordinate to its superior. These events include a wide variety of things that can occur in systems, such as button-presses, mouse-clicks, time-outs, etc. One important kind of event is the completion of a command that was performed in a separate thread. You can use rider notices to get any of this information if polling is feasible. Polling means that a superior periodically (repeatedly) queries its subordinate by saying "tell me whether an event occurred" or "tell me whether you're done." The information returned in the poll-command is a rider notice. You can employ polling on two conditions:

1. The rate of polling can be low enough that it will not use an objectionable amount of CPU-time or I/O bandwidth.

2. You can tolerate the worst-case time-lag between the occurrence of an event and discovering that event in the following poll-command. This maximum time-lag is the longest period at which you can poll.

Cycles of Dependencies   One advantage of rider notices mentioned above is that they eliminate cycles of dependencies. The problem this is referring to is that on a large project, groups of files are usually compiled into libraries, which are linked to form the final executable image. As mentioned in Section 6.11.3 (page 160) and in Chapter 7, some poor linkers fail if there is a cycle of dependencies among libraries. This means that some library *A* has a dependency on library *B* (probably a command-call), and *B* depends on *A* (probably a notice-call). Such cycles are never a problem among the files that are compiled into a single library. But libraries are (presumably) large subsystems in the program, and an upward notice into a different library can be a problem because it often creates a cycle. Using rider notices (perhaps with polling) is one solution. Another is to always use indirect notices for those notices that cross library-boundaries. The best solution is to use a better linker.

6.11.2   Free Notices

In Section 3.4.2 on page 44, I stated that if a notice passes between two objects, neither of which commands the other, then it is termed a "free notice". You should probe the purpose of each one, because free notices can be warnings about the following:

- A free notice represents an interaction between two objects occurring outside the normal hierarchical division of responsibilities. Thus, free notices might indicate that the hierarchy was poorly defined.

- If the notice-call is hard-coded (i.e., not indirect), then the source-code of the notice's sender contains a dependency on the receiver of the notice, which is likely to be unrelated to the sender's role. Unrelated dependencies cause some problems which are discussed on page 145.

- Each free notice creates additional coupling between objects. Watch out for control coupling, wherein the notice might alter the logic within its object.

- A free notice might actually be a veiled command. In addition, such a notice can entice you into the trap of temporal chaining described on page 147.

Free notices commonly travel horizontally between peers which have a common superior, making them peer-to-peer. The HD metric of such notices is 2, indicating that their quality is acceptable. Other free notices go farther, resulting in higher HD metrics and creating unrelated dependencies. That said, here are some reasons to employ free notices in your design:

Collector Objects Free notices are often sent to collector objects. A collector object usually implements a GUI or cross-cutting concern, and notices can be sent to it from various places in the program. Because such notices funnel into one location, they do not contribute to messiness. The Collector pattern is discussed in Section 7.2.1 on page 188.

Distributor Objects Collector and distributor objects both funnel notices, differing only in direction (inward versus outward). Consequently, neither adds to messiness. The Distributor pattern is discussed in Section 7.2.2 on page 190.

Dataflows Peer-to-peer free notices are frequently used to implement dataflows, so such notices are not a cause for concern. For more information, refer to Section 7.3.1 on page 198. However, if free notices travel farther than between peers, the data is flowing between unrelated objects, and the design should be reviewed carefully. As an aside, making such long-distance notices indirect lets you easily redirect dataflows for debugging or logging purposes.

Bypassing Bosses To improve performance, or to avoid tramp coupling (which is often illegal), free notices can be used to bypass one or more layers of management, as you see in the hard-disk controller in Figure 6.10.

Tidbit One object may need a tidbit of data that is procured or generated by some other object. Tidbits often represent events or changes in status. The objects may be well-designed and have low coupling, except that this tidbit needs to be passed between them. This topic is discussed more on page 163.

Unrelated Constraint Two objects may face a mutual constraint that is unrelated to their roles, forcing them to coordinate their activities. But take care that you not violate the need-to-know constraint in the Identify rule.

Reveal Communications Free notices clearly reveal communications between two objects that would otherwise be concealed if the communications were to follow the command hierarchy.

I discuss some of these reasons in detail below, along with some examples.

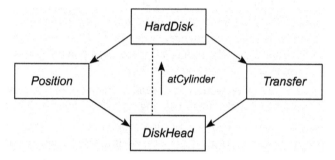

Figure 6.10: Hard disk controller

Bypassing a Boss

An uncommon use of free notices is to bypass a boss, as illustrated in Figure 6.10. The *Position* object must queue the access-requests to the disk and rearrange them to reduce the number of long seeks performed, thus increasing the overall throughput of the drive. *Position* partially sorts the access-requests by position, and issues them (as commands) to *DiskHead*, which does the mechanical seeks. When the head has reached the proper position, *DiskHead* sends a free notice (*atCylinder*) to the top-level manager (*HardDisk*), which in turn commands *Transfer* to perform the transfer. *HardDisk* also coordinates the activities of *Position* and *Transfer* to prevent them from concurrently commanding *DiskHead*. This design is an example of the Resourceful Boss pattern, described in Section 7.1.2 on page 180.

The free notice *atCylinder* is appropriate because (1) it satisfies the need-to-know constraint in the Identify rule, (2) performance is improved compared with routing it through *Position*, (3) we avoid having an illegal tramp notice in *Position*, (4) the design is clear, and (5) it's unlikely to cause problems in maintenance.

Unrelated Constraint

You might be tempted to use free notices to help resolve a conflict between unrelated activities. Resist this temptation.

For example, to reduce cost, suppose the manufacturer of a digital camera used a small internal power-supply that lacked sufficient capacity to provide the current needed to accelerate the zoom-motor and charge the flash-capacitor concurrently. This electronic limitation has created an interaction between unrelated functions of the camera: zooming and charging the flash-cap. The first design for dealing with this limitation used free notices between the *ZoomMotor* and *Capacitor* objects, as shown in Figure 6.11. The dangling arrows indicate that this is only a fragment of the entire design; it only shows the relevant objects.

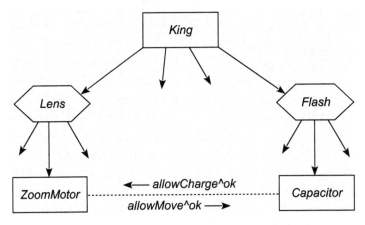

Figure 6.11: Free notices to handle current-limitation

To avoid overloading the power-supply, the objects *ZoomMotor* and *Capacitor* tell each other when they are starting by sending export-style free notices *allowCharge* and *allowMove*. Each of these "allow" notices will not return from its method-call until the callee is inactive, which grants the caller permission to start. This permission is supplied by the returned response *ok* in Figure 6.11. As usual, I'll ask you whether you see any problems with this design.

One problem is that we are violating the rule that external objects may not directly communicate with objects inside a subsystem. Both "allow" notices are sent to internal objects. Violation of this rule strongly suggests that you are creating an unrelated dependency in your code.

And sure enough, the second problem is that we violated the principle of avoiding unrelated dependencies. *ZoomMotor* and *Capacitor* both call methods in the other's object, even though the roles of the two objects are unrelated. The "allow" notices have an HD metric of 4, which is very high, telling us that the two communicating objects are unrelated.

A solution is to introduce a higher-level object to manage current-consumption called *Current*. It receives "allow" notices announcing that an action is about to occur, and that action can only occur after it replies *proceed*. Figure 6.12 shows this modified design. Note the unusual situation of a command riding on the method-return of a notice; thus, *proceed* is a rider command. For this reason, *proceed* is allowed to be sent to an internal object. So the new *Current* object solves both of the problems in the original design. If you are uncomfortable with using rider commands, you could modify this solution by renaming each *proceed* to *ok* and identifying it as an export-style free notice as was done in Figure 6.11.

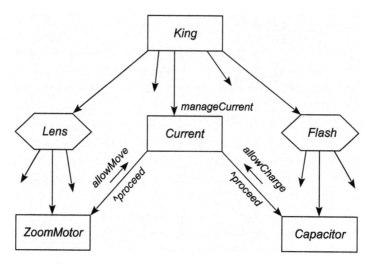

Figure 6.12: Current-manager removes free notices

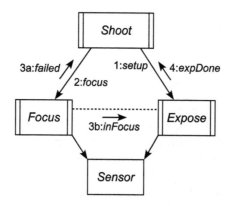

Figure 6.13: Digital camera with a suspect notice

Veiled Commands

In the list of warnings on page 155, I stated that a free notice could be a veiled command. Let's look at a sneaky example. Figure 6.13 shows a small part of the design of a digital camera. When the *Shoot* object is told to shoot a picture, the following commands and notices are sent. The sequence numbers in the diagram correspond to the steps listed below:

1. *Shoot* commands *Expose* to *setup* an exposure.

2. *Shoot* commands *Focus* to auto-focus by calling its *focus* command.

3. When *Focus* is done focusing, it sends an *inFocus* notice to *Expose*, giving it the go-ahead to start the exposure. If the auto-focus failed, *Focus* sends a *failed* notice back up to *Shoot*.

4. When *Expose* is done, it sends an *expDone* notice up to *Shoot*.

In light of the hazards of free notices listed above, think through this design and ask what problems it might have. The problem I see (and which I deliberately inserted) is that the *inFocus* notice is actually a command. This is a sneaky attempt to have one peer command another peer. A boy commanding his brother is likely to result in a childhood fight. Having one peer command another is equally unwise.

When checking this notice against the list of warnings, we see that *inFocus* starts an action in *Expose* which is not covert aid because there is no job in progress from a prior command-call. We conclude that *Focus* is commanding *Expose*. This is in fact an example of temporal chaining as described on page 147 wherein an object, upon finishing its chore, commands another object to perform the next chore. Instead, each object should perform its chore and then notify its boss, which is responsible for commanding the next chore.

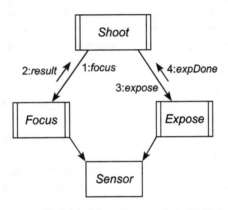

Figure 6.14: Digital camera with poor free notice removed

The troublesome *inFocus* free notice is peer-to-peer, and you can remove any peer-to-peer notice by routing it through the mutual superior. The resulting design is shown in Figure 6.14. This modified design follows the Boss pattern described in Section 7.1.1 on page 177. All high-level control is in *Shoot*, which is the boss. Its two workers, *Focus* and *Expose*, merely obey commands and report back results. The *focus* command given to *Focus* only focuses and does not also commence an exposure. It's a clean design that follows the IDAR rules.

Alternatively, we could have renamed *setup* to *expose* with a role of "exposes the sensor," and kept the *inFocus* notice unchanged. Then, *inFocus* would be telling *Expose* when it could proceed. Although this approach is legal, it is not ideal because you would still have an unrelated dependency in *Focus*. Using the Boss pattern yields a better design because it's usually better to have a boss rather than a coworker tell an object when it can proceed.

Did you notice that three out of the four objects in this design are named with verbs instead of the usual nouns? These names are forcefully clear, and such verb objects are described more in Section 5.2.1 on page 113. Both noun objects and verb objects arise from Service-Based Design (SBD) described in Section 8.2 on page 232. In essence, SBD teaches you to think of an object as providing a service whose name can be either a noun or verb.

6.11.3   Ways to Send Notices

Direct (hard-coded) notices can cause some problems:

- They create more dependencies, and the more dependencies that are in code, the less reusable it becomes.

- For *Worker* to send a notice up to its *Boss*, the class for *Worker* must have a dependency on *Boss*. But *Boss* already has a dependency on *Worker* in order to command it. As described above, such a notice creates a cycle of dependencies which can cause low-quality linkers to fail when the methods are in different libraries.

- Communicating with multiple superiors is clumsy. When using ordinary hard-coded calls, a subordinate object must contain a notice-call to every superior it has, and somehow select the appropriate one. Such clumsiness might be tolerated when there are only two superiors, but it's unacceptable for three or more superiors.

In this section, we examine various ways of sending notices, paying particular attention to the problems listed above, and to any additional problems or constraints the techniques introduce. For completeness, a little information already presented is repeated. As an aside, some of the techniques described below use the principle or technique of delegation.

Unless stated otherwise, all of the techniques listed below avoid creating upward dependencies, and allow subordinates to have multiple superiors.

RID: Rider Notice   The simplest technique for sending a notice is to have it ride on the method-return of a preceding command-call. This technique is ideal when (1) blocking the superior's thread during the command's execution is acceptable, (2) a notice is always a response to a prior command, and (3) only one such notice is needed. Fortunately, all of these conditions are often true, so rider notices are often used. But a violation of one of the conditions listed above will cause this technique to become very clumsy or unusable.

HC: Hard-Coded   This is also a simple way to send a notice: A subordinate hard-codes a call to the notice in the superior. If the superior is not a static class, you must save that superior's instance-pointer somewhere. This technique is suitable only when a worker can have only one superior (or possibly two), as code becomes clumsy if it needs to select among multiple superiors. Fortunately, this one-superior condition is usually true in practice, so this technique is usually feasible. Note that hard-coded notices create upward dependencies.

MS: Mailbox/Semaphore   When a superior calls a subordinate's command, the parameters include a pointer to a mailbox or semaphore located in the superior. The subordinate sends the notice by posting to that mailbox or semaphore. Unfortunately, one can't include data in a notice using a semaphore, making a mailbox more desirable for general use. A severe restriction on this technique is that the superior must have its own thread.

```
1    /***** Subordinate *****/
2
3    class Subordinate {
4      public:
5        typedef void (*NoticePtrT)(int result);
6        void commandMe (NoticePtrT np, int stuff);
7        // more
8      private:
9        NoticePtrT noticePtr;  // commandMe saves np here
10   };
11   void Subordinate::commandMe (NoticePtrT np, int stuff) {
12     noticePtr = np;  // save notice-ptr for the call later
13     // more
14   }
15   void Subordinate::someRoutine() {
16     // code
17     noticePtr(result);  // this sends notice to superior
18     // more
19   }
20
21   /***** Superior *****/
22
23   class Superior {
24     // important: noticeMe is static
25     static void noticeMe (int result);
26     static Subordinate servant;
27     // more
28   };
29   void Superior::noticeMe (int result) {
30     // do something with the notice
31   }
32   void Superior::yetAnotherRoutine() {
33     servant->commandMe (&noticeMe, stuff);
34     // more
35   }
```

Listing 6.1: C++ code for PM technique

PF: Pointer to Field When a superior calls a subordinate's command, the parameters include a pointer to a field located within the superior. Sending the notice consists of writing to that field. This technique has the severe disadvantage of requiring that the superior poll the field. But this technique is ideal whenever quick response isn't needed and thus polling can be slow.

DEL: Delegate C# and Python support delegates, and the interface feature in Java can be used to closely mimic a delegate. For such a language, a superior can pass a delegate as a parameter in a command to a subordinate. A delegate contains pointers to both a notice in the superior and its instance. This technique is simple to use and has no restrictions.

PM: Pointer to static Method When a superior calls a subordinate's command, the parameters include a pointer to a static method to be called later as a deferred

Technique to send notice	Restrictions
RID: Rider Notice	One notice per command, and no queuing of commands
HC: Hard-Coded	Subordinate may only have one superior, and adds dependencies
MS: Mailbox/Semaphore	Superior must have a thread
PF: Ptr to Field	Superior must poll field
DEL: Delegate	C# and Python support delegates, but most languages don't
PM: Ptr to static Method	Superior must be static or have one instance (usually true)
PMO: Ptr to static Method & Object	Casts to/from void*; more complex than the techniques above

Table 6.1: Techniques of sending notices

callback. Since static methods don't use an object's instance, an instance-pointer isn't needed, but the lack of an instance-pointer means every superior must either (1) be a static class or (2) have only one instance so that it can fetch its own instance-pointer within that static method. Fortunately, most managers (objects that manage others) are static or have only one instance, so this restriction is not severe in practice.

PMO: Pointers to static Method and Object This is the same as PM described above, but the parameters of the command also include a pointer to the superior's instance, type-cast to void*. The subordinate's call to the notice (the deferred callback) includes this instance-pointer in its parameters, giving the superior access to its correct instance. This technique is the most general, but requires that two pointers be passed down, stored and used. It's more complex than PM, but doesn't have the restriction of requiring single-instance superiors.

The PM technique is popular enough to warrant an example in C++, shown in Listing 6.1. The subordinate defines the type NoticePtrT (line 5) to hold the pointer to the notice. The superior contains the static method noticeMe (lines 25 and 29), whose signature matches NoticePtrT, and whose address is passed as a parameter in the call to commandMe (line 33). In the subordinate, the commandMe method (line 11) saves the method-pointer in noticePtr (line 12), which is used in the callback later (line 17) which sends the notice.

RID is the simplest technique, and should be used whenever its requirements can be satisfied without adding complexity. If RID isn't feasible, then HC is excellent and should be used in most situations where a subordinate will most likely have only one superior. MS, PF, DEL and PM are about equal in complexity, as they all require a pointer to be passed in a command. You should use DEL if your language supports it. Otherwise, PM is preferable because the other two expose data in a superior, reducing information-hiding a little. PMO is the most complex technique, and should be used only in the uncommon cases when kludges would cause the other techniques to be even more complex to use. In practice, RID, HC, and DEL-or-PM satisfy the needs of almost all notices, and should be considered in that order.

Finally, although these techniques were presented for sending notices, they also apply to sending commands. However, indirect commands are (or should be) rare. So in practice, these techniques (except HC) will apply solely to notices.

6.12   The Tidbit Problem

A common problem in software is that one object has some tidbit of information that another unrelated object needs. An example is the home heating-cooling system shown in Figure 13.6 on page 344. In it, *MainPanel* knows the time, and the unrelated instances of *LivingPattern* need it. How can this tidbit be communicated to those instances? In that design, we used a global variable. Here are some options:

- Use a global variable. This popular technique has the disadvantages of common coupling which were listed in Section 4.2.1 on page 90.

- A superior can pass a pointer-to-tidbit to the supplier and user objects. But doing so violates the Indirection principle of good coupling, concealing the very existence of this coupling. A global variable would be better.

- Use an indirect free notice, either import-style or export-style. This technique violates the Indirection principle, thus making the coupling hard to follow. Also, passing down the pointer might add dependencies to a superior.

- Use a direct free notice, either import-style or export-style. This technique adds an unrelated dependency to the caller. In a corporation, he who needs a tidbit is expected to ask him who has it. This social expectation of "ask for it" suggests that you employ a direct export-style free notice.

- For objects that are peers, a free notice can be rerouted through their superior. But doing so hides communication between objects. A benefit of a free notice is that it reveals such inter-object communication on the graph, so I often leave such a free notice alone instead of removing it by rerouting it.

There is no good solution to the tidbit problem in this sorry list. The least-bad solutions are probably a global variable or a direct free notice.

The design in Figure 6.15 is an example of communicating tidbits in free notices. It shows several free notices in the software that controls an environmental chamber. Such a chamber is about the size of a refrigerator, though far more costly, and has a front door which opens to reveal a large metal interior. A chamber accurately controls the temperature and humidity of its interior, and can continuously change these between specified levels over a settable number of minutes. Companies torture-test their products inside these chambers.

In this design, the *Thermometer* object sends *temp* notices to the *TempServo*, which controls the temperature, and to the *CtlPanel* which displays it. Because two objects need temperature, *Thermometer* was made a subordinate of *EnvChamber* instead of *TempServo*, as would normally have been done. This organization created the free *temp* notices. Due to symmetry of chores, the identical design is used for controlling humidity by the *HygroServo* and *Hygrometer* objects. Let's check these free notices against the warnings listed on page 155:

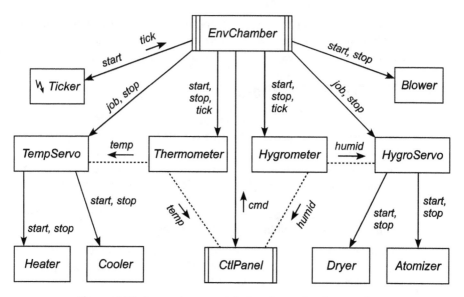

Figure 6.15: An environmental chamber using free notices

1. Clarity, cohesion, etc. are good, so the hierarchy is fine.
2. These free notices are peer-to-peer, so the extra dependencies are tolerable.
3. These notices do not introduce control coupling.
4. These notices are not veiled commands, as they obey the Identify rule.

We conclude that these *temp* and *humid* notices add little risk and are acceptable in this application.

6.13   Built-in Unit Tester

Most developers dislike testing. It's something that we are required to do, and we grind through it, and are glad when it's over. But testing can be better. You are designing software as a command hierarchy. As a result, every object (except the topmost) has one or more superiors. A benefit of this design method is that you can easily substitute a tester as an object's superior. Having done that, it becomes a fairly simple matter to test any level of the system, from a bottom-level object up to the highest subsystems. Figure 6.16 shows a unit tester object named *WombatTester* commanding a *Wombat* object, and also receiving its notices.

Such an arrangement is outstanding for black-box testing, but it suffers from a disadvantage in that its use requires that the build-script be changed each time a test is to be performed. That makes it inconvenient to use such a tester to quickly test small changes. We can do better than this.

Figure 6.17 shows a unit-test layer which has been added over the top of the public interface of an object. This layer consists of a *testMain* method containing the test-script, some test-variables called *testVars*, and methods needed to intercept notices sent by the object (*testNotice* in this case). The crucial feature which makes this

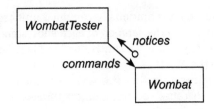

Figure 6.16: A unit tester object

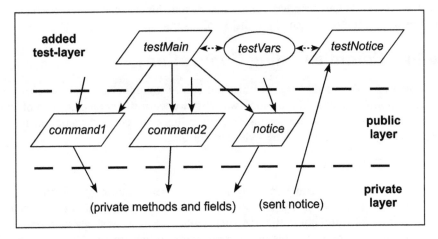

Figure 6.17: A unit-test layer within an object

design convenient is the fact that the test-layer is conditionally compiled using a flag that is hard-coded in the class itself. For example, in C or C++, you could easily compile-in the entire test-layer by changing the 0 to a 1 in Listing 6.2.

```
#if 0 // beginning of wombat-tester
   void Wombat::testMain() {
      // ... main test-routine ...
   }
   // ... some subordinate test-routines ...
#endif
```

Listing 6.2: Conditionally-compiled unit-tester

I have seen examples of where such a tester (for a substantial subsystem) consumed thousands of lines of code, having a variety of available tests, and running automatically when the program was run. For other objects, the tester consisted of only five lines of code.

A great advantage of this approach is that enabling or disabling the tester-code is effortless, and it can be used in the actual system without changing a build-script. As a result of this convenience, developers will use such a tester to test small changes to the object, resulting in higher software quality. Extreme Programming (XP) [1] demands thorough unit testing. To make such extensive unit testing less burdensome, I recommend putting a conditionally-compiled unit tester into each large or complex object, or at least into the subman of each subsystem.

Another benefit is that you are not constrained to black-box testing, because the tester is located inside the object being tested. The tester can check private fields in the object for correct values, or gather statistics from them. Such a gray-box tester can make testing easier because you can monitor things and detect events that are not visible from the public interface.

Because the tester is incorporated into the object's source-code, writing it is scarcely more arduous than writing the source-code for the object itself. Such ease of coding should remove much of our dislike of testing.

6.14   Commie Coding Conventions

The style of code greatly helps or hurts our ability to understand it, as you will see in the examples below. The primary way that we learn the detailed design of code is by reading it, so if you are porting or maintaining code, you will spend much time deciphering it. Therefore, coding style is important.

6.14.1   Sabotage

In the late 1980's, the former Soviet Union trained some saboteurs who entered the USA in order to sabotage the software of its government and defense contractors. After getting software-jobs in the USA, their sabotage was surprisingly successful, and is probably affecting you. This information came to light in Feb 2011 through the Freedom of Information Act, and we have obtained Russian-language transcripts of the classes for those saboteurs. This section consists of interesting excerpts of those transcripts revealing the techniques of the sabotage. The teacher of the classes was Boris Bloatsky, who apparently was also the genius behind their techniques.

In the introductory class, Boris says, "Comrades, if you try to put malware in the American's software, code-inspections will find it, and you'll be exposed. You cannot be straightforward. Instead, the best way to sabotage their software is to appear to improve it. Yes, you can make it worse by making it better! I have devised some techniques that appear to improve software by making it easier to learn, while actually making it harder to learn. You must hinder American software development by promoting these techniques as "best practices" and thus popularize them.

"First, you must understand how people learn the design of code. Then you can hinder that process. Studies conducted by the Kremlin have reported that software contains levels of structure, from small scale (a few lines or a routine), through medium scale (files and classes), up to large scale (system architecture). They also report that structure that's small enough to fit in the height of the monitor is easy to learn, because all of it can be seen at once. As its size increases beyond that, code-structure becomes progressively harder to learn because more and more of it must be kept in the mind (which is difficult), as less and less is visible on the monitor. They conclude that the more vertical space a code-structure uses, the less readable it is. A wise comrade in the Kremlin penned the following Law of Readability:

Vertical is valuable.

"That is, the more lines a given chunk of source-code consumes, the harder it becomes to learn its design. This law is the basis of all my ideas on how to reduce readability, and thus hinder capitalist imperialism.

6.14.2 Waste Height!

"Unlike our Communist monitors, western monitors are relatively wide. With a wide monitor, a developer's natural inclination will be to widen code to 120 or even 150 columns, and put comments on the right, on the same lines as the code on the left. In fact, an American article [17] recommends doing this to improve clarity, so somebody over there has also noticed the Law of Readability. Instead, you must tell the Americans that they must stay within the classic 80 columns. Doing so will force them to interleave comments with code. Forcing a reader to alternate between code and comments disrupts the flow of logic, obscures the code, and thus hinders learning its design. But most importantly, interleaving consumes more vertical space. The 80 column punched card was invented in the 1920s, and it's a well-established standard. Put it in the coding-standards used by projects you work on. Here is what the results look like. First, the clear style:

```
dist = calcHyp(dx,dy);              // Calc length of mouse-move
maxDist = getDistLim(viewType);     // Watch out for max move-dist
if (dist <= maxDist) {              // If not over max, we're okay
```

And the Soviet style with interleaved comments:

```
// Calc length of mouse-move
dist = calcHyp(dx,dy);
// Watch out for max move-dist
maxDist = getDistLim(viewType);
// If not over max, we're okay
if (dist <= maxDist)
```

"You see that the second (interleaved) version is less readable than the first, so that is the style you must promote. If anyone objects, tell him that the 80 column standard is needed for reusability and that long lines are hard for the eye to track. No one can argue against reusability, yet few managers know that modern software-tools are not restricted to 80 columns. Even fewer people understand that the eye tracks code and right-side comments separately, so long lines are not a problem. Your 80 column proposal will sound reasonable.

"When interleaving comments with code, you should insert a blank line after each comment-and-code pair of lines to make them stand out better. So each line of code consumes *three* lines on the monitor. This 3x bloat-factor is wonderful. Whoever said "use plenty of white space" deserves a trip to Moscow.

6.14.3 The Commie Coding Rules

The transcript goes on, "I have list of ways to enhance the unreadability of software, which I'll describe in a few minutes. Here's an example of how effective all these techniques are. First, the clear style:

```
//===== quicksort ========================================================
//
// Sorts array from index begPos to endPos using the quicksort
// algorithm invented by C.A.R. Hoare.
//
void quicksort(int array[], int begPos, int endPos)
{
    if (begPos < endPos) {
        int pivot = array[(begPos+endPos)/2]; // guess pivot at mid-array
        int l = begPos, r = endPos; // l and r are cursors that'll collide

        while (true) { // partition array around pivot
            while (array[l] < pivot) l++;
            while (array[r] > pivot) r--;
            if (l >= r) break; // cursors collided; partitioning is done
            swap(&array[l], &array[r]);
            l++; r--;
        }

        quicksort(array, begPos, l-1); // sort left half of partition
        quicksort(array, r+1, endPos); // sort right half of partition
    }
}
```

That code is very clear, which is *not* what we want. The *same* code is shown below,
but after applying my techniques for boosting unreadability.

```
//========================================================================
//
// @fn
// MODULE NAME: quicksort
//
// @details
// DESCRIPTION: sorts an array.
// Invented by C.A.R Hoare.
// Coded by Boris Bloatsky.
//
// @param
// array - the array to be sorted
//
// @param
// beginPosition - index of first element for sort
//
// @param
// endingPosition - index of last element for sort
//
// @retval
// RETURN VALUE:
// none
//
//========================================================================
//
```

```
void quicksort (
    int array[],
    int beginPosition,
    int endingPosition)
{
    // when beginPosition==endingPosition, we're done because array
    // has only one element

    if (beginPosition < endingPosition)
    {
        // best-guess pivot is middle of array
        int pivot = array[(beginPosition+endingPosition)/2];

        // leftCursor and rightCursor are the cursors.
        // they'll eventually hit each other.
        int leftCursor, rightCursor;

        // initialize the cursors to the entire area to be sorted
        leftCursor = beginPosition;
        rightCursor = endingPosition;

        // partition the array around pivot
        while (true)
        {
            // scan cursor rightward until hitting element >= pivot
            while (array[leftCursor] < pivot)
            {
                // step to the right
                leftCursor++;
            }

            // scan cursor leftward until hitting element <= pivot
            while (array[rightCursor] > pivot)
            {
                // step to the left
                rightCursor--;
            }

            // we're done if the cursors have hit each other
            if (leftCursor >= rightCursor)
            {
                // cursors collided, so exit the main partitioning loop
                break;
            }
            else
            {
                // no action needed in else-part. just continue
            }

            // swap elements at l and r so we can resume scans above
            swap(&array[leftCursor], &array[rightCursor]);

            // elements were swapped, so it's okay to advance cursors
```

```
        leftCursor++;
        rightCursor--;
    }

    // sort left half of partition
    quicksort(array, beginPosition, leftCursor - 1);

    // sort right half of partition
    quicksort(array, rightCursor + 1, endingPosition);
    }
    else
    {
        // no action needed in else-part. array has 0 or 1 elements.
    }

    // we're done. Return.
}
```

"The second (Soviet) example is well-commented and beautifully spaced-out. Each coding-technique it uses is justifiable separately, yet the result is nearly incomprehensible, while the first example above is clear because it is compact. These two examples of *quicksort* show how you can destroy readability by adding comments and helpful white space. And people think that adding comments *improves* readability! We want you communist saboteurs to get these techniques into the American coding-standards.

[Translator's note: The quicksort code above has been compiled but was not tested, and might not work.]

Bloatsky drones on, "Here is my list of rules for how to destroy readability while appearing to improve it. Establishing these coding-rules will hinder any American trying to learn the detailed design of some code."

- Restrict code to 80 columns. This has no benefit, but it forces interleaving of code and comments, forcing the reader to alternate between the two, hindering anyone trying to learn its design.

- Require that at least half the code be comment-lines. This rule will encourage developers to interleave comments instead of putting them on the right.

- The 3x technique: Put a blank line and a comment-line above many statements.

- Put opening curly braces on their own lines. You can argue that the code is more readable this way because the braces line up. But you know the truth: They waste valuable vertical space.

- Use blank lines liberally. Tell the Americans that blank lines can only improve readability.

- Comment what's obvious, because "it might not be obvious to everybody." Each such comment on its own line, of course.

- Compare booleans with the constant true, as in if (happy == true) instead of the normal if (happy). Doing so results in code that is slower, a bit less readable, and (most importantly) more verbose.

- Always put an else-part on each if-statement, and add a comment about why the else-part is empty. This shows somebody reading the code that you did due-diligence and considered what should happen when the conditional is false. And it wastes at least four lines while contributing nothing. Here's an example of how wasteful this unwise practice is:

```
if (whatever == true)
{
    // some code
}
else                                                    WASTE
{                                                       WASTE
    // an else is not needed here because no action is  WASTE
    // needed for the case of whatever==false.          WASTE
}                                                       WASTE
```

- Use long slow-to-read variable names such as *initializeConfigurationManager* instead of quick-to-read abbreviations such as *initConfigMan*. This verbosity will also cause some lines to become long enough that they must be split into two lines, consuming yet more height. It's easy to argue that fully spelled-out names are more readable, even though they are *less* readable.

- Function headers are another great opportunity to waste height, as that bloated example shows. The clear example is too compact, and its levels of visual loudness help people to learn. The function-name in its banner is loudest, whereas in the Soviet example, the worthless MODULE NAME is loudest. Add doxygen tags, and put them on their own lines. As always, "Use plenty of white space." Include everything you can think of in the header, such as INPUTS, OUTPUTS, EXCEPTIONS, RETURN VALUE, ad nauseam. Most people won't fill these fields in, and they are usually useless anyway, causing them to be mere consumers of precious height.

Bloatsky continues, "We believe that almost no American developers will realize the principle behind all of this: A comment on its own line has a cost. The cost is reduction of readability because less code-structure is visible on the monitor. If its benefit is lower than that cost, then the comment is a net loss of readability. Such a comment hurts more than it helps. That net loss is the basis of all the items in my list. Also, a blank line is a form of a comment that says "Here's a change in logic," and the same rule applies: Make it a net loss. Their ignorance of the Law of Readability ("vertical is valuable") means they will accept your harmful coding techniques. And please put in a good word for me, as I'd like to get that trip to Moscow. (Now you know why Boris' comrades called him "Boring Bloatsky" behind his back).

Bloatsky taught this about OOP: "We know that OOP is taking over, giving us more opportunities to make their software incomprehensible. Inheritance is a feature that creates a hierarchy of categories, which is seldom useful but looks interesting. You must convince those capitalist pigs to base their designs around these foolish hierarchies and not around service hierarchies. Software organized around this wrong kind of hierarchy will bog down in complexity. Inheritance hierarchies appear to be sophisticated, so you should have little trouble promoting them.

Many small files   The transcript ends with this suggestion: "Bloated code (using the techniques above) is hard to learn because a smaller amount of the design is visible in the small space on the monitor. Likewise, code-design is obscured yet more by small files. It's hard enough for somebody to learn code by scrolling up and down. It's even harder if that code is broken into little files, because switching back and forth between files is slower than scrolling. Encourage the Americans to use small files "because it's more modular and helps reuse." Our studies show that files containing a few thousand lines and a number of classes are the quickest to learn. You must encourage the opposite. At least put each class in its own file. Splitting a class into multiple files is even better.

6.14.4   A Serious Summary

I'm tired of seeing code that appears to have been written by our enemies! The point of this section is that some popular coding practices do more harm than good. Such "best practices" are actually worst practices. As you saw from the code-examples above, they cause a severe reduction in readability. Plenty of my own time has been wasted trying to learn code written this bloated way.

The source of these mistakes is that people don't know the Law of Readability and thus don't know the harm they're causing. For example, the technique of creating 3x bloat has the obvious benefit of adding comments. But its cost is not obvious. For every technique described above which makes code vertically larger, the additional largeness itself reduces understandability. Vertical space is needed for learning structure, and yet it's at a premium; hence the Law of Readability:

Vertical is valuable.

But vertical space can be overly conserved by putting too much code on each line. To avoid this trap, use the vertical direction for control-structure, and the horizontal direction for detailed computations and comments.

Some people prefer a coding style that puts opening braces on their own lines because they have formed the habit of looking up for an opening brace in the same column where they saw a closing brace. Instead of looking for an opening brace, a better habit is to look at indentation instead. Being guided by indentation is superior because (1) because "vertical is valuable," curly-brace languages such as C and C++ are more readable when they are more compact (with opening curly braces on the right ends of lines), and (2) you'll be comfortable reading non-curly-brace languages such as Python, Ruby, Basic, and others.

Opening braces should *not* be on their own lines; comments should be to the right of the code using a wide editor-window; add blank lines sparingly; use a compact function-header with correct levels of visual loudness; and files should be reasonably large to help readers learn the big picture by reading through each file. Remember the Law, "vertical is valuable," and your code will become more readable.

Finally, don't forget that inheritance usually makes a design worse instead of better because software is best organized as a hierarchy of *services* and not as a hierarchy of *categories*. The problems caused by inheritance, and alternatives to inheritance, are detailed in Section 6.6 on page 142.

6.15   Enhancements to the Language

Your class declarations will be clearer if you add the keywords commands and notices to the programming language. In C++, this can be done by adding the following two macros to a global include-file:

```
#define commands  public
#define notices   public
```

Such a change will allow you to declare classes that look like this:

```
class Mp3Player {
    commands:  // only called by my superiors
        static bool playFile(string fileName);
    notices:  // called by anything, but mostly by subordinates
        static void decompBufDone(byte *pBuf, bool happy);
        static void audioBufDone (byte *pBuf, bool happy);
};
```

Not only will this change make your code clearer, it also will allow a program to read your source-code and produce IDAR graphs automatically for you. Such a tool could also perform some checks such as ensuring that all public methods are identified as commands and notices, and that commands only go down.

I would like a language to have the ability to declare a field in a class to be read-only by nonmember methods, and yet writable by member methods. This feature would allow an object to set such fields to values once, perhaps by reading from a file or registry, while all other objects would treat those fields as constants. Another common use would be placing results of commands in such fields for other objects to read. Such fields presently must be declared public, enabling accidental writes to them. So in addition to public, I suggest that fields may be export (publicly read-only) or import (publicly write-only).

An object communicates with superiors, and with helpers such as subordinates, peers and perhaps other objects. Thus, an object has two interfaces: one for superiors, and one for helpers. Ideally, a language would support both kinds of interfaces.

6.16   Roster of Rules

This section contains some useful rules that didn't fit anywhere else in this chapter.

Service Hierarchy Back in Section 5.2.1 on page 113, I describe verb-type objects, whose names are verbs. Each contains a primary command fulfilling its entire role, and any other commands in it are supportive. Noun-type objects are the most common, and are taught by traditional OOP. In fact, it's best to think in terms of the service provided by each object. The only purpose of an object is to provide a service, so you are creating a hierarchy of services. Section 8.2 on page 232 discusses service-based design in detail. Theoreticians have known for decades that software is best structured as this kind of hierarchy.

Meaty Rule Although the Meaty rule was mentioned earlier in this chapter, it's important enough to justify this reminder. Avoid creating tiny classes that do nothing substantial. Make your classes meaty.

Boss When structuring your code using the Boss pattern (see Section 7.1.1 on page 177), divide the responsibilities among the boss and its workers so that (1) the boss is not a micromanager, trying to do too much, and (2) the boss is not laissez faire, saying "Wake me up when you're done." Create a reasonable division of responsibilities, just as competent corporations usually do.

Resourceful Boss If resources will need to be allocated, try using the Resourceful Boss pattern described in Section 7.1.2 on page 180. Centralizing the allocation of resources in the boss, along with control and error-handling, can save you days of debugging later.

Pancake If you have an object that commands many subordinates and contains much code, it will be low and wide in the IDAR graph, looking like a pancake. You might have a "God class" [26] on your hands. What levels of clarity and cohesion does it have? They are probably low. These are signs that the class should be split. However, this problem is less common than the beanpole phenomenon described below.

Beanpole If the IDAR graph contains a chain of commands that's long and thin, then it resembles a bean-pole, and probably means that there are too many levels of abstraction. Another clue is that the roles of such objects contain several qualifying clauses, indicating that the objects are overspecialized. Such objects probably violate the Meaty rule. Combine some levels.

Threads Keep the number of threads to a minimum, preferably only the number needed to achieve required parallelism. More threads mean more timing-holes, race-conditions, and deadlocks.

Concealing Design Avoid techniques that hide design. These include:

- Inheritance, which scatters related code that should be kept together, and turns direct calls into indirect calls.
- Indirect calls, which makes calls hard to follow when reading source-code.
- Hiding the main loop of a thread in a subordinate object that makes callbacks. Instead, keep the main loop explicit in the top level of each thread.
- Hiding routing of queued messages for a thread in a subordinate object. Instead, use a mailbox for the thread, and follow a message-fetch with an explicit `switch` or `case` statement. This structure clearly reveals where messages are fetched and processed.
- Small files hide the surrounding design by only showing a tiny portion of the code. Files should contain hundreds (or a few thousands) of lines.
- A bloated coding style (see the Commie Coding Conventions on page 166) conceals design by diluting it in a large quantity of inert ingredients.

Quality Criteria During the process of design, constantly evaluate your decisions in terms of clarity, cohesion, concealment, coupling, and need. Chapter 4 describes these important ways of gauging the quality of a design; learn them so well that they become part of your intuition.

Pattern Pressure from Peers "How many patterns did you use?" If you've been asked this question, that member of your team is following a fad instead of following what's right. Patterns have become a fad, so be extra careful to ignore such pressure and do what's right for the software.

Here are a few rules which have become well known in the software community, and which I strongly agree with:

KISS–Keep It Simple, Stupid This rule has been around for decades, but you'd never know it based on the unnecessary complexity of much software out there.

DRY—Don't Repeat Yourself Don't replicate a chunk of code. Instead, make it a method. If you find yourself copying and pasting code so you can make small changes to it, make it a method instead, and accommodate the changes with a parameter and if-then-else statements using that parameter.

YAGNI—You Aren't Gonna Need It Are you thinking of making your design more complex in order to make it more flexible? Thinking of adding a feature which might be needed later? Don't. Implement the present requirements, because it's too hard to predict future requirements, and what you thought will be needed probably won't be needed.

Knowing that complexity is the enemy, I'll end this chapter with one of the most important observations I've made in my career:

> *Usually the simplest design is best,*
> *so do your best to simplify.*

6.17 Exercises

1. What is temporal chaining? Does it violate any of the IDAR rules? What harm does it cause?

2. What are free notices? Are they allowed in designs? What are their dangers?

3. Unrelated dependencies should be avoided, but what is an important exception to this guideline?

4. What is the enemy of software? Why?

5. What are the disadvantages of using inheritance?

6. What are the alternatives to inheritance?

7. Most classes have only one instance. How can you use this fact to simplify your software?

8. What is the Law of Readability that was discovered by the Kremlin? What does it mean? In light of this law, where should opening curly braces be put?

9. How should you think about new classes you are defining?

10. The section about Unrelated Dependencies described the problem of upward bound notices. Why was there no mention of downward bound notices?

Chapter 7

Design Patterns

— the final reinvention of these wheels

If you have a tool-chest, there are some tools in it that you occasionally use, and others that you've used only a couple of times, if ever. But there are a few tools that you use on almost every job. So it is with this collection of design patterns: You'll use a few many times, and others seldom if ever. The Boss pattern is the screwdriver of design patterns. It is the tool you'll use most often, because the Boss pattern is compatible with both the way people think and with the best way of designing most software (as a hierarchy). But some other patterns are used often as well. For example, most GUI-based designs use the Collector and/or GUI App patterns. Objects that listen for activity on ports are often based on the Watcher pattern. Most threads use the Inbox pattern. And the Resourceful Boss pattern is an elegant way to resolve contention for resources. The 25 patterns described in this chapter are divided into these groups:

Structuring Commands	Ways of using commands
Structuring Notices	Ways of using notices
Dataflows	Some ways to implement dataflows
Threads	Patterns for multithreaded systems
Interfacing	Ways to communicate with other objects
Applications	Frameworks for entire applications

Most of the IDAR graphs shown in this chapter do not show which objects are active, because doing so (1) would add clutter and distractions to the graphs, obscuring their concepts, and (2) could imply that certain objects must be active, yet most patterns don't care which objects are active.

Patterns have become a fad in some social circles, and people are being pressured into using them inappropriately. It's bad news if you are asked, "How many patterns did you use?" This question means that you are being measured by your use of patterns, and the more you use, the better you look. If you reply, "three," you're wonderful. If "two," you're acceptable. Expect to be regarded as a diplodocus if your answer is "one" or "none." The authors of the landmark book *Design Patterns* [12] warned us about inappropriate use of patterns:

> *Design patterns should not be applied indiscriminately. Often they achieve flexibility and variability by introducing additional levels of indirection, and that can complicate a design and/or cost you some performance. A design pattern should only be applied when the flexibility it affords is actually needed.*

The correct approach is to use patterns appropriately. That is, only use patterns whose benefits exceed their costs. If none do, then use none. You might be comforted a little to know that you will be using at least one pattern—Boss. By creating an IDAR graph, it's impossible to *not* use the Boss pattern. If you can contrive to use one other popular pattern, such as the Resourceful Boss or Watcher, then you can reply "two" and stay out of trouble.

7.1 Structuring Commands

This group of design patterns relies heavily on the metaphor of a corporation. As I mentioned in Section 3.12.3 (page 66), IDAR graphs tend to resemble the organization of corporations because both are command hierarchies. But the metaphor goes deeper, and remains true of how bosses assign tasks to and communicate with their employees, and with how peers (under the same boss) work together. The metaphor even extends to how secretaries work with their bosses. Philosophically, IDAR graphs can be thought of as a way to organize the communications among specialized workers. Such communications are divided into two categories—commands and notices. This section discloses patterns used for organizing commands among superiors and their subordinates. A summary of these patterns follows:

Boss	Implements a service by delegating chores to workers
Resourceful Boss	Like Boss, but also handles resource-allocation
Dispatcher	Handles multiple objects implementing one interface
Layer	Grouping haphazardly used subordinates
Union	Call cross-cutting commands via a shadow-hierarchy

7.1.1 Boss Pattern

Out of all the design patterns, the Boss pattern is the most commonly used because, as mentioned in the introduction above, it is impossible to *not* employ this pattern as it is inherent to the heart of IDAR: having superiors command subordinates. IDAR graphs are hierarchies of authority, and that is what corporations and governments are, with bosses commanding workers, so IDAR graphs fit our way of thinking. A boss with three workers are shown in Figure 7.1. Two of the workers send notices back to the boss. Also, two of the workers (*Worker1* and *Worker2*) are also bosses, because they command *Subworker*.

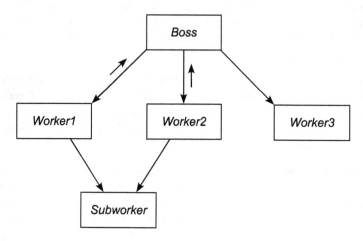

Figure 7.1: Two levels of bosses

Because *Subworker* has a fan-in of greater than one (i.e., it has multiple bosses), you will need to take care to ensure that any notices sent by *Subworker* are sent to the correct boss. As shown on this IDAR graph, *Subworker* returns no notices. But if you decide to have it return a notice in the future, there are several ways of dealing with multiple superiors, described in Section 6.11.3 (page 160). Also, if a worker can receive commands from multiple threads, you'll need to be careful to avoid creating a race condition. The Inbox pattern (Section 7.4.1 on page 207) is a popular way of handling this situation.

You should separate management from work by relying on the metaphor of a corporation. Objects at the bottom levels should perform detailed or algorithmic chores, and those above them should fulfill their broader roles by managing the activities of their subordinates. This approach helps you avoid the trap of mixing levels, where objects contain both higher level control and lower level details.

Requests to Superiors

Figure 7.2 portrays an interesting question about communication between objects that developers occasionally face. This is the sequence of events corresponding to the numbered labels in this IDAR graph:

1. Using the *open* command, the *Statistics* object tells *Document* to open a file whose name is passed as a parameter.

2. But *Document* discovers that the file it was given is encrypted, so it needs the decryption-key for it. For security reasons, keys are only transferred on a need-to-know basis, and this need was not known when the *open* command was sent. So *Document* sends a notice up to *Statistics* asking it for the key.

3. *Statistics* responds with the key in the *hereIsKey* message.

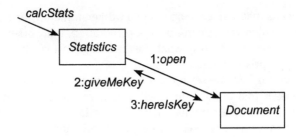

Figure 7.2: A subordinate requesting an item from its superior

The question about this design is whether *Document* is commanding its superior by asking it for the key. The notice in question is called "give me key," which starts with a verb and is phrased in the imperative, so it certainly appears to be a command. What do you think?

As was taught back in Section 3.13.6 on page 72, such a command-like notice is referred to as an "imperative notice" because it appears to be a case of a worker commanding its boss. But there are three cases where such a notice is acceptable: relaying, echoing, and requesting help. The *giveMeKey* notice is a request for help that is needed to perform a prior command (*open* an encrypted document), making it an acceptable imperative notice.

Another way to answer this question about commanding a superior is to compare this situation to a boss and a worker, as described above. First, the boss commands the worker to build a circuit. The worker realizes that he needs a soldering iron located in the locked supply-cabinet, so he comes back and says to the boss, "Give me the key to the cabinet." The boss finds the key and gives it to the worker, who builds the circuit. It is acceptable for a worker to make a request of his boss for some item needed to obey a prior command. Hence, "give me the cabinet-key" is not regarded as a command in the corporate world. Likewise, *Document* is not commanding its superior when requesting a decryption-key as part of performing a prior command, even though "give me the decryption-key" is phrased as a command.

Centralized Control and Error-Handling

An important and sometimes overlooked benefit of the Boss pattern is that control and error-handling among the workers are centralized in one place (the boss), instead of being dispersed among the workers.

When an error occurs in an object, it can clean up itself. However, the object is probably contributing to a job in concert with other objects, and the problem is how to tell those other objects to quit, thus cleaning up the job. Look again at Figure 7.1. Suppose *Worker1*, *Worker2*, and *Worker3* are performing chores that contribute to a job. Imagine what would happen if an error occurred in a worker and the boss lacked code to clean up the job. The worker would have to do that job-cleanup itself, requiring that it send notices to the other workers telling them to quit their chores. You can see how such dispersed error-handling would turn into a mess, with some overlooked error-cases going into production and angering customers. Here's an important rule:

The boss handles errors.

This rule means that if an error occurs in a worker, it merely reports it to its boss, which performs the job-wide clean-up. In a corporation, if a worker has a problem, he won't tell his coworkers to stop what they're doing. Instead, he'll notify his boss who will take appropriate action.

It's also natural to put the set-up and tear-down required for a job in the boss. So when the boss is told to do a job, it will configure and command its workers to perform chores needed to accomplish that job. The fact that commands cannot go sideways means that one coworker cannot command another to configure or tear-down, forcing those responsibilities into their mutual boss. But a coworker can send notices to others, so here is a rule about such notices:

A coworker may not tell another coworker about a problem.

This constraint forces problem-notices to be sent up to the boss. Centralizing control and error-handling in a boss also makes maintenance easier because it's easier to learn how the overall control and error-handling work when they are all in one place instead of scattered around.

7.1.2   Resourceful Boss Pattern

The Resourceful Boss pattern is similar to the Boss pattern, but it also moves all resource-management out of the workers and into the boss. As a result, subordinates may not procure a resource on their own (or by commanding their subordinates). Instead, they must politely ask their boss for it.

Multimeter and Power-Supply

Using the metaphor of a corporation, let's say a boss (named Jim) has a multimeter and a power-supply in a cabinet outside his office. Let's say Jim has two workers, Pavel and Leo. Jim gives both some work to do, and tells both to get the equipment they need from the cabinet. Here's what happens:

1. Pavel gets the multimeter.

2. Leo walks up and gets the power-supply.

3. Later, Pavel walks over to the cabinet needing the power-supply, and seeing that it's gone, goes back to his computer and plays games while keeping an eye on the cabinet, waiting for the power-supply to be returned.

4. Then Leo walks to the cabinet needing the multimeter, and seeing that it's gone, goes back to his computer and plays games while keeping an eye on the cabinet, waiting for the multimeter to be returned.

5. Pavel and Leo are waiting on each other, and we have a classic deadlock like that of two threads that have each procured one semaphore and are each waiting for the other semaphore.

What went wrong here? The problem is we didn't program Jim to be wise enough about allocating resources, so he left allocation up to his workers. The Resourceful Boss can do better. Let's try it again, but this time, Jim locks the cabinet and tells his workers to ask him for the equipment they need. Here's what happens:

1. Pavel asks Jim for the multimeter, and Jim gives it to him.

2. Leo asks Jim for the power-supply. At this point, wise Jim knows that trouble is coming because he knows that both workers will need both pieces of equipment. He decides to solve this problem in one of two ways: (1) Tell Leo to wait until Pavel is done, or (2) plan to take a piece of equipment from either Pavel or Leo and give it to the other worker to break the deadlock.

Wise Allocation

The first scenario above corresponds to the common technique of allocating resources using a semaphore. There are well-known situations where it can lead to a deadlock. The Resourceful Boss pattern solves such problems by making allocation more intelligent. Figure 7.3 shows both of these arrangements. Figure 7.3(a) portrays the usual method of protecting resources with semaphores located in the *Resource1* and *Resource2* objects. The *alloc* and *release* methods in those objects merely take and release the semaphores, respectively. Figure 7.3(b) portrays the Resourceful Boss which handles allocation itself. The two workers ask the *Boss* for a resource by sending it a *needRes* notice, which has a parameter indicating which resource is needed. The *Boss* responds (perhaps after a delay) with a *useRes* command, causing the worker to proceed and use the resource.

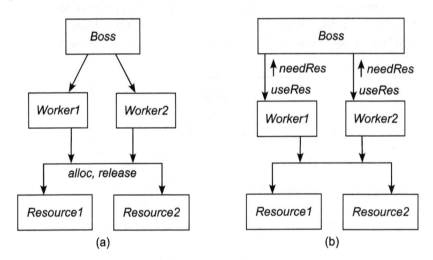

Figure 7.3: Foolish (a) and wise (b) allocation of resources

By putting resource allocation in the boss, we have the opportunity to use more knowledge about the worker's needs when allocating resources. For example, the code in *Boss* can privately allocate both resources to a worker when either is requested. Or if you're more ambitious, you can make arrangements with one or more of your worker objects to temporarily relinquish a resource upon command from the boss, which will permit the resources to be utilized in parallel, but at a cost of greater complexity in these objects. Both approaches solve the problem of deadlocks that occur with the simple-minded use of semaphores.

The essence of the Resourceful Boss pattern is that the boss controls (or owns) all resources. These include discrete resources, such as peripherals and I/O devices, and also memory. The Resourceful Boss can control a certain amount of memory, which might have been handed down to him by his boss. Using imperative notices (see Section 3.13.6 on page 72), workers ask their bosses for such resources. This design pattern turns allocation upside-down. Traditionally, a worker asked a resource for permission to use it. Thus, the request went *down*. Using the Resourceful Boss, the resource-request goes *up* (to the boss).

Per-Chore Allocation is Ideal

Resources, including memory, are often allocated and freed on a per-chore basis. For example, a printer has distinct print-jobs, each consisting of some number of pages. A photo-editing program has distinct operations, such as flood-filling an area. Each such job or operation is a chore, and often, a number of resources are needed only while the chore is being performed.

For such chore-delimited needs, subordinates should *not* request resources from their bosses. Rather, when a Resourceful Boss needs to do a chore, it will:

1. Ask its subordinates which resources they need for that chore.
2. Ensure that all resources are available (apportioning may be needed).
3. Give resources to the subordinates (using pointers for memory-blocks).
4. Command each subordinate to start doing its part of the chore.
5. When the chore is done, all resources allocated above are available.

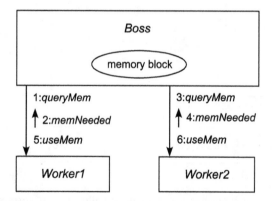

Figure 7.4: Per-chore allocation of memory

Figure 7.4 shows these actions. Step 2 is crucial. Because the boss is aware of all needs for resources before the chore is started, it can ensure that there will be no deadlocks or shortages of resources. This protocol brings two benefits:

- *There will be no memory-leaks!* Memory-leaks are a perpetual pesky problem pervading people's poor programs. But if the boss allocates memory from its private pool before the chore starts, then when the chore is done, the boss will simply reinitialize that pool to remove all allocations.

- *Memory-allocation will never fail.* The subordinates told the boss how much memory they will need, and the boss knows how much it has available. In fact, each memory-needed notice from a subordinate can consist of a minimum and optimal amount of memory, allowing the boss to intelligently scale the requests down to ensure that every subordinate has sufficient memory, while not exceeding what's available.

I once worked for a manufacturer that employed this technique in its wireless devices for many years. They used this technique in all levels of software, even at the topmost level. The big boss would hand a chunk of memory to a lower-level boss, which in turn would subdivide it further among workers based on their needs. This design worked well, even in lower-end devices having little memory. Based on that experience, I recommend that all allocation of memory and other resources be done using the Resourceful Boss pattern, especially on a per-chore basis when possible.

7.1.3 Dispatcher Pattern

Most uses of polymorphic inheritance and other forms of indirect commands can be removed by introducing a dispatcher, converting such indirect commands into conventional direct (hard-coded) commands. The phrase "dispatcher layer" came from Structured Design, but I cannot find it in my books on Structured Design. However, Richard Fairley's book [7] describes both a "dispatcher" and a "dispatcher subsystem". So I apologize for not providing the reference. I tried.

Each command in a dispatcher consists of a case or switch statement which selects the appropriate subordinate. Figure 7.5 shows the use of a dispatcher for the situation where one of three kinds of printers can be connected.

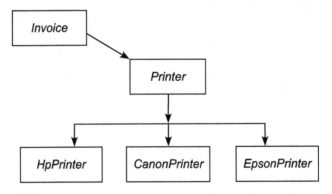

Figure 7.5: *Printer* is a dispatcher for printers

Listing 7.1 shows the code for the *printLine* and *skipLines* commands inside the dispatcher object, *Printer*. Commands inside a dispatcher object always look like this example, merely routing each command to the appropriate subordinate object.

Compared with indirection (which includes polymorphic inheritance), a dispatcher has the advantage of making the software much quicker to understand for somebody reading its source-code. Why? Look again at Listing 7.1. The choices of subordinates are obvious: HP, Canon and Epson. With indirection, you would only

```
void Printer::printLine(string text) {
    switch (kindOfPrinter) {
        case MakerHP:       HpPrinter.printLine (text); break;
        case MakerCanon: CanonPrinter.printLine (text); break;
        case MakerEpson: EpsonPrinter.printLine (text); break;
    }
}

void Printer::skipLines(int numLines) {
    switch (kindOfPrinter) {
        case MakerHP:       HpPrinter.skipLines (numLines); break;
        case MakerCanon: CanonPrinter.skipLines (numLines); break;
        case MakerEpson: EpsonPrinter.skipLines (numLines); break;
    }
}
```

Listing 7.1: Dispatcher for printers

see a call to a method using a pointer or some other mechanism, and it's not clear what method will be called or even what object will be involved. So a person reading and trying to learn such software must look around to find the choices, hopefully with the assistance of a smart text-editor, open another file and proceed. Such searching wastes time and is error-prone. I've done it several painful times. Learning other peoples' software makes you appreciate the clarity provided by the direct method-calls in a dispatcher.

A criticism that will be directed toward the Dispatcher pattern is that each of its public methods contains a case or switch statement with the same set of labels, which is hazardous duplication. In fact, one often reads the suggestion that multiple case/switch statements with identical labels indicate that inheritance should be used. However, this duplication is not a problem with the Dispatcher pattern because all of the case/switch statements are physically near each other in the source-code. There is little code between labels because there is only one method-call after each label, as you can see in Listing 7.1. As a result, if you need to change the labels, it's obvious which lines must change. Therefore, there is no danger of overlooking a case/switch statement, as can happen when such statements are scattered around the program. The duplication of labels is harmless.

Dispatching Notices   You can use this pattern to dispatch non-rider notices sent to multiple superiors. But the selector-variable in the notices' case/switch statements will probably change more often than in the command dispatcher described above because multiple superiors often command a dispatcher in an unpredictable order, forcing each subordinate to save the superior-selector that will be used later by returned notices. These extra steps are not needed when dispatching commands because the commander supplies the selector-variable for the subordinate. These same additional steps must be done when using indirection, so these are not disadvantages of using a dispatcher for notices, but you need to be aware that dispatching notices is more complex than dispatching commands. Consequently, I recommend using a dispatcher for commands and not for notices.

7.1.4 Layer Pattern

As I mentioned back on page 67, you will occasionally find that the major functions of your program are implemented by several superiors that command several subordinates that serve as tools for the superiors. Furthermore, the selection of tools (subordinates) used by each superior is haphazard, consisting of what it happened to need. A graph of such a design will look like the law firm in Figure 7.6.

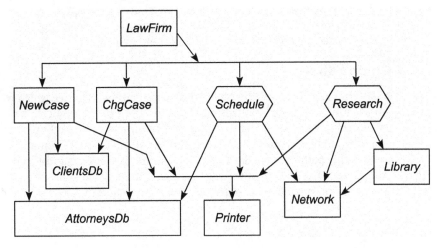

Figure 7.6: Superiors with haphazard usage of subordinates

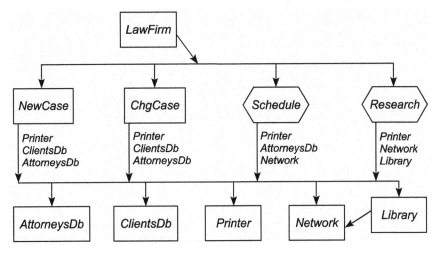

Figure 7.7: A rail shows that subordinates are a layer of tools

There is no rhyme or reason in Figure 7.6 below the row of superiors that starts with *NewCase*. The choice of tools that happened to be employed by each superior is not important to the design, and thus should not be prominent in the IDAR graph. In this situation, you can place all of the subordinates under a rail, as shown in Figure 7.7.

In this new graph, we clearly see that the overall structure of this program consists mainly of two layers: a row of superiors, and a row of subordinates whose services are available to all of the superiors. The specific subordinates used by each superior are listed under it, so both graphs convey the same information. But the layer graph reveals the overall design and intent.

When you find that your graph has haphazard lines below a row of superiors like Figure 7.6, check whether the subordinates are serving as a collection of tools or services. If so, the Layer pattern will clarify and clean up your design.

Layered designs have been employed for decades, especially in operating systems and networking stacks. IDAR graphs accommodate them well.

7.1.5   Union Pattern

The Union pattern partially solves the problem of cross-cutting concerns, which was described in Section 3.7.4 (page 52). This pattern allows you to (1) send commands to arbitrary objects, regardless of their location in the normal command-hierarchy, and (2) broadcast commands to all objects in the system. The name "union" was selected because this pattern is similar to a labor union. All members must sign up with the union boss. That boss and the members constitute a shadow-hierarchy that is supplemental to the core hierarchy of the system. Figure 7.8(a) shows its structure.

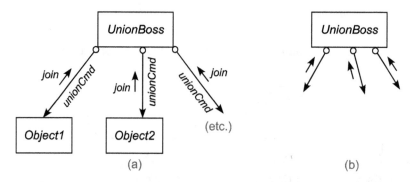

Figure 7.8: Union pattern (a), and as a popular object (b)

To join the union, the *initialize* command within an object sends a *join* notice to *UnionBoss* containing a pointer to a *unionCmd* command in the object, and some other items, all of which *UnionBoss* saves in a private data-structure. The imperative *join* notice is a request for help so that the object can perform future union-related commands. *UnionBoss* helps the object simply by remembering it, allowing it (or any other object) to be commanded indirectly via its *unionCmd* command.

You should *not* use the Union pattern to perform initialization and shutdown, because (1) *UnionBoss* cannot initialize (or shut down) objects in the proper order, and (2) the union is intended only for cross-cutting concerns, and not for such core concerns. The normal IDAR hierarchy is well suited for performing initialization and shutdown systematically in the proper order. My recommended technique for these operations is covered in Section 6.5 on page 141.

Here are some uses of the Union pattern:

Testing This pattern is superb for testing objects or subsystems. Objects can be told to inject (call) commands and notices with specified parameters, generate or process test-data, or mimic failures that are otherwise nearly impossible to create. Be careful about injecting commands because this capability can create a security-hole that a whale could swim through.

Debug You can change the debug-levels (or logging-levels) of selected objects while the program is running, saving you the trouble of editing source-code and rebuilding the project each time you want to change these levels. Also, *UnionBoss* can be connected to a port or back-channel, enabling an outside user to view diagnostic output.

Profiling Periodically checking whether each thread is presently active gives you statistics on CPU-usage. Such polling also lets you monitor stack-size and/or memory-consumption, which can be valuable for detecting memory-leaks.

Health-Checks In a round-robin fashion, the *UnionBoss* can command each object to check its health, which would be returned to *UnionBoss* in a rider notice. This test could wake up any thread inside the object to verify that it's not hung, as well as performing other quick tests.

Tuning Parameters affecting performance can be changed on-the-fly.

As mentioned above, *unionCmd* should only implement cross-cutting concerns, and never core concerns. In addition, it's desirable (but not required) that every object function correctly even if its *unionCmd* is never called.

To be most useful, the union boss should be at or near the top of the command-hierarchy. Drawing lines to all objects the union boss communicates with would add too much clutter, so this boss is shown as a popular object as in Figure 7.8(b). In the likely case that the union boss is also the topmost controller of the program, I suggest drawing that boss normally, but also adding the dangling commands and notices in Figure 7.8(b) so readers will know that boss is also a union boss.

Here is an example of a *UnionBoss* class:

```
class UnionBoss {
    public:
    typedef enum { U_SYNOPSIS, U_DEBUG_LEV, U_CHK_HEALTH } UnionCmdE;
    typedef int (*UnionCmdCb)(void *pThis, UnionCmdE cmd, int param);

    // Notice called by many/most/all objects in system:
    static void join(unsigned oid, UnionCmdCb pCmd, void *pThis);

    // Commands only called by topmost controller:
    static void outputSynopsis();
    static void setDebugLevel(int level);
    static void checkHealth();
    // ... and probably others ...
};
```

UnionBoss is a static class, making it easy to work with. The *oid* parameter uniquely identifies every object by number, allowing an outsider to target any object. Here is a fragment of code from a typical object that joins the union:

```
// A call to this means that UnionBoss is commanding me.
int SomeClass::unionCmd (void *pThis, UnionBoss::UnionCmdE cmd, int z) {
    switch (cmd) {
        case UnionBoss::U_SYNOPSIS:
        ...
    }
}

SomeClass::SomeClass() {    // Constructor
    UnionBoss::join (12345, &unionCmd, this);   // can also be in init cmd
}
```

The constructor joins the union via the call to the *join* notice. All commands from *UnionBoss* are funneled into the *unionCmd* command, which must be declared `static`. In C++, you must declare one dummy instance of a static class to cause its constructor to be called so it can join the union. This annoyance is not necessary with C# because it offers static constructors. The per-object overhead of this pattern is small, so all objects may join the union at little cost.

The *unionCmd* command will usually have no cohesion. The alternative is to pass an interface to *UnionBoss* containing pointers to all of the commands. But doing so adds clumsy work for all objects. Using one command-method with worse cohesion is simpler and easier.

7.2   Structuring Notices

Distant notices are free notices that are not sent to nearby objects, such as a superior, subordinate or a peer under the same boss. Their HD metric is 3 or higher. Since they travel farther, they have greater potential for making a mess. The Collector and Distributor patterns provide effective ways of managing distant notices. In addition, the Watcher and Secretary patterns solve common problems and—surprisingly—convey commands inside their notices. Here is a summary of these patterns:

Collector	Many notices funnel into this object
Distributor	Sends notices to many objects
Watcher	Sends events it receives up to a big boss
Secretary	Stores and gives chores to the boss

7.2.1   Collector Pattern

The Collector and Distributor patterns are analogous to and named after collector and distributor roads [14]. A collector road acts as a funnel, collecting traffic from several smaller roads onto itself. A distributor road is a reverse-funnel, dispersing traffic from itself onto several smaller roads. Objects can treat notices analogously, with a collector object funneling notices together into itself, and with a distributor dispersing notices to various objects in the program.

A collector object is one that receives distant notices from objects throughout the program. The Collector pattern is illustrated in Figure 7.9. Note that a collector is not required to command the objects that send it notices, as Figure 7.9 shows.

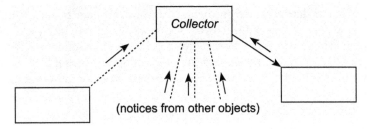

Figure 7.9: Collector pattern

The classic example of a collector object is a GUI. A GUI is typically the topmost object in a program, because it controls the program. Objects in various places can send notices up to the GUI informing it of progress of operations, status of various items, and any asynchronous events. Figure 7.10 shows a typical GUI receiving notices from various other objects, some (or many) of which it does not command, making those notices free. The *percentDone* notices from worker objects causes the GUI to update a progress-bar. Other notices inform the GUI of status-changes.

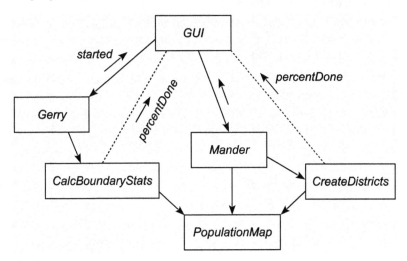

Figure 7.10: GUI collector object

By the way, such notices to a GUI are often *not* drawn in an IDAR graph. If you were to draw them, there would be so many lines that the graph would look cluttered. Furthermore, most developers know that many objects send notices to the GUI, so showing such notices on the IDAR graph only tells readers what they already know. Instead, such graphs mark the GUI as being popular by using dangling notice-lines.

Having a collector object in a program is permissible because it does not make the design messy. Having distant notices fly all over a program makes a mess, but having them funnel into one place is clear and understandable.

A possible problem is cycles of dependencies mentioned earlier in this book. If a GUI and lower subsystems are compiled into separate libraries, then the cycle of dependencies in this design can break a poor linker. The GUI commands worker

objects, so it has dependencies on them. Those worker objects often send notices
to the GUI, so they have dependencies on it. One way to remove such cycles of dependencies involving a GUI is to have worker objects use indirect notices, which adds
clumsy code to all the worker objects that send notices. A better way to eliminate
these cycles is to use the Proxy pattern as described in Section 7.5.4 (page 219).

7.2.2   Distributor Pattern

A distributor object sends notices to various objects in the program. An example
might be an object containing a timer that "ticks" once per second, and sends tick-
notices to various interested objects.

Direct Distributor

At first you might think that there's no problem with distributing notices. But if the
notices are hard-coded (direct calls) in the distributor object, then the notices can
cause the following troubles:

- Cycles of dependencies are likely to occur if the notices pass among multiple
  libraries, which can trouble poor linkers.
- A distributor object contains an unrelated dependency on *every* object to which
  it sends notices. If it disperses them to many objects, then it has dependencies
  on many objects unrelated to its role of sending notices.

On the other hand, if there are few recipients of notices and the cycles aren't a
problem, then using a direct distributor is acceptable. There is a trade-off between
the additional clarity and simplicity of using direct calls, and the problem of having numerous unrelated dependencies within the direct distributor object. You must
decide when it's time to switch to the Indirect Distributor pattern.

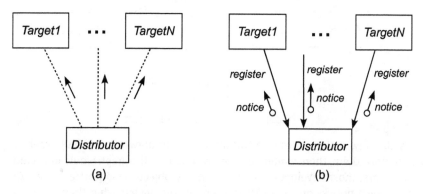

Figure 7.11: Distributor pattern, direct (a) and indirect (b)

Figure 7.11(a) shows the Distributor pattern using direct calls as described above.
Target1...TargetN are the target-objects for the notices.

Indirect Distributor

The problems caused by dependencies can be removed by requiring that recipient
objects register for notices. Such a registration includes the address of a notice to

be called, causing all notices sent by the distributor to be indirect. Registrations are required in Figure 7.11(b), removing all dependencies within *Distributor*. Each notice received by the *Distributor* is sent to all registered recipients. Such recipients are often called "subscribers", and sending notices is also referred to as "publishing". Hence, the Indirect Distributor pattern is also called "publish-subscribe" in the literature.

The Indirect Distributor pattern is helpful when you are not certain which objects will be interested in an event. Some examples of this situation are:

- In a product-line of devices, some features may be present only in the higher-end models. If a feature is present, its objects will register for notices with the indirect distributor.

- In a GUI, some objects might be present only when a certain form or dialog is being displayed. Sending a notice to a nonexistent GUI-object is pointless.

- For a large program having a large development team, it may be easier to tell other team-members (via documentation) to subscribe to events they need. The alternative is to ask each member of the team if he needs your events, which consumes much more of your time, and you must do it again when new members are added to the team. Using the analogy of a restaurant, it's easier for you to offer a buffet than to ask each customer what he wants to order.

It is tempting to make the distributor more sophisticated by allowing subscribers to choose which events they want, turning the distributor into a subscription service for objects wanting to listen to broadcasters. Instead of adding this complication, I suggest using a separate instance of the distributor for each kind of event. Hence, each instance of an indirect distributor listens to only one publisher.

Discussion about Distributors

A word of warning: Use the Indirect Distributor pattern as little as possible, because its indirect notices are very hard to follow. Ordinarily, an indirect notice is sent using a single stored pointer. But an indirect distributor contains an array holding an unknown number of pointers, which the code loops through, making it difficult to trace calls in a debugger and nearly impossible to follow calls in source-code. This pattern badly violates the Indirection principle of good coupling, making learnability plunge. Use the Direct Distributor pattern instead whenever feasible.

Figure 7.12 shows an example of the Direct Distributor pattern. This design is for a program that controls a specialized robot used on an assembly line consisting of a clamp that can open or close, which is rotated by a wrist, which is at the end of two arm-segments, each with an elbow. Some movements are performed for a given amount of time, and all movements are subject to time-outs in case of a mechanical blockage. The *Timer* supplies *centiSec* notices 100 times per second to all objects that need to monitor time.

Before you decide to employ either the Direct or Indirect Distributor pattern, be sure to read about the Watcher pattern described below. It eliminates the problems of multiple unrelated dependencies or indirection found in the Distributor patterns, and you might decide that it's a better approach for your design.

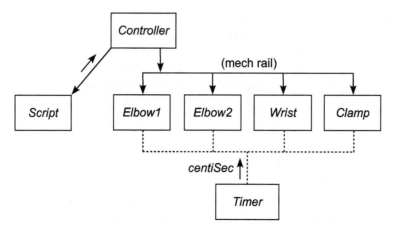

Figure 7.12: Example of a Direct Distributor

7.2.3   Watcher Pattern

In a military division or a kingdom, a watcher is a person who observes an area and reports any activity to a commander. The analogous object in software listens to some source of events such as an I/O port, a device or even a script of events. It sends them as notices to a high-level object, which in turn might forward them as commands down to action objects. A watcher object does not store, filter or alter the incoming events or messages that it sees. Rather, it immediately relays them unchanged up to its superior. In contrast, the Secretary pattern described later in this chapter (on page 195) stores incoming chores, and releases them according to some criterion.

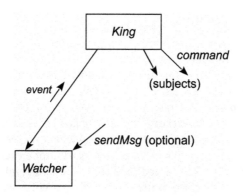

Figure 7.13: Watcher pattern

Figure 7.13 shows the Watcher pattern. The *Watcher* object sends the events it observes up to *King*. I chose call its superior *King* because in most software, such notices go up to a high-level object, probably the subman over a subsystem or the topmost controller over the entire program. You should name it after the program's role. This graph also shows that *Watcher* contains an optional *sendMsg* command. A watcher often listens to an I/O port, and *sendMsg* is used for outputting data.

The high-level object may forward the notices back down to worker objects as commands. After reading that, you should be asking, "How can a notice be turned into a command?" It depends on what's in the notice. If a packet arrives at an I/O port, the watcher over that port will send the packet to its superior as a notice that says, "This packet arrived for you." That superior will read what's in the packet, and may discover that it contains a command such as "Close the clamp." In this situation, the *Watcher* is serving as a mailman that merely relays I/O messages to its superior. This interesting topic of conveying commands inside of notices is discussed in detail in Section 3.13.6 (page 72). The superior receiving such an imperative notice may give it to another subordinate as a command.

For example, suppose you work for a manufacturer of paint which is writing a group of programs that control and monitor the equipment used for paint production. Programs running in the same computer communicate with each other with messages sent using IPC (inter-process communication), and those running in different computers communicate over Ethernet connections. The details of communicating with other programs are hidden by a low-level object named *Intercom* which can send and receive messages to/from any other program or computer.

Your program is called *ChemMonitor* because it monitors the levels of various chemicals, their ratios, temperatures, and pH levels, and adjusts controls based on these measurements. It also maintains statistics on such data. The primary worker-objects in your program correspond to the critical locations on the production line, which are *Solvents*, where the solvents are mixed, *Pigments*, where pigments are mixed, and *FinalMix*, which produces the resulting paint.

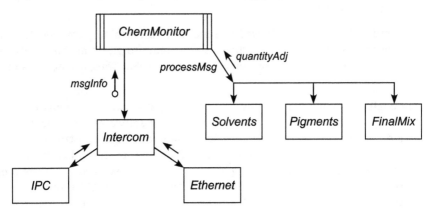

Figure 7.14: Example of a watcher

Figure 7.14 is the IDAR graph of this program. *Intercom* and its subordinates are responsible for communicating with other programs. *ChemMonitor* controls the entire program, which includes routing incoming messages to the correct worker-objects like a boss delegating incoming chores to his employees. Each worker-object can send a notice back to *ChemMonitor* recommending adjustments of various quantities on the production line. *ChemMonitor* forwards these notices to *Intercom* as commands. By the way, the *msgInfo* notice is indirect to gain portability, as *Intercom* will be used in several programs.

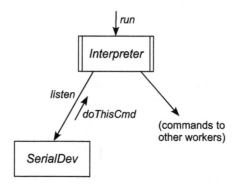

Figure 7.15: A common kind of watcher

The design fragment in Figure 7.15 shows a common situation utilizing the Watcher pattern. At start-up, the *Interpreter* was commanded to run, so it initialized itself and in turn commanded *SerialDev* to listen for arriving packets on the serial I/O port. An arriving packet contains a command which *Interpreter* performs. When a packet arrives, *SerialDev* notifies *Interpreter* using the *doThisCmd* notice, and then *Interpreter* performs the command in the packet.

The Watcher pattern has these advantages over the Distributor pattern:

Learnability Notice-calls in an indirect distributor are difficult to follow. Because a watcher has only one notice-call, it's not hidden in a data-structure, making it easier to follow.

Flexibility A watcher is allowed to send notices containing commands to its superior, exactly as a boss authorizes a secretary to give him commands (see the Secretary pattern in Section 7.2.4 on page 195). Thus, a watcher is more flexible than a distributor.

Simplicity A design that employs the Watcher pattern can be simpler than one using the Distributor, resulting in lower cost of software. A watcher's events are forwarded down the usual chain of command. But a distributor creates new communication-paths to the destination-objects, increasing the number of communication-paths among objects. That increase makes software more complex, and thus harder to learn and maintain. Figure 7.16 shows the extra complexity produced by the additional lines of communication created by making *Intercom* a distributor. Compare this graph with Figure 7.14.

On the other hand, a disadvantage of the Watcher pattern compared with the Distributor pattern is that it can be more complex instead of simpler, contrary to the claim of simplicity made above. This additional complexity occurs when there are multiple layers of hierarchy between the watcher's superior and the objects to receive the notices. This situation is shown in Figure 7.17.

This graph shows a notice passing through two layers of tramp-methods before reaching the desired object, called *Target*. Sending the notice directly to *Target* using a distributor object would have been more straightforward. We see that there is a trade-

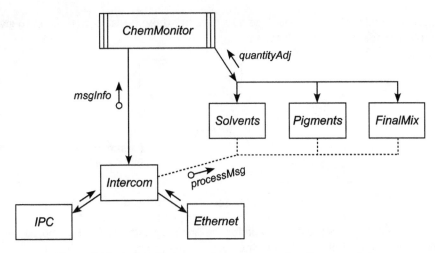

Figure 7.16: A distributor can be more complex than a watcher

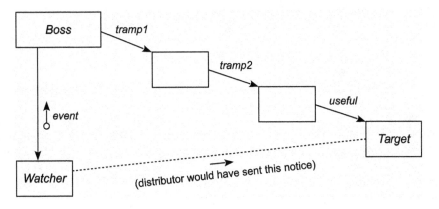

Figure 7.17: Tramp-methods needed for a watcher

off in the advantages and disadvantages of the Distributor and Watcher patterns. You should weigh both approaches and select the one that is simpler.

A warning: Apply the imaginary-arrow test to any watcher to ensure that you are not laundering commands. See Section 3.13.7 on page 74 for details.

7.2.4 Secretary Pattern

The Secretary pattern is interesting because it appears to reverse roles, having a worker command its boss. Imagine a traditional secretary from the 1950s. She maintains the boss's schedule. One day, at a few minutes before 10:00, she tells the boss, "Go meet with Mr. Figby at 10:00." To all appearances, she commanded her boss. That sentence starts with a verb and is imperative. Did she command him? She also deals with customers for the boss, and one day, an important customer comes in wanting to talk with him. She tells her boss, "Talk to Mister Bigdeal now." Did she command him? Consider that the boss previously told her to manage the schedule and to handle

initial contact with customers. The boss gave her these tasks, expecting her to give
him such orders. So it is with software.

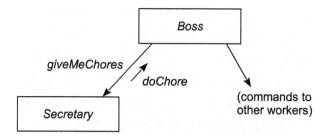

Figure 7.18: Secretary pattern

Figure 7.18 shows the IDAR graph for the Secretary pattern. The *Boss* object delegated the responsibilities of acquiring and tracking its chores to the *Secretary*. As is
true of the 1950s secretary, these responsibilities often are maintaining a schedule
or interfacing to a source of chores or both. In addition, a secretary can function well
as a resource-manager. In general, a secretary object is responsible for:

- Acquiring chores from other objects, which may include its boss
- Storing those chores
- Releasing those chores to the boss when they can or should be performed

One or more objects in the system can create chores that the boss needs to do.
These chore-makers are designed to either command or notify the secretary of new
chores, placing the chore-makers above and below the secretary in the graph, as you'll
see in the examples below. The secretary and chore-makers might have been delegated chores from the boss. Or they might receive chores from an outside source. The
examples below show both cases.

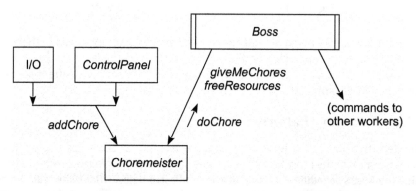

Figure 7.19: Secretary allocates resources to chores

In Figure 7.19, at start-up, *Boss* commands *Choremeister* to "Give me chores."
Chores may be submitted to the system using an I/O or the control panel, both of
which command *Choremeister* to *addChore*. Chores are stored inside *Choremeister*.

When the resources required by a chore become available, *Choremeister* informs *Boss* by sending it a *doChore* notice containing the required resources. Chores might be given to *Boss* out of chronological order. *Boss* performs the chore, and when it's done, *Boss* commands *Choremeister* to free those resources by sending it a *freeResources* command. If chores are queued, this freeing is likely to cause *Choremeister* to send another *doChore* notice to *Boss*.

Because the chores in Figure 7.19 are created outside the *Boss* and *Choremeister*, you should apply the imaginary-arrow test (see page 74) to check for the misdeed of laundering commands. Draw an imaginary arrow from the source of the chores to the *Boss*, verifying that it points down. In this example, the source of chores is a human pressing buttons on the control panel, or another computer sending a packet over the I/O. The source is outside the computer, and you should verify that that source has greater authority than the receiving object.

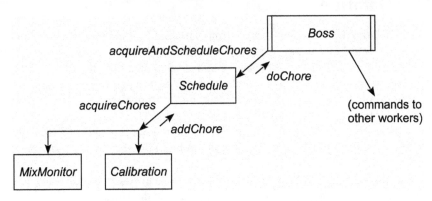

Figure 7.20: Secretary maintains a schedule

Figure 7.20 portrays another style of the Secretary pattern which is similar to the original example of the 1950s secretary. The secretary is the *Schedule* object which maintains a schedule of chores to be done. These are given to *Boss* at the appropriate times using the familiar *doChore* notice. This design comes from a system that mixes chemicals, and certain chores must be done at certain times, including checking mix-ratios and calibrating sensors. So the *MixMonitor* and *Calibration* objects submit chores (with intervals in them) as *addChore* notices to *Schedule*.

You need not apply the imaginary-arrow test in this case because all jobs were delegated, originating with *Boss*. The *Boss* delegated acquiring and scheduling chores to *Schedule*, which in turn delegated acquiring chores to two subordinates. The role of their *addChore* notices is "tells me that chore C must be done every N minutes." The role of *doChore* is "tells me that chore C must be done now." Employing the Secretary pattern always consists of subordinate(s) storing chores, and sending an imperative notice to a boss whenever a chore must be done. The topic of imperative notices is discussed in Section 3.13.6 on page 72.

In general, the Secretary pattern can be used for any object that receives a series of chores to perform, and those chores can only be started when specific conditions have been met. These conditions include any combination of:

- Availability of resources required by the chore, such as money, memory, CPU-time and devices
- The time at which the chore must be done (scheduling)
- Occurrence of prerequisite events
- Physical conditions, such as a temperature being in-range
- Selection of a chore based on its priority

A secretary may also queue chores. However, if queuing is all you need, it can be done more simply by using the Inbox pattern (see page 207). Finally, a secretary is allowed to reject incoming or stored chores based on some criterion of acceptability, feasibility, ageing, system-load, etc.

7.3   Dataflows

What is a dataflow? How does it differ from variables that are passed as parameters, or saved in fields? A dataflow is commonly considered to be a large amount of data that is processed identically. The source of such data is often outside the software. Examples of common dataflows include: pixels from a digital camera; financial data, such as commodity-prices; repetitive measurements from a sensor; an audio or video stream; and blocks of data sent to/from a server or an I/O device. All such data is large and is processed identically. As a reminder, the Dataflows principle of good coupling requires that all dataflows be drawn on your graph in order to make those couplings easier to follow.

In your design, you will create objects which perform stages of processing on such data. The question you face is: How can you pass such data among your objects? The following four patterns should accommodate any design you wish to create:

Peer-to-Peer	Passed between peers under a common superior
Micromanaged	Routed through a mutual superior (micromanager)
Piped	Routed through a mutual subordinate (pipe)
Vertical	Passed between superior and subordinate

7.3.1   Peer-to-Peer Dataflow Pattern

This popular form of dataflow uses peer-to-peer notices between workers under the same boss. The boss does not participate in individual transfers in the dataflow. Each worker (peer) is one processing-stage, as shown in Figure 7.21.

The peers themselves implement the dataflow. The sequence of events for passing one buffer between *Stage1* and *Stage2* is:

1. From some source of data, *Stage1* fills a buffer.
2. *Stage1* sends it to *Stage2* using the *xferBuf* notice (i.e., it calls *xferBuf*).
3. *Stage2* processes the buffer and is done with it.
4. *Stage2* informs *Stage1* that the buffer is now unused by sending the *availBuf* notice to *Stage1*.

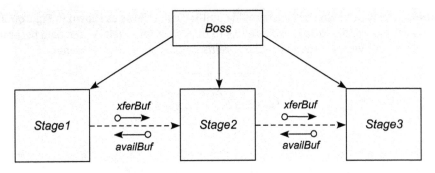

Figure 7.21: Peer-to-peer dataflow, push-style

The dashed arrows represent the effective dataflows. The notices are indirect, as signified by the bubbles on their arrows. I recommend employing such indirection to prevent unrelated stages from having dependencies on each other. But if you are certain that a pair of stages will always and only communicate with each other, then hard-coded notices may be used.

The *availBuf* notice may be omitted in some cases. For example, it could be made a rider notice when *xferBuf* returns. In other words, when the *xferBuf* notice returns, the caller knows that the buffer is unused. This design is simpler, but it precludes concurrency in the two stages, unless buffers are copied to internal storage.

The Peer-to-Peer Dataflow pattern is useful for simple dataflows where dealing with buffers adds little complexity to the stages involved. Therefore, I recommend that this pattern be employed when a single buffer is passed back and forth between a pair of stages, or two buffers are handled in a ping-pong fashion (alternating), or when the writer stage maintains a queue of buffers.

Between any two adjacent stages, I assume that the writer stage (on the left) outputs data to the reader stage (on the right), so that the resulting dataflow proceeds left to right, as is portrayed in Figure 7.21. Having defined the terms "writer" and "reader", ping-pong buffers (also called swing buffers) follow these two rules:

1. The writer stage always owns one buffer and the reader owns the other.
2. When the writer stage is done writing and the reader stage is done reading, the ownership roles are swapped, and processing resumes.

You can implement ping-pong buffers by having the writer stage send an *xferBuf* notice to the reader after filling its buffer. When the reader stage is done reading its buffer, it will cause the call to *xferBuf* to return (which is a rider notice), and then each stage will know to operate on the other buffer.

Push- and Pull-Styles

A dataflow is a push-style if the writer of the data sends it without first being requested to do so by the reader of the data. Hence, the writer pushes the data into the reader. With a pull-style dataflow, the reader must first ask for data before the writer will send any. We think of the reader as "pulling" the data out of the writer.

The dataflows shown in Figure 7.21 are push-style because the writer stage (on the left) takes the initiative and forces the data into the reader on the right. This

arrangement can be reversed to provide pull-style dataflows as shown in Figure 7.22.
A reader first sends a *giveMeData* notice to the writer on its left. When data becomes
available, the writer responds with a *hereItIs* notice containing the buffer.

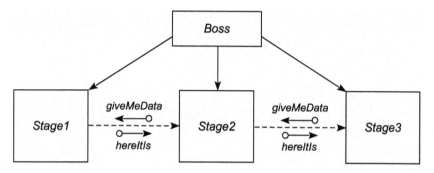

Figure 7.22: Peer-to-peer dataflow, pull-style

Which style to use (push or pull) depends on where any buffering is done, and
whether the source or destination of the data can be stopped at will. If the source is
a file or a device that can be stopped quickly, then a pull-style will be suitable. But
if the source is an I/O device that provides data outside the control of your software,
then your source is not stoppable and you should use a push-style dataflow, unless
you provide buffering in the source.

Finishing

Pay careful attention to how a dataflow is terminated. At some point, the leftmost
stage will finish. Then what should the objects do? Here are some ideas:

Boss Controlled The leftmost stage notifies the boss that it's done by sending
it a *finished* notice. The boss then sequentially tells the following stages to
finish. Each such *finish* command causes a stage to complete the processing of
its buffers and send all of them to the next stage. When this flushing of internal
buffers is complete, the stage sends a *finished* notice to the boss, so it'll know
to proceed to the next stage.

Chaining The leftmost stage tells the next stage (in a notice) that it's done. Such
a *done* notice is identical to the *finish* command described above. When any
stage is finished, it notifies the next stage. As a result, a chain of *finish* notices
proceeds left to right. The rightmost stage notifies the boss that it's done. At
that point, the boss knows that all stages are quiescent.

Final Flag Each buffer contains a *final* flag indicating whether it's the final buffer
in the sequence. When a stage sees that *final* is true in an input-buffer, it will
flush its own output, setting *final* to true in its final output-buffer. When the
rightmost stage sees that *final* is true, it cleans up and notifies the boss.

Which of these solutions do you prefer? The chaining solution resembles temporal
chaining, which is described in Section 6.8 (page 147). The boss controlled solution
causes the boss to micromanage part of the process (finishing), but not the entire

process, which is inconsistent. The final-flag solution is elegant, but it requires that the *final* flag be present and set correctly in the headers of all buffers.

7.3.2   Micromanaged Dataflow Pattern

The description of the Peer-to-Peer Dataflow pattern above ended with the note that if the boss monitors each step of finishing the flow, it becomes a micromanager. The obvious evolution of this approach is to allow the boss to control *all* buffer transfers, not only the final ones. Such an approach yields the Micromanaged Dataflow pattern, and its IDAR graph is shown in Figure 7.23.

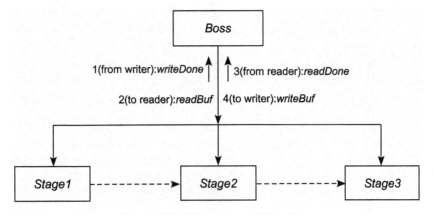

Figure 7.23: Micromanaged dataflow

All notices are sent to the boss, never to a peer. Suppose a pair of stages, called writer and reader, transfer a buffer. Each such transfer involves four messages, which are numbered in the IDAR graph and explained below:

1. When writer is done filling a buffer, it sends a *writeDone* notice to *Boss*.
2. *Boss* tells reader to read that buffer (the *readBuf* command).
3. When reader is done reading it, reader sends a *readDone* notice to *Boss*.
4. *Boss* tells writer to fill that buffer (the *writeBuf* command).

Although there are twice as many messages involved in the dataflow, this pattern has the following advantages over the Peer-to-Peer Dataflow pattern:

- The stages are completely independent, making it easier to change the stages, or to mix buffer-transfer protocols among stages.
- Peer-to-peer notices are eliminated, thus removing the complication of passing addresses needed for indirect notices, and also eliminating controversy.
- Debugging is easier because you can easily monitor all activity in one place: the buffer-transfer methods in the boss.
- Error-handling is simpler because all of it is done in one place—the boss. Upon error, a stage notifies the boss, which knows how to shut down the pipeline. Individual stages don't need to concern themselves with set-up and tear-down.

Despite these advantages, you must weigh the extra complexity that is added to a boss to manage the various transfers in the pipeline. Fortunately, the amount of added code is typically small. Perhaps the main disadvantage of the Micromanaged Dataflow pattern is its *perceived* increase of complexity in the boss.

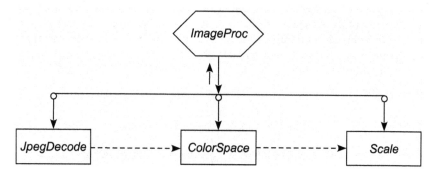

Figure 7.24: Image-processing subsystem with micromanaged dataflows

Figure 7.24 is the IDAR graph of an actual image-processing subsystem which you have probably used unwittingly because it is hidden inside of Microsoft Windows®. The pipeline is dynamic, so the number of stages and their contents can differ in each instantiation, which is why the commands are indirect. Every stage both inputs and outputs its buffers from/to the boss, so the boss contains some carefully written buffer-management code. The beauty of this design is that the buffer-management algorithms only needed to be implemented once (in the subman, *ImageProc*), simplifying every object in the library of available stages.

7.3.3   Piped Dataflow Pattern

The Micromanaged Dataflow pattern described in the prior section added some buffer management code to the boss. You can achieve greater flexibility and simpler bosses if such code is moved into a separate object devoted solely to buffer transfers. This arrangement is the Piped Dataflow pattern, and data flows through the pipe object like water. Figure 7.25 shows dataflows using a typical *Pipe* object. Because this example pipe was designed to be as general purpose as possible, there are *six* messages involved in transferring one buffer from a writer (on the left) to a reader (on the right):

1. *Writer* commands *Pipe* to give it an empty buffer.
2. After filling it, *Writer* commands *Pipe* to accept the now-full buffer.
3. *Pipe* notifies *Reader* that a newly filled buffer is available.
4. *Reader* commands *Pipe* to give it a filled buffer.
5. After reading it, *Reader* commands *Pipe* to accept the now-empty buffer.
6. *Pipe* notifies *Writer* that a newly emptied buffer is available.

When starting, *Boss* commands *Pipe* to *start* a new session, and this call to *start* is given the address and size of memory to use. *Pipe* is also given pointers to the methods to call for the indirect *writerAvail* and *readerAvail* notices.

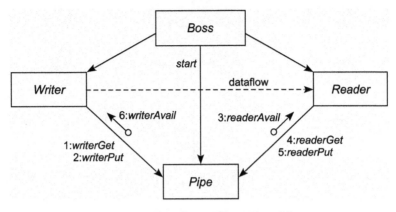

Figure 7.25: Dataflow using a *Pipe* object

As before, we need to decide how to finish a dataflow. *Pipe* itself can handle it for us. When *Writer* finishes, it commands the *Pipe* to close. That causes *Pipe* to wait until *Reader* has fetched and returned all buffers queued for it. Then *Pipe* notifies *Reader* that the pipe has closed, causing *Reader* to finish.

While this *Pipe* is very general, the six messages per transfer make it clumsy to use. This protocol can be simplified. For example, the *get* and *put* commands can be combined, so that returning a buffer also fetches the next. This idea also introduces a couple of complications, such as what to do when there are no more buffers. If null addresses are used to signify "no buffer", then the number of messages per buffer-transfer drops to four, as shown in Figure 7.26. Having only four messages per buffer-transfer makes this interface more appealing.

1. *Writer* commands *Pipe* to accept the old (filled) buffer and to return a new (empty) buffer back to *Writer*.

2. *Pipe* notifies *Reader* that a newly filled buffer is available.

3. *Reader* commands *Pipe* to accept the old (empty) buffer and to return a new (filled) buffer back to *Reader*.

4. *Pipe* notifies *Writer* that a newly emptied buffer is available.

These pipe-based designs are neither push-style nor pull-style because the pipe separates the writer and reader, so neither forces data to/from the other.

You can create your own pipe object with any interface you want. For example, you might want the pipe to block the caller when a requested buffer is not available instead of immediately returning a null address for the buffer. I believe that the *Pipe* interface shown in Figure 7.26 is a good compromise between flexibility and simplicity, so I'll recommend it as a good place to start.

7.3.4 Vertical Dataflow Pattern

All of the dataflows described above proceeded horizontally between two more more stages, like an assembly line. Data can also flow vertically between a superior and a subordinate, as shown in Figure 7.27.

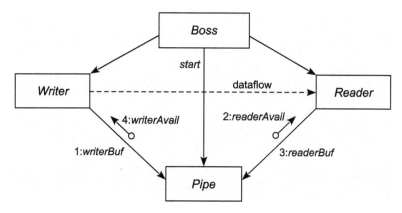

Figure 7.26: Simpler *Pipe* object

The pull-style dataflows in this figure use the same messages as did the pull-style peer-to-peer dataflows shown in Figure 7.22. The reader first sends a *giveMeData* notice to the writer. When data becomes available, the writer responds with a *hereItIs* notice. Because data can flow up or down, the reader and writer may be the superior or subordinate. These pull-style dataflows can be simplified if you allow the calls to *giveMeData* to block the calling thread. Such blocking allows the *hereItIs* notice to be a rider that is carried on the return of the call to *giveMeData*. In this arrangement, you simply call *giveMeData* and it returns the data.

Vertical push-style dataflows are very simple, using the single method *takeData* which is a notice (for upward flow) or a command (for downward flow).

Vertical dataflows may be less common than horizontal dataflows, but they have their uses, which include networking stacks, communicating with I/O ports, and printing. Figure 7.28 shows the commands and notices used in these dataflow examples. Figure 7.28(a) shows an input-only I/O port, which I suppose should be called an "I" instead of an "I/O". Data flows upward, but I changed the messages from the prior discussion. In this example, when a packet arrives at the port, the *Port* sends a notice to *Dispatcher* telling it that data is available, but this notice does *not* contain the data. The reason for excluding the data is that the *Dispatcher* might not be ready to take it. When the *Dispatcher* is ready, it calls *giveMeData* which returns the data in a rider notice (when the method returns). Because the data is only transferred when the reader (*Dispatcher*) requests it, this is a pull-style dataflow.

Figure 7.28(b) shows two layers in a networking stack. Data flows in both directions, and both use simple push-style flows involving a call to *takeData*. Such a stack typically involves multiple buffers, so these push-style transfers imply that each layer has its own queue of buffers.

Figure 7.28(c) shows *ScoreSheet* commanding *Printer* to print the score-sheet. This interface is the simplest possible: push-style from superior to subordinate. Because multiple buffers will be transferred, *Printer* must either queue the buffers or block until they've been transferred to the operating system's printer-queue.

As with horizontal dataflows, you can choose between push-style and pull-style based on buffering and whether a source or destination can be stopped instantly.

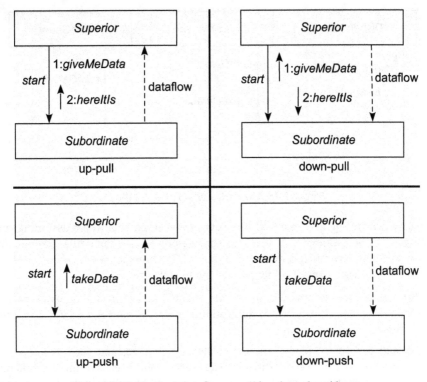

Figure 7.27: Vertical dataflows, pull/push and up/down

Finally, remember to bias yourself in favor of the simplest approach. It's all too easy to select a complex approach, such as the Piped Dataflow pattern, when something simple such as peer-to-peer ping-pong buffers would work just as well.

7.4 Threads

Around the year 2004, microprocessors hit a speed-wall, and have stayed there ever since. Unless there's a breakthrough in electronics, clock-speeds of microprocessors will never rise much above 3.5 GHz. This limit is caused by the heat generated from switching transistors at high speed. Making transistors smaller has little effect on heat produced per unit area on the silicon die. Manufacturers are putting more transistors in their chips, but running them at around the same speed. As a result, they are forced to increase the parallelism in their designs. One way they increase parallelism is by executing multiple instructions in each clock-cycle. This approach has been used a good deal, and it probably has little additional room for improvement. Another approach is to put more cores in a chip. If the operating system supports it, multiple threads can run simultaneously, one thread per core.

As a result of microprocessors having more cores instead of more speed per core, concurrency (parallelism) has become more important in software designs. If performance might be a problem, you should try to design your software to run on multiple

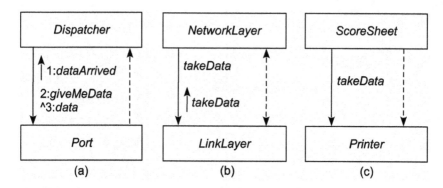

Figure 7.28: Examples of vertical dataflows

cores by performing multiple CPU-intensive chores in parallel. (I am assuming your software will be running on a multi-core processor.) A reasonable rule to remember when deciding how much concurrency to have is "a chore per core".

There are three terms used for parallelism in software:

Process A process runs within its own isolated and protected address-space in memory. Inter-process communication is more awkward and slower than inter-thread communication.

Thread Multiple threads can run inside of a process, and each can share its address space with other threads in its process. But threads running in different processes cannot interact with each other except by using clumsy inter-process communication.

Task A task refers to either a process or a thread. This term is ambiguous.

Both processes and threads have their own stacks and may run on multiple cores concurrently. An active object contains a process or a thread, and is represented in an IDAR graph with one or two extra vertical lines at the left and right sides of its rectangle or hexagon, as you saw earlier in Figure 3.19. An example of an active object in a design is the *MAC* in Figure 3.15.

Because the term "thread" is most popular, and because threads are also the most popular form of concurrency used in software, I capitulated and use the term "thread" throughout this book. The word "task" would have been more suitable for this section due to its ambiguity, but using it would have meant going against most modern usage of this terminology.

This section presents the following thread-related patterns:

Inbox	One thread fed by a message-queue
Multiwait	One thread can wait for multiple events
Shared Thread	Sharing a thread among multiple objects
Thread Pool	Multiple threads allocatable by their boss

The Inbox pattern is the most popular, but you will find the others to be useful in some situations. Also, the Multiwait and Shared Thread patterns simplify designs by reducing the number of threads.

7.4.1 Inbox Pattern

The Inbox pattern is the primary technique for thread-bridging, which simply means performing a chore on a different thread. Using the analogy of a corporation, imagine a worker in a service-group who sits at his desk. When somebody needs some work done, he fills out a piece of paper and places it into this worker's inbox at the side of his desk. The worker performs the chores in chronological order.

The software analogue consists of an object containing a thread that fetches messages from a message-queue. The public methods of the object add entries to the queue, each requesting that an action be performed. Often the method containing the thread simply calls private worker-methods within the object to do the actual work. Figure 7.29 shows this design.

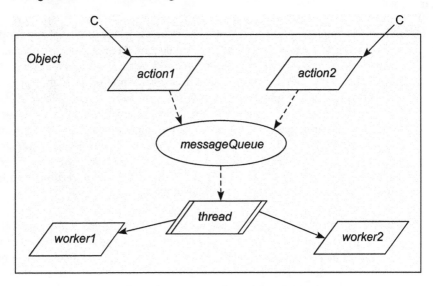

Figure 7.29: Inbox pattern

```
void YourClass::thread() {
    while (true) { // infinite loop
        msg = messageQueue.getNextMsg();
        switch (msg.action) {
            case ACTION_1_NUM: ...
            case ACTION_2_NUM: ...
        }
    }
}
```

Listing 7.2: Main thread for Inbox pattern

You should use the Inbox pattern when (1) you don't want to block the callers of your public methods (commands or notices), and (2) it's possible that one of your public methods could be called when you're not ready to handle it. Since you want your methods to be nonblocking (i.e., they must return immediately), you need the thread-bridging feature of the Inbox pattern. Each command or notice is not processed on the caller's thread, but on a thread internal to your object, which is creatively labeled *thread* in Figure 7.29.

Each entry in *messageQueue* usually consists of an action-number followed by the data for the message. The code in the thread is usually an infinite loop which fetches a message, and then executes a `switch` or `case` statement, as illustrated in the code in Listing 7.2.

This pattern is very powerful, and can be used for almost all cases of multithreading. In addition, it's convenient to use. Due to its power and convenience, this pattern is very popular, so much so that most multithreaded code you'll see is structured like this. Unfortunately, there are a couple of problems with this pattern, the first of which can be severe:

Overflow The queue can overflow. You need to be especially careful of any conditions that might cause a flood of messages to be sent. At program start-up, many messages might be sent to your object before your thread is given a chance to run, causing your queue to overflow. Or perhaps some other higher-priority thread can run for a while, preventing yours from running and allowing your queue to overflow. Or perhaps another thread might block for a while, and when it finally runs again, it might pour its backlog onto your object. Also, any object that sends a message periodically will overflow your queue if you stop your thread in a debugger, making debugging difficult. You will be irritated when you discover that stopping at a breakpoint forces you to rerun the entire program because the message-queue always overflows.

Overuse It is so convenient and powerful that it is overused. Folks habitually use this pattern even when queuing is not necessary and simpler approaches would work just as well. Perhaps they are lazy. But it's more likely that most developers are not aware of alternative designs. The Multiwait pattern covered next allows you to eliminate the queue, making overflow impossible, and it also reduces the number of threads you'll need.

7.4.2 Multiwait Pattern

The purpose of the Multiwait pattern is to reduce the number of threads in your design. The problem is that developers tend to create numerous specialized threads. For example, one thread will wait on a high-priority message-queue, another on a low-priority message-queue, and still another on some event. The Multiwait pattern allows one thread to do the work of all of these specialized threads. The IDAR graph for the Multiwait design pattern is shown in Figure 7.30.

This design looks almost identical to the Inbox pattern, but its operation is rather different. The private fields *work1* and *work2* correspond to chores the thread can perform, and each contains a data-structure indicating (1) whether some work needs to be done, and (2) the details of that work. You can think of these work-fields as items on a check-list of chores around the house, where you're allowed to do your chores out of order.

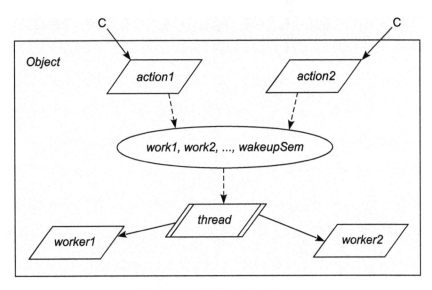

Figure 7.30: Multiwait pattern

The thread in the Multiwait pattern runs in an infinite loop, where each iteration does the following:

1. Wait on the wake-up semaphore. A command or notice releases the semaphore, awakening the thread. The semaphore-release tells the thread that it might have a chore to do.

2. Examine each work-field. If it indicates that there is work to do, then do that chore and clear its work-indication.

For example, let's say your object has multiple bosses giving it commands, and that it also has multiple subordinates giving it notices. In order to respond to bosses quickly, you want to have *two* message-queues called *bossMsgs* and *subMsgs*, with the *bossMsgs* queue having higher priority. In addition, a tick-command comes in once per second which you use for monitoring status. You need to watch three things. How can one thread do all that? First, let's declare the fields:

```
MsgQueueT     bossMsgs;  // messages from bosses
MsgQueueT     subMsgs;   // messages from subordinates
volatile bool tickedOff; // true if tick occurred
```

These are the "work" fields described above, and each iteration of the thread will check these sequentially.

Listing 7.3 contains the code. Notice the careful logic around the checking of the two queues. Each time the *subMsgs* queue is checked, the *bossMsgs* queue is rechecked in case a message from a boss arrived while processing a message from a subordinate. With this logic, a boss-message waits for only as long as it takes to process *one* subordinate-message (plus a tick-message). Also, I want to stress that within your command and notice methods, it's crucial that releasing the semaphore be the *last* thing the method does.

```
void MultiMan::commandFromBoss(int stuff) { // public command
    bossMsgs.enqueue(stuff);
    wakeupSem.release();
}

void MultiMan::noticeFromSub(int stuff) { // public notice
    subMsgs.enqueue(stuff);
    wakeupSem.release();
}

void MultiMan::tickCmd() { // public command
    tickedOff = true;
    wakeupSem.release();
}

void MultiMan::thread() { // private
    while (true) { // infinite loop
        wakeupSem.wait();

        while (true) {
            while (! bossMsgs.empty()) {
                // (code to fetch msg from bossMsgs and process it)
            }
            if (subMsgs.empty()) {
                break; // both queues are now empty
            }
            // (code to fetch msg from subMsgs and process it)
        }

        if (tickedOff) {
            tickedOff = false;
            // (code to process tick)
        }
    }
}
```

Listing 7.3: Code to handle two queues and a timer

The Multiwait pattern allows one thread to process any combination of messages, queued or not, from any number of sources. Furthermore, if you use boolean fields for various messages such as ticks, they cannot overflow a message-queue.

But the Multiwait pattern has a disadvantage. The separate work fields are not processed in chronological order. Instead, they are processed in priority-order, where the priority is determined by the order the items are checked in the thread's loop. All items needing to be processed in chronological order must be placed in the same message-queue. In practice, this disadvantage is minor, and is outweighed by the advantage of having fewer threads.

An operating system that supported waiting on multiple semaphores and/or message-queues simultaneously would be ideal for the Multiwait pattern. Thoughtfully, Windows offers *WaitForMultipleObjects*, and Linux offers *select* and *poll* which can be used in conjunction with files, pipes, sockets, semaphores (*eventfd*), timers (*timerfd*), and signals (*signalfd*). These system-calls can wait on multiple events from multiple kinds of event-sources, such as both message-queues and semaphores. They simplify the implementation of the Multiwait pattern, and provide more flexibility because you can wait on events that are generated outside of your object.

7.4.3 Shared Thread Pattern

In multithreaded systems, there are situations in which multiple objects need to execute in the same thread, instead of allowing each object to have its own thread. These situations include:

Conserving memory If there are many objects that can run concurrently with others, allocating a separate thread to each may consume too much RAM in a small embedded system. Each thread allocates a task control block (TCB), which is dozens of bytes, and a stack consuming several kilobytes.

Mutual exclusion due to shared resource A group of objects may need exclusive access to a shared resource. Using a semaphore is the classic solution to this problem. Another solution is the Resourceful Boss pattern described on page 180. Sometimes the simplest solution is to prevent concurrency among such objects by having them share a single thread.

Mutual exclusion due to nature of design You might have a group of objects which must run their commands to completion before another object in the group is allowed to run. This situation arises when a partially completed command leaves the system in an indeterminate or inconsistent state, which would cause a failure if another object in the group were to run. A simple solution in this situation is to force all objects in the group to share a single thread.

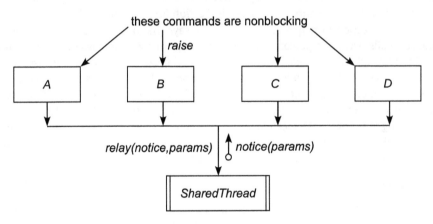

Figure 7.31: Shared Thread pattern

Figure 7.31 shows the commands and notices among objects using the Shared Thread pattern. Commands sent to objects *A-D* do not block. As a result, these objects must perform their commands on some other thread, which in this case is the shared thread. As you guessed, the *SharedThread* object contains the shared thread, and it probably also has a message-queue like the Inbox pattern (page 207), although this queue is not required by this pattern. A command is forwarded down to *SharedThread* as the *relay* command, and when the thread is available, the indirect notice (passed in *relay*) is called on the shared thread, thus providing the thread to a superior of

SharedThread. I know that description was cryptic. Below, I describe this sequence of actions in more detail, using the *raise* command in object *B* as an example:

1. Some object calls *B.raise*.

2. The *B.raise* command either saves its parameters in member fields inside *B*, or packages them in *params*. It then calls *relay* in *SharedThread* with the following parameters:
   notice – the address of a notice-method located inside *B*.
   params – any additional data associated with the *raise* command.

3. The *relay* command in *SharedThread* puts its two parameters (*notice,params*) onto its message-queue.

4. When the main loop of the thread fetches this message from the queue, it calls *notice* with the *params* data.

5. This notice-method is located inside object *B*, so *B* now has exclusive control of the thread.

6. The notice performs the actions in the role of the *raise* command.

In this pattern, the notice conforms to the IDAR rules because (1) it conveys information ("you now control the thread"), as the Identify rule prescribes, and (2) it covertly performs the *raise* command's actions on its behalf, as the Aid rule allows. If you wish to think of it as an imperative notice, then this design is an example of echoing a boss's command as discussed in Section 3.13.6 on page 72.

The Indirection principle of good coupling says that direct calls are preferable to indirect calls because a person following couplings in the code does not know where an indirect call will go. This pattern is an exception to this principle because, when a reader sees a call to the *relay* command, he knows that it will result in a call to the notice specified in a parameter of *relay*. So he'll go to that notice in the source-code and continue learning the code without hindrance due to the indirection.

Taking the address of a method is only one among several techniques for sending a notice indirectly. Another is to use a delegate in C# or Python. The various techniques for sending indirect notices are described in Section 6.11.3 on page 160.

Shared Thread or Inbox?

The Shared Thread pattern and the Inbox pattern both allow one thread to perform multiple actions. For example, Figure 7.29 shows two actions that a thread using the Inbox pattern can perform. The Inbox pattern also has the same advantages of conserving memory and providing mutual exclusion. So why would you choose the more complicated Shared Thread pattern?

The Shared Thread pattern has the big advantage of supporting multiple objects. These are labeled *A* through *D* in Figure 7.31. But the Inbox pattern forces all commands to be located in a single object. Merging the interfaces of multiple objects together into a single object might not be feasible due to poor resulting cohesion or for other reasons, making it undesirable to use the Inbox pattern. Such a situation compels you to use the Shared Thread pattern.

Race-Condition

Finally, I should warn you about a race-condition that's easy to create. Examine the code shown in Listing 7.4, and ask yourself what is wrong with it. This code is the *raise* command in object *B* in Figure 7.31, and the corresponding notice *raiseNotice* which does the actual work on behalf of the *raise* command.

```
volatile int distance; // private member field in class

void B::raise (int distanceParam) {
    SharedThread.relay (&raiseNotice, NULL);
    distance = distanceParam; // save in private field
}

void B::raiseNotice (NoticeMsg& params) {
    motorCounts = distance * ENCODER_RATIO; // convert units
    // ... code which moves motor ...
}
```

Listing 7.4: A race-condition

Do you see the problem? The *raise* command sets the *distance* field after it calls *relay*. If the shared thread has a higher priority than the caller of *raise*, it will execute immediately and call *raiseNotice* which will then read the not-yet-set *distance* field. The solution to this race-condition is to swap the two lines in *raise*, so that it first writes to *distance* before awakening the thread in *SharedThread*.

In this design pattern, calling the *relay* method in your shared thread object should be the *last* thing your commands do. The inversion test described on page 93 would have caused this problem to occur, but it still might be difficult to debug (or even detect) if the value of *distance* doesn't change often. Also, note that we declared the field *distance* to be volatile. We did this to force the compiler to write its value before the thread-switch could possibly occur.

7.4.4   Thread Pool Pattern

The Thread Pool pattern allows you to dynamically assign a group (pool) of threads to chores needing to be done. You can think of it as a king and his palace. The king rules the region, and he has a number of princes in the court of the palace waiting for assignments. When the king needs something done, he'll call for an idle prince and give him the chore, which might be to run a message to a neighboring kingdom, or to inquire about taxes due from a recalcitrant territory, etc.

A pool of threads is useful in situations such as these:

Image Processing An image can be divided into horizontal strips, where each strip is assigned a thread from a pool for concurrent processing. Users appreciate the resulting speed-up.

Image Rendering The various graphical objects in an image can be rendered into pixels by assigning one thread to each object, reducing total rendering-time.

Repetitive Chores You might have a time-consuming chore which is done repetitively, and which takes a variable amount of time. Sometimes, a chore can take long enough that it overlaps the starting-time of the next chore. Therefore, these must be handled with multiple threads.

Accelerating CPU-Intensive Work If you have a chore that requires much CPU-time, try to divide it into several pieces that can be executed concurrently in multiple threads.

Many Capabilities A device might have many capabilities that need threads, but only a few of them will ever be running concurrently. A good example is a digital camera. Assigning a few threads from a pool when needed is more efficient than having many dedicated threads.

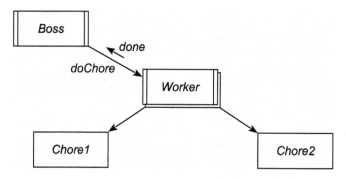

Figure 7.32: Thread Pool pattern

Figure 7.32 shows the design of this pattern. The *Boss* object handles the allocation of the threads, all of which are members of class *Worker*. All of them run the same code, and thus can perform any and all chores, such as *Chore1* and *Chore2*. The *Boss* commands a waiting thread to *doChore*, giving it information about the chore to be done, including an object-pointer as needed. When done, the thread sends a *done* notice up to the boss, which might contain results of the chore.

The *Boss* object contains an array of records, each containing a pointer to and the status of a thread in the pool. In fact, you can think of this as an array of objects, each containing one thread.

7.5   Interfacing

These patterns pertain primarily to interfacing among objects, and all are intended to provide a convenient interface for their superiors. The Façade, Adapter and Proxy patterns were introduced in the landmark book, *Design Patterns* [10], and they carry over into IDAR graphs exceptionally well. Here is a synopsis of the four interfacing patterns:

Façade	Merges the interfaces of several objects
Component	A subsystem with no hard-coded dependencies
Adapter	Changes an interface to make it more suitable
Proxy	Provides a local interface for a remote object

7.5.1   Façade Pattern

The Façade pattern combines the interfaces of several objects together into a single interface. It puts several objects under one roof.

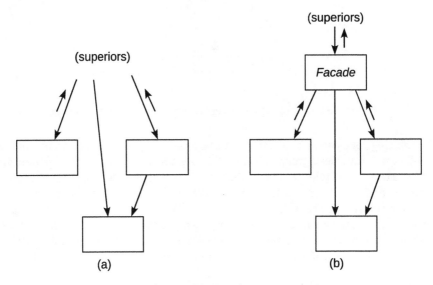

Figure 7.33: Façade pattern

Figure 7.33(a) shows some objects receiving commands and sending notices, and Figure 7.33(b) shows them with covered by a façade. A façade merely funnels commands and notices.

A façade object differs from other patterns in that it contains no intelligence. Its methods are tramps, relaying calls down to its subordinates. It is allowed to have tramp notices on the basis of isolation (see page 100). Furthermore, a façade passes the *need* criterion because (1) each subordinate contributes to the overall service, and (2) the façade provides the service of coalescing interfaces. On the other hand, the head-objects in all other patterns are smarter because they actively control and participate in actions.

There are a couple of reasons why you might want to hide some objects under a façade. A minor reason is that putting a façade over several objects to provide a single interface can make it easier to reuse a group of objects. The major reason for a façade is to provide a higher level of abstraction by creating a new conceptual object composed of several subordinate objects. For example, a swamp cooler contains a water-pump and a fan which can be individually controlled, but putting these two objects under the same interface means that the other objects in the system can work with the swamp cooler using only one *SwampCooler* object, instead of its component objects.

Figure 7.34 shows three objects related to encryption: *Keys*, which stores the keys used for encryption, and *Encrypt* and *Decrypt* which perform the actual encryption and decryption. While other objects can use these three objects individually, the *Crypto* façade which covers them provides all of these cryptographic services in one place, making their use more convenient.

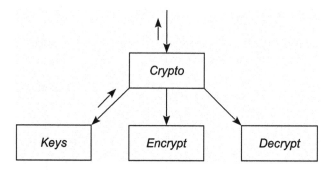

Figure 7.34: Crypto façade covering encryption-related objects

Reducing cohesion is a danger of using a façade. You can easily end up with an interface that provides a group of actions that are not closely related. In addition, you will get a trait-based role if you make the façade cover some category, such as "control-panel actions" which may include unrelated actions such as "eject" and "calibrate". Note that this reduced cohesion does not mean you should not use a façade, because the benefit from the added convenience of having things in the same category in one place may exceed the cost of reduced cohesion, making a façade the correct choice. As with other aspects of software design, you must carefully make a trade-off.

7.5.2 Component Pattern

The term "component" became popular in the 1990s, and we use it here to refer to a subsystem having no hard-coded dependencies on outside objects. All dependencies in a component are supplied by a superior and accessed indirectly, as you'll see below. Although it can be a standalone executable file, it's usually better to link a component into the rest of the system as doing so allows you to command it using ordinary method-calls instead of resorting to clumsy inter-process communications. Figure 7.35 illustrates the objects involved in a component.

A component appears to be an ordinary subsystem, except that all services it uses (shown as a dashed cloud) are commanded indirectly, as evidenced by the bubbles on their command-arrows in Figure 7.35. Employing indirect commands removes all hard-coded dependencies from the subsystem, making it a component. This absence of such dependencies forces the needed services to be passed into the subman during initialization in the form of pointers to external objects. In the literature, supplying pointers to dependencies in this manner is known as "dependency injection" [9].

The advantage that a component enjoys over a subsystem is that its absence of dependencies on other objects in the system makes it more portable. Porting a component only requires that you recompile it. Its disadvantage is loss of learnability: While studying the source-code of the component, you may see a command to an outside object, and you won't know which object will be commanded, forcing you to tediously look around to see which object was supplied at initialization. On the other hand, with a direct call in an ordinary subsystem, you can simply right-click on the call and click on "go to definition" and you're there. You must make a trade-off between portability and learnability.

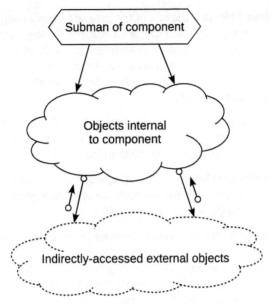

Figure 7.35: Component pattern

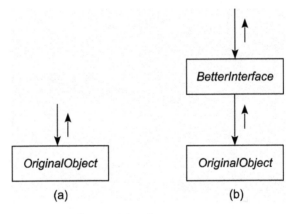

Figure 7.36: Adapter pattern

7.5.3 Adapter Pattern

The Adapter pattern is frequently known by its synonym, "wrapper", but I prefer the term "adapter" as its connotations are more accurate. Its purpose is to change an interface. It's like an electrical adapter, such as a USB adapter that converts the traditional large USB connector into one of the newer, tiny connectors. Figure 7.36(a) shows an original object with an unsuitable interface, and Figure 7.36(b) portrays how the interface was improved by passing commands (and notices) through the adapter object, *BetterInterface*. There are several reasons why you would want to use such an adapter in your software.

Isolating a Mess Shielding the rest of the program from a poorly designed object or subsystem is a good reason to use an adapter. During maintenance (or even during initial coding), you often encounter poorly designed areas of software created by (hopefully) others. A good way to prevent such a mess from polluting the rest of the system is to hide it under an adapter that provides a clean interface to everything else.

Unsuitable Interface While porting or leveraging code, you can acquire an object that is clean enough, but its interface doesn't fit the way your program was designed. Creating a different interface using an adapter solves that problem.

Multiple Operating Systems All operating systems have different interfaces, and if a program is intended to run on multiple operating systems, it will be necessary to provide an OS-adapter for each OS.

Multiple Languages When creating new software and scavenging for objects from various sources, you often encounter code that is not object-oriented, or was written in another language. Often you will have a body of code written in ANSI C, but you want it to blend well with your object-oriented design coded in C++. Writing a C++ adapter for such code solves that problem.

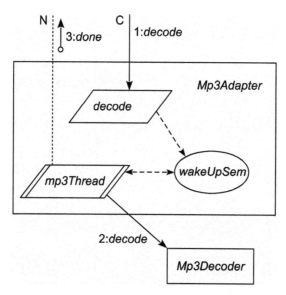

Figure 7.37: Adapter for MP3 decoder

Figure 7.37 shows the internal structure of an adapter for a decoder of MP3 files. The problem is that the *Mp3Decoder* object (at the bottom of the graph) blocks the caller's thread (i.e., the call to *decode* does not return) until the decoding is done. That blocking makes this object clumsy to use in this system, so an adapter was written which (1) does not block the call to *decode*, and (2) sends back a *done* notice when decoding is done. This adapter contains a thread (*mp3Thread*) which performs the actual decoding. The call to the adapter's *decode* method posts the *wakeUpSem* semaphore, which wakes up the thread and causes it to call *Mp3Decoder.decode*.

Adapters can become complicated. If the subordinate objects are missing a piece of capability, the adapter will need to provide it. Often timing needs to be different, forcing an adapter to use a message-queue or semaphore. Data-formats might differ as well, forcing the adapter to perform a good deal of decoding and re-encoding.

Adapters can also be difficult to code correctly. The problem with them is that the developer must thoroughly understand both the existing interfaces of the objects being adapted, and the new interface being created. So the developer needs to climb *two* learning curves. Only then can the developer hope to figure out how to convert between the two interfaces.

Finally, if you want to reuse some code, but its interface doesn't fit, you have two choices: Use an adapter, or modify the code. Modifying the code requires more thought and effort, but the results are better. The trade-off between the two choices needs to be made intelligently. Unfortunately, some people are lazy or perhaps enjoy claiming a high rate of reuse. Whatever their motivation, they consistently overuse adapters when they should be overhauling the code they're porting. Their product is a mess of objects held together with bubblegum and bailing wire. I suggest using adapters infrequently, choosing instead to do it right whenever feasible. If you take pride in your work, you will resist importing substandard code.

7.5.4   Proxy Pattern

You can use the Proxy pattern when you need to interact with another object which is separated from your program in some way. Such a "remote object", as I'll call it, might be running in another thread, in a different process, or even on another computer. The proxy hides the location of the remote object from you, making it appear as though you are interacting with the remote object directly. The proxy pretends to be the remote object, presenting the same interface for other objects in the program to use, but internally the proxy relays commands and notices to and from the remote object. The words "agent" and "relay" describe what a proxy does.

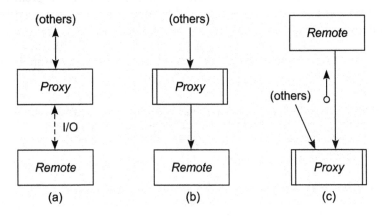

Figure 7.38: Proxy pattern

Figure 7.38 shows some common arrangements of proxies. The term "(others)" in this figure signifies various objects that would like to interact with the remote object, and do so using the proxy. The following are some situations that warrant the use of the Proxy pattern:

Isolation An object might be executing in another processor or computer, connected by some kind of I/O or a network. A proxy makes it appear that you are accessing that remote object directly, while hiding the resulting I/O transfers from you. Figure 7.38(a) is a dataflow diagram (not an IDAR graph) illustrating this kind of proxy.

Forced Thread-Bridging If an object requires that incoming calls be made on a certain thread, but you want to call it from other threads, a proxy is a good way to do the required thread-bridging, as illustrated in Figure 7.38(b). Many GUIs require that all calls be made from the same thread, forcing all GUI-calls to be bridged to that GUI-communicator thread.

Increase Parallelism To increase performance, you can run some objects in their own threads or processes, to be scheduled on other cores in the CPU. A proxy can do this thread-bridging or process-bridging for you.

Eliminate Cycles of Dependencies Long-range upward notices, such as those directed to a collector object as described in Section 7.2.1 (page 188), can create cycles of dependencies between libraries that can cause low-quality linkers to fail. This is likely to be a problem for a GUI compiled as a separate library. A low-level proxy eliminates these cycles, as portrayed in Figure 7.38(c).

As mentioned above, if a GUI or subsystem is compiled as a separate library, then upward notices directed to the GUI can cause cycles of dependencies which might trouble a poor linker. Figure 7.39 shows a way to eliminate such cycles without adding clumsy indirection to all senders of notices.

In this design, instead of sending notices directly to the GUI at the top of the hierarchy, they are sent to a proxy at the *bottom* of the hierarchy. The proxy forwards each notice using indirection to avoid creating an upward dependency between the two libraries.

Figure 7.39(a) shows two worker-objects commanded by a GUI. They both send notices back up to the GUI. Figure 7.39(b) illustrates the use of a bottom-level proxy to relay these notices. Instead of sending a notice upward, each worker sends the notice downward as a command to *Proxy*, which forwards it to *GUI*. When the program started, *GUI* commanded *Proxy* to register itself as the target of its notices. This registration included the address of the notice-method as a parameter.

But multiple notices need to be called in *GUI*, not just one, and the registration above contains the address of only one method. Consequently, *Proxy* is required to marshal (pack) the parameters of each notice into a single buffer to be forwarded, and *GUI* needs to demarshal (unpack) to obtain the original parameters. An alternative to this trouble is for *GUI* to pass an interface in its registration call to *Proxy*, instead of a method-address. Most languages allow you to do this. Java and C# implement

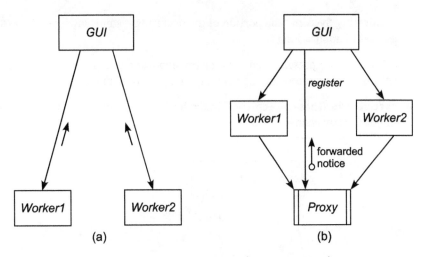

Figure 7.39: A proxy for GUI (collector object)

interfaces directly. In C++, you need to declare a pure abstract base class, and then create a derived class containing the actual notices to be called. No matter how you do it, forwarding multiple notices to *GUI* will require some nontrivial programming.

In Figure 7.39, did you notice that the notices sent by the worker objects became *commands* when they were sent to *Proxy*? How can that be? The semantics changed subtly. When sent to *GUI*, a typical notice meant "Conversion is 27% done." When sent to *Proxy*, that notice becomes the following command: "Tell *GUI* that conversion is 27% done." The workers are commanding *Proxy* to forward the notice, so that message is a command. This situation of a command conveying a notice is the opposite of a notice conveying a command as described in Section 3.13.6 on page 72.

Finally, using a proxy has another advantage. As mentioned above, many GUIs require that all incoming method-calls be made from the same thread. In a multi-threaded system, such calls need to be bridged to the sole thread responsible for making GUI-calls, and a thread-based proxy can perform this service well.

7.6   Applications

These popular patterns are frameworks for designing entire programs.

GUI App   Provides the overall structure of a GUI-based application
Database App   Framework for database applications
Web App Server   Framework for web-page scripts
IPO App   Input-process-output application

7.6.1   GUI App Pattern

GUI-based applications are very common, and most are similar to Figure 7.40. This pattern contains the following three objects (or groups of objects):

GUI Operating System The portion of the operating system which provides GUI-services to applications.

GUI Contains the presentation logic of the application. It manages the GUI by setting up all windows and associated items, and handling their events.

Worker objects These objects contain the business logic of the application. They do not directly change the GUI.

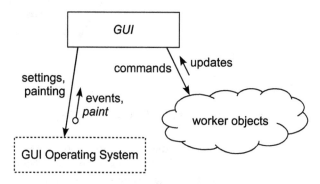

Figure 7.40: GUI App, variant 1

The operating system provides the basic GUI capabilities, which in an IDAR graph is portrayed as a dashed (external) object at the bottom level labeled *GUI Operating System*. In this arrangement, the application first commands the *GUI Operating System* to create various windows and items that can be displayed. The application also registers callback functions which the *GUI Operating System* calls for events such as mouse-clicks, keyboard characters, and so on. These callbacks are treated as notices in the IDAR graph, labeled *events* in this IDAR graph.

After the application has finished performing this set-up, CPU-control returns to the OS, and does *not* remain executing in the application. Rather, the OS runs the thread in a loop inside the bottommost *GUI Operating System*. All activity in the application occurs using callbacks from this OS object.

A typical event, such as a mouse-click, proceeds as follows:

1. The *GUI Operating System* detects the event and calls the appropriate registered callback, resulting in a notice being sent up to the *GUI* object.

2. The *GUI* object handles the event. Often, the event will require that an action be performed by the business logic of the program, so the *GUI* will command a worker to perform the action.

3. The cloud of worker objects is a conspicuous feature of this IDAR graph. These worker objects implement all the business logic of the program. A worker optionally sends *update* notices back up to *GUI*. Percent-done is a common example of such a notice, which the *GUI* could use to update a progress-bar. When done, the worker returns control to the *GUI* using a method-return.

4. Frequently, the *GUI* will need to change the display. It does so by sending the appropriate commands to the *GUI Operating System*. When the *GUI* is done with such activities, it returns control to the *GUI Operating System* by returning from the callback done in Step 1.

5. The *GUI Operating System* resumes its main loop in which it monitors the system for events.

The IDAR graph also shows a *paint* notice being sent from the *GUI Operating System* to the *GUI*. Such notices indicate that a portion of the screen needs to be redrawn. This notice is handled as follows:

1. The *GUI Operating System* calls a callback informing the app that a specified area needs to be redrawn. This is a *paint* notice sent up to *GUI*.

2. *GUI* sends various painting commands down to the *GUI Operating System* which redraws the given area.

3. The redrawing is likely to need information from the business logic, so *GUI* will probably command worker objects to get that information.

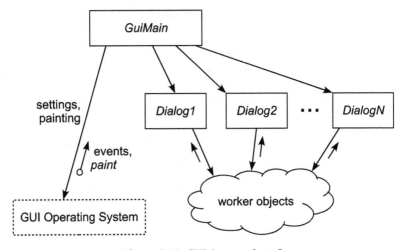

Figure 7.41: GUI App, variant 2

The *GUI* object is usually large enough to consist of multiple objects. In this case, the IDAR graph looks similar to Figure 7.41.

The various *Dialog* objects shown in this IDAR graph handle the windows, tabs or dialog boxes implemented in the GUI. The topmost object is now named *GuiMain*, and mostly serves to route events arriving from the *GUI Operating System* to the appropriate *Dialog* objects. In fact, many GUI frameworks do this routing for you. For example, Microsoft MFC ® defines BEGIN_MESSAGE_MAP and END_MESSAGE_MAP macros which map events (messages) into function-addresses. In cases like this, the GUI framework *is* the topmost object in your application.

After reading about this pattern, did you notice that this GUI App pattern is a special case of a Watcher? The *GUI Operating System* is the watcher which watches for events from the user. The *GUI* or *GuiMain* objects are the high-level objects which deal with those events and command workers to perform actions.

Finally, this pattern separates presentation logic from business logic. This separation is important because it means you can change one without the risk of adding a bug to the other. Entangling the two together can easily turn a nontrivial application into a mess. Also, this separation allows the business logic to be commanded by a script as well as by your GUI, so it improves both flexibility and robustness.

7.6.2   Database App Pattern

Applications based on databases and GUIs tend to have a similar design that follows the Database App pattern. Briefly, it consists of a GUI at the top, controlling the entire program. Below this GUI, there are several objects for dialog boxes or forms, all of which access database objects one level beneath them. Those database objects might directly access a local database, or they might access a datacenter. Figure 7.42 shows this pattern.

The *Comm* object accommodates communication that is often needed with devices or services other than a database. The most common example is the need to print documents on a printer attached to the computer. Other possibilities include USB devices, email, and access to banks for transfer of funds.

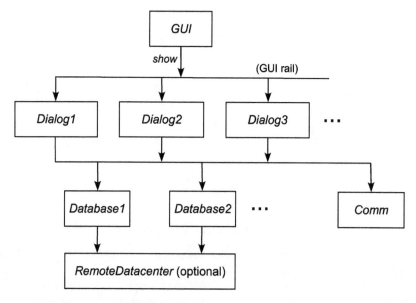

Figure 7.42: Database App pattern

The Database App pattern applies when (1) most GUI screens let you view, change or store data, and (2) the program does little computation or activity itself. Such a program is oriented around maintaining a database. This pattern is more widely applicable than you might think, because the term "database" covers a huge range of sizes, starting from a simple local file all the way up to a large datacenter in a city. As a result, this pattern covers a broad swath of common programs.

7.6.3   Web App Server Pattern

Back in the early days of the Internet, a web server was capable only of fetching static pages, meaning that the pages didn't change. They soon became smarter by adding forms, which allowed users to input data to the website, and for the site to change the page in response. Such dynamic pages are served with a web application server. Note the word "application" inserted between "web" and "server". Such web app servers are commonly used on the Internet for businesses of all kinds to display products and handle details of purchases. Such work requires that the server run a script which computes the contents of each page. Those scripts are the software that you must design and code.

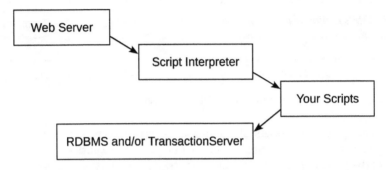

Figure 7.43: Framework of a Web App Server

Figure 7.43 shows the typical components of a web application server, which are:

Web Server This server handles all the details of communicating with the out-side world. It deals with the IP interface, and handles GET, POST and other commands associated with the http and https protocols.

Script Interpreter Your software that controls a website is usually coded in a scripting language, hence the need for a script interpreter.

Your Scripts This is the software that you will design and code. Everything else around it is framework that is supplied for you. Note that your scripts run on the server-side, not the client-side.

RDBMS Relational DataBase Management System. If you need a database that is more sophisticated than a simple file, this is it. These databases range from small freeware packages that run on your local computer, up to large datacenters maintained under contract with companies expert in such systems.

Transaction Server If you are running a site that can perform financial trans-actions, you'll need some kind of server to handle them, and to interact with financial institutions (usually credit-card companies).

All pages and actions of your website are controlled by your scripts. Figure 7.44 shows a design pattern for use within such scripts.

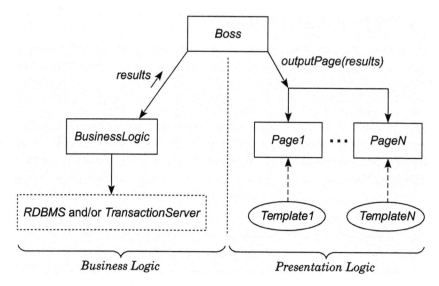

Figure 7.44: Web App Server pattern

This design consists essentially of two subtrees of objects, both controlled by the *Boss*. The left subtree performs the business logic of the website. The right subtree handles the presentation of the results. The script (1) inputs the results obtained from the business logic, (2) selects a page to display in response (*Page1* to *PageN*), and (3) creates that page by reading a corresponding template and filling in its blanks with the results obtained from the business logic. A common page would be a confirmation that a purchase was successful. Another page could display an error of some kind. Still another page could display more products for sale.

A very popular arrangement for websites is termed LAMP, which stands for Linux, Apache, MySql and PHP/Perl/Python. Apache is a web server; MySql provides a database; and PHP/Perl/Python are popular scripting languages, as is Ruby on Rails. All of these components run under the Linux operating system, and all are free (which explains their popularity).

PHP encourages business logic and presentation logic to be mixed together, but I think that's poor practice because (1) it means that changing one can accidentally introduce bugs in the other, and (2) such mixing reduces the learnability of both. I strongly recommend that you keep business logic and presentation logic separate, as shown in Figure 7.44.

The Web App Server pattern has some similarities to the popular MVC (Model-View-Controller) architecture. The *Boss* corresponds to the controller; the business logic corresponds to the model; and the presentation logic corresponds to the view. It has been well-known for decades that developers should keep the *display* of information separate from the code that *computes* that information. Philosophically, this separation is related to the concept of "image versus substance", where image is how a thing appears, and substance is what it actually consists of. A similar dichotomy is "form versus function", where form refers to the appearance of a thing, and function refers to what it does.

7.6.4 IPO App Pattern

IPO stands for "Input-Process-Output" (not "Initial Public Offering"), and this pattern is suitable for any program consisting of the following three stages:

Input This stage pulls data into the program from some outside source. It might consist of merely reading a file, or it could be information from a database, or it might be a sophisticated collector of sensor-data, or it could display forms on a monitor to get information from a user. This data is transferred in a dataflow to the next stage.

Process This stage is the heart of the program. It receives data from the input stage, processes it, and sends results to the output stage. The processing can be anything. Business applications might generate data for invoices or paychecks. Or the processing might be conversion of data from one format to another.

Output This stage receives processed data and sends it to some outside destination. The data might go to a printer to print paychecks, or it could be displayed on a monitor, or it might simply be written to a file or database.

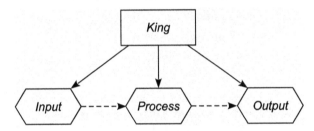

Figure 7.45: IPO—Input-Process-Output

Figure 7.45 shows this simple but popular pattern. The three stages are portrayed as subsystems, but for smaller programs, they can be single objects. Each dataflow can be a series of buffers. Or it could be a file that is written by the producer and read by the consumer. It could even be a global variable.

The controller of the program is called *King*, but your name should be an abbreviation of its role. It simply calls the three stages sequentially, or perhaps in a loop if multiple jobs will be run. It also handles set-up, shutdown and errors.

7.7 Summary

I'd like to reiterate that the patterns shown in this chapter should be treated as suggestions, and not as formulas to be followed rigidly. For example, a façade object was described as having no intelligence; it is merely a pass-through. But if you want to put a couple of commands in it that do actual work, you'll end up with an object that's a hybrid of a façade and an adapter. But does it matter? Maximizing clarity, cohesion, concealment, and need, while minimizing coupling are what is important. Patterns are merely suggestions so you won't need to reinvent the wheel.

Structuring Commands

Boss	Implements a service by delegating chores to workers
Resourceful Boss	Like Boss, but also handles resource-allocation
Dispatcher	Handles multiple objects implementing one interface
Layer	Grouping haphazardly used subordinates
Union	Call cross-cutting commands via a shadow-hierarchy

Structuring Notices

Collector	Many notices funnel into this object
Distributor	Sends notices to many objects
Watcher	Sends events it receives up to a big boss
Secretary	Stores and gives chores to the boss

Dataflows

Peer-to-Peer	Passed between peers under a common superior
Micromanaged	Routed through a mutual superior (micromanager)
Piped	Routed through a mutual subordinate (pipe)
Vertical	Passed between superior and subordinate

Threads

Inbox	One thread fed by a message-queue
Multiwait	One thread can wait for multiple events
Shared Thread	Sharing a thread among multiple objects
Thread Pool	Multiple threads allocatable by their boss

Interfacing

Façade	Merges the interfaces of several objects
Component	A subsystem with no hard-coded dependencies
Adapter	Changes an interface to make it more suitable
Proxy	Provides a local interface for a remote object

Applications

GUI App	Provides the overall structure of a GUI-based app
Database App	Framework for database applications
Web App Server	Framework for web-page scripts
IPO App	Input-process-output application

7.8 Exercises

1. What is the difference between an adapter, façade, and a proxy?

2. Which pattern is hard to *not* use?

3. Your subsystem needs to monitor a USB endpoint for arriving messages containing actions that your subsystem must perform. What pattern is appropriate for this?

4. The above subsystem needs to be modified to save the arriving messages, and only perform them when enough memory is available and the system has been idle for a few seconds. What pattern would accommodate these requirements?

5. What is the main advantage and disadvantage of the Micromanaged Dataflow pattern?

6. The same software controls all three models of sprinkler timers made by a company. These models use different circuit boards, which have different ways of controlling the electronic switches (i.e., transistors) which operate the valves. What pattern is appropriate for these sprinkler timers?

7. Your object will be sent commands by its boss, and will receive notices from a watcher under your object's control. Commands and notices may not block, but you don't want notices from your watcher to be processed ahead of commands from the boss. What pattern will help you design your object?

8. What is the main difference between a watcher and a secretary?

9. Part of your design has two objects, each with its own thread. Occasionally, each object must write information to two log-files at the same time. What pattern is appropriate for this situation?

10. *Ethernet* and *Statistics* objects have a common superior which wants messages arriving at the *Ethernet* object (from buffers in the operating system) to be transferred into *Statistics* which tallies data from the messages. What pattern is appropriate for this situation? Should the dataflow be pull- or push-style?

11. *Health* is a high-level collector object which receives notices from many other objects regarding their health. But *Health* is a precompiled binary library, and your project's 12 year-old linker can't tolerate a cycle of dependencies among such libraries. How can you solve this problem?

12. You want to write a GUI-based program for people who collect a large number of old items, such as coins, stamps, cameras, sports cards, model cars, etc. Such collectors would like to look up or list information such as purchase-date, condition, location, and so on. What pattern would be suitable for this collector program?

Chapter 8

Beyond Design

— objects are like people

<hr>

If you are in a hurry, and simply want to learn about the IDAR method, I suggest that you skip this short chapter. It covers a variety of interesting topics beyond the ordinary design of software. Because these topics have little in common, they have low cohesion (but high clarity).

If you are philosophical, as I am, this chapter will fascinate you. In the introduction, I promised that this book would be practical. I guess you could call me a "practical philosopher", because I never let myself drift away from practical design and implementation. And that includes this chapter. Although I discuss the philosophical foundations of some OOP-related topics rather deeply, the discussion never drifts far from the practical.

8.1   Why We Need a Command Hierarchy

All large human organizations are command hierarchies. Governments, armies, and companies—all consist of layers of command. Small-scale experiments of noncommand organizations have been attempted, but they don't scale to large sizes and they lack longevity.

This is human nature. In an unfamiliar organization, we instinctively ask, "Who's in charge here?" We know that a group of people cannot effectively achieve a goal without a manager providing guidance. Likewise, when we see a number of objects in a software design, we instinctively want to know which objects control others. We humans require that groups of people or objects be organized into a command hierarchy in order to form an understandable and effective organization. Without a hierarchy, a large organization of people or objects will be chaos. That is why IDAR graphs are easier to create and understand than network-like diagrams in UML.

After I explained IDAR graphs to a highly respected developer, he replied:

> *This is the first time that I've understood object-oriented programming. Whenever I saw a diagram with objects sending messages to other objects, I'd ask, "What's controlling all this?" It never made any sense.*

People need a hierarchy of control. Without it, an organization makes no sense to us. It is possible to understand a small or medium size organization expressed in UML, but it requires much more effort. In contrast, we can understand a command hierarchy (of any size) almost instantly.

Why-What-How Triad

Why is a hierarchy of control so much clearer to us? This is an important question because the command hierarchy is the foundation of the IDAR method. A convincing answer can be found in the field of cognitive engineering.

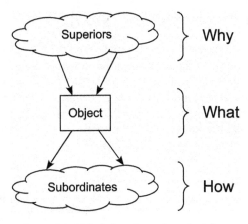

Figure 8.1: Triad showing why-what-how

Although cognitive engineers have not directly addressed the issue of representing software designs, they have created a way to model complicated socio-technical systems, and a software design can be regarded as a kind of socio-technical system. To model such systems, cognitive engineers have defined the "means-end abstraction hierarchy" (AH) [31]. Each object in an AH, termed an "element" or "node", defines a "why-what-how triad" consisting of (1) the object's superiors, (2) the object itself, and (3) its subordinates, as illustrated in Figure 8.1. To see how these triads provide insight, consider an object in a design and its corresponding triad:

Superiors→Why? The object's superiors tell us *why* it exists. The nature of those superiors shows how the object is used and how it fits into the broader context of the design, thus revealing why the object is present.

Object→What? The object's role and its detailed description tell us *what* it does.

Subordinates→How? Its subordinates tell us *how* the object works, because its role was parceled into the narrower roles of its subordinates. Those narrow roles (1) represent how it accomplishes its chores, and (2) reveal aspects of the object's design. Both provide insight into how the object works.

The roles of its subordinates are the means by which an object accomplishes its end (role), hence the phrase "means-end" used by cognitive engineers.

This explanation of our mental process of understanding a hierarchy is detailed and requires careful reading. But in practice, when we examine a command hierarchy, we learn from its triads instinctively, quickly, and effortlessly.

The why-what-how triads surrounding objects in an IDAR graph convey much more information than a UML diagram. UML lacks triads, so it cannot tell you why an object exists nor how it works. To see the magnitude of improvement yourself, I encourage you to compare the UML diagrams in Figures 1.1 and 1.5 with their IDAR equivalents in Figures 1.2 and 1.7. These graphs start on page 3. Finally, when we add notices and dataflows to a command hierarchy, the resulting IDAR graph brings far deeper understanding than a UML diagram.

8.2   Service-Based Design (SBD)

What is an object? Traditional OOP says that an object is a thing (noun) capable of performing actions (which are its methods). But where shall we put an action that is not done by an obvious thing? Back in Section 5.2.1 on page 113, I described verb-type objects that perform one action via one primary command, both of which are named after their action. A verb-type object solves the puzzle presented by Timothy Boronczyk in his insightful article, "What's wrong with OOP" [3], in which he provides this example of an action involving three objects:

spread (Knife, Jam, Bread)

The *spread* operation uses a knife to spread jam on a slice of bread. Which object should contain the *spread* method? Putting this method in *Knife*, *Jam*, or *Bread* is not appropriate because it uses all three objects equally. The answer is to create another object called *Spread* (or *Spreader*) containing the *spread* command.

Here is a real-life example: You need to stream video, and you must negotiate the compression-mode with the provider, based on the speed of your connection. Where should we put the *negotiateMode* command? It does not belong in *Ethernet* because negotiating a mode is too high-level for *Ethernet*; it merely transfers packets. Putting negotiation in a contrived *Mode* object would mean telling that mode to "negotiate yourself," which is a strange way of thinking. The solution is shown in Figure 8.2: Create a separate *NegotiateMode* object containing the *negotiateMode* command. It will also contain any supporting commands, such as setting capabilities.

The solution to both of these examples is to create a separate object containing the one command in question. As mentioned in Section 5.2.1, such an object could also contain supportive public methods, not to mention private methods involved with the object's service. The name of the object is a verb (or perhaps an agent noun), named after its sole action.

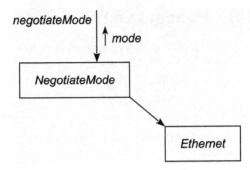

Figure 8.2: Negotiating a compression-mode

Two Kinds of Thinking

In the discussion above, I said that telling an object to "negotiate yourself" is a strange way of thinking. In fact, this is exactly how traditional OOP would have us create this design. When a computation does not belong anywhere else, we are encouraged to make an object out of its *result*, and then tell it to "compute yourself," which is an unclear design. The root problem is that traditional OOP tries to force-fit a stateless action into the state-based object-model. When there is no state, we are pressured to contrive some state out of the inputs or outputs of the action.

Therefore, in Section 5.2, I encouraged you to think of objects whose names are nouns and verbs. This dual-mode thinking is necessary because traditional OOP lacks any accommodation for stateless objects, as it only understands stateful objects. Can we improve on dual-mode thinking?

Service-Based Design

Thinking in terms of nouns yields a stateful object that provides a service. Thinking in terms of verbs can yield a stateless object that provides a service. Both provide a service. When designing, we can accommodate both kinds of thinking if we think in terms of services. Think of every box in an IDAR graph as being a service.

In OOP, the word "object" was a bad choice. It narrows our thinking, hurting our designs. We should have selected the word "service" instead.

I propose that we change from "Object-Oriented Programming" to "Service-Based Design" (SBD) from now on. The state-based (noun-based) OOP is too constraining. This is why I began Chapter 3 referring to a "hierarchy of services" rather than a "hierarchy of objects". I want your thinking to be centered around services, which will help you find better objects than what traditional OOP can yield. When creating a new design top-down, ask yourself, "What subordinate services can assist this broad service?" When designing bottom-up, ask yourself, "How can these services be combined, used, or enhanced to provide a higher level of service?" When doing white-box design, ask yourself, "What service can I wrap around this data? What service can I extract from this pseudo-code?" Service-Based Design unifies the noun-based and verb-based approaches.

Heed what David West wrote on page 272 of [32]: "Objects live to serve."

8.3   How IDAR Changes OOP

In the section above, I concluded by saying you should employ service-based thinking. In fact, IDAR changes the way you think about object-oriented design and programming in some fundamental ways, as shown in the following table:

Traditional OOP	IDAR
An object is a thing (a noun) possessing attributes and behaviors.	An object is a service-provider.
You design a flat network of classes.	You design a hierarchy of services.
Objects collaborate as one team using message-passing.	A superior commands its subordinates; notices are ancillary communications.

The differences in thinking parallel the differences in diagramming. Figure 8.3 shows the design of a simple voicemail subsystem in two forms. The UML diagram on the left shows all collaborations among classes, but it's hard to understand because it cannot show why-what-how triads, command-relationships, or dataflows—all of which are essential to understanding this program. The IDAR graph on the right clearly shows the breadths of roles from top to bottom, and the two dataflows of instances of the *MP3* class. When I have taught the IDAR method in classes, attendees have remarked that IDAR graphs make it easy to understand how programs work. And I have heard it whispered that "UML is useless".

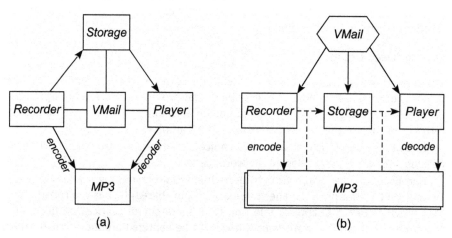

Figure 8.3: Voicemail subsystem as UML (a) and IDAR (b)

Perhaps the greatest change in OOP caused by the IDAR method is the transition from viewing objects as a flat network of collaborating equals, to arranging them into a hierarchy of services, with the broadest service on top and the narrowest on the bottom, communicating with commands to initiate actions and notices to convey needed information. In Chapter 1, I explain why the network approach encourages disorganization in the "chasm of disorder", and that IDAR's command-based hierarchy of services cleans up the messy network, resulting in understandable designs. The voicemail program above provides a small comparison illustrating this improvement in understandability. I should not need to mention that if developers can understand their software, it will have fewer bugs and be completed sooner.

IDAR has little effect on some aspects of object-oriented design. For example, some authors suggest using a CRC card for each class, which is a 3x5-inch index card containing (C) the class name, (R) the responsibility (i.e., role) of the class, and (C) its collaborating classes. With the IDAR method, the collaborators could be replaced with a list of the object's subordinates, and the remainder of the card would be unchanged, making it a CRS card: Class–Role–Subordinates.

Controllers

The topic of controllers is controversial in the OO world. Purists believe that the use of a controller is forbidden, and that objects should only collaborate as equals, each handling all normal and abnormal conditions within themselves, independently of the surrounding objects. On page 112 of his book, *Object Thinking* [32], esteemed object technologist David West states that

> *Hierarchical and centralized control is anathema in the object paradigm.*

He is fiercely opposed to any command-based hierarchy, as he repeats the above statement (in different words) multiple times in his book. In contrast, on page 179 of *Object Design* [35], Wirfs-Brock and McKean casually advise us to

> *Invent controllers if you need them.*

Clearly, there is disagreement among the thought-leaders about controllers. But a careful reading of West's work shows that he opposes controllers because they indicate that you are trying to create a hierarchy of subroutines, with controllers at the top, and then force-fitting that design into the object model. He rightly opposes this approach because its underlying thinking is not object-oriented. The IDAR method creates a hierarchy of services, so its thinking is based purely on services provided by objects, rather than on a call-tree of subroutines.

On a related topic, Section 4.1.4 (page 83) mentioned that you should not name an object "controller" or "manager" or similar merely because it controls subordinates. The role of the object should describe the service it provides, and should not mention how it does so. Controlling subordinates is one way an object can provide its service, but another implementation could provide that service entirely within the object. However, if an object controls things or data that its superiors will know about, then a name (and role) like *ArmCtrl* or *FontManager* would be acceptable.

8.4   Unification of Procedural and OO Design

In Section 5.2.1, on page 113, we described verb-type objects which consist primarily of one method that performs an action. If you have several such verb-type objects calling each other down a hierarchy, then as you proceed to lower levels, you'll probably find that objects consist solely of one method. Above those, objects might consist of a primary method and a few support-methods. Above those, objects consist of the usual mixture of methods and fields. Thus, when going down a hierarchy, the IDAR graph smoothly and gracefully turns into a call-tree of procedures (subroutines). That is, the graph gently transitions from objects into procedures. Hence, IDAR graphs can depict both object-oriented and procedure-oriented designs, and they can effortlessly represent any mixture of the two. We make the following fascinating conclusion:

> *The IDAR method unifies the procedural and object-oriented approaches to designing software.*

Until now, procedural and object-oriented were considered to be separate and unrelated ways of designing software, and they've been treated almost as if one were the antithesis of the other. People believed that they are so different that they cannot coexist. To accomplish a chore, you thought in terms of either (1) calling a hierarchy of procedures, or (2) defining collaborating objects. Never both. People believed the two approaches were irreconcilable.

Unifying them seamlessly is an important advantage of the IDAR method, as it acquires the strengths of both ways of designing. Portions of a design may be primarily procedural as appropriate, and the remainder of the design can be object-oriented, with no conflict between the two. The result will be designs that are better than what is possible when using only an object-oriented approach.

8.5   Engineering, At Last

I'd like to make the bold claim that software development was an art before the IDAR method appeared, and that the IDAR method has changed this art into a proper field of engineering. To verify this claim, let's compare art with engineering:

Art   is created subjectively, with no rules that can assure the artist that his artwork will be good. There are a variety of helpful rules that help an artist to avoid some common mistakes, such as matching colors and maintaining aesthetic balance. These rules prevent some of the bad, but they do little to ensure the good. Thus, the success of art depends heavily on the instinct-based skill of the artist. We observe that there are few great artists, and many mediocre ones.

Engineering   is applied science, and is based on "design rules" which ensure that the design will be reasonable. For example, electrical engineers use design rules regarding spacing and lengths of traces on circuit boards. Mechanical engineers use design rules to determine dimensions and types of materials based on stress and maximum deflection of parts. These rules ensure that designs will be reasonable in the sense that they will be functional and won't waste space on a circuit board or waste material in a part.

The following phrase succinctly describes the criterion for engineering:

> *Engineering employs rules that ensure you'll create a reasonable design.*

Before IDAR came along, software could be represented by various UML diagrams, and it had a folklore of guidelines regarding a smattering of topics such as coding standards, global variables, side-effects, sizes of routines, and so on. But these heuristic guidelines say little about designs above the level of objects, so they help mostly at the lowest levels. Overall design can be *represented* using UML, but cannot be *guided* by it, so design is determined primarily by the skill and instinct of the designer. Is this way of creating software most similar to art or engineering? Obviously, we have just described an art.

David West supports this eye-opening assessment on page 55 of his book [32]:

> *Software development is neither a scientific nor an engineering task. It is an act of* reality construction *that is political and artistic.*

Furthermore, the concept of "code smells" is based solely on the human instinct for what is clean versus dirty. Some authors have reduced the "smell" of code to a set of heuristic guidelines, as artists have done for centuries. But such intuition-based maxims do not constitute engineering.

With IDAR, we still have the many low-level guidelines as before. In addition, we have gained an enforced hierarchy created by the Down rule, governed by the constraints provided by the Identify, Aid, and Role rules. These four rules make creating a poor design more difficult, and they make creating a good design easier. The four IDAR rules are supplemented with the criteria of clarity, cohesion, concealment, coupling, and need, along with some metrics such as fan-in, fan-out, HD, CR, and FNR. Taken together, these constitute the design rules we need to guide us into creating good software instead of messes as described in Chapter 1. The improvement in design is substantial enough that the decades-old phrase "software engineering" is no longer an oxymoron. IDAR has changed us from artists into engineers.

Process Versus Engineering

As of this printing, the subject called "software engineering" should be called "software development process". Most universities offering a major in computer science offer a class on software engineering, which is often based on a book. We can see what is being taught by looking at the outline of such a book. Here are the parts (not chapters) in [30], which is Sommerville's popular 840-page book, *Software Engineering*:

1 – Overview	5 – Verification and Validation
2 – Requirements	6 – Managing People
3 – Design	7 – Emerging Technologies
4 – Development	

The only item in that list that could contain anything about rules for creating good designs would be Part 3 on Design. That would be the only part that might discuss engineering. The remainder of those items discuss various aspects of the *process* of developing software. The following is the list of chapters contained in Part 3:

11 – Architectural design	14 – Object-oriented design
12 – Distributed systems architectures	15 – Real-time software design
13 – Application architectures	16 – User interface design

These topics look promising. But when looking through these chapters, we see that none of them provides rules to ensure that your design will be reasonable. The text presents several approaches along with some discussion of the advantages and disadvantages of each. But there is no unifying set of rules that span the various approaches. Rather, the book presents a hodgepodge of approaches and suggestions applying to various specific types of software, such as real-time or event-driven. These chapters are describing an art and not a field of engineering.

Summarizing, the field of "software engineering" consists mostly of the phases of the development process, plus some added art, and little or no engineering. An aphorism might say, "Software engineering isn't engineering. It's process." So I suggest (1) renaming this field to "software development process", and (2) creating a new field called "software engineering" that starts with IDAR, a true form of engineering.

8.6   Proposal: A Course in Designing and Coding

I have noticed with dismay that college graduates do not know how to design well or how to write good code. Surprisingly, our computer science curricula have no courses covering these two crucial topics, so college students learn these skills piecemeal (if at all) in their programming assignments. Consequently, students graduate knowing little or nothing about the two topics in computer science that are most important to industry. Therefore, I propose that universities provide a required (non-elective) course named "Designing and Coding" covering:

- The IDAR method of design and related topics contained in Chapters 3 to 7 of this book, teaching students how software is to be engineered
- The various techniques of good coding, including how to comment well, sizes of methods and files (page 151), the principle that vertical is valuable (page 166), avoiding verbose identifiers, "code smells", and many others
- An overview of topics in the (renamed) field of software development process

This course must not only teach rules and principles, but it also must give numerous assignments in creating/drawing designs and in writing code. As the old adage says, "Practice makes perfect." Measured by its usefulness to industry, this will be the most valuable class offered in the CS curriculum.

8.7   Parallel Human Organizations

In an IDAR graph, all pairs of objects that pass messages are designed to have either a commanding or notifying relationship between them. The theory underlying this partitioning is interesting because it posits that there are only two kinds of relationships in the world: imperative and informative.

Imperative (Commanding) If one object has authority over another, then their relationship is imperative, which is related to the word "emperor". The one may command the other, and never vice versa. Obviously, these are the downward commands in your IDAR graphs.

Informative (Notifying) If neither object may command the other, and yet messages are passed between them, then their relationship is informative. Either object may inform the other about something. These are free notices in your IDAR graphs; they do *not* parallel command-lines.

This division is also true of people. Common imperative relationships among people include: manager and employee, sergeant and soldier, and parent and child. Common informative relationships include: two employees under the same manager, buyer and seller, children playing a game, and newscaster and viewer.

The IDAR rules closely parallel the rules that have evolved over the millennia for human organizations such as armies, governments, and corporations. Table 8.1 shows the IDAR rules in the left column, and the corresponding organizational rules in the right column. This close agreement with long-established rules for human organizations tells us that the IDAR rules are on a sound footing; the rules match the way people perceive and understand complex organizations.

	IDAR Rule	**Organizational Rule**
I	Every public method is a command, or a notice which must supply needed information.	Communications among people are commands or needed information.
D	Commands go down in the IDAR graph.	People may only command their subordinates.
A	Methods may aid previously commanded duties.	Workers may help coworkers perform their duties.
R	Objects must fulfill their roles, doing no more and no less.	People must fulfill their roles in the organization.

Table 8.1: The IDAR rules parallel human organizations

8.8 System Modeling

Because IDAR graphs parallel human organizations, and because dividing all communications into commands and notices is a good model of communications in real life, IDAR graphs can be used to model systems. They can be used as what's known as a "system modeling language". For example, Figure 8.4 portrays the commands and notices among entities when a customer places an order with an online retailer.

In fact, IDAR graphs can even portray relationships and communications among people, even when computers are not involved. For example, Figure 8.5 portrays your marriage. Notice that nothing happens to the patio.

8.9 Three Rats

I am old enough to remember when OOP took over the software world by storm around 1990. It was strange to watch. People appeared to throw away all the wisdom our field had carefully acquired about design, and plunged recklessly and uncritically

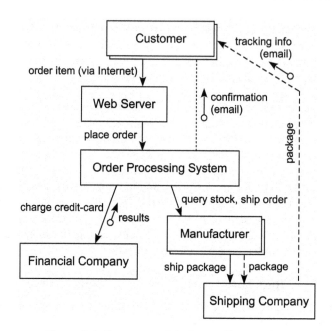

Figure 8.4: System model of an online retailer

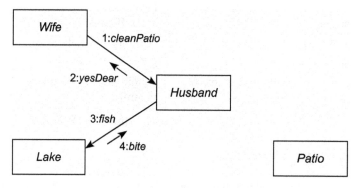

Figure 8.5: Your marriage

into the new waters of OOP. As people should have expected, some mistakes had been made in the early development of the theory of OOP, and these mistakes eventually became venerated dogma. Unfortunately, three mistakes were severe enough to be considered blunders. These are the three rats that have been hiding inside OOP for many years, surreptitiously causing great damage.

For a long time, I didn't recognize these rats. I only knew that something about OOP made me uncomfortable. However, I did see that inheritance caused designs to become contorted and hard to learn, so I opposed it. But until I had invented the IDAR method and could use it as a comparison, I could not identify what specific problems were skulking in OOP. After many years, I can finally clearly explain the three blunders made by the creators of OOP. Briefly, they are (1) the loss of a hierarchy of services,

(2) stressing inheritance when it's best avoided, and (3) being object-oriented instead of service-based, causing developers to think in terms of passive things instead of active services. Below, I also show how the IDAR method solves these problems.

Rat 1: Loss of Hierarchy

Back in the 1970s, we had a hierarchy of services. A subroutine performs a service, and most programs consisted of a hierarchy of subroutine calls, so those subroutine hierarchies were also service hierarchies. Also, Constantine's Structured Design was popular back then, which was a reasonably systematic way of creating a hierarchy of subroutines that implemented a dataflow consisting of processing steps. It was well-suited for business applications of that day.

OOP swept subroutine hierarchies and Structured Design out of existence, as I mentioned in Chapter 1 on page 6. Despite its mistakes, the invasion of OOP publicized the concept of an object consisting of a group of closely related subroutines that share internal variables. Before that, this concept (without inheritance) was known as a "module" or "package". But we lost subroutine hierarchies, and the greatly touted feature of inheritance could not replace them. Because traditional OOP has no other kind of hierarchy, we lost all *useful* hierarchy. That is why traditional OOP is naturally messy, as I explained in the Introduction starting on page 4.

The IDAR method creates a useful kind of hierarchy, resulting in a great improvement to the structure and clarity of software.

Rat 2: Stressing Inheritance

Historically, far too much importance has been laid on inheritance, to the point where folks believe that if you aren't using inheritance, you aren't object-oriented. I stagger at the thought of how much damage has been done to software over the decades from developers trying to force-fit inheritance inappropriately into their designs.

Back in the 1990s, people believed that an inheritance hierarchy is as useful as the subroutine hierarchy it replaced, which it isn't. In Section 6.6 on page 142, I discuss four problems that inheritance causes, including the fact that it produces a hierarchy of categories, which is far less useful than a hierarchy of services. Fortunately, we are seeing a backlash against inheritance nowadays in both books and lectures, so folks are finally perceiving that the costs of this rat usually exceed its benefits.

Here are some ways to remove the need for inheritance:

- Use the hierarchy of services provided by the IDAR method. The literature refers to this technique as "composition".
- Use the Dispatcher pattern, which selects one of several subordinates.
- When you need to call methods indirectly, use function-pointers in C and C++, delegates in C# and Python, and the `interface` feature in Java.

Consequently, we should regard inheritance as a rarely needed tool, and we would be wise to question its presence in modern object-oriented languages.

Rat 3: Object-Oriented Instead of Service-Based

In Sections 5.3 and 8.2 (pages 116 and 232), I stated that your goal should be to define services, not objects, where a service's name can be a noun or verb. I proposed that such thinking be called Service-Based Design (SBD). Thinking in terms of objects instead of services hurts a developer in two ways:

- The strongest connotation of "object" opposes actions. When people hear the word "object", they think of an inert object such as a rock, chair, or bottle. Such inert objects are incapable of performing an action, creating a mental stumbling-block. Subconsciously, a developer thinks, "An object can't perform an action, yet my object must do something. How am I supposed to define it?" Thus, the anti-action nature of the word "object" causes confusion. On the other hand, the word "service" correctly connotes a thing that can perform actions, encouraging a developer to define those actions.

- The word "object" strongly suggests thinking in terms of nouns, neglecting verb-type objects, causing folks to overlook objects that would improve their designs. This problem has been exacerbated by the noun-centric teaching that has dominated traditional OOP.

  To make matters worse, the absence of verb-type objects prevents developers from unifying the procedural and object-oriented approaches at the lower levels of designs as described on page 235, so the damage from this noun-oriented mistake is greater than we might first think.

  The IDAR method encourages developers to think in terms of services, and with the unification of approaches mentioned above, it yields designs superior to what traditional OOP normally produces.

The Rats are Gone

Summarizing, the IDAR method solves the three great blunders of traditional OOP, and based on trial designs and pilot testing in industry, I am confident that it adds no new blunders of its own. These are the reasons why the IDAR method is a substantial leap of progress in the (new) field of software engineering.

8.10   Exercises

1. What are the two fundamental kinds of interactions between people that are also true of designs using IDAR graphs?

2. The *characterize* method is given an array of bytes, and computes a record containing its characteristics, such as the number of bytes, whether they are binary or text, etc. A common design would be to make the record a class containing the *characterize* method, and tell an instance of that class to compute its fields by calling *characterize*. Getter methods could be used to fetch the results. Is a better design possible?

3. What is the best way to perform an operation on multiple objects where the operation doesn't belong in any of those objects?

4. What are the three rats?

5. Why do people find a command hierarchy easy to understand?

6. What great change does the IDAR method make to object-oriented thinking?

Chapter 9

Advice to Managers

— dig for truth

One of my motives for writing this chapter is to explain the IDAR method in nontechnical terms so that all managers can understand it, with the goal of encouraging managers to review designs. The desire to avoid upsetting their colleagues puts pressure on reviewers in peer-reviews to *not* point out ways of simplifying designs. The resulting designs are technically correct but overcomplex, leading to missed deadlines. Hence, I encourage managers to examine designs, and I'll show you how.

A bigger motive is to publicize the common problem of fanatics. Fanatics are smart people who are fixated on some aspect of software design and overuse it. I've seen them cause great harm, so my intention is to help you identify them *before* they damage your project and hurt your career.

There are some techniques you can use to deploy the IDAR method in your organization. The IDAR method has the unusual trait of blending well with traditional methods of software design, allowing you to try it on a piece of your project without assuming any risk.

As a bonus, this chapter ends with a practical description of how to think clearly.

9.1 You Can Understand IDAR Graphs

In the next section, I offer a good reason for you to review your employees' designs. But you might protest, saying "I can't understand designs. It's been many years since I've done technical work, and it would take me forever to get back up to speed." Not so! One of the advantages of IDAR graphs is that nontechnical people can understand them. You can understand IDAR graphs. Below, I briefly explain IDAR graphs in terms that managers and other nontechnical people can understand. I explain them twice, first very briefly, and again not so briefly. While not complete, these explanations will allow you to understand most of what's in an IDAR graph.

9.1.1   A Very Brief Explanation

An IDAR graph is similar to a corporate organizational chart, but with the following enhancements: Allow subordinates to have multiple bosses. Bosses command their subordinates, but there are also other noncommand communications among people, including those from subordinates up to their bosses. Draw such noncommand communications (called "notices") with floating arrows. Finally, pretend that each person (box) in the chart is very specialized, and can only do one specific chore. Each such specialist corresponds to an object in a program.

9.1.2   A Not So Brief Explanation

This explanation consumes several paragraphs, but it explains IDAR graphs in greater depth. Please read the last item carefully, as it explains a new concept not present in corporations.

Org Charts An IDAR graph is similar to an organizational chart for a corporation. Everybody understands those. Like an org chart, it uses a horizontal line when a boss commands multiple subordinates.

Multiple Bosses These organizational charts allow subordinates to have multiple bosses. That's easy to understand, though rare in companies.

Specific Roles The people in these org charts are called "objects", and they are very specialized, like idiot savants. Each is drawn as a box, and can only provide the exact service described in its role. A role is a brief description of the service an object offers to its boss(es).

Commands Each object can only understand a few commands (from its bosses). These commands together allow an object to fulfill its role. Downward arrows are drawn from each superior to its subordinates.

Notices These org charts are embellished with short floating arrows showing the noncommand communications (called "notices") among objects. Most notices are responses from subordinates to their bosses. The remaining notices are called "free notices" which are other objects talking with each other.

Messages Commands and notices together are called "messages", and each object has a fixed repertoire of specific messages it can send. These messages have been written beforehand by the programmer. Examples include "print document" (a command) and "user clicked on link" (a notice). The arrow for each message is often labeled with a name representing the message, such as *printDocument* and *userClickedOnLink*. This situation is like giving an office-worker an email program that can only send pre-written emails with a few blanks to be filled in.

Active Each worker is unbearably lazy, and won't process a message unless its
sender is present to goad him. So the sender can do nothing else until that lazy
object finishes. There can be a chain of these stoppages, where *X* is waiting on *Y*,
meanwhile *Y* sent a message to *Z*, and is waiting for *Z* to finish with that message.
On the other hand, an "active" object is not lazy, but will work independently,
allowing a sender to do other things. Active objects are more flexible than lazy
objects, but they add complexity. In an IDAR graph, an active object is denoted
with double or triple vertical lines on the sides of its box.

Indirection The arrow for a message may have a bubble opposite its arrowhead,
indicating the message is "indirect", meaning it can be sent to any object. A normal (direct) message can be sent to only one particular object. For example, a
subordinate with only one boss will use direct notices to that boss, but it would
use indirect notices for multiple bosses. This arrangement is like restricting a
pre-written email to only one recipient (direct), versus being able to send it to
any email address (indirection). Direct messages are easier to learn and debug
in a program, so they are preferable when a message has only one destination.
Indirect messages are more flexible, but they increase complexity. They also
reduce clarity because it's hard to tell where a particular message will go.

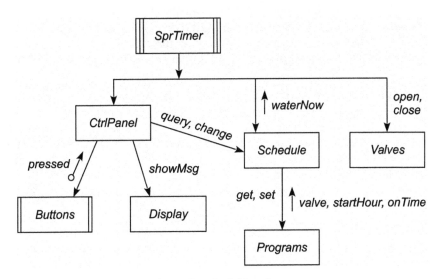

Figure 9.1: Sprinkler timer

These concepts are straightforward, except indirection which requires careful
reading. As an example, Figure 9.1 shows the design of the embedded software that
controls a sprinkler timer. From what you learned above, you can see that:

- *SprTimer* commands *CtrlPanel*, *Schedule*, and *Valves*.
- The *Schedule* object is also commanded by *CtrlPanel*.
- *CtrlPanel* also commands *Buttons* and *Display*.
- *Buttons* sends an indirect *pressed* notice up to *CtrlPanel*, its boss.

- *Programs* is commanded only by *Schedule*, and sends it the direct notices *valve*, *startHour*, and *onTime*.

- *SprTimer* and *Buttons* are active (able to operate independently). Therefore, after *CtrlPanel* commands *Buttons*, *CtrlPanel* can do other things while *Buttons* is performing that command. If *Buttons* were not active, *CtrlPanel* would stop until *Buttons* was done with the command.

These observations reveal how most of this design works. For example, when *Button* reports a button-press in its *pressed* notice, it's a good guess that *CtrlPanel* might command *Schedule* to change an entry. Likewise, when *Schedule* sends a *waterNow* notice to *SprTimer*, it's a good guess that it will respond by commanding *Valves* to open a valve. You've learned a great deal about this program, and you haven't even seen its list of object-roles. An IDAR graph is understandable.

Now that you've had an overview of IDAR graphs, you can be given an IDAR graph along with a list of roles of objects and their commands, and you can understand both the structure and operation of that program.

As an aside, the acronym IDAR comes from these words, which are the four rules governing this method: "Identify, Down, Aid, Role". These rules are:

Identify	*Identify* commands & notices in an object. Notices convey needed info.
Down	Commands must go *down* in the graph.
Aid	Methods may secretly *aid* previously commanded actions.
Role	Objects and commands must fulfill their *roles* (synopses of behaviors).

9.2 Managers Should Review Designs

We all know that peer-reviews should be conducted on designs (and code, but this book is concerned about designs). These reviews rely on the fact that developers tend not to make the same kinds of mistakes, so they will notice bugs created by others. Thus, reviews should remove most software problems early in the project.

9.2.1 Pressure to Avoid Simplicity

That sounds good in theory. But in practice, a social phenomenon constrains reviewers. People on most teams have become friends with each other. As a result, most developers don't want to upset another developer. Thus, reviewers are under pressure to criticize a design as little as possible. Consequently, reviewers tend to only point out places where a design is wrong, where "wrong" means it fails to fulfill the requirements or fails to follow a standard. Crucially, *reviewers are pressured to avoid pointing out where a design can be simplified.*

Pointing out a way to simplify a design (1) makes the creator of the design look bad, thus angering a friend, and (2) does not identify a place where the design is technically wrong. From a reviewer's point of view, such a criticism has a social cost and no benefit. So a reviewer says to himself, "It looks like it should work, so I won't say anything about all this unnecessary complexity." Such reviews result in designs that are technically correct, but overcomplex for what they do. The ultimate result is that implementation and debugging consume more time, causing your project to miss deadlines or to ship with more bugs (or both).

You Should Review   The solution is to have designs reviewed by somebody who does not fear insulting a developer on the project. The obvious choice is *you*. You learned enough about IDAR graphs in the prior section that you can review designs. But what should you look for in a design?

9.2.2   Too Much Complexity

Back in Chapter 6, I described several forms of excess complexity in detail. Knowing the damage that overcomplex designs cause, your goal in reviewing designs is to find unnecessary complexity. You should always question indirection and active objects. In the sprinkler timer for example, *Buttons* has only one boss, so we should not need the flexibility of its indirect notice. If you ask the developer about this, he might reply, "The flexibility isn't needed now, but this indirection makes that object more reusable, and it might get a second boss later." Your response to such unneeded flexibility and complexity is "YAGNI—You Aren't Gonna Need It." I say more about YAGNI and other good principles of design in Section 6.16 on page 175.

Peer-reviews will find flaws in designs, so you don't need to try to find flaws. You only need to look for unnecessary complexity, as we did in the sprinkler timer. Here's how I suggest that you conduct a manager-review of a design:

- Review the design with the developer sitting by you, so you can question him.
- Read the listing of roles of objects, and note any objects that do little, such as forwarding a message. A do-little object with only one boss should be merged into its boss.
- Point out each active object, and ask why it needs to be active.
- Point out each bubble (signifying indirection), especially on commands, and ask the developer how it can be removed.
- Point out each notice that's not sent to a boss, and ask for its justification.
- Don't let the developer confuse you with technical jargon. Insist that explanations be in plain English.

Finally, be sure to read the next section about fanatics. Then when you review designs, you can watch out for fetishes that sometimes afflict the smartest developers, as well as the common overuse of indirection, active objects, and do-little objects.

9.2.3   Too Little Complexity

As a manager, you will always wonder whether the developers working for you know what they are doing. Specifically, you need to know if a developer has thought his design through to sufficient detail, or whether he is overlooking areas that will cause schedule-slips later in the project due to unexpected extra implementation and redesign of existing code that didn't mesh with the additional design. You also need to know whether his design is correct. His IDAR graphs will tell you both.

You might not understand all the details of an IDAR graph, but you understand its hierarchy, commands, secondary communications in the form of notices, and dataflows (shown as dashed arrows). Unlike a UML diagram, an IDAR graph communicates how a program will operate. By examining an IDAR graph, you can follow how the program will respond to various events, commands, and situations.

That brings me to my point: You can determine whether a design is lacking features or sufficient detail. In the prior section, I recommended that you review the design together with the developer. During this review, you can ask him to trace the paths of various operations on the graph, requiring that he explain its operation in sufficient detail. You need to be assured that the design is complete. Therefore:

1. If he dismisses an important feature with the software-equivalent of waving his hands and saying "then a miracle happens," the design is not complex enough. It is incomplete. The developer has not thought it through.

2. If his answer to a question or the path taken for an operation is tortuous or hits a dead end, the design is poor or incorrect.

9.3   Fanatics

Fanatics have caused me much frustration over the years. Over my career, I have seen some exceptionally intelligent developers fail—one here, one there. It's an odd kind of failure, and decades of observation were needed before I began noticing that these failures were part of some patterns. It's the phenomenon that I call "fanatics". I'll first describe the patterns I've seen, and then proceed into detail about the various kinds of fanatics you might encounter.

9.3.1   The Patterns

Over my long career, I have seen the following patterns of unobvious failures in both developers and their managers:

1. A smart person can have an obsession with some aspect of software that causes him to create overcomplex designs. These people are fanatics. They can be obsessed about almost anything, such as templates, inheritance, flexibility, abstractions, levels of trivial methods, dynamic binding, and others. Any aspect of software which is interesting is a candidate for overuse.

2. Managers believe that high intelligence does not vanish anywhere. They have not been taught that smart people can have foolish obsessions and therefore can have weak points, what I call "drop outs in intelligence".

3. Managers reject criticism of smart people and support their mistakes, probably due to item 2 above—not knowing that intelligence can have drop outs.

4. A software project can fail due to a fanatical architect. This can be a painful lesson. For example, if the architect is an abstraction fanatic, the architecture will have too many levels and will be overcomplex, slowing everyone down and lengthening the schedule unnecessarily.

Noticing such patterns requires decades of experience in industry. As a result, professors and teachers often don't know these things because they've spent little time in industry, or perhaps because they haven't pondered why failures have occurred. You were not taught any of this in school because it's unknown.

9.3.2 Overdoing It

Here is my definition of a fanatic:

> *A fanatic is a person who consistently overuses some aspect of software.*

Most of the fanatics listed below are the kinds that I have encountered, although I have added a few kinds described by reliable colleagues. As the list shows, the particular aspect of software that fanatics overuse varies widely.

Abstraction Fanatic An abstraction is an implementation of a service or operation in an object that hides the details of how it's done. When such objects command others, the design has multiple levels of abstraction. To create good designs, a developer must have the ability to create well-defined abstractions.

However, an abstraction fanatic produces designs having too many layers of abstractions, each doing little. He was taught the concept of "information hiding", and took it to an extreme. With all those levels, his software is hard to learn and hard to change. Somebody trying to learn his software gets lost in the layers. This kind of fanatic falls into the "layers of crap trap" [5], as a frustrated colleague so aptly phrased it. Abstraction fanatics are common.

An abstraction fanatic might be trying to simplify software by breaking up methods into simpler ones, but he cannot see that the resulting large call-tree itself is a form of complexity that makes the software hard to learn and understand. He cannot see that there's a trade-off between internal complexity of methods and the external complexity of their calls. I discuss this on page 151.

Inheritance Fanatic Object-oriented programming has a concept of "inheritance" which follows a taxonomy of objects, creating a hierarchy of categories, described in detail in Section 2.6 (page 25). As you can imagine from that brief description, some smart people could go overboard about this, creating fancy inheritance-hierarchies instead of doing things the simple way. A person who values simplicity will first sketch a basic IDAR graph. An inheritance fanatic will first sketch an inheritance diagram. That can make them look smarter than others who keep their designs simple.

Flexibility Fanatic They try to make their software accommodate all possible additional requirements, real or imagined. Doing so makes their software over-complex. Furthermore, the extra effort is usually wasted because we humans are bad at predicting the future, and therefore future requirements are not what we anticipated, so the software must change anyway. But it takes longer to write, change, and debug because it's too complicated.

Managers and developers should be aware that adding complexity to make software more flexible, makes it *less* flexible due to the additional complexity. The inverse statement is a thought-provoking paradox:

Making software less flexible makes it more flexible.

Here is that paradox with parenthetical explanations:

Making software less flexible (simpler) makes it more flexible (because simpler software is easier to change).

A flexibility fanatic will never understand that less can be more.

Reuse Fanatic—Producer There are two kinds of reuse fanatics around. This one insists on making his designs reusable. He will say "we might want to reuse this" as a justification to adding complexity to help with reuse. Never mind that most software will never be reused. There will not be a worthwhile benefit from the cost paid by over-modularizing to make objects and subsystems maximally reusable.

This fanatic is similar to the Flexibility Fanatic described above, and he has the same problem of not perceiving that adding complexity to improve reusability reduces reusability, defeating the fanatic's purpose.

Reuse Fanatic—Consumer This "developer" insists on reusing code that ought not to be reused. He can't see that most code out there should be refactored (overhauled would usually be more appropriate), so he slaps adapters around them and cobbles together a mess. Then he's proud of all his reuse, and can't see that he's made a pot of software spaghetti held together with bubblegum and bailing wire. Debugging that mess will take months.

Thread Fanatic The concept of many threads harmoniously working and communicating concurrently appeals to this intelligent mind. Each thread is simple, so the software is simple, right? Wrong. This developer doesn't appreciate that potential race-conditions and deadlocks increase with the *square* of the number of threads. Such software is likely to have intermittent crashes and hangs that are all but impossible to find. After months of debugging, when the software is finally (mostly) working, it will lose performance and eat more CPU-time due to the many context-switches caused by all those threads.

Template Fanatic Templates in C++ appeal to some personalities, so they use them for normal code. They don't realize that templates are hard for normal people to understand, are hard to debug in a debugger, and should generally be avoided. They represent unnecessary complexity, except for the rare times when one needs to push multiple data-types through the same algorithm.

Fad Fanatic These fanatics stay current. They like to adopt the latest technologies, techniques, frameworks, and whatever else is in vogue. They make you feel like a dinosaur if you don't go along with them. They can't see that adopting the latest craze causes unnecessary turmoil in an organization, that new technologies are poorly tested and are therefore risky, and that new things often fail an objective cost/benefit analysis.

Others I doubt that I've listed all possible kinds of fanatics here, so you'll need to keep alert for anyone who overuses some aspect of software. As a possible example, XML is a fad as of this writing, and it is being overused. Also, there are people around who are fixated on dependency injection (DI) [9], and who love its benefits but ignore its costs. So there are probably some XML or DI fanatics here and there, hidden in cubicles, doing their damage.

Based on the ratios I've seen over the years, I estimate that 10 to 25 percent of the smartest developers in an organization are fanatics of some sort. Hopefully this percentage is on the low side in your organization. By "smartest", I'm referring to developers who are in the top five percent. These are the cream of the crop. They are the top performers. Their reasoning always sounds intelligent and plausible. But as you saw in the examples above, fanatics can slow down or destroy the project you're managing.

9.3.3 Abstraction Fanatics

Abstraction fanatics (and their close relatives, inheritance fanatics) are common, so it's worth creating a fictitious example to illustrate the sort of design that you can expect out of such a fanatic. This program managed a small display-unit containing an LCD and a keypad. The display was mounted in an isolated hazardous area, and was connected to a computer (located in a separate room) using a standard serial I/O. Commands sent to the unit allowed it to display icons, small images, and lines of text in a couple of sizes. The display sent a message to the computer (1) in acknowledgement of each command it received, and (2) whenever a key was pressed. It was not a complex device.

Figure 9.2 shows the original design of the software in the computer that controlled this display. Note that this is *not* the software inside the display-unit itself. Those who create designs like this one clearly have a good sense of levels of abstraction because of the careful hierarchies they create. Notice the thoughtfully laid out levels. If you notice them more closely, you'll see some shortcomings with this design.

- What does the *KeyProc* object do? It merely forwards a key-press message from *Parser* to *DisplayUnit* as the *key* notice.
- Likewise, the *AckProc* object only forwards an acknowledgement from *Parser* to *DisplayUnit*.
- The *Driver* is responsible for communicating with the device over the serial port, so why is the *Parser* object handling some of that communication separately from *Driver*?
- The *Ticker* object passes its ticks through the *TickProc* object, which does nothing but forward them to the *DisplayUnit*.
- Likewise, the *UDP* object passes messages to the stack of *StatProcl* message-handlers, which only forward them to *DisplayUnit*.

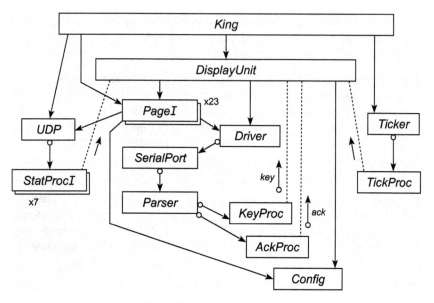

Figure 9.2: Too many layers

In fact, this design has seven layers and 13 rectangles. And all it does is control a display with a keypad. This is a classic case of an abstraction fanatic who loved to produce too many layers. As I stated in the Introduction, traditional OOP discourages the use of levels of abstraction because UML diagrams are incapable of portraying such levels. Despite this hindrance, abstraction fanatics not only produce layers of abstraction, they produce too many of them. Such people are obviously intelligent, but something is wrong with their minds. Do they enjoy complexity? Can they not see that complexity lengthens schedules by generating more work for everyone? I am unable to understand such minds.

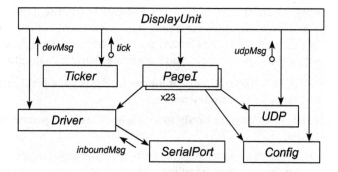

Figure 9.3: A better design

Another serious flaw in this design is its excessive use of indirection (dynamic binding). Notice the many bubbles on both commands and notices. These represent pointers to objects or functions which have been registered somewhere within the caller-objects. This style of programming makes code hard to understand because you don't know where a call will go, and hard to debug because you don't know where to put a breakpoint. Indirection needs to be kept to a minimum, but some fanatics enjoy it and maximize its use, making their code abstruse.

Figure 9.3 is an improvement of this design. The most obvious change is that the design is much simpler. It now has only four levels and seven rectangles. The number of indirect calls is now restricted to only two notices, which is one fourth as many indirections as before. All other calls are direct, making the code easier for a developer reading it to follow its calls.

But have we shrunk the design by giving the objects too much work to do? Let's look at what each object does in comparison with the original design.

- *Config* handles system-configuration as before, and is unaffected.

- *SerialPort* now sends output from the display as notices instead of commands. So the code in *SerialPort* is almost identical.

- *Driver* now contains the code for the parser. Because I've worked on similar parsers in the past, I know that a parser like this one would only contain around 80 to 100 lines of code. That is not an excessive increase in *Driver*.

- *PageI* child instances are not affected.

- *Ticker* now sends ticks to *DisplayUnit* instead of some other object. That is an insignificant change in its code.

- *UDP* needs to do the message-filtering that the *StatProcI* child instances used to perform. But such filtering can be done with only a few lines of code, so the extra burden is insignificant. Alternatively, the filtering could have been done in *DisplayUnit*, making *UDP* more reusable because it would contain no application-specific code.

- *DisplayUnit* now performs the initialization that was done by *King*. It's appropriate for the manager to do this small chore, so this change is reasonable.

Summarizing, this design has about half as many objects and layers, one fourth as many indirections, and all this was done without making objects too large or reducing their clarity or unity of purpose. The new design is considerably better than what an abstraction fanatic would have produced.

An important lesson here is that IDAR graphs allow you to identify designs that contain too many layers of abstraction. If your instinct says that there are too many layers for what the design is supposed to do, look closely at the roles of the objects. If you see objects that do little, they should be combined in order to simplify the design. And perhaps more importantly, such a design tells you to keep an eye on that developer. You might have an abstraction fanatic on your hands.

9.3.4 My Advice

It's crucial for you as a manager to know that fanatics produce excess complexity. A fanatic on your project will produce designs that are too large, have too long a schedule, and that are too unreliable. On top of all that, the software will be too difficult to maintain.

Fanatics also tend to be the smartest people on your team. Because of their high intelligence, they can produce their overcomplex code quickly enough to be considered top performers on the team. And the final bitter fact is, because fanatics are so smart, managers often make them leads! In that role, they drag down the entire project. I have seen and experienced this multiple times. Given that most people are sheep, they quietly do what they are told. Either they don't see the simple way, or they don't try to change anything because they know that complaining will do no good because they know the manager always follows the lead's suggestions. Given these facts, my advice to managers is:

- Be aware that some of your smartest developers might be fanatics who overuse an aspect of software.

- When selecting a lead, look at the designs and code he has created to be certain that you're not selecting a convincing-sounding fanatic. Ask the developer's coworkers about this as well.

- Adopt the rule that "The simplest design wins." Design takes little time, so have multiple people create designs independently, and select the simplest. Note whose designs are being selected, and whose are being rejected. An alternative idea is to require that all suggestions arising from design-reviews that simplify designs shall be adopted (unless they violate the requirements).

- Encourage people to report excess complexity to you privately. Most people don't have the courage to say anything in front of the group, but some will do so privately. Take special note of somebody who often uses the word "simple". He might have the valuable gift of simplicity.

- Look at designs yourself. If your instinct says that a design is overcomplex for what it does, it probably is. Fanatics create excess complexity, and you can look for it directly in IDAR graphs. I said more about such manager-reviews starting back on page 246.

- Hire and promote developers who have a firm grip on practical reality, who don't overuse or underuse anything.

- In interviews, ask questions about aspects that fanatics often overuse. For example, ask the candidate what he thinks about inheritance, or how he would subdivide a problem into levels of abstraction.

I might as well add another disturbing observation: I have never seen a fanatic be cured. You might have noticed in my advice above that I never suggested that you help the fanatic to be healed of his fanaticism. Now you know why.

9.3.5   The Curse of Complexity

Fanatics cannot see the simple way. Something is faulty in their intelligent minds that causes them to consistently choose a complex approach. They appear to have a curse of complexity clinging to their minds. This is a form of poor judgment, and I've pondered what causes it. It's certainly not education, because the same college that produced a fanatic also produces normal developers. My definition of clear thinking is "unbiased assessment of all costs and benefits." Fanatics don't do that, so they are not thinking clearly. My own theory about the cause of their mental fog is:

1. Fanatics are smart enough that mental pursuits and concepts appeal to them. Ordinary people are not like this, but instead prefer practical hobbies such as restoring classic cars, watching sports, gardening, and so on. Highly intelligent people who are in danger of turning into fanatics also enjoy (or even prefer) intellectual hobbies, such as inventing methods of designing software.

2. Fanatics have a weak grip on practical reality. In other words, they lack common sense about what is efficient and effective, and what is not. I believe they are similar to the proverbial absent-minded professor who is so engrossed in his own thoughts and theories that he is unaware of his surroundings.

3. Merging both of the above traits into one brain yields a person who is likely to latch onto a concept that is intellectually fascinating, but impractical.

Saying this briefly, fanatics are smart enough to be obsessed by a fascinating idea, but they lack the common sense required to see the damage they cause. This theory explains (1) why fanatics overuse an aspect of software, (2) why fanatics are only found among the smartest people, and (3) why fanatics can't see the harm they cause (weak grip on reality). This theory also suggests that interview questions should be posed that test a candidate's grip on practical reality. Low-level questions are a good idea, such as "write a for-loop in assembler language" or "write a routine that outputs a tone to a speaker having a given frequency and duration."

A colleague who has seen a few fanatics has this theory about them:

> Fanatics are insecure. They need to prove to themselves that they are smart by creating overcomplex designs.

Either way, fanatics always produce only one product: overcomplexity. And that lengthens both your schedule and your bug-list. Overcomplexity bogs down the whole team both during initial implementation and during maintenance. And because people cannot remember all interactions of code in a complex environment, bugs will be more frequent. Overcomplexity thus hurts you over the entire life of the product. Therefore, we can say that

> Overcomplexity is the curse that keeps on cursing.

9.3.6 The Gift of Simplicity

Just as a few developers in the crowd are fanatics who have the curse of complexity, a few other developers have the gift of simplicity. The gift of simplicity will give a developer a dislike of unneeded complexity, and the creativity to produce a simple design. It will drive a developer to simplify and simplify until the design is minimal. He will fulfill Albert Einstein's saying:

> Everything should be kept as simple as possible, but no simpler.

In an interview for the book, *Programmers At Work* [18], Bill Gates said:

> *The hardest part is deciding what the algorithms are, and then simplifying*
> *them as much as you can. It's difficult to get things down to their simplest*
> *forms. You have to simulate in your mind how the program's going to*
> *work, and you have to have a complete grasp of how the various pieces of*
> *the program work together. The finest pieces of software are those where*
> *one individual has a complete sense of exactly how the program works. To*
> *have that, you have to really love the program and concentrate on keeping*
> *it simple, to an incredible degree.*

I strongly agree. In fact, as I mentioned earlier in this book, I penned a paradoxical proverb which I used as my email-signature for years:

> *It's easy to create complexity, and hard to create simplicity.*

Despite the mental effort required, there's a great advantage to creating simplicity: It makes the developer more productive. If a simplified design has only a third as much material in it, then there's only a third as much code to write and debug, so the developer will get done in about a third of the time. That's a 3x boost in productivity. With higher quality. I've seen cases where that 3x was realistic. A developer who is able to design but lacks the gift of simplicity can create a working design, but it won't be notably clean or simple. Here are some traits I've noticed about people with the gift of simplicity:

- Such a developer's usual response to other people's code is "why wasn't it done this simpler way?" They can quickly see simpler approaches.

- They are frustrated with the excessive complexity of most code they encounter.

- Their code seldom uses inheritance because it's seldom the simplest design.

- Most of their classes are static because they know that an instantiable class makes everything more complex. This topic is discussed on page 138.

- Their code has a minimum of layers, where each layer fulfills the Meaty rule of doing something substantial (see page 152). When you look at the content of a layer, you see useful work and not merely calls to lower layers.

- Their code is flexible enough but not overflexible.

- They refuse to follow fads because they accurately perceive both the costs and benefits of any idea. Fad-followers see benefits but not costs. Fanatics badly overestimate the benefits of their obsession.

9.3.7   Freddie and Sam

This section is a short story about two fictitious developers on the same team, Freddie Frugaler and Samuel Sophisticate. Their boss knew that design takes a tiny fraction of the entire schedule, so he had both of them create designs of a new software package they were to develop. Both designs were to be presented to managers for evaluation, and one would be selected.

Sam created a beautiful group of UML diagrams showing all his class hierarchies (inheritance trees) based on "is-a-kind-of" relationships which he divined from the requirements. At the evaluation, he presented these in an impressive slide-show. Sam had obviously thought the problem through completely and in detail. One manager remarked, "It's complicated. It must be good!"

During the presentation, Sam made little remarks revealing that he was following "best practices" in software design by utilizing the "is-a-kind-of" relationships lurking deep inside the problem, and by further subtle phrasing let it be known that he had a low opinion of those who don't follow that established OOP-religion. Secretly, Sam wanted to make Fred look like a dinosaur.

Freddie created straightforward IDAR graphs on *three* slides. Just three. He used no inheritance, and all but one of his classes were static. The slides looked attractive enough, but having only three of them caused concern. At the evaluation, managers asked him if the design was sufficiently thought-out. Freddie insisted that it satisfied all the requirements, and he demonstrated that by tracing every operation from beginning to end on his three IDAR graphs.

During the presentation, Fred's approach was as simple and straightforward as his design. He answered questions simply and directly, with no subtle insinuations.

When they discussed these designs privately, the managers were worried that a design that simple might not be complete. They had confidence in Sam because it was obvious from talking to him on prior occasions that he was close to being a genius. But Sam's canny slight against Fred caused the managers to be a little skeptical of Fred. The effect of Sam's words was subtle enough that the managers were not conscious of their own skepticism. Consciously, they listened to Fred willingly enough, but the subconscious seed of skepticism in their minds meant that Fred had a higher bar to jump than Sam. When discussing their decision, the managers felt it was safer to choose Sam's design, despite Fred's having demonstrated that his simple design did everything required.

The project was released a couple of months late. The quality was tolerable, as the software didn't crash too often. It crashed on occasion, but customers didn't complain much because they quickly learned to save their work often, allowing them to resume from where they left off after a crash. During the later phases of the project, some developers on the team began to realize that if Fred's design had been used, the project would have finished a little *early*, giving developers time to polish it up to outstanding quality. But their managers will never know that.

Sam is an inheritance fanatic.

Freddie has the gift of simplicity.

9.4 Resisting Decay

Most of us have heard of and seen the common phenomenon of decay, which is the degradation of design and code that usually occurs as developers add changes and enhancements to a program over a period of time.

The original design might or might not have been good enough. It scarcely matters because when a change needs to be made, it is hacked in as easily as possible, in a manner inconsistent with its original design. The change is a kludge. Then another kludge is added later. An enhancement is also kludged in, with managers telling the developers, "Just make it work." For every change, developers are told, "Just make it work" instead of "Do it right" because kludging is faster—in the short term. But the mess invades and grows like a metastasizing cancer, causing each change to take longer and to introduce more bugs, reaching the point where the tangled code is unmaintainable.

Maintenance does not need to be like this.

To solve this problem, a manager only needs to require that changes conform to the IDAR rules. Note that this assumes that the original design used the IDAR method. This constraint prevents developers from hacking up a kludge, but forces them to properly change the design, perhaps with a small amount of refactoring consuming a few hours of effort. The design and code stay clean.

But you might complain that this is not realistic. If you are facing an urgent deadline, or you have a critical bug where every hour of down-time is a significant expense for the company, you don't have time to do it right. I understand such pressure. In this case, go ahead and put in a quick hack to solve the problem. But then, once the time-pressure is off, require that your developers remove the hack and do it right. This will require some self-discipline on your part, but it will prevent the code from decaying into an impossible mess.

9.5   Deployment

How can you deploy the IDAR method in your organization? Are you even convinced that it provides a benefit? Is your organization convinced? Is the culture of your organization open to experimenting with new ideas, or are the people entrenched in their ways? These are some of the questions and pressures you will face when attempting to adopt the IDAR method.

9.5.1   Benefits

Before we launch into the topic of how to deploy the IDAR method in your organization, first let's talk about the benefits it provides. This method offers several specific benefits, but when you are questioned about the wisdom of using the IDAR method, remember that it ultimately provides one important overall benefit:

shorter schedules

The logical question is: Why does the IDAR method shorten schedules? There are several reasons:

- The IDAR method hinders messiness in designs because it forces designs to be structured as command hierarchies. This benefit is similar to the way block-structured statements such as if-then and while forced statements to be structured as a hierarchy of blocks, eliminating the messiness caused by goto statements in the 1960s.

- Command hierarchies encourage clear thinking about the responsibilities of groups of objects. Traditional OOP has no concept of a group of objects, except at the package (subsystem) level.

- An IDAR graph forces developers to structure software in levels of abstractions. The mess-prone network-structure of traditional OOP actually discourages the creation of such levels.

- IDAR graphs make designing easier (and thus faster) by providing a structure in which objects are defined. One can design objects top-down, bottom-up or both, all within the context of an emerging hierarchy. A developer can follow a five-step process (page 117) which provides guidance in creating a design. Traditional OOP has none of this.

- IDAR graphs are easier to understand than traditional OOP diagrams, because they correspond with the way we think. Humans think in terms of hierarchy (page 230). Ease of understanding means that designs tend to be better, having fewer bugs, shortening schedules.

- The IDAR method allows (and even encourages) the use of both procedural and object-oriented thinking (page 235). Such broader and more creative thinking tends to produce better designs.

There is another benefit that's more subtle. Because traditional methods of design impose no hierarchy, designs naturally tend to be messy because any object can send a message to any other object. However, some developers have an instinct for command hierarchy, and by intuition they constrain their designs to be similar to IDAR graphs. As a result, the messiness of design depends on who happens to be on the team. If a couple of people with instinct for hierarchy happen to be leads, the schedule will be shorter than if you happen to get designers who lack that instinct. Thus, the schedule is difficult to predict. In fact, software is notorious for being difficult to schedule accurately, with underestimates of 30% or more being common due to designs being more complex than anticipated. The IDAR method forces all designs to be command hierarchies, hindering messiness and allowing reviewers to probe more deeply for flaws. These features should reduce happenstance variations in your schedules. To say it briefly, the second benefit is:

schedules that are more accurate

Improved accuracy of schedules should allow a company to bid lower on contracts, because less padding of estimates will be necessary, thus making the company more competitive. Improved accuracy will tend to increase the quality of products when schedules are fixed, because the crunch time (hurried time) at the end of a project will be less severe.

This benefit can be shown in the form of its effect on risk curves. Such a curve plots confidence of success of a project on the vertical axis, versus expenditure on the horizontal axis. Obviously, as expenditure rises, the confidence of success rises. But the effects of the IDAR method on this curve are interesting.

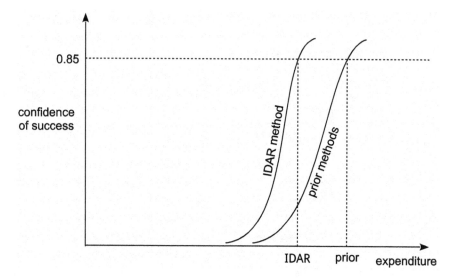

Figure 9.4: Effect of the IDAR method on a risk curve

Figure 9.4 shows hypothetical risk curves for prior methods of design and the IDAR method. I am using a realistic confidence-value of 0.85 for determining the expected expenditure for a project. Point 'prior' shows the expenditure for prior design methods, and point 'IDAR' corresponds to the IDAR method. As anticipated, the IDAR method results in lower expected expenditure, but note that there are two reasons for this reduction. First, the risk curve has shifted left due to reduced time spent implementing and (especially) debugging. The second reason is more subtle: The reduced variability in time spent implementing and debugging causes the curve to be *steeper*. This higher slope has the effect of moving the location of the 0.85 confidence-point left even more. From these curves, we see that the IDAR method causes a double-reduction in cost and schedule.

Some people will regard the statements above as sales-talk; that is, exaggerations and lies. And with all the lying in our culture, I don't blame them. To convince yourself or others that IDAR graphs are a good way to design, I suggest reading Part II of this book, which describes the design of several applications in detail. You'll see how design always proceeds naturally, both top-down and bottom-up, and that the resulting designs are easy to understand. These chapters also explain the thinking behind the decisions being made, along with mistakes and corrections, so you'll be seeing a true design process unfold. You'll also see that the IDAR method works well in a wide variety of systems, from GUI-intensive to embedded.

9.5.2   Opposition to IDAR

Opposed by Tradition

The item in the bulleted list above regarding broader thinking might cause trouble. Traditional object-oriented design defines objects that are conceptual or physical things. Such thinking is thing-oriented. The IDAR method broadens one's thinking to include objects that are verb-oriented. While such wider thinking results in better designs, it might also result in conflict with people who insist that you follow object-oriented tradition.

For example, Chapter 11 is an example application of a drawing program which contains an object named *Stretch*. "Stretch" is a verb and not a noun, and it certainly is not a thing in any sense. A *Stretch* object is pure action. Followers of OOP tradition will dislike such verb-type objects. Such people might make complaints about the design along the lines of "That's not really an object," or "This is not an object-oriented design," or "You're not following the OOP way."

Also, the IDAR method causes inheritance to be used much less than it was with traditional techniques. In fact, many IDAR designs will not use it at all. Unfortunately, inheritance is a strong tradition in OOP because it was promoted heavily, and it is so firmly entrenched that some people believe that if a design does not use inheritance, then it's not object-oriented. When learning about the IDAR method, such people will complain that it is regress and not progress.

None of these complaints are based on the goal of meeting the requirements in the shortest possible schedule. Rather, they are based solely on tradition. I am somewhat of a visionary, so I say to myself, "If this is a better way, then I'll adopt it and throw out tradition." Traditionalists are the opposite, clinging to tradition even when logic and truth say there's a better way.

In response, I suggest that you remain steadfastly goal-driven. Point out that the resulting design is simpler and/or clearer, and it therefore results in shorter schedules for initial coding, debugging, and maintenance. Perhaps you will get the person's attention off tradition and on the goal.

As an aside, an easy way to deal with the issue of inheritance is to require that any use of the keyword `virtual` in C++ or `extends` in Java must have your prior approval. Polymorphic inheritance requires the use of those keywords.

Opposed by Documentation

Your organization or project might be required to document its designs in some way. These requirements might be standards imposed by the department or company. Contractors for the government always have extensive and specific requirements for documents to be delivered as part of the software. You will probably be required to document your software in the form of UML diagrams. Does this requirement preclude the use of the IDAR method?

Certainly not. UML can represent any design produced by the IDAR method. The following table shows how the IDAR method affects the common UML diagrams:

Class diagram	Unaffected
Dataflow diagram	Unaffected
Sequence diagram	Unaffected
Package diagram	Unaffected
Communication diagram	Adapt from IDAR graph

Clearly, only the seldom-used communication (collaboration) diagram is affected, and you can modify an IDAR graph to make it a communication diagram, saving you the effort of producing it separately.

It's important to realize that documentation-standards apply only to your final designs. They do not dictate how you should create your designs. You are free to create the design using any process you wish, such as the IDAR method. Only your results matter.

Small Design Documents

While we are on the topic of documentation, I strongly suggest keeping your design documents small. If they are large, developers will resist making changes to the design because the corresponding changes to the documentation would be too much work. Instead, developers will code ugly hacks during maintenance that don't affect the design documents. I recommend that a design document consist of:

1. IDAR graphs of the system and its subsystems
2. Lists of roles for methods and classes
3. Descriptions of covert aid provided by methods
4. Dataflow diagrams (as appropriate)
5. Explanation of principles of operation

As part of (5), you will often need to illustrate the sequences of actions that compose each major operation in the software. Each such sequence will consist of an IDAR graph with sequence numbers on commands and notices, accompanied by a table explaining the commands and notices.

A small document is maintainable. A large document is unmaintainable. A small document also conveys the design more quickly because—it's small.

Opposed by Risk

If you are concerned about the risk of adopting the IDAR method, you are being prudent. You know that you should not make major changes without testing them first. IDAR gives you two options to reduce risk: You can stop using the method at any time, and you can deploy it on a small piece of a project.

It might surprise you that once you start using this method, you are *not* locked into it. You can stop using it whenever you wish, and continue the design using traditional techniques, without slipping your schedule. Hence, you have a free fallback option. As a result, the IDAR method can only help you, and will not hurt you. Trying this method has no risk.

It is safe because it can be employed as a supplement to an existing process. You can still use your existing process of design, but also add the IDAR method to the brainstorming portion of the process. If you don't like it, you can stop using it. Neither adopting this method nor dropping it is disruptive to an existing process. The only additional activity is to scribble IDAR graphs on pieces of paper, and make sure they obey the four IDAR rules. That activity can be added or stopped without affecting anything else. No harm done.

The second approach to reducing risk is to use this method to design only a portion of a system. You could try this design method on one subsystem, or even a section of a subsystem.

The reason this approach works is that the objects in an IDAR graph are happy to communicate with other objects in the system. Therefore, you don't need to design the entire system this way. You can start with a small piece and see how well it works. I suggest designing one subsystem this way, and looking at the results.

Maintenance is another opportunity to try this piece-at-a-time approach. Adding a new feature is a common need in maintenance. Try having an employee design that feature with an IDAR graph.

Another chore in maintenance is fixing bugs. When making bug-fixes, a developer often encounters design that is so messy that the region needs to be cleaned up. This process is called "micro-refactoring", and refers to small-scale clean-up. It's often very small-scale. Try micro-refactoring a little area with the IDAR method.

After a couple of these pieces work out well when using the IDAR method, both you and skeptics in the organization will start becoming receptive to larger adoption of this method. The basis of this receptivity will be demonstrated feasibility and benefits, and not sales-talk.

The safety mentioned above should encourage even the most hesitant manager to try using the IDAR method on a portion of a design. This safety means the manager will be taking no risk, but will hopefully get a benefit. Thus, the cost-benefit analysis of trying this method is favorable.

Opposed by the Team

If you are managing a project, and if you are convinced of the benefits of the IDAR method, then you can simply require that all your developers use it.

But the team might resist you. Although it's clear to you that the IDAR method provides a benefit, parts of it are contrary to the prevailing OOP-religion, so some folks might oppose your decision. As a manager, you know the importance of having everyone "on board" (i.e., in agreement) so that the team will work together effectively, so it's difficult to issue decrees, unless that's the culture of your organization. In such a difficult situation, you need to use techniques that are more subtle than issuing decrees as you would if you were working in a Dilbert cartoon. I suggest introducing the IDAR method to your project as follows:

- Tell the developers on the project that "we are going to try using the IDAR method that we've been hearing about." Introducing the IDAR method with the phrases "we are going to try" and "hearing about" implies that your team is keeping up with progress in the field (which it is). This gentle and humble approach is less likely to provoke opposition than an edict.

- Have the team attend a class on the IDAR method. This class only needs to be two or three hours long to cover the essentials of the method and still allow some time for questions and discussion. An entire day would allow the class to cover everything in detail, along with working through a couple of example designs. The class serves two purposes. First, it teaches the IDAR method to the team. Second, the class creates social momentum in the team. This momentum makes it socially difficult for developers to oppose this method because doing so would be opposing the momentum of the entire team.

- An alternative to a class would be to assign chapters of this book to read, but I'm afraid that most people will skim instead of reading, because we have become a nation of skimmers instead of readers. To motivate people to read well, you'll need to require that they pass a test (oral or written). In fact, I recommend requiring that the developers pass a test regardless of whether a class is offered or reading assignments are given. I'm afraid that a test is the only way to motivate people to learn the topic thoroughly.

- Tell the team that because a small mistake in design has a larger effect on the program, you want all designs to be reviewed by peers, and all must be IDAR graphs. Peer-reviews cause developers to expect their colleagues to produce IDAR graphs, representing another form of pressure on potential opponents.

- Require that all designs be documented as IDAR graphs along with lists of roles. This approach will at least cause people to follow the four rules.

These gentler techniques should get the team to adopt the IDAR method with minimal grumbling.

Here's another bit of good news. Over my career, I have noticed that most people are sheep. They do what they are told. When a project manager decided to use some technique, the whole team docilely used it, even when doing so made no sense. I've seen this happen a few times. Unlike these follies I've seen over the years, the IDAR method makes sense (is beneficial), so I would expect little trouble from the team.

9.5.3   For Developers: Only Results Matter

Though this chapter is written to managers, this related section is for developers who wish to adopt the IDAR method. We must distinguish *means* from *ends*. Most organizations only care about your results, and they don't care how you got them. They only care that you created a good design, and they don't care if you did so by using the IDAR method, asking your friends, or consulting the great pumpkin. In fact, you can scribble IDAR graphs on pieces of scratch paper, document the resulting design, and hide the papers in your desk. The company will be happy with you because your results are good.

This is the sneaky approach that you can use in an organization that is resistant to change. It will benefit you because your designs will improve. If you work in a tradition-bound organization that insists that object names be nouns, then the verbs that the IDAR method gives you for verb-type objects can be changed into "agent nouns" by adding "er" or "or" to their names. For example, *Stretch* becomes *Stretcher*, which is a noun and will keep you out of trouble. You'll lose a bit of clarity doing this, but it's better to get along with people. Such object names are discussed more in Section 5.2 (page 112).

Of course, it's best to have the organization improve, so I suggest showing one or two of your colleagues what you are doing. They should understand that improving their designs can only make them better developers and make them look better to their bosses. Spreading the use of the IDAR method will improve the productivity and quality of your group's software.

9.6   Clear Thinking

Making good decisions requires clear thinking. But what is clear thinking? This is a fascinating question for those of us who are philosophical. After pondering it as it relates to life in general, I've settled on this description of clear thinking:

Facts   Dig for the facts, making sure they are factual.

Reasoning   Use sound logic, avoiding fallacious reasoning.

Importance Stress what is important, usually determined by size of effects.

Let's explore these three items in more detail.

Facts Our culture is full of bald lies and subtle lies, making it difficult to know the truth. A teenage friend recently observed that "False is the new normal." You need to dig for truth by investigating and testing all questionable claims. Get all the facts, taking care to be unbiased.

Reasoning You can draw wrong conclusions using fallacious reasoning. Someone might say, "I believe software developers are stupid because I know one and he is stupid." This example of incorrect reasoning is known as "hasty generalization". There are many other errors. Too many others. They could fill a class in college. The "List of fallacies" in wikipedia.org, and fallacyfiles.org are good introductions to this interesting and important topic. Use sound reasoning to avoid being deceived by persuasive (but faulty) arguments.

Importance As part of bias or lying, a proponent (or opponent) of an idea often downplays or omits an important fact. You must correctly assess the relative importances of everything, omitting nothing. When deciding what's important, you should consider the effects of all aspects of each of your alternatives, without overlooking any unpleasant aspect or effect that you would prefer to ignore. This includes the aspect of time, which generally means weighing big long-term effects higher than small short-term effects.

A related topic is the definition of a lie. I've decided that a lie is a DFI—Deliberate False Impression. Ponder those three words.

But pertaining to decision-making at work, my broad description of clear thinking often narrows down to this simple definition:

Clear thinking is objectively assessing all costs and benefits of a proposal.

For example, you are a manager, and one of your employees proposes that your project use interposers for method-calls between objects. An interposer is an object that stores the address of another object. When a method is called in the interposer, it is forwarded to the object whose address is stored. An interposer thus forwards method-calls using a stored pointer. The employee explains that the use of interposers makes objects independent of each other, because none contains a hard-coded call (or reference) to another. Thus, objects can easily be swapped with unit-testers or alternate implementations. Because objects have no dependencies, they are much more portable, making reuse easy. One needs to only use the object, without needing to also get other objects it uses. He summarizes by saying that interposers offer several benefits, so they should be used on your project. Before reading on, consider how you would respond to this proposal.

Clear thinking tells you to objectively assess all costs and benefits. You rightly suspect that this employee is not being objective because he is (1) overstating benefits, and (2) understating costs by ignoring them. This employee is not thinking clearly.

Another employee overheard this conversation and said, "Definitely not! Interposers double the number of layers in every design, greatly increasing complexity and thus cost. Furthermore, every call becomes indirect, making code hard to follow, boosting cost even more. Due to these additional costs, interposers must be rejected." What do you think about this comment?

The second employee only considered the costs and ignored the benefits, so he also is not thinking clearly. Like the first employee, he is not being objective. One often encounters this situation at work (and in life) where one person says "look at the benefits" and another says "look at the costs," and neither is thinking clearly because neither is objectively evaluating both costs and benefits. Both forms of unclear thinking will cause you to make wrong decisions. The first will cause you to adopt bad ideas. The second will cause you to reject good ideas.

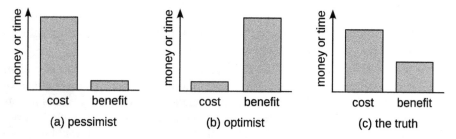

Figure 9.5: The truth is hard to find

The underlying problem you face is shown in Figure 9.5. Some people will be pessimistic about a proposed idea, and their assessment of it is shown in Figure 9.5(a). They are underestimating its benefit and overestimating its cost.

On the other hand, the person who is promoting the proposal is likely to be thinking along the lines of Figure 9.5(b), and is therefore overstating its benefit and downplaying its cost. Some smart developers become fascinated with an idea or aspect of software, such as the example of interposers, and will encourage you to push their fascination onto the entire project. These are the fanatics that I described in detail earlier in this chapter in Section 9.3, and their thinking fits Figure 9.5(b) perfectly.

Sometimes a person appears to be objectively assessing both costs and benefits, but due to his bias (or dishonesty) he is *not* being objective. Such a person can easily deceive you. If you are wise, you will be distrustful of everyone's objectivity. This is especially true if money is involved, such as a presentation from a vendor.

As a manager or lead, you are forced to learn the topic well enough to assess things for yourself. Or at a minimum, talk to other team members *privately* about the proposal to get an unbiased assessment of it. You must force yourself to be objective so that you can estimate both costs and benefits as accurately as you can, so that your thinking will be that of Figure 9.5(c)—the truth. I encourage such objectivity when deciding whether to employ the IDAR method.

In the discussion above, I used the words "assess" and "estimate" a few times. Such words imply that costs and benefits must be estimated *subjectively* instead of *objectively*. Objective estimation of monetary costs and benefits take too long for routine engineering-decisions, forcing us to base them on instinctive assessments instead. Any bias in you will sway such estimates, hurting your project.

Because costs and benefits are estimated subjectively, people on the project can argue endlessly about the merits and problems of an idea. In this case, most people won't bother arguing, and will stay on the sidelines, leaving the argument to whomever cares about the question. The decision will go in favor of whomever is most respected or can argue most convincingly. This is a bad way to make decisions! Get involved yourself, carefully maintaining your objectivity.

Sometimes a bad idea will have an eloquent proponent and an inarticulate opponent. Making matters worse, fanatics are usually the most talented people on the project, so they also tend to be eloquent orators for their obsessions. Such a situation is a severe test of your objectivity. Make the effort to learn both sides, regardless of eloquence or lack thereof.

While listening to a proponent and an opponent, be careful to *not* fall into the convenient trap of simply averaging together their estimates of costs and benefits. Doing so biases you in favor of the most extreme fanatic. Instead, get the facts from disinterested people and other objective sources.

Products, tools, processes, and ideas come and go in our profession, often to be recycled under a different name a decade later. These are often foolish fads. Be wary of following fads. Evaluate such bandwagons objectively and skeptically.

Be careful with all of your technical decisions. Clear thinking requires effort, and it's even more difficult when fanaticism, money, or fascination is involved. You must dig for truth, because it's buried.

9.7 Additional Recommendations

As discussed in the Introduction, your goal is to meet the requirements in the shortest possible time. IDAR graphs are only a part of the solution. Below, I list common problems I've observed, and my suggestions for solving them. Some of these are discussed elsewhere in this book in detail. The purpose of this list is to provide managers with a short list of bullet-items to implement in software teams.

Forbid a Coding Tool Forbid your developers from using a tool like Rhapsody® for entering design and code. One developer characterized such a tool as "More work; same result." The reason for the slowdown is that you must click on several items in the tool to do something that would take only a moment to write in source code. Therefore, have your developers write source code directly in a text editor. Although a coding tool can generate graphs, they can also be produced manually or by a tool (program) that reads source code.

Agile Use an agile technique that allows requirements and design to be changed easily while implementing and debugging. I suggest having a brief weekly meeting that airs any problems and adjusts developers' goals. Meeting daily is too frequent. You should not impose a rigid process on your team, but don't relax the controls so much that the team becomes sloppy.

Fanatics As described in Section 9.3, fanatics are smart people who overuse some aspect of software, creating excess complexity, and bogging down the project. The solution is to ensure that such people have no role in design. However, managers find such people difficult to identify and squelch because they are the top performers. Managers need to be aware that high intelligence can have gaps. When such a gap has been identified, a manager needs to have enough mettle to properly deal with the person.

Vertical Bloat The usual coding standards for C-like languages waste much vertical space, making the code-structure hard to learn, thus making learning and maintenance harder. In Section 6.14 (page 166), I discuss the Commie Coding Conventions in detail as a fictitious story about communist sabotage. I then recommend a compact style which is more readable.

Messy Designs Designs are often messy due to the lack of an enforced hierarchy of abstractions, as described back in Chapter 1. The solution is to deploy the IDAR method.

9.8 Exercises

1. Would you use interposers on your project? Why or why not?

2. Adding layers of abstraction to a design makes each object smaller, and thus makes the design simpler. Therefore, we should encourage designers to use layers of abstraction liberally. Do you agree or disagree? Why?

3. What primary effect do fanatics have on designs?

4. What curse do a few designers have, and what gift do a few others have?

5. Explain why "Making software less flexible makes it more flexible."

6. A developer on your team privately tells you that the lead of your project is creating an architecture that's too complicated, and that he has a couple of ideas on how to simplify it. How should you respond?

7. A manager responded to a design by saying, "It's complicated. It must be good!" Was this response wise or foolish? Why?

8. You are a manager interested in the IDAR method, but you don't want put your project at risk. What would be a good approach?

9. How can you adopt this method for your entire project without increasing risk?

10. You are a developer or manager who has adopted the IDAR method for a subsystem. Another developer protests your decision, saying "This method is different from the way OOP has gone for the last 25 years, so it's heading the wrong way. You are regressing. This is a mistake." What will be your reply?

Part II

Applications

Introduction to Applications

Some people learn better by reading theory, and others learn better by example. At this point, you've seen plenty of theory, including the rules for creating and drawing IDAR graphs, the process of design, some guidelines of what to do and avoid, and a set of useful design patterns. This part of the book shows all of these principles in practice in designing four nontrivial programs representing both GUI-based and real-time embedded designs. By reading through the process of designing these programs, you'll gain a practical understanding of how the design process proceeds in reality, along with insights into trade-offs one must make along the way.

The following chapters describe the design of these applications:

Chapter 10: Pen Plotter A machine which uses motors to move a pen to make a drawing on a sheet of paper. It is controlled by commands sent to it from a computer or from its control panel.

Chapter 11: Drawing Program Lets you draw shapes in a manner like OpenOffice Draw, LibreOffice Draw, or the drawing features in Microsoft Word. It is much more complex than paint programs because it stores shapes in their original forms, allowing you to change their position, size, rotation, color, etc.

Chapter 12: Digital Camera This is a basic digital camera. While easy to use, these cameras contain a great deal of electronics and mechanics that must be controlled by the software as part of the process of taking, processing and storing a picture. In addition, the software supports reviewing pictures, working with files on a memory card, and other functions.

Chapter 13: Home Heating/Cooling System An 8-bit microcontroller controls a forced-air heater and compressor-based cooler. This program shows that the IDAR method is suitable for highly constrained systems.

Please take note that these are *not* toy programs. These are not *like* programs used in real life; these *are* programs used in real life. The designs you see in the following chapters could be used to create salable products. The reasons for showing such full-size designs are to (1) demonstrate that the IDAR method works well for large designs, and (2) show you how to design full-sized software.

Also, I've sprinkled some lessons I've learned from experience among these applications, which should help you avoid common traps in design, as well as serving as helpful guides that will make you a better developer.

Chapter 10

Pen Plotter

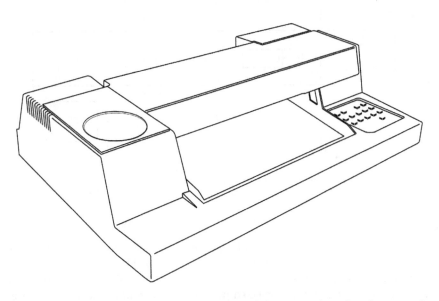

Pen plotters were electromechanical devices which let you make a drawing on a piece of paper. I said "were" because they stopped being made around 1990 when ink-jet plotters made them obsolete. A pen plotter moved the paper back and forth using a servomotor, and moved a pen back and forth in the other axis using a second servomotor. By moving these two motors, and lifting the pen up and down, it could draw anything that could be drawn with a pen. In addition, a carousel of pens was available, so the plotter could switch pens at any time, letting you plot in various colors and/or with different widths of lines.

An application running in a workstation or PC would send plotting commands to the plotter in a language called VDL—Vector Drawing Language. These were simple commands with X-Y coordinates that told the plotter to draw straight lines, arcs, circles and text.

A plotter also had a control panel which allowed you to load and unload paper, and manually choose which pen to use, in case the application didn't choose one. In

271

addition, you could digitize coordinates from an existing drawing by manually moving both motors using buttons while looking through a hollow pen-like device called a "sight", allowing you to precisely position the sight at positions on the drawing. This slow way of transferring a drawing into a computer would tax the patience of Job, but it worked and was more accurate than using graph paper.

A microprocessor inside the plotter controlled everything. Our task is to design the software for that microprocessor. For that, we need to start with its requirements.

10.1   Requirements

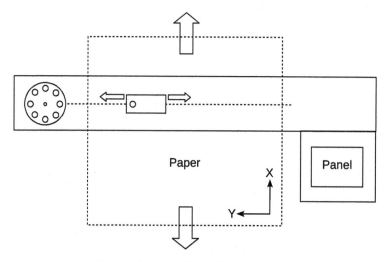

Figure 10.1: Top view of a pen plotter

Figure 10.1 shows the top view of a plotter, with paper loaded. As drawn here, the paper moves vertically, which is the X-axis, also called the paper-axis. The X-axis motor rotates a grit-covered tube which the paper is pressed onto, thus moving the paper. A carriage holding the selected pen moves horizontally, which is the Y-axis, also called the pen-axis.

The paper- and pen-axis motors are closed-loop DC servos, which means that they are ordinary motors that have encoders on their shafts used for feedback control. Some electronics counts the ticks produced by each encoder, thus keeping track of each motor's position. Software can read each position register at any time. Software is required to implement each servo by doing the following 500 or 1000 times per second: Read the position register, do some calculations, and change the voltage on the motor.

The carousel holding some pens is located at the left side of the plotter. To change pens, the following steps are done:

1. Rotate the carousel to the empty stall corresponding to the current pen.

2. By moving the carriage leftward, transfer the current pen out of the carriage and into the carousel.

3. Withdraw the carriage out of the carousel, allowing it to rotate.

4. Rotate the carousel to the desired pen stall.

5. By moving the carriage leftward, transfer the pen out of the carousel and into the carriage.

6. Withdraw the carriage out of the carousel.

The carousel can be rotated using a stepper motor. A stepper motor is easy to control in software. Using a periodic interrupt, you tell the motor to move one step in each interrupt, and it moves one step. No feedback mechanism is needed. There are sensors in the carousel-area to detect the following:

- Whether the carousel is present or absent
- Whether the carousel is at its reference angle
- Whether a pen is present or absent at the selecting position, which is at the 3:00 position in Figure 10.1

The position of the stepper motor is unknown at power-up. It's also unknown if the user has removed and replaced the carousel, because the user might have rotated the motor a little. In this case of an unknown position, when the carousel is replaced (by the user), the software rotates the carousel continuously until the reference angle sensor goes high. At that point in time, the motor and carousel are known to be at the reference angle. Also, while rotating the carousel, the software notes and remembers which pens are present and absent.

The carriage has a pen-lift mechanism on it which allows the pen in the claw to be raised or lowered by a solenoid, which in turn is controlled by software. After raising the pen, you need to wait a certain number of milliseconds before moving the X- or Y-motors to be certain that the pen is off the paper. Likewise you must wait a bit after lowering the pen. The carriage also has a sensor indicating whether its claw is holding a pen.

The control panel has the following buttons:

- Load—loads paper.
- Unload—unloads paper.
- 1-8—pressing one of these buttons selects the corresponding pen (which might mean first putting away the current pen). Pressing the button corresponding to the selected pen puts that pen away.
- Left, Right, Up, Down arrows—moves X- and Y-motors manually.
- Enter—pressing this button records the current position of the motors for transfer to the computer.

Unfortunately, the buttons on the control panel don't interrupt the processor, so the software must poll them. Experiments show that polling a button 20 times per second is frequent enough that even brief button-presses will not be missed.

The paper is pressed onto the grit-tube by a pair of pinch wheels. The software can move these wheels up or down by applying voltage to a DC motor and then polling the up-sensor or down-sensor, which indicate whether the wheels are up or down.

Paper is loaded using the following steps:

1. The user places a sheet of paper into the plotter.
2. The user presses the Load button.
3. Software lowers the pinch wheels.
4. Software moves the paper up (negative X direction) until the front paper-present sensor goes low.
5. Software then moves the paper down (positive X direction) until the rear paper-present sensor goes low. These two sensors allow the software to determine the height (X-size) of the paper.
6. Software then moves the carriage from right to left (positive Y direction), until the paper-present sensor in the carriage indicates that it is no longer seeing paper. This allows the plotter to determine the width (Y-size) of the paper.
7. Software moves the paper back and forth twice over its entire length to embed the grit-tube tracks into the paper.
8. At this point, plotting may begin.

Paper is unloaded using the following steps:

1. The user presses the Unload button.
2. Software moves the paper to its center position, so it won't fall off the plotter when released.
3. Software raises the pinch wheels.

We won't describe the VDL commands in detail here, but the incomplete list below shows what some of the commands do:

- Set maximum plotting velocity of each pen.
- Select pen N.
- Put away current pen.
- Unload paper.
- Set clipping rectangle.
- Set dash-pattern for subsequent lines.
- Raise pen.
- Lower pen.
- Move to (x,y).
- Get status/position/pen/etc.

Those VDL commands arrive at an I/O. The "get" commands in VDL also output values through the I/O.

10.2   Starting the Design

Do you feel lost? The good news is that you have a tolerably complete requirements document. I did that for you, and I hope you are thankful. Let's follow the steps described in Chapter 5. It says we should start with a requirements document (we can check that one off), and talk to our users. This is a book, so we cannot do that. Chapter 5 also says that we should look for verb objects and several kinds of noun objects. How many kinds of noun objects do you remember? They are described on page 114, and common examples include data-storage, agent nouns, and concrete nouns. Keeping both verb and noun objects in mind, we will make a list based on reading the requirements. These will be mostly concrete objects due to the large number of electronic and mechanical devices in this pen plotter.

Let's move on to finding those objects. Step 1 of the five-step process of design (page 117) tells us to find the obvious objects on the top and bottom of the IDAR graph, which are:

- *Plotter*—This top-level object controls everything. That one was easy. Now let's think about bottom-level objects.

- *Servo*—The X- and Y-axis motors are servos, so we'll need a servo class that produces two instances.

- *Sensors*—Many sensors are scattered inside the plotter, and the electronics schematic (not reproduced in this book) tells us that all are read in a similar manner, so let's make an object that can read any of them.

- *CarouselMotor*—The carousel is the only stepper motor in the machine, so we'll need a separate object to control it.

- *VDL* subsystem—The VDL command-interpreter is an obvious choice for a subsystem. We'll think about its design later.

- *PenLift*—Here's a bit of electronics that will need some code to control it. The *Ticker* object described below will provide a time-delay after raising or lowering the pen. There is a pen-present sensor in the claw, so this class can read it using the *Sensors* object. But why bother adding a method for that in this *PenLift* object when anybody can read the sensor using the *Sensors* object? This is a question of organizing by device-type versus functional category. We'll need to think about this some more.

- *WheelLift*—The pinch-wheel motor is another bit of electronics that needs code to control it. While this motor is moving, our code must poll the up-sensor and down-sensor to determine when to stop the motor.

- *CtrlPanel*—All those buttons need to be polled 20 times per second, and this object will do that. When a button is pressed, this object will coordinate with *Plotter* and perform the action.

- *IO*—The I/O needs an object to handle dataflows in both directions. Note that arriving VDL commands might conflict with actions being done on the control panel. Letting *Plotter* sort out such contentions would be appropriate.

- *Pen?*—There is no circuitry for each pen, although there is a pen-present sensor in the carousel. This is not a bottom-level object, but it's close. Let's think about it some more in a few minutes.

- *Ticker*—After thinking things over for a few minutes, we realize that several items need to be monitored regularly or need times, which are: X-motor, Y-motor, carousel stepper, control panel, and time-delays after raising or lowering the pen. A simple way to handle all this is to have one hardware-timer interrupt the CPU at the highest rate needed (1000 times per second), and count downward to provide the lower rates. A ticker object can do those things. We'll want to think about whether to use the Direct Distributor, Indirect Distributor, or Watcher patterns for this *Ticker* object. There are five objects that need tick notices, and perhaps more if we missed some, which is high enough to make me reluctant to use the Direct Distributor. On the other hand, the Direct Distributor will give the highest performance, but we'll need to think about having all those dependencies in the *Ticker* object.

Now let's identify the obvious threads. The *Plotter* object is one obvious possessor of a thread. Another is the *VDL* subsystem. For the rest of the system, it's hard to tell. We'll think about this again later.

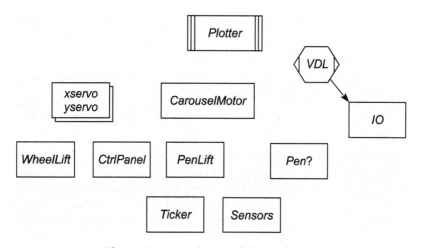

Figure 10.2: Pen plotter: obvious objects

We are done identifying the obvious objects. Figure 10.2 is a rough first-pass drawing of these objects that we have defined so far. I put *Plotter* at the top for obvious reasons. I drew a command from *VDL* to *IO* because that command is obvious. I put *Ticker* and *Sensors* on the bottom because they will have no subordinates, and many objects will need their services.

10.3   First Trial Design

Step 2 of the five-step process tells us to define objects between the obvious top-level and bottom-level objects we identified above. Section 5.4.2 (page 118) offers several ideas for identifying such unobvious objects, one of which is the operations the software is supposed to perform. What operations should this pen plotter do? We can find them in the list of VDL and front panel operations:

- Select a pen.
- Put the selected pen back into the carousel.
- Load a sheet of paper.
- Unload a sheet of paper.
- Set maximum plotting speed for each pen.
- Set clipping rectangle. This operation will probably be implemented within VDL, and I cannot think of any use for it outside VDL.
- Raise and lower the pen. The *PenLift* object can do this, so this operation is already covered.
- Move to (x,y).
- Move continuously in (x,y) directed by the control panel.

Let's start with operations done by the control panel, because they *must* be implemented outside the *VDL* subsystem. They are: Selecting a pen, putting the pen away, loading and unloading the sheet, and moving continuously in both axes.

The pen must be selected or put away, so it appears that we will need the *Pen* object we considered in the "obvious" list above. Now we face a decision: Shall we have eight pen objects, one for each stall in the carousel, or just one? Let's go with only one *Pen* object, representing the currently selected pen. However, this *Pen* object will remember which pens are installed in the carousel.

Another capability we need is a movement in (x,y). Let's call that the *Move* object, and it is responsible for moving the X- and Y-motors in tandem to the target position, and for continuous moves directed by the control panel.

Looking at the list above, we see that we also need to be able to load and unload a sheet of paper. Loading is a complex operation because it requires several movements to determine the size of the paper. Let's create a *Load* object which performs both loading and unloading. The unload operation is simple and is the dual of the load operation, giving the object's role good cohesion.

Now let's list the superior-subordinate pairings:

- *Move* commands *xservo* and *yservo*.
- *Pen* commands *PenLift*, *CarouselMotor*, and *Move*.
- *Load* commands *WheelLift* and *Move*.
- *CtrlPanel* commands *Load*, *Move*, and *Pen*.
- *VDL* commands *Load*, *Move*, and *Pen*.
- *Ticker* sends notices to several objects.
- *Pen*, *Move*, *Load*, and *WheelLift* command *Sensors*.

I mentioned earlier that VDL and the control panel could try to command the mechanics at the same time, and that *Plotter* would need to decide between them. This protocol means that *Plotter* commands both *CtrlPanel* and *VDL*, and that both *CtrlPanel* and *VDL* must first ask *Plotter* for exclusive access to the machine before proceeding. Also, both *CtrlPanel* and *VDL* will need to notify *Plotter* when they no

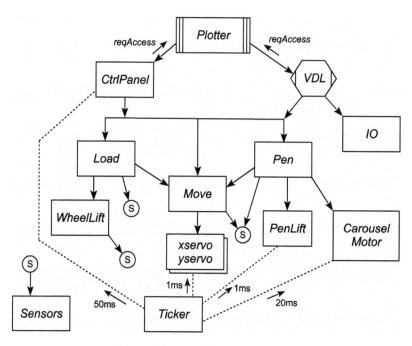

Figure 10.3: Pen plotter: trial design

longer need exclusive access to the machine. This approach follows the Resourceful Boss pattern described in Section 7.1.2 on page 180.

At this point, Figure 10.3 shows our trial design. It is surprising how the short list of commands above turned into so many lines in the graph. I created the *Ticker* using the Direct Distributor pattern. If the dependencies prove to be too burdensome later, this decision can easily be changed. The commands to *Sensors* are shown with "S" lollipop labels because their command lines would clutter the graph too much. Alternatively, we could show *Sensors* as a popular object.

10.4   Refining the Design

At this point in our design, we have completed Steps 1 and 2 of the five-step process described in Section 5.4, producing a trial design. Step 3 tells us to reread the requirements and hand-check their fulfillment, including error cases. Rereading and hand-checking the requirements (while thinking of error conditions) is especially fruitful, as it reveals several omissions in our design, which are listed below:

- The *CtrlPanel* object needs its own thread, otherwise it will perform actions from the ticker's thread, which is an ISR (Interrupt Service Routine). That would never work because some operations block the calling thread.

- The X- and Y-servos are intimately tied together because the motors must accelerate and decelerate in tandem. Therefore, the accelerations of the two motors are interlinked. So let's put the servo code in the *Move* object and rename it to *XYservo*. The old servo objects become private records inside *XYservo* named *xmotor* and *ymotor*.

- The *Pen* object might be trying to do too much, as it also monitors removal and replacing of the carousel, and performing the pen-scan when the carousel is replaced. Let's split *Pen* by moving the carousel-handling portion of it into a new *Carousel* object.

- The *CarouselMotor* object needs to move its motor to a known position, so it will need to command the *Sensors* object. Because its tick notice is called every 20 ms, it can poll the other carousel-related sensors as well and report them to the *Carousel* object. But polling the other sensors is not in its role, so we'll need to think about this polling some more. The *CarouselMotor* object sends two notices to *Carousel*: *moveDone* and *sensorVals*.

- VDL needs a tick notice so it can time-out and release access to the mechanics in case the I/O stops supplying it data for a while.

- That tick notice to VDL will be a long line that's difficult to graph, so let's use lollipop labels for tick notices and normal lines for commands to *Sensors*.

- Notice that both *CtrlPanel* and *VDL* command a rail containing the objects *Load*, *Move*, and *Pen*. Thinking about this for a moment, we realize that these objects implement all the plotting operations, so let's label it the "plotting rail".

- *WheelLift* will also need tick notices so that it can time-out in case the raising or lowering of the wheels is taking too long, which would indicate that the mechanics are jammed. The ticker is already supplying a 50 ms notice to another object, so we can use that one here as well to avoid requiring that *Ticker* implement a different period.

- We also should add more notices to the graph. For example, the I/O sends a *char* notice to *VDL*, and several objects send *done* notices to indicate that their operations have finished.

Figure 10.4 is the result of all these changes. A remarkable aspect of this graph is that a surprising amount of information and complexity can be represented clearly in only one IDAR graph. There is no other kind of graph available that can portray this much useful information.

We also observe that most notices are named *done*. Such a *done* notice is needed whenever an object starts a time-consuming operation and does *not* block its caller. Finally, roles are evaluated in terms of their clarity, cohesion, and concealment, so I've listed the roles of all these objects in Table 10.1.

10.5 Final Design

Let's look things over once again. We have not paid enough attention to threading. In particular, let's think some more about all those *done* notices below the plotting rail.

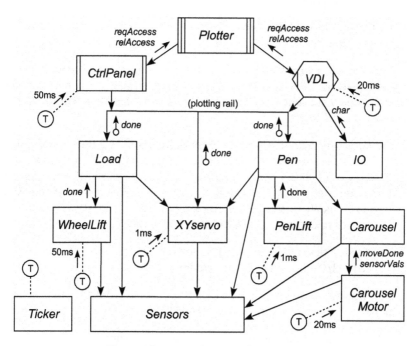

Figure 10.4: Pen plotter: refined design

We observe that no objects below the plotting rail contain threads. Consequently, they must block their superiors until their operations are done. Do we really want to do that? For example, while the X- and Y-motors are drawing a line, is there anything else the machine can do? Or while a pen is being selected, is there anything else that can be done? The only thing that must be done while these operations are active is to poll the buttons on the control panel, and that's done in an ISR, so that will be happening anyway. So I see no problem with having all objects below the plotting rail block their callers. A result of this decision is that all those *done* notices become riders because they will ride on method returns.

The user can remove or replace the carousel at any time, and after it has been replaced, we should rotate the carousel one revolution to see which pens are in it. This is called a "pen scan", and if a thread does not do this, then it must be done in an ISR. Doing this in a thread would result in simpler code, which means the *Carousel* object should have a thread. It should also send a *changed* notice to *Pen* when the carousel is removed or rescanned.

All other operations are initiated by the control panel or VDL, which have their own threads. At this point, we have evaluated where all threads can be blocked, so hopefully we won't need to alter the threading model again. We should take a moment and ponder the fact that we have designed an interactive real-time system using only four threads. And we could have gotten away with only three threads if we were willing to do the pen scan in ISR code. Having few threads is a sign of good design because the fewer threads you have, the fewer race-conditions you'll be creating.

It's interesting to note that a significant change to the threads could be made this

Object	Role
Plotter	Oversees entire plotter.
CtrlPanel	Polls buttons and performs their actions.
VDL	Executes incoming VDL commands.
IO	Receives or transmits bytes from/to the I/O port.
Load	Loads/unloads sheet and determines paper-size.
Pen	Selects or puts away a pen.
PenLift	Raises or lowers the pen claw in the carriage.
Carousel	Manages the carousel.
CarouselMotor	Rotates the carousel motor in either direction.
XYservo	Controls both X- and Y-motors in tandem, and it can stop a move when a sensor changes.
WheelLift	Raises or lowers the pinch wheels.
Sensors	Can read any sensor.
Ticker	Supplies periodic tick-notices to objects.

Table 10.1: Roles of objects in pen plotter

late in the design, with negligible effect on the design. This is an important point: Threads can be decided later in some systems. First identify your objects and how they communicate with each other (their commands and notices). Decisions about threading can wait, unless queues for data will be needed. In that case, you'll need to plan your threads earlier.

A lingering question is whether we want *CarouselMotor* to poll the sensors that detect whether the carousel is present and whether a pen is in the current stall. We did this out of convenience because a tick notice is being sent to *CarouselMotor*. But such polling is not in its role, so let's fix it. Let's add a notice to *Carousel* that's called every 50 ms by *Ticker* so it can poll those sensors itself, thus eliminating this source of poor cohesion in *CarouselMotor*.

A detail we've forgotten is that the drawing rules state that an object containing an ISR should have a little lightning-bolt inside its rectangle. Let's add those to the *Ticker* and *IO* objects.

Figure 10.5 is the result of these decisions, and represents our final design. Notice that all *done* notices below the plotting rail are now riders, and that *Carousel* is now an active object because it contains a thread. Also, *CarouselMotor* still reads a sensor. It needs to do this when the motor's position is unknown. It rotates the motor until the reference-angle sensor changes, which establishes a known position.

A nagging detail we left unaddressed is how the *Ticker* object should distribute its notices. It is still using the Direct Distributor pattern, but now it has seven clients, resulting in seven unrelated dependencies in its code. If we're unhappy with that, we could change it to the Indirect Distributor pattern wherein each client that needs tick notices registers in advance for them. If we were to ask the other developers on the team about this change, they would probably tell us that this indirect approach would be "more work; same results." So let's leave it as-is.

Step 4 of the five-step process requires that we attempt to improve and simplify the

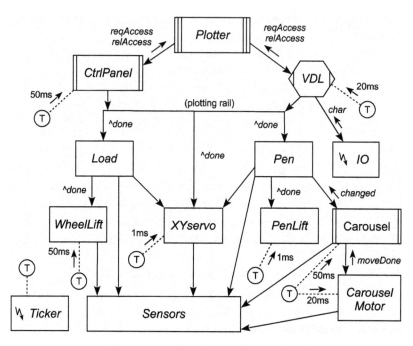

Figure 10.5: Pen plotter: final design

design. We already changed the *done* notices from indirect to riders, and kept threads to a minimum. I can't think of any additional improvements or simplifications.

Finally, this design is probably *not* final, despite my claim above. As this software is coded and debugged, we will probably encounter details we overlooked during the process of design. But the resulting changes will almost certainly be minor. It's hard to believe that we could get this far while overlooking some major feature or aspect that would force a major change in the design.

That's what peer-reviews are for. At this point, this design should be reviewed by others as a recheck for omissions and misunderstandings. Also, if a mistake is found later, peer-reviews are a good technique for blame-shifting or at least blame-sharing. Yes, I am half joking, but seriously, peer-reviews are good for uncovering our blind spots, but only if the reviews are thorough. The danger is that the reviewers will skim the requirements and glance at the design, and say that it all looks fine. Such a review is worthless. Reviewers must take enough time to learn the design well and think through the various operations using steps similar to the five steps you followed when creating the design.

Wrap-up   It took only a few hours to create this design. In that time, we were able to identify top-level, bottom-level, and mid-level objects fairly quickly because IDAR graphs provided us with guidance about organizing them. Most of our time was spent evaluating details of how objects need to interact with each other, and checking that all the items in the requirements were fulfilled, including everything that could go wrong. We now have a solid design that you can implement with confidence.

Did you notice that we spent no time thinking about the four IDAR rules? That's because they agree well with our instincts, so our design naturally obeyed them. We had to make a couple of changes to satisfy the Down and Role rules, so we did not completely satisfy the IDAR rules by instinct, but we came close.

In a large system, each subsystem is about as complex as this pen plotter we just designed. In such a system, you need a top-level IDAR graph showing the interactions among the subsystems, and once that's done, the developers on the project can independently design their subsystems. Using this process, very large programs can be designed cleanly using IDAR graphs.

I hate to disappoint you, but we're not done with this pen plotter. We still need to design its VDL subsystem.

10.6 VDL Subsystem

VDL is an abbreviation for "Vector Drawing Language", which is the set of commands a computer can send to the plotter over the I/O. All features for drawing are accessible through VDL commands.

10.6.1 Requirements

Each command starts with a short name or mnemonic of at most four letters (to make name-lookup easy), followed by parameters (separated by spaces), and terminated by the next command or a semicolon. Table 10.2 is a summary of all the commands.

The VDL commands for a simple drawing are shown below, and its output is shown in Figure 10.6.

```
init fac 0.2 pen 1 circ 1000 1000 1000 m 500 500
text "VDL" m 500 1000 1500 1000 up unld;
```

Figure 10.6: Sample plot

We were considering adding commands which would draw rectangles and polygons, and fill them with single-hatch or cross-hatch patterns. But we took the advice given in Section 5.1 (page 112), and asked our customers what features they wanted in a pen plotter. The gist of what they said is, "Forget the fancy stuff; we do all that in our own software. Just give us lines, arcs, and text, and we'll do the rest." So we removed such filled areas from the commands, making our software simpler and shortening our schedule. Keeping in touch with your customers is wise.

Except for a small buffer inside the *IO* object, arriving commands are not buffered within the plotter, although they could be if you wanted to optimize the movements of the mechanics. But for now, a command is executed as soon as it is fetched from the I/O's buffer. The queuing that occurs in the I/O's buffer will improve performance

Command	Description
init	Initialize all settings.
vel *p vel*	Set maximum plotting velocity of a pen.
pen *p*	Fetch pen *p* (1-8); 0 puts it away.
unld	Unload paper.
fac *fac*	Set scaling factor.
clip *x1 y1 x2 y2*	Set clipping rectangle.
dash *n len*	Set dash-pattern for everything but text.
up	Raise pen.
down	Lower pen.
m *x y* ...	Move to (x,y); pen drops for more points.
arc *xc yc xf yf*	Arc to (xf,yf) centered at (xc,yc).
circ *xc yc r*	Circle of radius *r* centered at $(xc\ yc)$.
fset *f s*	Select font *f* and character set *s*.
tsiz *p*	Set text size to *p* points.
tdir *angle*	Set text direction to *angle*.
text "*text*"	Draw text.
gtex "*text*"	Get size of text string.
gcor	Get coordinate range (max clipping rectangle).
gpos	Get current position.
gpen	Get current pen-number.
gsta	Get status.

Table 10.2: VDL commands

slightly because it means that the next command is usually available in the buffer as soon as the execution of the current one finishes.

This list of commands tells you enough that you can create the design at the level of objects (i.e., an IDAR graph). You'll need more detailed requirements to design the methods within the objects, such as the layout of the coordinate system, details about the syntax, and so on.

10.6.2   Starting the Design

Once again, we'll follow the five steps described in Section 5.4 (page 117). But knowing that this is a subsystem, the top-level design which we created above shows us what objects and other subsystems will be needed by this subsystem. Having such environmental objects already specified makes the design of the subsystem a bit easier because you are starting from something instead of nothing.

We can start by drawing the subman at the top (denoted as active), and the external objects which will provide services for this subsystem with dashed lines. Those external objects are *Pen*, *XYservo*, *Load*, and *IO*, and are shown in Figure 10.7.

Now we need to identify some objects between the subman at the top and the dashed objects at the bottom. Let's think about the various kinds of noun objects. One kind that should be considered is data-storage: The amount of data that VDL

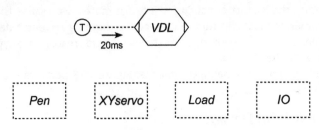

Figure 10.7: Environment of the VDL subsystem

keeps on hand is negligible, and they'll be fields within the objects we define. But there's one major exception: the fonts. They contain much read-only data which will need methods to access, so we've just identified a class named *Font* and some instances of it. Let's add them to the IDAR graph using the stack-notation signifying multiple instances.

To get more ideas of objects, we can read the requirements, which in our case consists mostly of the list of commands in Table 10.2. We notice that some commands occur in related groups. The obvious approach is to make each group an object, even though doing so is likely to yield objects that are trait-based and thus might have poor clarity. This approach produces the following list:

- Text: **fset**, **tsiz**, **gtex**, and **text** commands.
- Arcs: **arc** and **circ** commands.
- Pens: **vdl** and **vel** commands.
- Coordinates: **fac**, **clip**, **gcor**, and **gpos** commands.

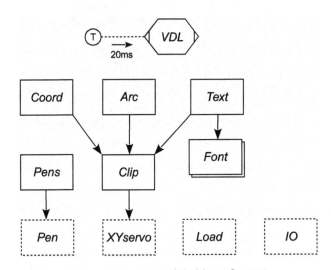

Figure 10.8: Some trial objects for VDL

Section 5.4.2 (page 118) describes several methods for finding unobvious objects. One such method is to think of how to combine low-level services in useful ways.

After pondering the VDL commands for a few minutes, we realize that *all* of the drawing commands must clip their output to the clipping rectangle defined by the **clip** command. This observation suggests that we should create a verb-type *Clip* object which commands the *XYservo*.

After adding some reasonable commands, Figure 10.8 portrays the fragment of design that we have so far.

10.6.3   First Trial Design

To arrive at our first trial design, we need to provide objects to implement all the VDL commands, and as a double-check, make sure that we are commanding all four of the bottom-level objects. First, let's go through the remaining VDL commands, and put them in objects.

- Page: The **unld** command can go into a page-handling object. This will be a tiny object consisting of one call into the external *Load* object, unless we can find some more page-handling logic that belongs in it.

- Dash: The requirements say that "everything but text" is drawn with the current dash pattern set by the **dash** command, so let's create an object that creates dashed lines. *Dash* will command the *Clip* object we defined above.
  Next on the list is the **m** (move) command. The *Dash* object is a good place to put it, because the only thing this command does is draw line(s) with the current dash pattern.

- A couple of control commands are **init** and **gsta** (get status). The VDL subman is responsible for overall control, so let's put these commands in there.

As I mentioned, we should go through the four external bottom-level objects to make sure that all of them are being commanded. Here's what we see:

- *Pen* will be commanded by the *Pens* object, which is reasonable.
- *XYservo* will be commanded by the *Clip* object, as expected.
- *Load* will be commanded by the *Page* object, as anyone would expect.
- *IO* will be commanded by..., let's see, I'm looking...Hmm, we must have forgotten something, because nothing is commanding the *IO*. Oh yes, we forgot the parser! Let's put the parser in there.

Hooking everything together with the expected commands gives us Figure 10.9, which is our trial design.

10.6.4   Refining the Design

This trial design has problems. Some big problems. It's not even a legal IDAR graph. Did you see why? The *Parser* is commanding *VDL*, which is the topmost boss over this subsystem. When *Parser* receives the **init** or **gsta** (get status) commands, it tells *VDL* to perform the command. That is what Page-Jones calls an "inversion of authority". We can fix it by following the Watcher pattern, where the *Parser* watches for one of those two commands, and reports them to *VDL* as notices. This might seem like a

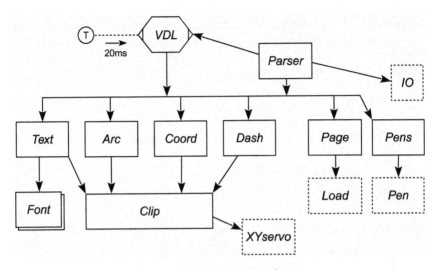

Figure 10.9: Trial design of VDL

semantic shell-game to you where nothing has actually changed. But conceptually, the superior in the Watcher pattern has told the subordinate to relay commands to it, similar to the Secretary pattern. And since *Parser* can now relay some commands to *VDL*, it might as well relay *all* commands to *VDL* to keep the design as simple as possible by not having two ways of executing commands.

Another mistake you might have noticed is that the *Arc* object is not commanding the *Dash* object as it should, but is directly commanding *Clip* instead. Thus, arcs and circles will not be drawn dashed.

Let's think about a move command. *Dash* will perform it, which commands *Clip*. But *Dash* never communicates with *Coord*, so *Dash* is not able to scale the (x,y) value from scaled units into motor units. Both *Dash* and *Arc* receive coordinates from *Parser*, so both of them must command *Coord*. The **text** command does not contain an (x,y) coordinate, but draws text at the current position, so it doesn't need to command *Coord*.

Section 5.4 tells us to consider all conditions and modes as we are hand-executing the design. One condition is a line passing outside the clipping rectangle. What happens in the *Clip* object when a line passes from outside the clipping rectangle back to within it? The *Clip* code will raise the pen, move it to the entry coordinate, and draw a line starting there. But that means that *Clip* will need to raise and lower the pen, and our graph shows that it does not command *Pen*. Let's fix that.

This mistake is a good example of the wisdom contained in the five steps in Section 5.4. Another example is the **vel** command, which sets pen velocity in the *Pens* object. *Clip* needs to know this, so as a result of hand-executing this command, we realize that *Pens* needs to tell *Clip* what velocity to use.

Figure 10.10 shows the result of these refinements in design. The design has changed substantially, which is normal. We first scribbled down a design that was somewhat close. Then we checked it against the requirements, and hand-executed the operations, which revealed several mistakes. Finding mistakes is normal. It's easier to create a design with mistakes and to improve it, than to try to make it perfect on the first attempt. The human mind can't keep all the required details in mind, so we forget details such as telling *Clip* about a change in velocity. That's why we hand-check the design against the requirements.

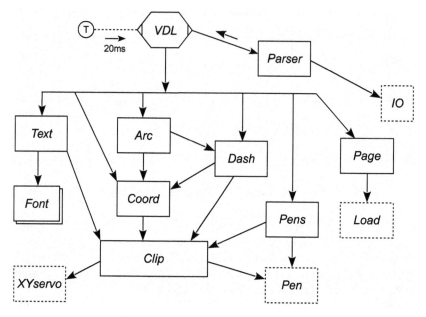

Figure 10.10: Refined design of VDL

10.6.5   Final Design

This design is good. Hand-checking against the requirements shows that it should perform as intended. Step 3 of the design process tells us to stare at the design and ponder anything that is bothersome. Two things bother me. First, we need to add notices, even if they are merely rider notices.

The second is more substantial. It's the *Text* object. Does anything about it bother you? It's too big. It's trying to do too much. The font specifies each character in the form of lines and cubic curves, so there will be some nontrivial code to draw each character. In addition, the characters need to be positioned correctly, and that's nontrivial if a variable-width font is selected. Let's see if we can extract some useful subordinate objects out of this overlarge *Text* object.

Text consists of characters, which are drawn individually. That suggests that we should have a *DrawChar* object which knows how to draw a character. I mentioned that each character in a font consists of lines and cubic curves, so let's define a *Cubic* object (commanded by *DrawChar*) which knows how to draw a cubic polynomial.

Also, a font describes characters in a coordinate system, and those coordinates will need to be converted into motor-coordinates for plotting. Let's add an *Xform* object which does this conversion. Note that the **tsiz** (text size) command will be implemented inside this object.

I think that splitting apart the *Text* object in this manner will yield objects having a reasonable size.

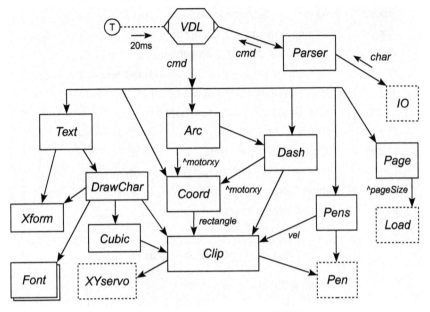

Figure 10.11: Final design of VDL

Figure 10.11 shows our final design, and Table 10.3 is its list of roles.

You have seen a realistic example of the process of designing software using the IDAR method, complete with all the mistakes along the way.

10.6.6   Simplicity is the Goal

Let's examine the following sentence quoted from the discussion above:

> *That suggests that we should have a* DrawChar *object which knows how to draw a character.*

That sentence reveals the big difference between thinking in terms of noun-type versus verb-type objects discussed in Section 5.2 on page 112. Let's examine these in the context of the *DrawChar* object:

Verb-type We need to draw a character, so let's create a *DrawChar* object which contains a primary *draw* command which is passed a pointer to the character-data in the font. Other commands in this object will support *draw*.

Noun-type We have data in a font describing a character. Let's create a *Char* object containing a pointer to that data, and we'll think of *Char* as being that character itself. Furthermore, the character *Char* knows how to draw itself via its *draw* command (and using private methods as needed).

Object	Role
VDL	Subman which oversees this subsystem.
Parser	Assembles each command into a record.
Arc	Implements arc and circle commands.
Dash	Draws with current dash-setting.
Coord	Implements scale-command and transforms coordinates.
Text	Implements all text-related commands.
Xform	Coordinate transform for characters.
DrawChar	Draws a character.
Cubic	Draws a cubic polynomial for a character.
Font	Provides access to characters in a font.
Page	Implements unload command, and provides page-info.
Pens	Implements pen-related commands.
Clip	Clips lines to a rectangle.

Table 10.3: Roles of objects in VDL

Which kind of thinking do you prefer? Which kind is correct for object-oriented software? Here is my suggestion: Choose the way that produces the simplest design. Back in the Introduction on page 11, I reasoned that the goal of design is to "Fulfill the requirements in the shortest possible schedule." Then I stated that because schedule is approximately proportional to complexity, this goal is equivalent to saying "Fulfill the requirements with the simplest possible design." The simplest design is usually the best design.

DrawChar can be a verb-type object because it has one primary command, which is its one action: draw. For more information about verb-type objects, refer to Section 5.2.1 on page 113. Making *DrawChar* a verb-type object offers two advantages:

1. The *DrawChar* object has no fields, making its design simpler.
2. Because *DrawChar* has no fields, it need not be instantiated, so you need not store and manage an instance, making the design even simpler.

In this *DrawChar* example, the verb-type object was simpler for two reasons, so it was selected. In other situations, a noun-type object will be simpler and should be selected. For example, consider the *Font* class. A verb-type object would require maintaining a separate pointer to the font data, and the font "object" would only contain methods which accept that pointer as a parameter. Noun-oriented thinking says, "A font is an object containing characters, and which knows how to supply the data for each character," and consequently, the object contains pointer(s) to the data. As a result, a noun-type object would represent the simplest design.

I strongly suggest thinking in terms of services, which means keeping both nouns and verbs in mind. You were probably taught only noun-oriented thinking, to the neglect of verb-oriented. Gaining fluency in services (comprising both nouns and verbs) will make you a better software developer.

10.7   Designing an Object

That finishes the design and discussion of the VDL subsystem. Before we continue to the next chapter, let's create a detailed design of one of the above objects. We see that the *Clip* object is crucial because all moves go through it. Let's design it.

First, we need to list its commands and notices (i.e., its interface). Table 10.4 lists the public methods contained within the *Clip* object.

Method	Role
setRect	Sets the clipping rectangle.
setVel	Sets velocity to use in subsequent lines.
getCurPos	Returns the current position (x, y, up).
move	Moves to (x, y, up).

Table 10.4: Interface for *Clip* object

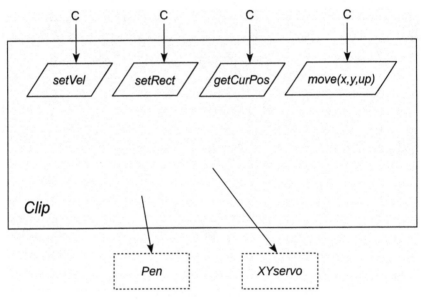

Figure 10.12: Interface and environment of the *Clip* object

Figure 10.12 shows the public interface of the *Clip* object, and the objects which it will be commanding. This figure is mostly a restatement of Table 10.4, but it's helpful for those of us who think graphically.

Now, what shall we put between our public methods and the external objects that we'll call? Let's think about the private fields this object will need. The getters and setters tell us some of the fields, which are (1) the clipping rectangle, (2) the velocity, and (3) the current position (x,y,up).

Section 5.6.3 (page 130), which describes how to find methods within an object, suggests looking at all the operations the object is supposed to perform. In the case of *Clip*, the only nontrivial operation it has is *move*. So let's think through what the *move* method does. It is given an (x,y) location. It moves from the current position to that new (x,y), with clipping. The current position is already a field, so we should not need any more fields.

Do we need any private methods? To help with clipping, we need a *calcZone* method to calculate the four-bit zone-code of a point, where bit-0 in the zone-code means the point is above the clipping rectangle, bit-1 means it's below, bit-2 means it's to the left, and bit-3 means it's to the right. Zero, one, or two bits can be set in a zone-code. Also, *move* needs to calculate an intersection along one of the four edges of the clipping rectangle, so we can put that in another method called *intersect*. With those two methods, the remaining work that *move* needs to do is the logic associated with selecting intersections to compute based on zones, and making the movements. Leaving that code in *move* should be reasonable.

The result of incorporating these decisions into the design of the *Clip* object is shown in Figure 10.13.

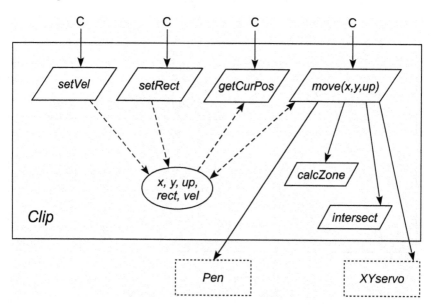

Figure 10.13: Final design of the *Clip* object

That design is much simpler than what we had to do for the pen plotter or its VDL subsystem. It's common for objects to have simple designs comparable to this one. For example, let's look at a few more objects in *VDL* and estimate how many private methods they'll need.

Dash Public methods will compute dash pattern lengths, and its public *draw* method will contain a loop that computes the actual dashes that are drawn. But I don't foresee any need for private methods.

Text This object has several public methods that support commands such as **fset** and **tsiz**. I suspect that both of these methods will command *Xform* to compute the height of characters in the current font in native units, so no private method will be needed for this chore. But both the **text** and **gtex** commands parse a quoted string, so we will need a private method to do that.

Coord I think its public methods can do all the work, so no private methods will be needed.

From this example, you can see that method-level design is typically simpler and easier than object-level design. For many objects, there is little design-work to do because they need no private methods. But if an object is considerably more complex than these, do *not* be in a hurry to split it. If its clarity and cohesion are good, and its internal design is clear, there would be no benefit to splitting it apart.

Don't forget that structure itself is a form of complexity, as was explained in Section 6.10 (page 151). So splitting an object might not provide any benefit of improved clarity, but it will certainly impose a cost arising from the additional complexity due to the extra structure. Try to gauge this trade-off objectively, as I've seen too many people subdivide designs excessively, not understanding that they were increasing complexity instead of reducing it.

10.8 Exercises

1. In this pen plotter, why are almost all notices riders?

2. List the commands, notices and actions that occur after the characters "unld" arrive at the I/O.

3. Identify a group of objects in this design that could compose a reasonable subsystem (aside from VDL).

4. *Ticker* contains many unrelated dependencies because it employs the Direct Distributor pattern. How can these dependencies be removed without using the hard-to-follow Indirect Distributor pattern?

5. To cut cost, it was decided to replace the carousel motor with a gear connected to the X-axis motor. The gear is engaged or disengaged by an electric solenoid which is under software control. What changes will need to be made to the IDAR graph?

6. *Plotter* does nothing but grant exclusive access to *VDL* or *CtrlPanel*. The design could be simplified by eliminating *Plotter* and having *VDL* and *CtrlPanel* handle access themselves. What do you think of this idea?

Chapter 11

Drawing Application

— water, wagon, weapon

You have probably used both a painting application and a drawing application. The way you use both is similar, but a painting application is not able to change an item after its creation. That's because as soon as you create an item, such as a circle, it is converted to pixels (dots), and from then on, the application has no knowledge of what the dots on the display mean. It has forgotten about the item you created.

On the other hand, a drawing application remembers every item you create, allowing you to select and modify it in any way and at any time you wish. For example, you can delete, rotate, resize and reposition items, as well as changing their color, line-widths, dash-pattern, etc. You can even select a group of items, and make changes to the group. Furthermore, selecting a group allows you to change alignments, sizes and spacing of items relative to each other. For example, you can align the top edges of all the items, center them along a common centerline, equally space them horizontally, or make them all the same height. Such features are far superior to what a painting application can do.

The design of this drawing application employs the GUI App pattern. Below, we start with a primer on GUIs to provide an overview of their operation and to give you some additional details needed for this application.

11.1   Primer on GUIs

A drawing application makes heavy use of a GUI (Graphical User Interface). If you have programmed a GUI, particularly at the event-level, you can skip this section, as it provides an overview of GUI-programming.

The GUI system is the part of an operating system that manages the GUI on the monitor. Most GUI systems are similar. Your application tells the GUI system what windows and other GUI-objects to create and manage. The GUI system tells your application about events that happen to your objects, such as mouse-clicks, keyboard input, etc. That is, a GUI system reports *events* to your application. Figure 11.1 is an IDAR graph portraying the environment for a GUI-based application.

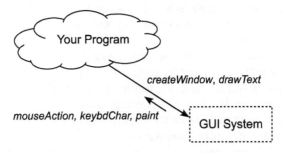

Figure 11.1: GUI environment

Events and Callbacks In this graph, the application has commanded the GUI system to create a window. The GUI system in turn reports events that occur within the window (such as mouse movements) back to the application. These events are reported in the form of callbacks, which means the GUI system calls a subroutine in your application from its thread. You gave it the address of the subroutine in a prior call, and every window or object which you created in the GUI has at least one callback subroutine associated with it. In IDAR graphs, these callbacks are shown as notices because they notify your application about interesting events.

In some GUI systems, all standard events (such as keyboard and mouse actions) use a single callback subroutine, with the particular event indicated in a parameter having many predefined values. For example, Microsoft Windows reports a right-click event as the constant value WM_RBUTTONDOWN in its callback. Other GUI systems use a separate callback subroutine for each event.

Painting One important callback is "paint". This notice tells your application that a rectangular portion of its window has become invalidated, meaning that its pixels on the screen are incorrect. So you need to "paint" those pixels to make the display correct, and you do so by drawing the items located in that area. There are many subroutines in the GUI system that let you draw lines, text, and area-fills.

In the drawing application that we're designing, we'll need to figure out which items are located in the area that needs repainting, and draw those. If the drawing is being printed, then all the items in the drawing need to be painted to the printer instead of to the view on the monitor.

To further complicate matters, the coordinate system we'll use in the drawing application is not the pixels on the display or printer. It has a high resolution so we won't need to concern ourselves with the granularity of coordinates. So we must convert between these coordinate systems. To make matters worse, the coordinate system used in Microsoft Windows specifies the locations of the gaps *between* pixels, and not the pixels themselves, making it easy to have off-by-one errors in the arithmetic that does the coordinate conversions. Painting is not a trivial chore.

Threading   The threading model in many GUIs will seem strange to you if you've never programmed a GUI before. Your application has *no* thread. At start-up, your main program sets up everything, and then calls a subroutine in the GUI system telling it to start running the GUI. The GUI system then runs in an infinite loop, and your application operates solely from callbacks as described above. These callbacks are similar to ISRs (interrupt service routines), and you must do everything in them because you don't have a thread.

Like ISRs, the most important rule with GUI-callbacks is: *Don't block.* A callback must do its chore without waiting for anything, and then return. While a callback is executing, the entire GUI has stopped, waiting for your callback to return. Applications that must perform large chunks of computation, such as transcoding a movie to another format, need to do some tricky programming to avoid having the GUI be unresponsive during the entire computation.

Actually, a GUI-based application is allowed to have threads, but there are constraints on them, and the constraints vary based on which GUI system you are using. Our drawing application doesn't do any large blocks of computation, so it doesn't need a separate thread, and as long as we don't block in a callback, we'll be fine.

11.2   Requirements

A complete description of this drawing application would consume the remainder of this book, so a summary must suffice.

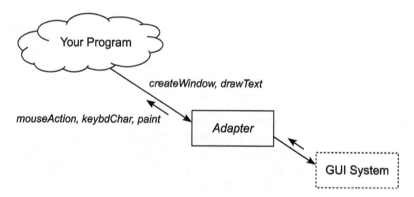

Figure 11.2: GUI environment with an adapter

Our application is intended to be multi-platform, meaning that it will run under several operating systems and several GUI systems. But we also want to minimize the amount of effort required to port to each of these GUI systems. How do you suggest satisfying these requirements? I suggest that we examine each of the GUI systems to be targeted, and select the one having the most generic kind of interface to serve as the basis for this application. Then we'll write adapters for the other GUI systems. The overall IDAR graph representing this plan is shown in Figure 11.2.

Definitions Before proceeding, we should define some terms and concepts pertaining to this drawing application.

View The drawing application has a large prominent area that shows a portion of the drawing. We'll call this area the "view".

Page The drawing is done in a rectangular area called the "page". If the user is zoomed in, the view will show only a portion of the page. When printing the drawing, the entire page will be painted.

Item The user can create a variety of items on the page, such as lines, filled-in areas, and text. Each of these things could be called an "object", but we use "object" to refer to parts of the application. To avoid confusion, we'll use the word "item" to refer to a single item that can appear and be manipulated on the page.

Selection and Handles The user can select one or more items on the page. Such selected items are displayed with a dashed rectangle around them, and with handles. Handles are small green circles displayed at the corners or midpoints of the item which the user can grab with the mouse in order to move, resize, or rotate the item.

Order Items have an order, and items are always drawn in that order, from first to last. Hence, later items overwrite earlier ones, making them appear to be on top of the earlier ones. The user can alter the order of items so that they are drawn in the desired order. For example, I have used a white-filled rectangle to erase a portion of an item. Clearly, the rectangle must be drawn *after* the item it erases. The operations that change order are labeled "bring to top", "bring to bottom", "move upward" and "move downward". The "bring to top" operation puts the selected item at the end of the list so it will be drawn last, and thus appear on top. "Move downward" shifts the selected item(s) one step toward the beginning of the list.

Modes Some of the menus and icons in the GUI allow the user to set the following modes. These modes apply to the entire application, and not to selected items.

- View grid-dots and/or grid-lines. To help the user place items on the page, a grid is defined. The grid's lines can be displayed, or their intersections can be displayed as dots.

- Snap settings. Positioning items on the page is easier when they are able to snap to various places. The user places the item close to where he wants it, and then it conveniently snaps to the correct location. Snap-locations can be grid-dots, grid-lines, item-sides, and item-points. Item-points are typically the corners and midpoints of items.

- Default attributes for lines, filled areas, and text. These attributes include color, line-width, dash-pattern, fill-pattern, font, and others. Whenever a new item is created, its attributes are initially set to these defaults.

- Drag-rectangle action. The user can hold down the left mouse-button and drag, which demarcates a rectangular area displayed with a rubber-band rectangle (i.e., dashed guidelines). This setting tells the application what to do when the mouse-button is released. There are two choices:
    - *Select Mode* Select all the items contained within the rectangle.
    - *Create Mode* Create a new item of a chosen kind. To create a new item, the user (1) clicks on an icon specifying the desired kind of item, which both identifies which kind to create, and also puts the application into this create mode, and (2) drags a rectangle where the item should be placed. When the mouse-button is released, the item is created and appears in that rectangle, and the application changes back to select mode.
- Multi-point. In this mode, the user is clicking successive points in order to define a curve or closed area having an arbitrary shape. A double-click leaves this mode and freezes the shape.

Actions   Some of the menus and icons in the GUI cause actions to occur. There are two groups of actions: nonselection and selection. The nonselection actions are:

- File operations, such as New, Load, Save, Save-As, and Export. Export supports the GIF, EPS, and JPEG file-formats.
- Printing.
- Show or hide various toolbars containing icons.

The selection actions affect the selected items in the drawing, and are:

- Change drawing order of items: bring to top, bring to bottom, move upward and move downward.
- Align to one of various choices (top edge, vertically centered, etc.).
- Equally space the items horizontally or vertically.
- Make the items equally wide or equally tall.

Mouse   There are several possible actions using the mouse that can be done within the view:

- Single-click selects an item.
- Control-click adds the given item to the existing selection, or removes it from the selection if it's already selected.
- Shift-click selects all items in the drawing.
- Double-click causes a text-cursor to appear within the text (if any) inside the item, allowing the user to change the text by typing on the keyboard.
- Drag (when anything is selected) moves the selected items.
- Drag-rectangle selects items or creates a new item, as described above.
- Drag-handle means that the user is dragging one of the selection handles. This action resizes or rotates the item, depending on the handle.

Context Menu Right-clicking the mouse when its cursor is inside a selection brings up a context menu, which contains the following items:

- Change attributes for lines, filled areas, and text.

- The selection actions allowing the user to change: order, various alignments, equal spacing or equal sizing.

11.3 Laying the Foundation

This application is centered around its GUI, so we need to be careful how GUI-related activities are organized. We'll be starting with the environment shown in Figure 11.2, which shows the system's native GUI system with an adapter over it. As I have shown earlier in this book, because the GUI controls a GUI-based application, I prefer to have a GUI object at the top of the IDAR graph. This arrangement agrees with the GUI App pattern described in Section 7.6.1 (page 221).

Let's start designing by following the instructions given in Steps 1 and 2 of the five-step process (page 117), which describes how to find obvious and unobvious objects. The *Adapter* and *GUI* objects are obvious, and they are already on our IDAR graph. Let's see if we can identify any more obvious bottom-level objects.

About the only thing that comes to my mind are the settings and modes. The settings include things such as the size of the page, type and spacing of grid-lines, default attributes of items, and other application-wide settings that do not change often. Modes are things that change often, such as the select-vs-create mode used when dragging the mouse across the view. Let's create two data-storage objects to hold these called *Settings* and *Modes*. These two objects will be accessed by many others, so we will not graph their superiors. Figure 11.3 shows our design so far.

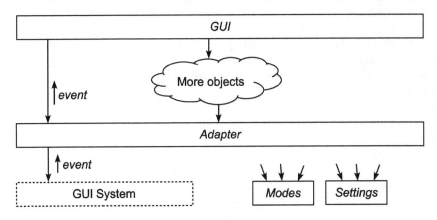

Figure 11.3: Drawing application: the beginning

At this point in the design, we are making fundamental decisions about the structure of the application. A mistake in this architectural phase would cause a large redesign, so let's rethink what happens with GUI activities to reassure ourselves that we haven't made a blunder.

1. The GUI system controls the thread.

2. The GUI system notifies the *Adapter* using callbacks, informing it about various events in the GUI.

3. The *Adapter* converts and forwards those notices to the *GUI* object at the top of the IDAR graph. This arrangement is the Watcher pattern applied twice, first between the GUI system (on the bottom) and *Adapter*, and again between *Adapter* and *GUI*.

4. The *GUI* object (at the top) handles the event, which it will sometimes process itself. But most often, *GUI* will merely dispatch an event to one of its subordinate objects.

5. Those subordinates command the GUI system to do various things, most of which involve painting items on the display.

When the *GUI* object receives a notice for an event, it will handle the easy ones itself, and forward the others to objects yet to be designed in the cloud shown in Figure 11.3. When the event has been handled, its method will return up the call-chain back into the *GUI*. Its notice returns to the *Adapter*, which returns to the GUI system. This structure appears to handle events well, and with a top-down structure for dispatching them, we're not going to block the GUI. The overall design looks fine. Now we need to think about what goes into that cloud.

11.4   Subdividing the GUI

Section 5.4 tells us that one way to find more objects is to extract operations out of a top-level object. In this GUI, we observe that the view is the most conspicuous area in this application, and it's where all the interesting activity occurs from the user's point of view. Let's separate view-handling from the remainder of the GUI by creating a *View* object.

Thinking some more about what happens in the view, we realize that all the items need to be stored and managed somewhere. So we will create a data-storage object called *Items* which holds all items in the order in which they are drawn (first to last). The *Items* object will need to be able to change this order in response to commands to bring to top, move downward, etc.

Also, much of the activity in the view happens to the selected objects. Selection is an important activity in the view, as well as operations on selected objects. A *Selection* object would be an appropriate place to perform such operations.

Both *View* and *Selection* need to command *Items* to create and change items.

Painting is an important operation that we'll need to handle well. When a *paint* command is given to *View*, it needs to determine which items are affected and redraw them. An important question is: Which object should know how to paint items? The *Items* object is an obvious choice. Adding the *paint* capability to it makes it much more than a data-storage object, and we'll need to think about whether and how to partition its painting responsibility.

Looking at top-level operations, we notice that the application needs to print the drawing, as well as open, save, and export it. Let's move these capabilities into *File* and

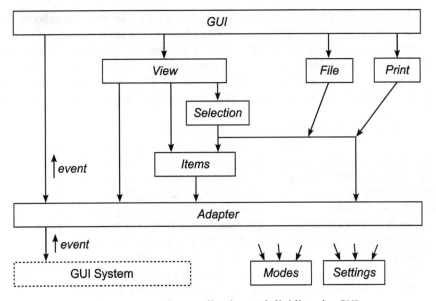

Figure 11.4: Drawing application: subdividing the GUI

Print objects. The *File* object needs to know how to read and write several formats of files, so we'll need to add them to our design later. Both *File* and *Print* need to command both *Items* and the *Adapter*. Figure 11.4 shows that our design is becoming substantial, but we are not even close to being done.

11.5 Working with Selections

Most activity which the user does in this drawing application is centered around the *View*, *Items*, and *Selection* objects. To add detail to the design in this area, we can go through the various operations on items. The core operations done in the *View* object are (1) creating items, (2) selecting items, and (3) changing their geometry. And we must not forget painting.

11.5.1 Selecting

Let's list the steps involved in selecting one or more items:

- The user clicks a spot or drags a rubber-band rectangle to define an area.
- The application examines all items to determine which is closest to the click-location, or which are located inside the rectangle. The qualifying items are selected.
- The application draws handles on the item (or area) to be used for repositioning, stretching, and rotation.

When determining which item(s) are selected, *Selection* and *Items* will need to work closely together. *Items* will return items in sequence, and *Selection* will determine whether each is part of the selection. We don't want to store the list of selected objects in *Selection* because managing two lists would add more complexity than simply tagging each item in *Items* indicating whether it is selected.

The painting of selection handles can be separated into an object named *Handle* which knows how to paint a handle. This *Handle* object can also determine whether a mouse-click (i.e., a button-down event) hit a handle. It's appropriate to make *Handle* subordinate to *Selection*, which can report to *View* whether a mouse-click hit one of those handles.

View can display the rubber-band rectangle used for selecting objects.

After a selection is made, *View* can perform the mechanics of moving, stretching, and rotating some image representing the selected items. To be most useful, we should display an image of the selected items which is thinned in some way. That thinned image would be manipulated by moving the selection handles with the mouse. For example, we could thin the image by drawing it with black and white dashed lines and not doing any area-fills. Alternatively, the image will appear ghost-like if we make half of its pixels transparent. The possibilities are determined by the capabilities of the GUI system which underlies the *Adapter*.

These operations of displaying and changing a selection will add a large quantity of code to the *View* object, so let's move these operations into separate objects which will be commanded by *View*. We'll name them after their operations: *Move*, *Stretch*, and *Rotate*. These verb-type objects that manipulate selections will need to snap their movements to the grid points, which means they need to know their locations. Fortunately, the grid settings are stored in the popular *Settings* object, making them available to all objects.

That reminds us that we've neglected the display of grid-dots and grid-lines. We'll add a *Guides* object which knows how to draw those. Before painting items, *View* will command *Guides* to paint the guides. The effect of this painting-order is that the items will appear to be drawn on top of the guide marks instead of under them, which is probably what the user expects.

11.5.2   Creating

While we are at it, we should think about the two ways of creating new items. The most common method is called "drag-rectangle" in the requirements above. The user drags a rubber-band rectangle with the mouse while holding its left button down, and when the mouse button is released, the program creates an item of the previously chosen kind. The second method is only used to create arbitrary curves and areas, described as "multi-point" in the requirements. Two objects can perform these two operations, named *RubRect* and *MultiPt*. The new objects we've defined are:

RubRect	Rubber-band rectangle for selecting or creating a new item.
MultiPt	User enters multiple points to create any shape.
Move	Moves selection rectangle around as mouse is dragged.
Rotate	Rotates selection rectangle as mouse is dragged.
Stretch	Stretches selection rectangle as mouse is dragged.
Guides	Displays grid-dots or grid-lines (if enabled).

Figure 11.5 shows our design thus far. The "IA rail" label was added to this graph because *Items* and *Adapter* together are used by many other objects, and thus form

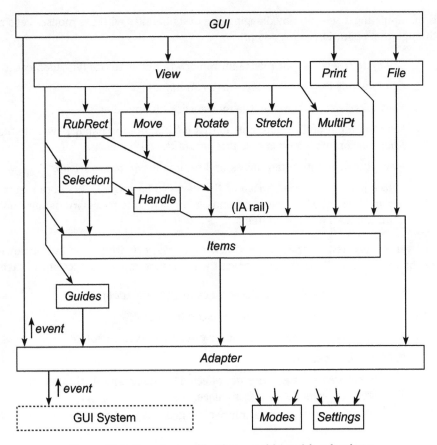

Figure 11.5: Drawing application: working with selections

a rail in this IDAR graph. It is common for a few objects to form a foundation on which higher objects sit. Such a foundation is a rail, and forms a natural layer in the software. The design of this application is converging on a three-layer structure with the *GUI* and *View* objects at the top, the *Items* object in the middle, and the *Adapter* and GUI system at the bottom.

11.6   Final Design

By now, you might have noticed that our design is proceeding top-down by extracting portions of objects' responsibilities, thus creating subordinate objects. To continue that process, we need to look at Figure 11.5 and assess which objects are still too large (i.e., trying to do too much). I see two such overlarge objects: *File* and *Items*.

File needs to read and write several file-formats, so an obvious way to subdivide *File* is to extract the knowledge of each of those file-formats, which will define objects named *EPS*, *JPEG* and *GIF*.

Step 3 in the five-step design process tells us to verify correctness by executing operations by hand. One of the more complex operations in this drawing application is manipulating a selection by dragging one of its handles with the mouse. Let's go through that operation step-by-step:

1. GUI system sends a "left mouse-button down" notice to *GUI* (via *Adapter*).

2. *GUI* forwards that event to *View* (as a command).

3. *View* asks *Selection* whether the mouse-click hit anything.

4. *Selection* replies (via a rider notice) that it hit a rotation handle. We note that *Selection* commands *Handle*, so this part of the design is fine.

5. *View* puts itself into rotate-mode, and commands *Rotate* to set-up.

6. *Rotate* paints a thinned image of the items to be rotated. We note that the design shows that *Rotate* commands *Items*, which is necessary because only *Items* knows how to paint items.

Over the next few seconds, many mouse-move events (with the left button down) will be given to the *GUI* as the user moves the mouse around. Let's trace one of them:

1. GUI system sends a mouse-move notice to *GUI* (via *Adapter*).

2. *GUI* forwards that event to *View* (as a command).

3. Because *View* is in rotate-mode, it forwards that event to *Rotate*.

4. *Rotate* does the following:

   - It tells *Items* to paint the area affected by the previously thinned image in order to restore the original image.
   - It tells *Items* to paint a thinned rotated image of the selection over the original image.
   - It tells *Items* to paint the handles.

Now we realize that we've made a mistake. Can you see what it is? The grid was not painted. The painting done above erases the grid, so it needs to be repainted. This tells us that *View* should not command *Guides* to paint the grid, but rather that *Items* should command *Guides* first before it paints items. By making *Guides* a subordinate of *Items*, we are treating the grid as if it were a permanent item.

11.6.1   Subdividing 'Items'

The best way to subdivide *Items* is not obvious. Let's list the operations for which it is responsible:

- Storing all items in an ordered list
- Creating, deleting, and modifying items
- Changing the order of selected items
- Remembering which items are selected
- Retrieving items for superiors
- Serializing and deserializing items for saving in a file

- Painting a rectangular area to the display
- Painting a bitmap to be used for printing
- Painting selected items into a thinned selection image, but with position, size, or rotation changed

That's a lot. The first five bullets above pertain to managing the data for all the items, and represent a small amount of code. The remaining three bullets are painting for several purposes. Painting may sound like an easy chore, but remember that there are a variety of items and their attributes to work with, including generating dashed lines and area-fills with various patterns. Painting is much code. An obvious way to offload this responsibility would be to create a *Paint* object containing all the paint code, but that would make all the methods in *Items* pertaining to painting tramps. That is, all paint methods in *Items* would have tramp coupling because they would merely be pass-throughs. Let's see if we can extract painting responsibilities in a finer grained manner.

We can list the kinds of items in existence and make shape-classes out of them, which will be *Line*, *Ellipse*, *Rect*, *Text*, *Curve*, and *Area*. The *Curve* class represents an arbitrary curved line which the user defined by clicking various locations. *Area* is like *Curve*, but is a closed area which can be filled. Whenever *Items* wants to paint an item, it can dispatch the chore to an instance of one of these classes. Each of the above classes contains all of the following commands:

paint	Paint the item.
boundRect	Return the item's bounding rectangle.
pointSel	Does (x,y) select this item?
rectSel	Does the given rectangle select this item?
getAttrTypes	List of attribute types supported.
getAttr	Gets an attribute-set.
setAttr	Sets an attribute-set.
getSize	Returns the number of bytes in an item.
move	Move item.
rotate	Rotate item.
stretch	Stretch item.

There are three possible approaches for organizing these commands and instances for the various shape-classes listed above:

Interface If the language supports it, we can create an interface named *ShapeI* containing the declarations of the above commands. Every shape-class would implement this interface.

Inheritance We can define an abstract base class named *Shape*, and from it derive the shape-classes.

Dispatcher A dispatcher can select the appropriate command based on a field named *shapeType* present at the beginning of all the shape instances.

The interface and inheritance approaches will cause the compiler to add a `vtbl` pointer to each object, making serialization and deserialization more difficult, forcing us to add *serialize* and *deserialize* commands. If we choose the dispatcher approach, then all calls to the commands listed above would be direct instead of indirect. Unfortunately, many `case/switch` statements would be needed inside the dispatcher, one for each of the many commands in the interface listed above. Also, each shape-class would need to type-cast the passed-in instance-pointer into its own type, which is a nuisance and causes us to lose some type-checking. Weighing these costs and benefits, I suggest choosing the interface approach, or the inheritance approach if the language doesn't support interfaces. The resulting indirection reduces readability, but I'd say the problems associated with supporting multiple instances through a dispatcher are worse. The Dispatcher pattern is superb for single-instance classes, but it's weak when its subordinates have multiple instances. Fortunately, few classes have multiple instances in most software, so a dispatcher is usually the best approach.

If we think about the various kinds of items to be painted, we notice that the situation is more complex than we expected (as usual). We see that most kinds of items are actually hybrids, consisting of two or three simpler kinds of graphics. For example, a rectangle consists of four lines, all of which use line attributes of width, color, and dash pattern. A rectangle can be filled, so it also has the fill attributes of color and hatching pattern. A rectangle can also hold text, so it also has the text attributes of a string, text color, font, and so on. To summarize, we see that there are three sets of attributes (settings) available, resulting in the following classes:

LineAttr	line settings:	width, color, dash pattern, dash length
FillAttr	fill settings:	fill-type, color, hatch pattern and spacing
TextAttr	text settings:	string, color, font, character set, point-size

Every item will contain an instance of one or more of these classes, and these attribute-objects will be subordinate to (commanded by) the item-objects. Each of these attribute-objects handles the attribute settings shown in the list above. What do you think of the idea of also having these attribute-objects do the actual painting? That will cause the *FillAttr* class to know how to fill an area with a solid color or a hatch pattern. I like this idea because it puts specialized painting knowledge together with the settings being used. To help make this idea clear, the code in the *paint* method within the *Rect* class is shown in Listing 11.1.

11.6.2   Review

We have now finished the design of the drawing application. Or more accurately, we now have a complete trial design of this application. By way of review, the following are the five steps in the design process described on page 117:

1. Define the obvious objects on the top and bottom.
2. Define the unobvious objects in between them.
3. Verify correctness by hand-executing every operation.
4. Improve and simplify. Most developers fail to do this.
5. Iterate if needed.

```
void Rect::paint(DevContext *dev) {
    // The private fields in Rect are:
    // xpos, ypos, width, height, fillAttr, lineAttr, and textAttr
    int x = xpos;
    int y = ypos;
    int w = width;
    int h = height;

    // Fill the interior of the rectangle.
    fillAttr.paint(x, y, x+w, y+h, dev);

    // Draw the four sides of the rectangle.
    lineAttr.paint(x, y, x+w, y, dev);
    lineAttr.paint(x, y, x, y+h, dev);
    lineAttr.paint(x+w, y, x+w, y+h, dev);
    lineAttr.paint(x, y+h, x+w, y+h, dev);

    // Draw any text inside the rectangle.
    textAttr.paint(x, y, x+w, y+h, dev);
}
```

Listing 11.1: *paint* method in *Rect*

Regarding Steps 1-2: We are done defining objects. I suggest having a team-lunch to celebrate, even though we only spent two hours designing.

Regarding Step 3: While rereading requirements and hand-executing the operations, we notice a few things:

- We should be using two different coordinate systems. We want the items stored in *Items* to use a high-resolution coordinate system to avoid troubles with the granularity of the pixels on the display or printer. But all painting is done in native pixels. Hence, conversions need to be done, and the formulas for these conversions will change based on page-size, display-size, display-resolution, and zoom-level. Let's put all that logic and arithmetic into a *Coord* object. Because *Coord* will have a variety of superiors, we can isolate it on the graph as a popular object next to *Modes* and *Settings*.

- The requirements also say that we should have the ability to show or hide some toolbars, and that a right-click on the mouse should display a context menu. We can have the *GUI* object do those operations.

- Changes in order can be implemented within the *View* object, which will command *Items* to move selected items around in its list.

- Adjustments to alignment and spacing can be done in the *View* object.

Hopefully we caught all the details, although I wouldn't doubt that small changes to this design will be needed during implementation. That's normal. We humans are not able to anticipate and plan all details in advance. The waterfall model of software development fails due to this fallacy of perfect planning. Use some kind of agile process instead.

Regarding adherence to the IDAR rules, we have been careful to ensure that all commands go down. All notices (except from *Adapter*) are riders, so those notices cannot be a problem. The event notice sent from *Adapter* to *GUI* follows the Watcher design pattern, so it's acceptable.

Regarding Step 4: Pondering improvements makes me realize that the objects which manipulate selections (*Move*, *Rotate*, etc.) do not command the *Selection* object. That's odd. We see that the *Selection* object only creates a selection, and that the knowledge of which items are selected is in the *Items* object, which the selection manipulation objects can command. Therefore, the design will work, but I wonder if it would be cleaner (simpler) to have those manipulators command *Selection* instead of *Items*. We put the knowledge of which items are selected into *Items* to avoid having to maintain *two* lists of items: the main list, and a list of selected items. This is an interesting trade-off, and it's not obvious which approach is simpler. I'll leave the design alone for now.

Clarity, cohesion, concealment, coupling, and need are evaluated in this step. Doing this means writing the roles for all the objects, which I list below on page 309. After reading through those roles, the one with poor cohesion is *Items*. Its role is "Stores items, paints them, and computes selections." That sounds like a list of poorly related actions. However, all of these actions act upon items, so perhaps the role-statement should be changed to "Manages items", despite the reduction of clarity. I'll keep this object as-is, but I still don't feel comfortable about its cohesion.

Most of the coupling is parameter and field, which are fine. However, *Modes* and *Settings* are merely glorified global variables, and thus employ common coupling. On the other hand, the number of such variables is small, and they are needed in various places, so we can leave them as-is. But let's agree to keep settings and modes inside other objects if they are used only by one object. For example, the grid settings are only used by the *Guides* object, so let's keep them in there, even though that will mean adding tramp methods in *View* and *Items* to pass those settings to *Guides*.

Regarding Step 5: We are done! The final design is shown in Figure 11.6. It's hard to believe that such a complex design contains *no* threads. From the *GUI* on down, everything is a call-hierarchy of methods originating from callbacks (notices) from the GUI system. The call-hierarchy ends up making calls (commands) back into the GUI system, forming a large cycle.

Also, we did not show the design for the *JPEG*, *EPS* and *GIF* objects. One would hope that the operating system or GUI system would supply such conversions for us. If not, they are available in open-source form, so there's no reason for us to design and implement such objects. *JPEG* in particular would be a substantial project. I know, because I've implemented a JPEG encoder and decoder. Don't try it unless you can spare a few months.

11.7   Extracting a Subsystem

Looking at that IDAR graph, we notice that *Items* has an isolated hierarchy under it, which tells us that *Items* and its subordinate hierarchy can be made into a separate subsystem. Doing so makes the final design appear somewhat simpler. But in this

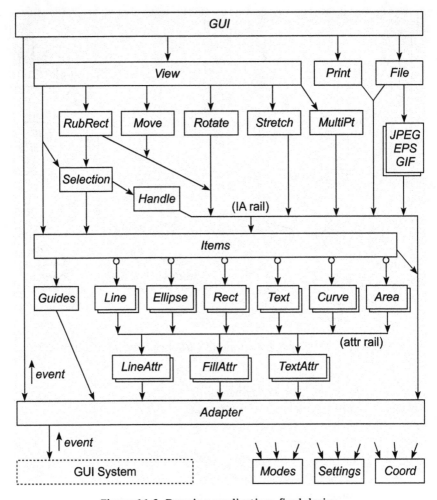

Figure 11.6: Drawing application: final design

case, the sole purpose of the subsystem is to split the IDAR graph into two pieces to make it more understandable, or at least less overwhelming. But to give you a wider perspective on complexity, all electrical schematics that I've seen are more complex than this because they usually have *hundreds* of lines, so I have little sympathy for anyone who complains about the complexity of this IDAR graph. Nonetheless, I went ahead and extracted the *Items* hierarchy as a separate subsystem, yielding the IDAR graphs shown in Figures 11.7 and 11.8.

The design of objects is always based on their roles, and I've said that these should be included in the documentation for a program. So for reference, here are the roles of all objects in this application:

GUI	Oversees the application, handling all incoming events.
View	Handles all actions in the view area.
Print	Performs printing operations.

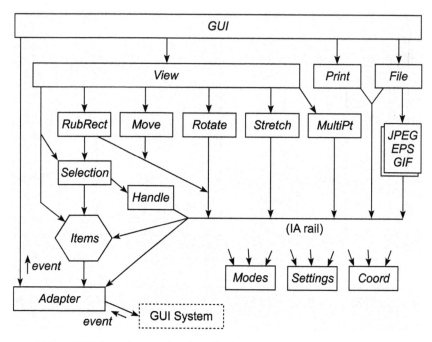

Figure 11.7: Drawing application: final design, using *Items* subsystem

File	Performs file-related operations.
JPEG	Encodes and decodes a JPEG file.
EPS	Encodes and decodes an EPS file.
GIF	Encodes and decodes a GIF file.
RubRect	Rubber-band rectangle for selecting or creating a new item.
Move	Moves thinned selection around as mouse is dragged.
Rotate	Rotates thinned selection as mouse is dragged.
Stretch	Stretches thinned selection as mouse is dragged.
MultiPt	User enters multiple points to create any shape.
Selection	Identifies selected items and handles.
Handle	Paints handles and computes hits on handles.
Items	Stores items, paints them, and computes selections.
Guides	Displays grid-dots or grid-lines (if enabled).
Line	Stores and paints a line.
Ellipse	Stores and paints an ellipse (or circle).
Rect	Stores and paints a rectangle (or square).
Text	Stores and paints a line of text.
Curve	Stores and paints a curve consisting of points.
Area	Stores and paints an area consisting of points.
LineAttr	Stores line-related attributes, and paints with them.
FillAttr	Stores fill-related attributes, and paints with them.

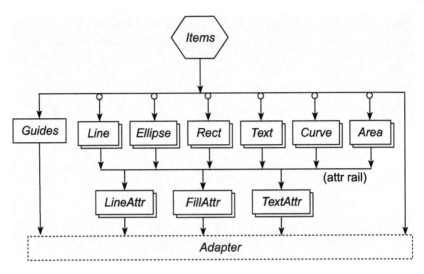

Figure 11.8: Drawing application: final design, *Items* subsystem

TextAttr   Stores text-related attributes, and paints with them.
Adapter   Converts underlying GUI system into a standard interface.
Modes   Holds settings that often change.
Settings   Holds settings that seldom change.
Coord   Converts between coordinate systems.

11.8   Designing Objects

Each of the objects listed above needs to be designed. The good news is that most of those designs are simple and obvious. In fact, most of those designs consist of simply the public methods, with no private methods. But a few objects have nontrivial designs at the method-level, and *Items* appears to be one of them, so let's design it first. Then we will design the *FillAttr* object, as it also appears to be nontrivial.

11.8.1   'Items' Object

The public methods in *Items* fall into two groups: list management and painting. The list management is not complex, consisting mostly of traversing and altering the list of items. A linked list would be straightforward and should work well. The list management will probably do most of its work in the public methods; consequently, a method-level IDAR graph showing their design will not be interesting. So we will design the painting portion, which consists of the following three public methods, shown with their roles:

paintRect   Paints a rectangular area to the display.
paintBitmap   Paints a bitmap to be used for printing.
paintThinned Paints selected items into a thinned selection image,
                but with position, size, or rotation changed.

These methods have access to the list holding the items, to the *Adapter*, and to the various shape-classes such as *Line, Rect, Ellipse,* and so on. Because all three of these paint methods act upon different destinations and/or in different modes (i.e., thinned or normal), their set-up code will differ. But then they all need to paint one or more items. For that, we'll create a private *paintItem* method which paints an item passed in as a parameter.

There's nothing more to be done at the method-level. The next step would be to write pseudo-code. So our method-level design of *Items* is done, and is shown in Figure 11.9.

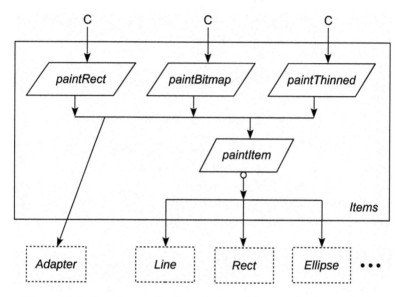

Figure 11.9: Drawing application: design of *Items* painting methods

Notice the small circle under the *paintItem* method. It indicates that the calls to *paint* in the shape-classes are indirect, which assumes that we used the interface or inheritance approaches, as recommended in the discussion above.

Remember that this IDAR graph only shows the painting portion of *Items*, but its list-management design will be equally simple.

11.8.2 'FillAttr' Class

Another class with a nontrivial design at the method-level is *FillAttr*. The work-horse method in it is *paint*, which fills the interior of a polygon according to the given attributes, which specify filling with a solid color, single hatching, or cross-hatching. As we think about what private methods might be useful to *paint*, we can list the kinds of fills it should paint. There are three, but hatch and cross-hatch both use the same underlying hatch-fill algorithm. So let's define two private methods:

fillSolid   Fills polygon with solid color.
fillHatch   Fills polygon with single hatching.

To fill with cross-hatching, the *paint* method can call *fillHatch* twice, the second time with 90 degrees added to the hatching-angle. No other private methods are needed, and the resulting design in shown in Figure 11.10. The other public methods in *FillAttr* are not pictured because they don't need any private methods, so their design at the method-level is trivial.

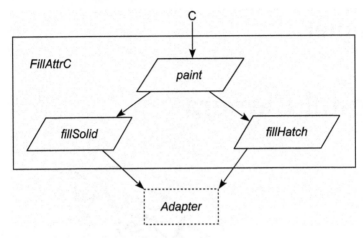

Figure 11.10: Drawing application: design of *FillAttr*

Although the design of *FillAttr* is simple at the method-level, it is certainly *not* trivial at the code-level. Filling polygons is complicated, unless the GUI system can do it for you.

11.9 Exercises

1. When following a mouse-move event, we made a mistake. We said that *Rotate* "Tells *Items* to paint the handles." But the *Handle* object is above *Items*, not under it, so *Items* cannot command it. How can this error be fixed?

2. This drawing app is missing groups of predefined shapes, such as various filled arrows, flowcharting symbols, call-outs, and so on. How would you add them to this design?

3. How would you incorporate an undo feature into this design?

4. Saving to a JPEG/JPG might be slow. How would the design change if this file-save were done by a separate thread?

5. *Selection* only computes the selection, but then does not remember or manipulate it. Rather, *Items* remembers the selection. This suggests that *Selection* should be subordinate to *Items*. How would this change affect the design?

Chapter 12

Digital Camera

12.1 Background

If you've ever disassembled a broken digital camera, you were probably shocked. The capacitor for the flash is typically charged to 330 volts, and has a capacity of 200-400 microfarads. If you short its wires together, the resulting spark sounds like a gunshot and leaves the wires welded together. You will not do that again.

The CPU inside such a camera has a great deal to do, not the least of which is managing that capacitor. Your mission, should you choose to accept it, is to design its software. Think about all the things that happen inside a digital camera before accepting this assignment.

A bit of good news is that all digital cameras contain an ASIC (Application Specific Integrated Circuit) which does all the math-intensive work for you. The ASIC is custom-designed by the manufacturer, and is divided into "blocks", each of which performs a specific chore and can be controlled by software in the CPU. So the job of our software in the CPU is to control everything, from the topmost level, all the way down to closing the electronic switch that discharges the flash capacitor into the flash tube, creating a flash of light.

All of the blocks in the ASIC are controlled by registers, which you can think of as special variables that cause actions to occur when you write to them. For example, writing a 1 to the register named *flashFireSwitch* causes the flash to fire (assuming that the capacitor was charged).

12.2 Electronics

Before we can start this design, we need to become familiar with the electronics and mechanics which we must control. Here's the long list:

Aperture The aperture is the f-stop you are using, which is a measure of how much light can pass through the lens. A larger f-stop number lets in less light. An aperture consists of two or more thin metal blades which form a hole through which the light passes. The CPU can write to a register in the ASIC which controls the transistors which control the positions of these blades, thus controlling the size of the aperture (hole) through which light passes.

Shutter Another register in the ASIC causes the shutter to open or close. Like the aperture, the shutter consists of a few thin metal blades. To obtain a given shutter-speed, the CPU writes to that register causing the shutter to open, waits the correct amount of time, and then writes to that register again to cause the shutter to close.

Zoom Motor This motor operates the zooming mechanism in the lens, and you can cause it to rotate in either direction, for zooming out or zooming in. This motor is also used to extend the lens when power is turned on, and to retract it when power is turned off. This block consists of registers which (1) set the voltage on the motor's windings, and (2) read its position based on the encoder, as discussed below.

Focus Motor As you might have guessed, this motor controls the focusing mechanism in the lens, and like the zoom motor, it is bidirectional.

Focus Beam Switch There is a light on the front of the camera used to illuminate the subject at night to enable the camera to focus on the subject. Without this light, nighttime photography would be impossible because the camera would be unable to focus. This light is controlled by an electronic switch which is controlled by a register which uses one bit to turn the light on or off.

Focus Predictor This block in the ASIC computes the amount of blurriness in successive exposures during the process of composing, and suggests a change in the focus motor's position. The software is responsible for reading this suggested change and controlling the motor. When the lens is focused as part of the final exposure, this block determines the focus position to be used.

Face Detector While composing, this block in the ASIC is constantly trying to detect a face in the image. It constantly updates the probability of a face (and its location) in registers.

Flash Charge Switch This is another electronic switch which causes the flash capacitor to (eventually) charge up to 330 volts. Several seconds are required to fully charge the capacitor. You'll need to charge the capacitor before firing the flash. While the user is composing the picture, your software is required to notice when the light-level is low enough that the flash will be needed, and to charge the capacitor anticipating firing the flash. You don't want to always charge the capacitor because doing so drains the battery faster.

Capacitor Voltmeter The rate at which the capacitor charges varies based on battery voltage, so the software needs some way to know when it's sufficiently charged. This simple circuit measures the voltage across the capacitor.

Flash Fire Switch Closing this electronic switch (via a write to a register) fires the flash. Obviously, software should only do this when the shutter is open.

Sensor The sensor is the expensive device that records the picture the instant it is taken. The software needs to set it up for an exposure, and there are several registers that control it. When composing a picture, the software puts the sensor in a mode that causes it to repeatedly expose images.

Display The display on the back of the camera shows menus, the picture as it is being composed, and a glimpse of the actual picture taken afterwards. It is also used for reviewing the photos on the memory card.

Memory Card A typical memory card can hold many gigabytes. Each picture is in a separate file on this card. There is a block in the ASIC containing a number of registers which allow you to perform various operations on the card.

JPEG The photos on the card are stored in the popular compressed JPEG format, which uses less space on the card than raw formats. There is a block in the ASIC which can both compress and decompress JPEG files. As usual, the ASIC provides a few registers to control these conversions.

Image Processing The image processing system in the ASIC consists of several blocks which the software must configure by writing to their registers. The purpose of image processing is to convert the image from the format provided by the sensor, called a "Bayer matrix", into both (1) the form needed by the camera's display (so the photographer can see the picture just taken), and (2) the form needed by the JPEG block for storage on the card.

Sound The ASIC contains a simple sound circuit that can play a buffer containing sound samples. This is used to make a "click" sound when a picture is taken.

Buttons There are about ten buttons on the camera, including the 2-step shutter button on top used to take a picture. A button press causes the CPU to be interrupted, and its interrupt service routine (ISR) is expected to read a register indicating which button was pressed.

Battery Voltage The software in the camera automatically turns the camera off when the battery is getting too low. This voltmeter provides an indication of how much charge remains in the battery. Software monitors this voltage as various operations are performed, and uses this information to predict how much longer the battery will last.

As mentioned in the list above, the Image Processing system in the ASIC consists of multiple blocks which software must control, which are:

Debayer The image which the sensor outputs does not consist of RGB (red, green, blue) triples as you would expect. Instead, each pixel is red *or* green *or* blue. That is, each pixel contains only one of the three colors. The pattern of these red, green, and blue dots on the sensor is called the "Bayer matrix". Because each pixel only contains one color, the ASIC must estimate the other two colors based on nearby pixels. This process is called "debayering". It is also called "demosaicing", because the color pattern on the sensor is often referred to as a "mosaic". The Debayer block inputs pixels containing an R or G or B, and outputs pixels containing complete RGB triplets.

Denoise The pixels contain noise, which looks like grain. In daylight, the noise is low enough that it's not a problem, but when the sensor is underexposed in poor lighting, the noise becomes visually prominent. This block removes enough of this noise so that it's not visually objectionable.

Sharpen To cut cost, manufacturers use cheap lenses with poor optical quality, resulting in blurry pictures. The Sharpen block in the ASIC removes this blurriness to improve the appearance of the picture. Note that such sharpening does *not* add more detail to the image, so there's a limit to how much manufacturers can cut lens-cost before their pictures become ugly due to lack of detail.

Color Space You are familiar with the RGB components of a pixel. RGB is called a "color-space". There are other color-spaces in use, and JPEG works with pixels in the YCC color-space. This block performs this conversion.

Scale The sensor has a fixed resolution, which is a certain number of pixels in its width and height. The display has a much lower resolution, and this block downscales the image to the display's lower resolution. Also, the user might wish to store pictures at a lower resolution to save space on the memory card, requiring a separate downscaling.

The two motors for the lens (zoom and focus) are actually closed-loop DC servos. That means that the shaft of such a motor has fan-like blades on it that interrupt a light-beam as the motor rotates, causing a light-sensor to emit tick-signals. That combination of fan, light, and sensor is called an "encoder". The ASIC counts the ticks arriving from the encoder, and thus keeps track of the motor's position. Hundreds of times per second, the CPU checks this position and adjusts the voltage on the motor so that its speed and position remain correct. This combination of motor, encoder and software is called a "servo". You saw them in the pen plotter in Chapter 10. The blocks for both motors in the ASIC are identical, and the mechanical characteristics of the motors themselves are similar. Thus, our software can use two instances of the same class for controlling these motors.

You might have wondered why the camera has a shutter. After all, it can take pictures constantly while composing, and during that time the shutter is always open, doing nothing. The answer has to do with shutter-speeds. The sensor only has slow shutter-speeds available electronically, so the faster speeds must be implemented mechanically. Fast speeds are essential because they freeze motion and camera-shake, making a mechanical shutter essential.

12.3   Requirements

The primary requirement is, of course, to take pictures. The features and operations supported by this camera are listed below:

Menu When the Menu button is pressed, the display shows a menu that can be navigated using the arrow buttons. The menu is used to change settings that seldom need changing, such as ISO speed, resolution, sound-mode, and others.

Compose In this default mode, the camera shows a preview of the picture on the display while it is being composed. The user can change the zoom while composing. Pressing the shutter button halfway causes the camera to focus. Pressing the button fully causes it to take a picture.

Shoot When the shutter button is pressed fully, the camera starts the shooting procedure consisting of the following steps:

1. If the focus wasn't determined while composing, do so now.
2. If exposure wasn't determined while composing, do so now.
3. Close the shutter and prepare the sensor.
4. Set the aperture to its correct size.
5. Set-up the image processing and JPEG blocks in the ASIC.
6. Expose the sensor by opening and closing the shutter for the correct amount of time determined by the exposure.
7. During the exposure done above, fire the flash if the exposure calculations decided it is needed.

8. As soon as the picture has been transferred out of the sensor, show it on the display for a few seconds.
9. Make a "click" sound if enabled.
10. Wait until image processing and file-writes are done.

Review In review (or playback) mode, a picture on the card is displayed. Pressing buttons on the back of the camera allows the user to go forward or backward among the pictures, zoom in or out, or delete a picture.

Regardless of the camera's mode, a battery-level icon is always present, displaying the estimated amount of charge remaining in the battery.

Also, if face detection is enabled, the camera will bias its focus toward faces if it detects any.

Most of the specifications for the camera, such as resolution in megapixels, auto-focus lag and others, are determined by the speed of the electronics, and not by the software. So we don't need to optimize the code for maximum speed. In this application, it's more important that the software be reliable and bug-free. As long as we don't do anything horribly inefficiently, the speed of the software will be sufficient.

12.4 Starting the Design

As described in Section 5.4 (page 117), the design process starts with writing down the obvious objects first, both top-level and bottom-level. For this digital camera, there will be one top-level object, *Camera*.

At the bottom-level, an obvious approach is to create a concrete-noun object for each block in the ASIC for monitoring and controlling the block. The result of this bottom-level effort is the following long list of objects and their roles:

Aperture	Controls the aperture of the lens.
Shutter	Opens and closes the shutter.
zoomMot	Controls the zoom motor (instance of *Servo*).
focusMot	Controls the focus motor (instance of *Servo*).
FocBeam	Controls the focus-assist light.
FaceDet	Configures the Face Detector block in the ASIC.
FlashCap	Charges the flash capacitor, and monitors its voltage.
FlashTube	Fires the flash.
Sensor	Controls the sensor.
ImProc	Controls the image processing system in the ASIC.
Display	Can put an icon, text and picture on the display.
Card	Manages the files in the memory card.
JPEG	Controls the JPEG block in the ASIC.
Sound	Plays sounds.
Buttons	Reports button presses as notices.
Battery	Monitors voltage and predicts battery life.

Perhaps you noticed that the list does not perfectly match the list of blocks in the hardware. In a few cases, functions or blocks were closely related, so I combined them into one object. These combinations are:

- The *FlashCap* object both monitors the voltage on the capacitor, as well as turning its charger on or off.

- The *Battery* object not only monitors the battery's voltage, but it also predicts battery life based on activity occurring elsewhere in the camera.

- The *zoomMot* and *focusMot* objects contain an implementation of a servo algorithm, giving them the ability to make complete moves with one command.

- The *Aperture* object sends a notice when the aperture has reached its commanded opening.

You might have noticed that we neglected to list the various blocks in the image processing portion of the ASIC. Yes, objects for them also need to be created, and they are listed below:

Debayer	Configures the Debayer block.
Denoise	Configures the Denoise block.
Sharpen	Configures the Sharpen block.
ColSpace	Configures the Color Space block.
Scale	Configures the Scale block.

To start with, let's decide how to handle the buttons. Rather than have the *Buttons* object distribute button-press notices all over the place (the Distributor pattern), let's have it send those notices directly to *Camera* which in turn will dispatch them appropriately. This is the Watcher pattern, and it has the advantage of producing fewer communication-paths among objects than the Distributor pattern. The disadvantage of this approach is that *Camera* needs to contain a piece of code that dispatches each button press to some subordinate object. However, *Camera* itself will handle presses of the Power button. Figure 12.1 shows the obvious objects that we identified.

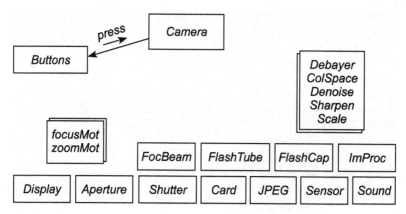

Figure 12.1: Digital camera: obvious objects

12.5 First Trial Design

Step 2 of the five-step design process is to define the unobvious objects. Section 5.4.2 reveals ways of doing so, and we will employ the top-down and bottom-up approaches.

The top-down approach requires us to consider the responsibilities of the top-level object, *Camera*, and to devise a way of extracting portions of those responsibilities that maintain high clarity, cohesion, concealment, and need, with low coupling. The most common approach, which we will use, is to break off distinct operations. The requirements list four modes of the camera: menu, compose, shoot, and review. Those modes operate mostly independently of each other, making them good candidates for objects below *Camera*. So let's define four objects which implement these modes:

Menu	Performs all menu operations.
Compose	Displays a preview of the picture being composed.
Shoot	Takes a picture.
Review	Displays pictures on the memory card.

Let's try to define some more objects in a bottom-up manner. Looking over the existing bottom-level objects, we see that there are three objects related to focusing, which are *focusMot*, *FocBeam* and *FaceDet*. But we don't have an object which can focus. Let's define a *Focus* object that controls these three objects, providing us with the capability of focusing.

Let's go back to the top-down approach, and see if we can identify objects that we can break out of *Menu*, *Compose*, *Shoot*, or *Review*. The requirements provide a list of actions which *Shoot* should do. Do you think those could identify objects? One step that suggests a subordinate object is the following sentence:

If exposure wasn't determined while composing, do so now.

Reading that sentence suggests that we should create an *Exposure* object which computes the exposure. Thinking about this a little more, we realize that the flash capacitor should be charged if we think we might need the flash. So let's put that charging responsibility into *Exposure*.

After perfectionistically moving objects around to avoid crossing lines, Figure 12.2 shows the IDAR graph we've created. We should be surprised at how much sophistication we have designed after only creating the obvious top-level and bottom-level objects, and doing a little more (mostly) top-down design. The IDAR method makes design easier than traditional methods.

In this IDAR graph, did you notice that *Display* is commanding *Battery*? Do you understand why? It's because in all modes, the display is required to show an indication of remaining battery life. The easiest way to do that is to have the *Display* object itself always show that icon. Remember, this *Display* object is smart. It does not merely control the display, but it knows how to display text, icons, and pictures. Its level of capability is high enough that giving it the added burden of handling the battery icon is appropriate.

Also, you will notice that I used the stacked-box notation for the *focusMot* and *zoomMot* objects. This notation makes it clear that they are both instances of the same class, despite having different superiors. To save space, I put the image processing blocks into a stacked box. This violates the IDAR drawing-rules because they are not instances of the same class; rather, they are in the same general category. However, this cheat is acceptable as the blocks are closely related.

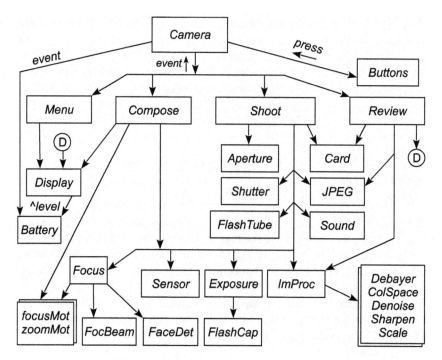

Figure 12.2: Digital camera: trial design

12.6   Refining the Design

As we ponder this IDAR graph, we realize that some things are missing. First, the *Menu* object allows the user to change a variety of settings, but nowhere in this design are they stored anywhere. We could store them in *Menu* itself, but doing so would mean low-level objects (such as *FaceDet*) would command a higher-level object (*Menu*), violating the Down rule. We will create a separate (and popular) *Settings* object. Do you remember what a popular object is, and how it's drawn?

What about dataflows? In fact, many dataflows are handled completely within the ASIC. For example, pixels flow from the sensor into the image processing blocks without passing through the CPU, so the software does not need to deal with those. But for the few dataflows that will involve the CPU, we can create a *Pipe* class that can perform the buffer transfers.

Another area that we haven't discussed is power-up and power-down. Earlier, we mentioned that *Camera* will handle presses of the Power button. Doing so means that (1) upon power-up, *Camera* will need to initialize electronics and extend the lens, and (2) upon power-down, *Camera* will need to ensure that writes to the memory card have finished, and then retract the lens. These actions imply that *Camera* needs to command more objects than we have shown. Rather than clutter the graph with lines that only apply to power-up and power-down, we'll add unconnected downward arrows emanating from *Camera* to show that it commands other objects. Also, the Union pattern (Section 7.1.5; page 186) would be suitable in this situation.

We haven't thought about threading yet. As is commonly true when designing with IDAR graphs, we were able to delay decisions about threads until late in the design. This ability to defer threading decisions is a helpful feature of the IDAR method, as it allows us to concentrate (I almost said "focus") on which objects command which others, instead of being distracted by *when* these commands are performed and what needs to be done in parallel.

Now we need to think about necessary parallelism. Obviously, *Camera* will have a thread because it always needs to respond to button presses, and as the topmost object, it will be the main (and only) process. Looking over the operations, we see that if the camera is in menu mode, then the *Menu* object needs to respond to button presses. So it needs to have its own thread. Likewise with the *Compose* object. Its thread will be busy updating focus and exposure, and with any zooming. At this point, we realize that it makes sense for *Shoot* and *Review* also to have their own threads.

The motors should not block their calling threads, so at first glance, people would say that they should have their own threads, but that's not true. Like several other objects in this camera, the motors have ISRs (interrupt service routines) which monitor the physical movements of the motors. Because these ISRs can also send "done" notices, the motor objects will not block their callers, despite lacking threads.

For the same reason, the *Sound* object does not need a thread. Its ISR monitors and controls playback, and can call a "done" notice in another object.

I have noticed that many real-time systems have too many threads because their developers didn't know that they could perform simple chores in ISR code. But elimination of threads is not the only advantage of doing such chores in an ISR. Another often-significant advantage is that the system becomes more responsive because an interrupt has a lower and more predictable latency than a context-switch needed for a thread. I encourage you to learn what can be done in ISRs, and to learn the proper trade-offs between processing in an ISR versus processing in a thread. These two methods of execution are sometimes called "foreground" (ISR) and "background" (thread). Remember that the rules for drawing an IDAR graph state that a lightning-bolt means an object contains an ISR, so you'll see a few of those in our graph. Figure 12.3 shows our design after making these changes.

12.7   Final Design

Do you think we're done with the design? So far we've only completed Steps 1-2 of the five-step process of design that's recommended for IDAR graphs (see Section 5.4, page 117). These steps provided us with an initial design. Actually, we're farther along than that because of the pondering and thinking we did a few paragraphs ago which uncovered some omissions in our design.

Step 3 of the five steps tells us to ensure that the IDAR rules are being obeyed, and to reread the requirements and hand-execute every operation, stepping through the design as if we were the CPU. A check confirms that the IDAR graph is legal. But while reading the requirements, we encounter this sentence:

> *As soon as the picture has been transferred out of the sensor, show it on the display for a few seconds.*

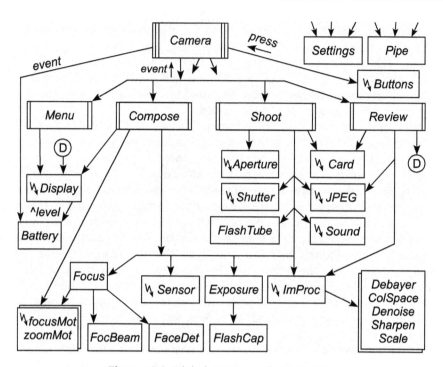

Figure 12.3: Digital camera: refined design

Upon hand-executing the actions for taking a picture, we realize that this brief display is not being done. We have found another omission in the design. I suggest creating a *Glimpse* object which provides a glimpse of the picture just taken.

Also, the sentence above said "for a few seconds." And how are we planning to implement such delays? So far, we aren't. That's another omission. Let's add a *Timers* object which will be commanded by any object that needs a delay. It will return a notice when the delay expires. Because it will be used by several objects, we can show it on the IDAR graph with unconnected incoming arrows signifying that it's used in a number of places (i.e., it's popular).

After reading and hand-executing operations some more, it occurs to us that the IDAR graph shows that the *Shoot* object commands *Aperture*, but that *Compose* does not. When composing in sunlight, the aperture will need to be closed down while composing to keep from overexposing the sensor. We realize that *Compose* also needs to command *Aperture*.

Step 4 in the five-step process tell us to ponder improvements, which we've already partly done.

But thinking through all the things done with a camera uncovers one more omission. When the memory card is inserted or removed by the user, *Camera* should be informed so that it will know whether to allow shooting. We will add two notices sent from *Card* to *Camera*. These notices result in crossed lines on the IDAR graph, which I tried hard to avoid.

Before we decide that we're done, let's think about the sizes of these objects. By "size", I'm referring to how much code needs to be in them. An object that is large might be a candidate for either splitting or turning into a subsystem. To estimate size, we should look at all the operations (capabilities) of an object, and estimate how much code will be required to implement them. Looking these over, we realize that the *Menu* and *Card* objects will probably be large. *Menu* is responsible for a menu system which is probably multi-level, which must be navigated with the arrow buttons, and which allows values to be changed. If the method-level design for *Menu* becomes too complex, as seems likely, we'll need to split it.

The other large object is *Card*, which is responsible for creating and updating a file-system. Admittedly, it is a specialized file-system, so some complicating operations are absent. But it's a file-system nonetheless, and I'm concerned that this complexity may be too much for one object. Once again, let's design its methods to get a better idea of how much complexity we are facing. If it's too much, nobody will complain if we split *Card*.

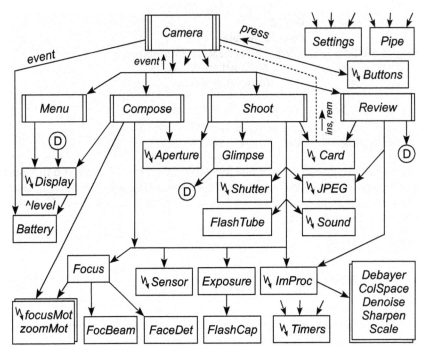

Figure 12.4: Digital camera: final design

Figure 12.4 shows our final design. It's worth reflecting on the fact that only a couple of hours of work have produced a design that covers a large program, and yet which shows enough detail to identify which objects contain ISRs. Somebody unfamiliar with the design would need only a few minutes to learn where everything is done in this camera, so he could quickly identify where a bug might be, or what would need to change to add a new feature. Imagine what it would be like if this design were expressed as a UML spaghetti-diagram like Figure 1.3 on page 5. Such a mess would be useless, and I've seen ample examples of such useless diagrams.

12.8   Designing Objects

As mentioned above, the *Menu* and *Card* objects might be large enough to be worth splitting. We will now design those objects at the method-level to assess their complexity before deciding whether to split them.

12.8.1   'Menu' Object

The role-statement of the *Menu* object is "performs all menu operations." The items in the menu are shown below:

Exit Menu	
Exposure Shift	Numeric adjustment (f-stops)
White Balance	Normal/Daylight/Tungsten/Shade
Metering	Smart/Center weighted/Average
ISO Speed	100/200/400/800/1600/3200
Face Detection	On/Off
Color	Color/Grayscale
Resolution	18Mp/12Mp/8.3Mp/5.8Mp/4Mp
Compression	High/Medium/Low/None(raw)
Sharpening	High/Normal/Low/None
Sound	On/Off
Auto Power-off	On/Off
Date/Time	Screen to set these
Reset Settings	Are you sure? (Y/N)

Remember that both *Camera* and *Menu* have their own threads, and that button presses are passed from *Camera* into the *Menu* object. To accept those button presses, we can define a *press* method within *Menu*, which accepts a *buttonNum* parameter, as shown in the code below.

```
void Menu::press (int buttonNum) {
    button = buttonNum;
    buttonSem.release();
}
```

In this code, the *press* method saves the button number in a member field, and then releases a semaphore to wake up the thread in *Menu*.

To enter menu mode, *Camera* can call the *press* method, passing it the button number for the "menu" button, informing *Menu* that the menu is now active. When the user selects Exit Menu item on the display, the *Menu* will send a *done* notice back to *Camera*.

While in menu mode, the items on the left side of the above list are displayed, and the user may scroll up and down to see all of them. One item is always highlighted. When the user presses the OK button, the choices for the highlighted item are displayed. The user selects a choice using the arrow buttons, and presses OK. Exceptions are Exposure Shift and Date/Time in which numbers are changed using the arrow buttons instead of distinct choices being listed and selected.

How do you suggest we design this menu object? The *press* method is done. I can think of two approaches for the menu code itself: the state-machine or subroutine approach. Both are described below.

State-Machine Approach The first approach is to use a main loop in the main method which waits for a button press. When it receives a button press (i.e., the *buttonSem* semaphore was released by the *press* method), it calls a subordinate method based on which menu is active. That method would never block, but would update the display and return to the main loop which waits for the next button press. This is the state-machine approach, because the main menu and subordinate methods must remember the state they're in so they'll know what to do when another button press arrives. Listing 12.1 is fragment of code showing the main loop.

```
int (*stateHandler)(int button);
void Menu::mainLooper () {
    ... some set-up code ...

    while (true) {
        buttonSem.wait();
        result = stateHandler(button);
        switch (result) {
            case RES_SUBMENU_DONE:
                ... change stateHandler for main menu ...
                break;
            case RES_ALLDONE:
                Camera::menuIsDone(); // tell Camera we're done
                break;
        }
    }
}
```

Listing 12.1: Main loop for state-machine approach

The advantage of the state-machine approach is that the thread only blocks in one place, so it can pre-filter button presses, and perhaps do other things. The disadvantages are (1) the states of all items must be kept in member fields instead of on the stack, and (2) the code is more dispersed and less clear because subordinate methods are not allowed to use loops or block.

Subroutine Approach The other technique is the subroutine approach. We will write a method corresponding to each item in the menu, and unlike the state-machine approach, that method will not return until the user presses the OK button. That is, each subordinate method blocks the thread while its display is active. Listing 12.2 is fragment of code illustrating this approach.

This code fragment shows one of the subordinate methods (*metering*) to illustrate how it blocks the thread using a call to buttonSem.wait(), and then executes a switch based on which button was pressed.

The advantages of the subroutine approach are that the code is easy to write and clearer, and that state variables are local to the methods. The disadvantage is that having a subordinate block the thread means that button presses cannot be pre-filtered and the thread can do nothing else.

```
void Menu::mainMenu () {
    int entryNum;
    while (true) { // infinite loop
        ... update the display ...
        buttonSem.wait();
        switch (button) {
            case B_UPARROW, B_DOWNARROW:
                ... update entryNum ...
                break;
            case OK:
                switch (entryNum) {
                    case EN_EXP_SHIFT: expShift(); break;
                    case EN_WHITE_BAL: whiteBal(); break;
                    case EN_METERING: metering(); break;
                    ... and more ...
                }
                break;
        }
    }
}

void Menu::metering () { // subordinate to mainMenu
    bool done = false;
    int meterVal = Settings::getMeterVal();
    while (! done) {
        ... update the display ...
        buttonSem.wait(); // thread is blocked here
        switch (button) {
            case B_UPARROW:
                meterVal -= 1;
                if (meterVal < 0) meterVal = MAX_METER_VAL;
                break;
            case B_DOWNARROW:
                meterVal += 1;
                if (meterVal > MAX_METER_VAL) meterVal = 0;
                break;
            case B_OK:
                Settings::setMeterVal(meterVal);
                done = true;
        }
    }
}
```

Listing 12.2: Subroutine approach

Because this thread needs to do nothing else, blocking it in a subordinate won't prevent other things from being done. And switch statements (which we need anyway) will filter button presses, so I think the benefits of the subroutine approach outweigh the state-machine approach. Hence, we'll use the subroutine approach.

The design is straightforward. We'll have a *mainMenu* method which contains the top-level loop for the thread. It calls a subordinate method for each of the items in the menu. That subordinate is responsible for everything in its menu item.

Figure 12.5 shows our design of the *Menu* object using the subroutine approach.

I would say that this object is not complex enough to split. Furthermore, even if we wanted to split it, where would we do so? We could make each menu item a separate object, but that would be overkill because we would get 14 tiny objects in place of this single bigger one. Even if this object climbs to a few thousand lines of

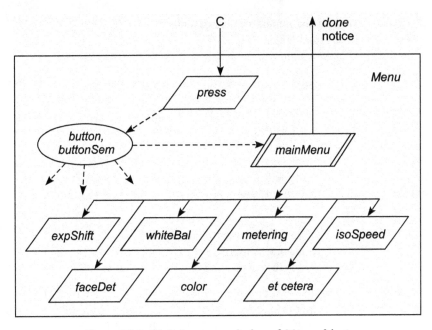

Figure 12.5: Digital camera: design of *Menu* object

code, keeping it as one object is still not a problem. The reason is that it's easier for a person to learn the contents of one substantial file by scrolling through it, than it is to learn the same amount of code by hunting through 14 little files. Many developers don't realize that breaking up a medium size file (containing a few thousand lines) into small files reduces understandability. Furthermore, if classes are small, I suggest grouping several classes commanded by one superior into one file. This technique of avoiding small files makes a design more learnable.

12.8.2 'Card' Object

When we reviewed the final IDAR graph, we thought that the *Card* object might be large enough to justify splitting. To determine that, we'll need to design it.

The *Card* object supports a file system on the memory card. The format of the file system is known as FAT, which stands for "file allocation table", signifying an important part of its data-structure. The large memory on the card is divided into pieces called "clusters", and the FAT contains a one-to-one map of these clusters, one FAT-entry per cluster. Each FAT-entry contains the location of the next cluster in the chain of clusters for the file, so the FAT-entries for a file are a linked list.

We can design the *Card* object either top-down or bottom-up. As usual, we'll do both. The top level is its public methods, which are:

folRead	Reads the contents (filenames) of a folder.
folWrite	Creates a new folder.
folEnum	Steps through files in a folder.
fileOpen	Opens a file for reading or writing.

fileClose   Flushes any buffers and closes a file.
fileRead   Reads from a file.
fileWrite   Writes to a file.

The *fileRead* and *fileWrite* methods will need to accept arbitrary buffer-sizes in their interfaces, but they are forced to work with a block-structured device underneath. To do that, they will need a buffer. We will add a private field named *buffer*.

Our design needs to transform calls to these public methods into operations on the electronics (registers in the ASIC) that control the card. The bottom-level methods will perform those electronics operations. After reading the detailed description of the card-related registers in the ASIC, and the operations they offer us, it's clear that we can create the following bottom-level methods to give us access to the "bare metal" electronics:

elecControl   Miscellaneous control functions.
elecReadBlocks   Reads one or more blocks of memory.
elecWriteBlocks   Writes to one or more blocks of memory.

That gives us the top-level and bottom-level methods. But it's too much of a stretch to go directly from the file-level public methods to the bottom-level electronics methods. What can we put between them to bridge the gap?

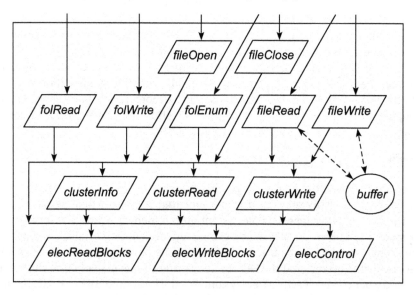

Figure 12.6: Digital camera: design of *Card* object

This is the most difficult part of any design. After thinking about the structure of the FAT-based file system, we notice that the prominent feature of this system is the parallel arrays of FAT entries and the clusters themselves. That suggests adding some methods which know about the FAT, and can read and write both the entries in the FAT and their corresponding data-clusters. Here are the detailed descriptions of these new methods:

- *clusterWrite* Its input is a list of data-blocks (to be written consecutively), each being the size of one cluster. This method (1) locates free clusters by searching the FAT, (2) writes the passed-in data-blocks to them, and (3) updates their corresponding entries in the FAT, forming a linked list.

- *clusterRead* Its input is a starting cluster-number. It reads a specified number of clusters which it locates by traversing their linked list in the FAT. The sequence of reads terminates early if the final cluster is encountered.

- *clusterInfo* Returns information about a specific cluster.

At this point, I think we've bridged the gap nicely. Figure 12.6 shows the design of the *Card* object. You'll immediately notice that calls are grouped in rails in this graph, so that you can only see calls between rails, but *not* the individual methods being called. That's deliberate. The individual calls are not particularly informative. What's more important is the layering in this design, and the interactions between layers. By grouping the calls into layers, we are saying that the public methods, for example, call many methods in the cluster layer.

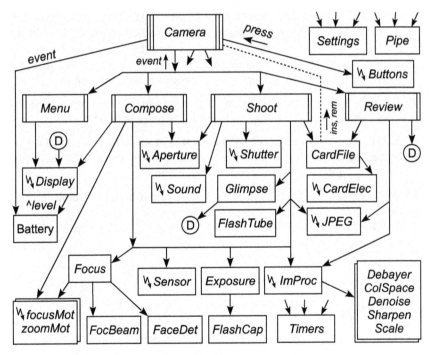

Figure 12.7: Digital camera: final design after splitting *Card*

Splitting?

Now that we have a method-level design, what do you think about splitting this object? I'd say that the code for this object will be large enough to make it a borderline case for splitting. So let's split it and see what happens.

Where would you split it? The object's design consists of three layers of methods (public, cluster, electronics), giving us two obvious divisions for a split: either between the public and cluster layers, or between the cluster and electronics layers. I'll split it between the cluster and electronics layers, but I don't have a strong reason for doing so. The interface into the electronics layer is a little simpler than the interface into the cluster layer. But the other split might be as good or better. It's hard to tell.

I won't show this *Card* design without the electronics layer, because the change is obvious. But splitting the *Card* into two pieces affects the main IDAR graph, so let's update that. I'll name the split objects *CardFile* and *CardElec*. Figure 12.7 shows our new final design.

12.9   Exercises

1. How would you modify this design to show the number of remaining shots on the card? Keep in mind that the sizes of JPEG files varies based on how much compression is being achieved, so you cannot simply divide the free space on the card by the size of a file.

2. The IDAR graph for the camera is large and crowded, which suggests that we should consider breaking off piece(s) of it into subsystems. The difficulty of course is deciding what the subsystems should be. A prospective subsystem should be large enough to significantly simplify the graph, but not so large that there's little graph remaining. What subsystems would you break off?

3. All modern digital cameras can record and playback video (with audio). How would you modify this design to incorporate these features?

4. As it is, the design causes the camera to stay in shooting mode until the image processing and writing to card are done. How would you modify this design to allow the camera to re-enter compose mode sooner?

5. *FlashTube* and *FlashCap* are separate objects, but both control aspects of the flash. What is your opinion about the idea of creating a new *Flash* object which handles all aspects of the flash? Both *FlashTube* and *FlashCap* would be commanded only by *Flash*.

6. Instead of creating a new superior over them as suggested above, would it be better to combine *FlashTube* and *FlashCap* into one object named *Flash*?

7. Most objects in this design are low-level in that they directly control hardware. *Focus* and *Exposure* are also rather low-level because they provide hardware-centric services. Some developers have proposed that all such hardware-related objects be placed into a single *HAL* subsystem. "HAL" stands for "Hardware Abstraction Layer", and it would serve as a façade for all hardware-access. Do you think this proposal improves the design?

8. All digital cameras can pre-fire the flash a few times to cause peoples' pupils to contract, reducing red-eye. How would adding this feature affect the design?

Chapter 13

Home Heating/Cooling System

— move to California instead

13.1 Background

The applications described so far in Part II run on 32-bit or 64-bit processors. One may ask the reasonable question of whether the IDAR method is suitable for small systems. To demonstrate its suitability, this chapter shows the design of a substantial system running on an 8-bit microcontroller. Such a processor is slow, and all resources are severely limited. Larger processors can tolerate wasteful design methods, but code written for an 8-bit microcontroller must be compact and efficient. This program uses no threads, and in fact has no operating system.

Booch [2] provides a complete design (and some source-code) of a home heating system which controls a furnace and per-room radiator-valves based on sensor-inputs. I have made the following modifications to his requirements: (1) The oil-fired furnace and radiators were replaced with a forced-air furnace fired by natural gas, (2) a compressor-based cooler was added, and (3) the time and day of week can be set on the main control panel. This system was designed from scratch using IDAR graphs, without consulting Booch's design. I'll admit that afterwards, I read Booch's design and made little changes to this one.

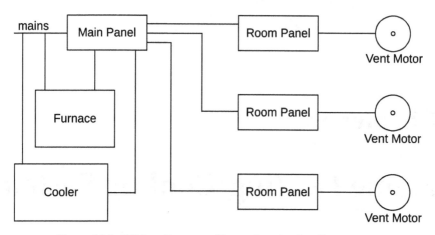

Figure 13.1: Wiring diagram of home heating/cooling system

13.2   Major Components

Figure 13.1 shows the wiring diagram for the home heating/cooling system. Lines in this diagram are wires running through attics and walls. The major pieces of hardware in this system are:

Furnace The furnace burns natural gas in a combustion chamber, which heats a heat-exchanger, through which cool air is blown. The outgoing warm air is then directed throughout the house by large pipes running through the attic. These pipes supply warm air to vents in each room.

Cooler The cooler consists of two main pieces. An evaporator unit is attached to the top of the furnace, and in fact is part of the furnace assembly. When the furnace-blower is turned on, air is cooled as it is blown through the evaporator, and the outgoing cool air is then directed through the same pipes and vents. A compressor/condenser unit is typically located outside the house.

Room Panel Each room has a small control panel with a temperature dial on it, which is set to the desired temperature of the room.

Vent Motor Each room has an air-vent. Each vent has a motor which operates a damper which opens or closes the vent. Once a room has reached its desired temperature, its vent is closed. To reduce the number of wires strung around the house, each vent motor is connected to its corresponding room panel instead of the main panel.

Main Panel The main panel has a small time-display, and some switches and buttons described below. It controls the entire system.

13.3   Electronic Components

The 8-bit microcontroller that you are programming is located on the circuit board for the main panel. The software is able to control the entire system using the following electronic components:

CPU Your software runs on this microcontroller.

Gas Switch This power transistor may be turned on or off using a GPIO (general purpose input/output) line on the CPU. Because this transistor is either on or off, it is being used as an electronic switch. Electrical engineers refer to it simply as a "switch". This particular switch controls the gas-valve in the furnace. There is a substantial time-lag between turning the gas on or off, and the blower turning on or off, as described below.

Cooler Switch This transistor is also controlled with a GPIO, and turns the cooler and blower on or off in tandem. Both devices start and stop immediately.

Vent Switches Each vent motor is controlled by two electronic switches (for opening and closing) located on the room panel's circuit board. The damper requires five seconds to change positions between open or closed.

Timer A timer is part of the microcontroller, and causes a repetitive interrupt with a programmable period. This timer will run the entire program.

NVM Nonvolatile memory holds its values when power fails. We will use it to store living-pattern data described later.

User Switches There are three mechanical switches on the main panel labeled "Heater On/Off", "Cooler On/Off", and "Energy-Saver On/Off". When both the heater and cooler switches are set to "off", the system is disabled. If both are set to "on", the house will be kept temperate regardless of the season. These switches are connected to GPIO lines which are used as inputs. In addition, each room panel has a "Living Pattern On/Off" switch which enables the Living Pattern feature for that room, described below.

LEDs The main panel has three green LEDs (light emitting diodes). The "ready" LED indicates that the system has power and has not malfunctioned. The other two indicate whether the heater or cooler is active, respectively. These LEDs are driven by GPIO lines.

LCD The LCD (liquid crystal display) displays the current time and day of week. The microcontroller has a built-in serial interface which controls the LCD. As an aside, note that the phrase "LCD display" is saying "liquid crystal display display". You should likewise avoid saying "USB bus".

Buttons A few buttons are used to change the time. To reduce cost slightly, the buttons and switches do *not* interrupt the microcontroller. Thus, you must poll them by reading their GPIO lines.

Serial I/O Each room panel is connected to the main panel via a low-speed serial I/O. In fact, there are only three wires connected to each room panel: power, ground, and serial. You must read devices on a room panel and control its vent motor by sending commands over its serial wire.

Serial MUX MUX is an abbreviation for "multiplexor", and this MUX selects which serial wire the microcontroller will use. Before talking to a room panel, you must first set this MUX to connect the serial I/O to the serial wire going to that room panel.

Desired Temp The temperature setting on a room panel is actually a variable resistor, which is digitized using an A2D (analog to digital converter). You can read the value of that A2D using a serial command.

Actual Temp You need to know the current air-temperature of each room. The temperature in a room is converted using an A2D, which you can read using a serial command.

Occupied IR The room panel also contains an IR (infra-red) sensor which tells you whether the room is occupied. You can read it using (did you guess?) a serial command.

Operation of the furnace needs more explanation. You can turn its gas-valve on or off at will using the gas switch. However, the blower motor is *not* controlled by this switch. Rather, it is controlled by a temperature sensor attached to the heat-exchanger. The blower is always on when the heat-exchanger's temperature is above a threshold, and it's always off when the temperature is below it. Thus, you don't have direct control over the blower. It's important to know that, after turning on the gas, the heat-exchanger takes close to a minute to become hot enough for the blower to turn on. Likewise, after turning off the gas, it takes close to a minute for the heat-exchanger to become cool enough to turn the blower off.

The cooler does not have such a time-lag. When you turn on the cooler, the blower starts running immediately, and the air leaving the furnace assembly becomes cool within a few seconds, which is a short enough time-lag to be ignored.

13.4   Requirements

After booting and initializing the system, keep the ready LED turned on as long as everything is running fine. If you observe a malfunction, such as temperature not changing appropriately in a room when heating or cooling, then the ready LED should flash to indicate a fault.

13.4.1   Heating and Cooling

The heating and cooling functions are enabled and disabled by the "Heater On/Off" and "Cooler On/Off" switches on the main panel. If the heater is enabled, then when the temperature of any room is a certain amount below its desired temperature (as set on its room panel), the heater will turn on, and the vents for all rooms that are below their desired temperatures will be opened. Also, the LED for "Heating" will light on the main panel. The cooler works analogously.

When both switches are set to "on", then every room in the house will be kept near its desired temperature, regardless of season. Oddly, doing so can require that both the heater and cooler be used within minutes of each other. For example, a south-facing room on the second floor may need to be cooled, while a north-facing room on the first floor may need to be heated. This system will cool the too-warm rooms while leaving the vents closed to the other rooms. Then it will heat the too-cool rooms, leaving the vents for the now-temperate rooms closed.

If the energy-saver switch is set to "on", the "certain amount" of temperature tolerance mentioned above is increased. The effect is that rooms are allowed to become colder before they'll be warmed, and likewise they are allowed to become warmer before they'll be cooled.

When running the heater or cooler, the vent will be closed for each room that reaches its desired temperature. When the final vent would have been closed, the heater or cooler is turned off instead.

Running the blower motor with all vents closed puts excessive stress on the motor, as well as wasting energy, so that is never done. Unfortunately, you don't have direct control over the blower motor when heating. In fact, you don't even know when the blower is running because there is no wire from the furnace to indicate this. Hence, you need to monitor temperature-rise to predict when the desired temperature will be reached, and turn off the gas about one minute prior to this predicted time (and keep the vent open).

13.4.2 Living Pattern

"Living Pattern" is a patented feature of this heating/cooling system, and the company constantly advertises it. Some people have irregular schedules, and this feature has questionable benefit for them, but it is worthwhile for everybody else. Marketing trumpets it as benefiting everyone in order to boost sales. You are required to implement it. Here is what it does.

Living Pattern allows a room to stay farther above or below its desired temperature if it expects the room to be unoccupied. The system restores normal temperature-tolerances for a room that it expects to be occupied soon, which has the effect of preheating or precooling that room. Thus, the Living Pattern feature saves energy, and it becomes ever more worthwhile as energy-costs rise.

Each room panel has an IR sensor indicating whether the room is occupied. The software records occupancy every 15 minutes, on a one week cycle. It can store four weeks' worth of occupancy data. For example, if today is Tuesday, Living Pattern has the prior four Tuesdays stored to use to predict whether the room will be occupied for each 15-minute period today. The prediction is based on how consistently the room was occupied or unoccupied. The system also examines stored data for the next and prior 15 minutes to improve the quality of its predictions.

This feature works well for those with regular schedules. Due to the weekly cycle, regular changes in schedule on weekends are easily accommodated. But for those with erratic schedules, a switch on each room panel called "Living Pattern On/Off" allows this feature to be disabled.

The Living Pattern feature requires that the system know the day of week and time. Therefore, the main panel has an LCD which displays the day and time, and also has a few buttons allowing you to set them. Your software needs to respond to those buttons appropriately, as well as keeping track of the day and time.

Also, it would be a pity for a brief power-outage to lose the four weeks of living-pattern data. Hence, the main panel's circuit board contains an NVM in which you must back-up the data occasionally. The NVM becomes unreliable after many writes, so you should perform your back-up infrequently. Once a day is appropriate.

13.5   Starting the Design

Let's start by thinking about the implications of this microcontroller. It runs with no operating system. When power is applied, the processor executes the boot code which does a small amount of initialization and then jumps to the entry point of the program. From then on, the processor is all yours. Hence, we have only one thread of execution. There are interrupts for the timer and serial I/O, and no others. That means most things must be done by polling. Reading temperatures, monitoring button-presses, changes in switches, and anything else—all devices must be polled.

Let's make an architectural decision have the timer interrupt control and execute all the software. Buttons must be polled about 20 times per second to avoid missing quick presses, so we'll program the timer to interrupt at that rate. When the ISR (interrupt service routine) returns, the processor will go into sleep-mode, which consumes almost no power. By not running the processor constantly, this architecture has the advantage that the microcontroller could continue running off a battery for a long time should the main power be disrupted. Running off battery-power is not a requirement, but allowing this flexibility costs us nothing because it does not complicate the software. With no cost and a possible benefit, we might as well use the timer interrupt to provide the thread for everything.

Programming an ISR is similar to programming a GUI-based application. The only firm rule is, "Don't block." Because this microcontroller has no operating system, the code can't block. However, it could spend a long time in some loop waiting for an event to occur. Doing so in an ISR is poor programming practice.

Because the timer interrupt is the only thread, we can make a second architectural decision to make all notices riders—all will ride horseback-style on method-returns. The lack of threads and interrupts already eliminates asynchronous notices. The only kinds of notices remaining are riders and those called from commands. The second kind can be eliminated by polling for events instead. Thus, notices are riders by using method-returns of poll-commands.

There is one exception to the rule that all notices in this design are riders. The timer sends a periodic *tick* notice up to a controller object, and this notice is sent as an explicit call, and is not a rider.

Step 1 of the five-step design process in Section 5.4 (page 117) tells us to identify the obvious objects, which are the topmost and bottommost. For the topmost, we can create a *Comfort* object which provides overall control of the system. *Timer* will send *tick* notices up to *Comfort* 20 times per second. Only the buttons need to be polled at 20 times per second; the sensors can be polled less often. *Comfort* will count ticks and call its subordinates at the lower rate. This design will not specify what that lower rate is, but it will probably poll every one to five seconds.

For the bottom-level objects, we need only to look at the list of electronic devices and define objects for them. Here is my first list, showing you both the object names and their roles. I included the top-level objects discussed above.

Comfort	Controls the entire system.
Timer	Sends tick notices.
Leds	Controls the LEDs on the main panel.

Buttons	Reads the buttons on the main panel.
MainSwitches	Reads the switches on the main panel.
LCD	Changes the contents of the LCD.
SerialCmd	Sends a command over the serial wire, and gets the response.
NVM	Writes or reads data to/from the NVM.
PowerSwitches	Turns the furnace or gas-valve switch on or off.

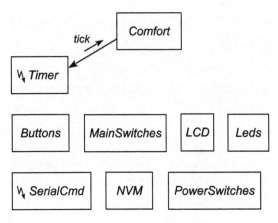

Figure 13.2: Obvious objects

Figure 13.2 shows these obvious objects as the beginnings of an IDAR graph. The only command shown is from *Comfort* to *Timer*. In this case, *Comfort* commands the *Timer* to initialize and start. The periodic tick notice from *Timer* to *Comfort* is also shown, but we haven't yet decided upon any other inter-object communications.

You will notice that some of the objects have plural names, such as *Leds*. These objects control several devices. For example, *Leds* controls several (three) LEDs. Traditional OOP would not have defined such objects. Rather, it would have defined a class to control one LED, and then it would have created three instances of that class, one for each LED. I chose not to do this in order to avoid creating trivial objects. The plural object *Leds* is already simple, and to break it up into three separate objects would have resulted in objects that were ludicrously trivial. But when over-subdividing in that manner, the structure of the program becomes more complex due to having multiple objects instead of one. Knowing that complexity is the enemy of software, we want to avoid the extra complexity that comes from excessive subdividing. There is a trade-off between complexity inside an object versus complexity outside it. In our examples of LEDs and switches, having fewer objects, each of which handles multiple items, results in the least overall complexity.

Interestingly, we have already made significant design decisions even with the obvious objects. We must keep in mind that our CPU is an 8-bit microcontroller, so simplicity is paramount. With such a processor, we must avoid any mistake that adds unnecessary complexity, and excessive subdividing is a common mistake.

Step 2 is to define unobvious objects between the top- and bottom-level objects, and connect everything with command lines.

13.6   First Trial Design

Chapter 5 tells us that we can find unobvious objects by looking at operations top-down, considering what needs to be done bottom-up, and by looking at nouns and verbs in the requirements. Let's start with the requirements.

Some important nouns (and potential objects) are the main panel and the room panels. Let's create a *MainPanel* object which handles setting the time, and the various buttons, switches, and LEDs on the main panel. We can also create a *RoomPanel* class which will have one instance for each room, and which performs the room panel operations, including controlling the vent motors. We just used the word "room". That's another plausible object. Let's create a *Room* class. Each instance of it handles all operations and measurements done on a room.

At this point, we have enough objects that we can connect them together into our first IDAR graph. Here are the commands:

- *MainPanel* commands *MainSwitches, Buttons, Leds,* and *LCD.* These are the electronic components attached to the main panel. *MainPanel* is responsible for setting the time, which means handling the time-setting button-presses and updating the LCD. This time-setting will consume the greatest amount of code in the *MainPanel* object.

- *Comfort* commands *PowerSwitches* which turns the furnace and cooler on and off. It also commands the instances of *Room* to perform the various per-room functions (opening and closing vents, measuring temperatures, etc.).

- Each instance of *Room* will control an instance of *RoomPanel*.

- Each instance of *RoomPanel* must command *SerialCmd* in order to communicate with the physical room panel.

Figure 13.3 shows our trial design. If you look at the command line from *Room* to *RoomPanel*, you'll see that each end is labeled "1". These numbers indicate multiplicity in the same manner as UML diagrams. In our case, they indicate that each instance of *Room* contains one instance of *RoomPanel*, and that each instance of *RoomPanel* is owned by one instance of *Room*. Thus, a pair of "1" labels indicates a one-to-one relationship between instances of the two classes.

13.7   Refining the Design

At this point in the design, it's helpful to ponder the IDAR graph for a while, thinking of all operations and commands which each object will perform. During this process, we become suspicious of the *RoomPanel* class. To see why, let's list the commands that the *Room* class accepts:

openVent	Opens the vent.
closeVent	Closes the vent.
getStatus	Returns status listed below.

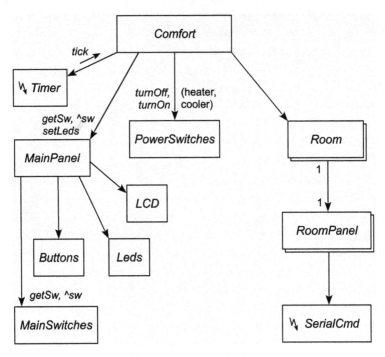

Figure 13.3: Trial design

The information returned by the *getStatus* command consists of:

ventOpen	Is the vent currently open?
curTemp	Current temperature
desTemp	Desired temperature

Now, ask yourself what commands the *RoomPanel* class accepts, and what information it returns. Both are the same. In effect, the *RoomPanel* class represents the room. But that is the purpose of the *Room* class. So the *RoomPanel* class is redundant and should be removed.

Step 3 in the five-step process of design described in Section 5.4 (page 117) tells us to double-check our design by rereading the requirements and hand-executing it. When doing so, we realize that we have not yet added the feature that marketing loves to promote—Living Pattern. The Living Pattern feature requires that some data be maintained on a per-room basis. That tells us that we could add a *LivingPattern* class which has one instance per room. We also note from the description that it should back up its data to nonvolatile memory on occasion as protection against disruptions in power. Doing so requires that *LivingPattern* command the *NVM* object, which we somehow omitted in the trial design.

What should the interface into *LivingPattern* consist of? I can think of two commands. The first command would be *update*, which tells an instance of *LivingPattern* whether or not the room is occupied in the current 15 minute time-interval. *LivingPattern* will record this bit in its memory.

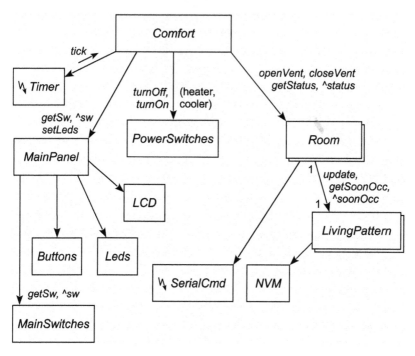

Figure 13.4: Refined design

The second command would be *getSoonOcc*, which returns (as a rider notice) a boolean indicating whether it expects the room to be occupied soon. "Soon" in this case would be enough time to preheat or precool the room, and is probably 15 or 30 minutes. The implementation of this command is not trivial because the prediction must be based on whether the room was occupied in this time-interval over the prior four weeks, and is allowed to be influenced by the data from adjacent time-intervals. Figure 13.4 shows our refined design.

13.8   Final Design

Going over the five-step design process once more, everything looks fine. But as I hand-executed all operations (Step 3), it occurred to me that the *MainPanel* object knows the current day and time, and that the instances of *LivingPattern* need this information. Those objects are far apart on the IDAR graph. So how can the day and time be communicated to the *LivingPattern* objects?

One way is to pass them through the normal command hierarchy. Doing so causes the day and time to be passed through the following objects: *MainPanel, Comfort, Room, LivingPattern*. We want to pass this data from *MainPanel* to *LivingPattern*, but it passes through two intermediaries. Do you remember what kind of coupling this is? Passing tramp data through one level can be tolerated, but two is becoming excessive, especially considering the high overhead of passing four bytes as a parameter (day, hours, minutes, seconds are one byte each).

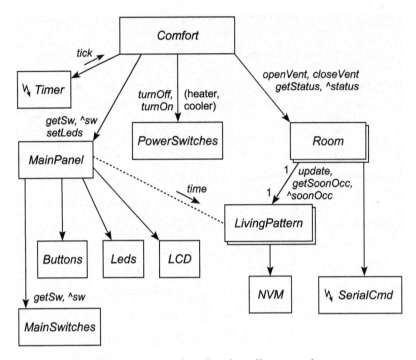

Figure 13.5: Passing time in a distant notice

Another way is to have *MainPanel* pass a *time* notice to *LivingPattern*. Doing so yields the IDAR graph shown in Figure 13.5. Seeing a notice streak sideways across much of the graph is disturbing. It's adding an unrelated dependency in *MainPanel*. The HD metric for this notice is 3, telling us that it's hopping across an uncomfortable amount of hierarchy and that we should attempt to remove it. Do you remember the HD metric? It's described in Section 4.4.1 on page 104.

I propose that the best solution to this problem is a global variable (gasp!). Doing so gives these two objects common coupling, which is low on the list of coupling-goodness. But this global is well-behaved because it has only one writer (*MainPanel*) and only one reader (*LivingPattern*). The problem with globals in general is that you can't tell what writes and reads them. But we can put this global on the IDAR graph, and thus anyone reading it will know what writes and reads it, solving that problem. Making it a global also means we don't need to pass a four-byte item as a parameter, which is clumsy on an 8-bit microcontroller.

There's another thing that disturbs me about this design. The *Comfort* object is doing more than I like. For example, to decide whether to start the heater or cooler, it must query every *Room* object about this. The design would be better if we were to push such tedium down a level below *Comfort*. I realized that an appropriate object between the *Comfort* and the *Room* objects would be *House*. The *House* object could tell *Comfort* whether the house needs heating or cooling, and could also set all the vents in the house to their proper positions. After making these changes, Figure 13.6 shows the final design of the home heating/cooling system.

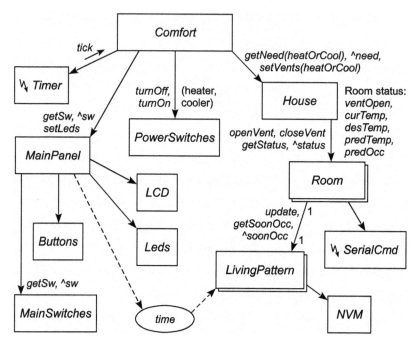

Figure 13.6: Final design of home heating/cooling system

I added more information about commands on the various lines. I also documented the information returned in rider notices (status). You are encouraged to put as much of this type of information on your IDAR graphs as possible without choking the graphs with text. Such information shows the communications among objects, which is the aspect of a design that is typically most difficult to learn.

This design is similar to the Drawing Application in that (1) the program has no thread, and (2) code is not allowed to block. The sophistication of applications possible under these severe constraints is surprising. I point this out because I see many designs that spawn threads profligately. Many threads are not necessary, and only serve to create timing problems that are difficult to debug. Keep the number of threads to a minimum.

One oddity about this design is that the fan-in of all objects is one. Most designs have a few objects with multiple superiors. This design happened to be a tree instead of a DAG.

As we should always do, I provide a list of objects and their roles below:

Comfort	Controls the entire system.
Timer	Sends tick notices.
Leds	Controls the LEDs on the main panel.
Buttons	Reads the buttons on the main panel.
MainSwitches	Reads the switches on the main panel.
LCD	Changes the contents of the LCD.
SerialCmd	Sends a command over the serial wire, and gets the response.
NVM	Writes or reads data to/from the NVM.

PowerSwitches	Turns the furnace or gas-valve switch on or off.
MainPanel	Sets time and handles other functions of main panel.
House	Monitors heating/cooling needs of the house.
Room	Monitors heating/cooling needs of rooms.
LivingPattern	Monitors living pattern and predicts occupancy.

13.9 A Little Code

At the beginning of this chapter, I raised the question of whether the IDAR method is suitable for an 8-bit microcontroller. To show you that it is, I provide a fragment of C++ code below for the heart of the *Comfort* object, which is the state-machine for the system. The *oneSecTick* method shown below is called once per second by the public *tick* notice located in *Comfort*.

```cpp
inline void changeState(uint8_t newState) {
    state = newState;
}

void Comfort::oneSecTick() {
    static uint8_t secDown;
    // Propagate the one-sec tick to our subordinates.
    MainPanel::oneSecTick();
    House::oneSecTick();

    // Check for a state-change.
    switch (state) {
    case ST_IDLE:
        bool coolEn = MainPanel::getSw(COOLER_SWITCH);
        if (coolEn && House::getNeed(COOL)) {
            House::startingAction(COOL);
            House::setVents(COOL);
            MainPanel::setLeds(LED_OK | LED_COOLER);
            PowerSwitches::turnOn(COOLER_POWER_SWITCH);
            changeState(ST_COOLING);
        }
        bool heatEn = MainPanel::getSw(HEATER_SWITCH);
        if (heatEn && House::getNeed(HEAT)) {
            House::startingAction(HEAT);
            House::setVents(HEAT);
            MainPanel::setLeds(LED_OK | LED_HEATER);
            PowerSwitches::turnOn(GAS_POWER_SWITCH);
            changeState(ST_HEATING);
        }
        break;
    case ST_COOLING:
        House::setVents(COOL);
        if (! House::getNeed(COOL)) {
            // Temperature has hit target in all rooms. Turn off cooler.
            PowerSwitches::turnOff(COOLER_POWER_SWITCH);
```

```
            House::finishedAction();
            MainPanel::setLeds(LED_OK);
            changeState(ST_IDLE);
        }
        break;
    case ST_HEATING:
        House::setVents(HEAT);
        if (! House::getPredNeed(HEAT)) {
            // Home predicts temp will soon hit target. Turn off gas.
            PowerSwitches::turnOff(GAS_POWER_SWITCH);
            changeState(ST_GAS_OFF);
            secDown = 50;  // yes, I know this should be a symbol
        }
        break;
    case ST_GAS_OFF:
        secDown -= 1;
        if (secDown == 0) {
            // It's been 50 seconds, so blower should be off by now.
            House::finishedAction();
            MainPanel::setLeds(LED_OK);
            changeState(ST_IDLE);
        }
        break;
    }  // end of switch
}  // end of oneSecTick
```

A high percentage of this code consists of method-calls because it's a top-level object. Lower level objects have a higher percentage of algorithmic code. But notice that all variables and parameters are 8 bits, and that there is *no* additional overhead due to this design being object-oriented, nor is there any additional overhead due to our use of the IDAR method. In particular, there is no use of function-pointers or virtual methods, so those two common sources of inefficiency are absent. The number of levels of method-calls is reasonable, because each level does something useful. If you wished, you could reduce the number of call-levels even more by using inline methods in objects such as *PowerSwitches*, *Buttons*, *Leds*, and *MainSwitches*. The code above will compile into efficient assembler language instructions.

13.10   Exercises

1. What's wrong with "LCD display"?

2. Did you notice that the final design shown in Figure 13.6 does not control the MUX? What object should control it? Would you recommend adding a *MUX* object? Why or why not?

3. Reviewers suggested that because all control in this program originates in the *Timer*, the *Timer* should be at the top of the hierarchy, sending *processTick* commands (not notices) down to *Comfort*. Would this design constitute a legal IDAR graph? Would it be a better design? Why or why not?

4. Some reviewers noticed that the *MainPanel* object does nothing with the values returned by *MainSwitches*. These switch values are tramp data passed up to *Comfort*. So it was suggested that *MainSwitches* be commanded directly by objects which need the values of those switches. For example, the heater and cooler switches are needed by *Comfort* and not *MainPanel*. So *Comfort* would command *MainSwitches* instead of *MainPanel*. The same suggestion applies to the LEDs: *MainPanel* doesn't set any of them itself, so other objects should command the *Leds* object directly. Do you agree with this suggestion? Why or why not?

5. This design does not account for the fact that opening or closing a vent takes five seconds. How would you change the design to account for this time?

6. A swamp cooler cools air by drawing it through wet excelsior. The water pump, which wets the excelsior, must be turned on 30 seconds before starting the blower, which is separate from the blower in the furnace. How would the design need to change to control a swamp cooler instead of a compressor-based cooler?

7. Each room panel has an IR sensor which detects whether the room is occupied. Somebody in marketing had the bright idea of using those sensors to make this heating/cooling system also function as a burglar alarm. A button would be added to the main panel to enable the alarm (indicating the house is not occupied). Entering a secret code using a few buttons would disable the alarm. Detection of an occupant would sound a siren. How would you change the design to accommodate this additional requirement?

Appendix A

Answers to Exercises

Chapter 2: Basics of OOP

1. A field is a variable located within a record or class. Yes, it can be public.

2. A type represents a pattern to be used for instances, and consumes no memory. An instance consumes memory.

3. An instance and an object are the same thing.

4. A record only contains fields. A class can also contain methods.

5. A class "contains" methods in the sense that the names of its methods are local to the class.

6. (b), the fields in the class. Methods (code) always exist in memory.

7. The syntax of the call of the method specifies which instance to use.

8. No, the sole private method cannot be called. That's not quite true; it can be called by a constructor or destructor, which you can learn about in a book about your programming language.

9. Message-passing is usually implemented as method-calls.

10. Additive inheritance creates a derived class by adding members to the base class. Polymorphic inheritance overrides methods in the base class with different ones in the derived class. Briefly, additive adds members, and polymorphic overrides methods.

11. Code employing composition is clearer than that using additive inheritance.

12. When not declared virtual: The *action* in *Base* in both calls.
    When virtual: The *action* in *Base* and *Derived* respectively.

13. Polymorphic inheritance is not feasible for this application because it replaces methods, whereas this application needs a way to map integers (command-IDs) into corresponding method-calls, which inheritance is incapable of doing.

14.
```
class Cooler {
    public:
        virtual void start() = 0;
        virtual void stop() = 0;
};

class SwampCooler : Cooler {
    public:
        virtual void start();
        virtual void stop();
    // other methods and fields as needed
};

class CompressorCooler : Cooler {
    public:
        virtual void start();
        virtual void stop();
    // other methods and fields as needed
};
```

Chapter 3: Core Concepts

1. A box usually represents an object or a static class.

2. The stacked rectangle notation is used for (1) multiple instances of a class, or (2) an interface which is implemented by several classes.

3. The Identify rule states that all public methods must be identified as commands and notices, and that a notice conveys needed information.

4. The Down rule, which states that commands go down in the graph.

5. A command can do anything, but is constrained to the hierarchy. A notice can be called from anywhere, but may only import or export needed information.

6. An import-style notice conveys information to the callee, whereas an export-style notice conveys it to the caller. A rider notice is information carried back to a caller via a method-return, whereas a bound or free notice supplies that information in a separate method. A bound notice follows a command-line, whereas a free notice doesn't.

7. The benefits of rider notices are greater simplicity, higher efficiency, reduced dependencies among objects, and ease of having a subordinate send notices to multiple superiors.

8. The rejection is incorrect. The *Intercom* object merely relays messages from a bigger boss without requiring that their recipient act upon them, which is acceptable. Refer to the Watcher pattern on page 192.

9. The role is poor, having low cohesion, because it combines the two unrelated actions of (1) verifying legality, and (2) sending notifications by email.

10. (1) The *PlayTrack* object does not need these notices to fulfill its role of playing a given track, violating the need-to-know constraint on notices given in the Identify rule, and (2) these notices are actually commands.

11. If the query-command is allowed to block, then the results of the query can be carried in a rider notice. Otherwise, a separate notice will be needed.

12. Triple vertical lines mean the object is active and contains a process.

13. The notice is acceptable only if the decompression is covert aid, and thus not in the notice's role.

14. Indirect commands make code difficult to learn because it's unclear which method will be called.

15. Requiring that the subman be a façade makes the subsystem independent of the other objects in the system.

16. Yes, this is a permissible way to provide pointers for subsequent notices sent into the subsystem. This technique does not add dependencies.

17. A parallelogram is never allowed in an IDAR graph because the phrase "IDAR graph" refers to an object-level IDAR graph (not method-level) which only shows objects, not individual methods within those objects.

18. Boxes are never nested in either kind of IDAR graph. Composition is represented in other ways.

19. The lightning-bolt would indicate that the method is an ISR.

20. The Role rule states that every object and public method shall have a brief description (role) which must be fulfilled exactly.

21. Not only does the Role rule require that you create roles, but roles enable you to gauge design-quality in terms of clarity, cohesion, and concealment.

22. The double lines mean that *macTask* is a thread (which we should have guessed by its name).

23. Blocking: Rider notices should be used because they are efficient and can easily handle multiple superiors. Non-blocking: Because there are multiple superiors, indirect notices should be used.

24. Aid-type actions are covert, and thus callers are unaware of them. Actions under the Role rule are overt, and callers rely on them.

25. Such a design is poor because *ProcessTimecards* does not need to use *getEmployeeSkills* in order to fulfill its role.

26. An imperative notice tells an object that it needs to do something.

27. An imperative notice from an object is allowable when relaying or echoing a command to its boss, or requesting help in fulfilling a command to itself.

Chapter 4: Gauging Goodness

1. The three criteria are clarity, cohesion, and concealment.

2. Clarity is how well a role communicates its actions. Cohesion is how closely those actions are related. Concealment is how well inner workings are hidden.

3. Vacuous roles use vague verbs. Trait-based roles rely on a shared trait. Managerial roles are controlling. Common roles use verbs.

4. Coupling is an interaction between methods.

5. The SPIED principles are: Minimize scopes of variables; avoid a flimsy promise; minimize indirection; minimize extent of coupling; and draw the dataflows.

6. Need is the degree that a superior needs its subordinate.

7. *HighSpeed* is trait-based, where the trait is "located in high-speed memory". Its clarity and cohesion are poor.

8. *Helpers* is trait-based, where the trait is the vague "helps objects", giving it no clarity and probably poor cohesion.

9. *Robot* has a common role with good clarity, but cohesion is poor because the role is a list of four actions with differing purposes. If its role were to be changed to "controls robot", it would be managerial with high cohesion.

10. The *emergencyShutdown* role is trait-based (temporal) with good clarity, but with no cohesion due to its unrelated actions.

11. *Employee* is managerial with high cohesion. Its clarity is probably medium or high because your guess of its actions will be close.

12. The role of *employeeInfo* is common with high cohesion and clarity because it performs one well-defined action.

13. *ItemMgr* is common with two complementary actions, giving it good cohesion and clarity.

14. The command is common with high clarity, but has poor cohesion due to its large number of actions that are weakly related.

15. The dataflows to/from the data-storage object were not drawn.

16. Your goal is to maximize the visibility of which methods are involved in each coupling.

17. Placing shared variables in a system-wide file violates the principle of minimizing scopes of shared variables.

18. The interposers violate the principle of minimizing extent of coupling.

19. The interposers exhibit tramp coupling (of calls).

20. Removing spikes violates the principle of not relying on a missing promise.

21. The two commands exhibit field coupling.

22. Making all methods virtual violates the principle of avoiding indirect calls.

23. The consorter architecture badly violates the principle of avoiding indirect actions. The code that I saw was very difficult to follow.

Chapter 5: How to Design

1. The two kinds of objects to look for are verbs and nouns.

2. Obvious objects are those on the top and bottom of the graph.

3. Unobvious objects can be found top-down, bottom-up, by white-box design, and by looking for nouns and verbs in the requirements document.

4. The five steps are: (1) find obvious objects, (2) find unobvious objects, (3) verify correctness and conformance to rules, (4) ponder improvements and simplifications, (5) iterate.

5. For a simple CSMA MAC, the *Schedule* object would not be needed, but the remainder of the design would be unchanged at the object-level.

6. The laser printer will need these bottom-level objects:
   USB—controls the USB I/O port.
   Image—creates a bitmap image to be printed.
   Fuser—controls the temperature of the fuser.
   MainMotor—runs the main motor that rotates the drum and pulls paper through the paper-path.
   DrumLED—controls the LED which expose the drum.
   PaperTray—picks paper, and detects any out-of-paper condition.
   ControlPanel—controls LEDs and monitors the buttons on the control-panel.

7. The printer will need a topmost *Printer* object to control its overall operation.

8. It is natural for *Printer* to have a thread. A middle-level object that prints a page should have its own thread. *Image* should have a thread so the next page can be input while a page is being printed. Button-presses can be detected by a timer-interrupt, so the *ControlPanel* will *not* need its own thread.

9. Figure A.1 is the IDAR graph for the laser printer.

10. Here are some suitable subordinate objects:

Assets	Stores all the assets.
AddAsset	Adds a new asset to the list.
DeleteAsset	Deletes an asset from the list.
ModifyAsset	Modifies an existing asset.

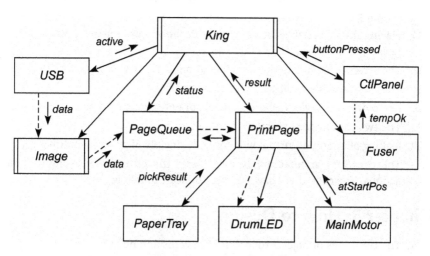

Figure A.1: Laser printer

Chapter 6: Good and Bad Practices

1. Temporal chaining occurs when an object, upon finishing its duty, commands another object to start the next action that needs to be done. It violates the

Role rule, and creates unrelated dependencies in the code, which makes maintenance more difficult.

2. Free notices do not parallel command arrows. They are allowed in designs, but they can add unrelated dependencies to objects, and might actually be hidden commands.

3. Cross-cutting concerns are acceptable unrelated dependencies.

4. The enemy of software is complexity because it lengthens schedules and reduces reliability.

5. Inheritance scatters related code around the program, makes learning a design more difficult for maintainers, and can be a security risk. Also, using inheritance inappropriately (perhaps due to peer-pressure) causes designs to be unnecessarily complex.

6. Inheritance can be avoided in most cases by coding changes directly into a class instead of inheriting from it, or by using a dispatcher.

7. Make a single-instance class static, meaning it will not be instantiated. Therefore, its methods are not called using an instance, and its fields are statically allocated. It simplifies code because an instance does not need to be created, managed, and passed around to users of the class. You don't need to remember to free it, eliminating a source of memory-leaks. Also, calling code runs a bit faster.

8. The Law of Readability is, "Vertical is valuable." It means that wasting vertical space on the monitor hurts readability. Opening curly braces should be put on the right sides of lines, and not on their own lines.

9. Your thinking should be service-oriented because each object provides a service. You should constantly ask yourself, "What services are needed here?"

10. A boss already has a dependency on its worker, so adding a downward bound notice will not add a dependency.

Chapter 7: Design Patterns

1. An adapter changes an interface; a façade groups interfaces together; a proxy is a "front" for an object that is remote in some way.

2. The Boss pattern is hard to avoid.

3. A Watcher should be used to monitor the USB and relay messages to a high-level object.

4. A Secretary should be used to store the messages (which contain chores), and release them when the system is idle and memory is available.

5. The Micromanaged Dataflow pattern removes unrelated dependences from processing-stages, but adds more complexity to their superior.

6. A Dispatcher would allow a single *turnOn* method in the dispatcher-object to be routed to one of three objects that knows how to operate each kind of circuit.

7. The Multiwait pattern will allow your object to wait on two message queues for the boss and watcher, with the boss's queue having higher priority.

8. A watcher forwards all messages (without storing them), whereas a secretary stores chores, and forwards them when they're ready to be performed.

9. The Resourceful Boss should be used to assign the log-files to one writer or the other.

10. The Peer-to-Peer Dataflow pattern could be used. Pull-style would be appropriate because we know that the data-source for the *Ethernet* object has buffering.

11. A bottom-level proxy for *Health* can be used which forwards notices to *Health* indirectly, eliminating the cycle of dependencies.

12. The collector program maintains a database and does little else, so the Database App pattern would be appropriate.

Chapter 8: Beyond Design

1. The two fundamental kinds of interactions are imperative and informative.

2. This is a case of an object being told to "Compute yourself." A solution is to create a separate static class containing the *characterize* method which returns a record containing the computed characteristics. In this case however, the record needs to be defined anyway, so it can be made an object that computes itself.

3. The operation is a pure action that belongs in its own separate class.

4. The three rats are (1) loss of useful hierarchy, (2) overstressing inheritance, and (3) being object-oriented instead of service-oriented.

5. A command hierarchy is easy to understand because each why-what-how triad reveals why the object exists (based on its superiors), what it does (based on its role and detailed description), and how it works (based on its subordinates).

6. Traditional OOP produces a network of collaborating objects, whereas the IDAR method produces a command-based hierarchy of services.

Chapter 9: Advice to Managers

1. The cost of interposers exceeds their benefit, so they should not be used. In practice, objects are ported in groups, not individually, so making objects more independent provides a negligible benefit in the future. The benefits to the present project are also small because objects should have clear interfaces making them easy to swap with unit-testers and alternative implementations. Everything the second employee said about high costs is true, so interposers offer high costs with low benefits, and should be rejected.

2. Disagree. Adding layers of abstraction makes objects simpler, but it also adds more interactions among objects, making the design more complex. Structure is a form of complexity which must be accounted for.

3. Fanatics make designs overcomplex.

4. A few have the curse of complexity due to their obsession with overusing some aspect of software. A few others have the gift of simplicity.

5. Software designed to be less flexible is simpler, which makes it easier to change, which by definition means it is more flexible.

6. Consider yourself fortunate if somebody on your project might have the gift of simplicity. You should thoroughly learn and evaluate the technical details, and if the lead is indeed creating excess complexity, take action to change the architecture. And carefully watch the lead's future work.

7. "It's complicated. It must be good." is about the worst response possible because it rewards those with the curse of complexity, and punishes those with the gift of simplicity. The result will be missed deadlines and lower quality. It also shows that the person making the comment has no understanding of the possibility and value of simplicity. A better response would be, "It's complicated. It might be bad."

8. Try having one subsystem designed using this method, and then evaluate the results. You can drop this method at any time, so you will not be taking a risk even on that subsystem.

9. Adopt the policy that if this method is blocking progress for some piece of software, then we'll stop using this method for that piece.

10. You could reply, "Your argument is based solely on tradition, instead of on the goal of meeting requirements with the shortest schedule. This approach shortens schedules, and that's why I use it." Such a person needs to be directed away from tradition and toward the goal.

Chapter 10: Pen Plotter

1. It was decided that it was permissible for most objects to block their callers, so their method-returns are rider notices.

2. 1 *IO* sends *char* notices to *VDL*.
   2 *VDL* parses this "unload page" command.
   3 *VDL* commands *Load* to unload the page.
   4 *Load* commands *XYServo* to move move to center.
   5 *XYServo* returns a rider done-notice to *Load*.
   6 *Load* commands *WheelLift* to raise wheels.
   7 *WheelLift* returns a rider done-notice to *Load*.

3. The *Text* object is the top-object in a tree that only commands *Clip*, so the following would compose a reasonable subsystem: *Text*, *Xform*, *Char*, *Cubic*, *Font*.

4. *Ticker* could be changed to follow the Watcher pattern, and send its notices to *Plotter*, which would distribute them down the command hierarchy.

5. The *CarouselMotor* object would be replaced with a *CarouselSolenoid* object. Also, *Carousel* would need to command *XYServo*.

6. Removing *Plotter* would force *VDL* and *CtrlPanel* to exchange notices with each other regarding access. These notices would represent unrelated dependencies in their objects, which is a poor practice. Also, the code in *Plotter* probably handles power-up and health-monitoring chores, and there is no other suitable place for such code, giving us a second reason to keep *Plotter*.

Chapter 11: Drawing Application

1. Since *Items* needs to command *Handle* in order to paint the handles, the *Handle* object should be moved down to make it subordinate to *Items*.

2. *GUI* or a new subordinate object would need to display the choices of predefined symbols. When one is selected, its data can be deserialized from a table similar to reading a file.

3. Undo is a cross-cutting concern. A separate *ChgList* would store the recent change-history. *Items* would command *ChgList* for every change made.

4. In order to prevent the data from changing while saving, the page would need to be rendered as a bitmap first. This could done by having *JPEG* command *Items*. *JPEG* could then use a thread for the JPEG-conversion and file-writes. This thread could be inside the *JPEG* object, or could be subordinate to *JPEG*. The thread would send periodic progress-notices to *GUI* so it could update a progress-bar.

5. Making *Selection* subordinate to *Items* would create a few tramp methods in *Items* which pass down selection-requests. This change would also cause *Handle* to move down in the hierarchy because *Selection* commands it. In essence, this change would treat selection-handles like the guides: As pseudo-items that *Items* would paint in addition to the actual items. One would need to take care that these pseudo-items are *not* painted for printing and saving to pixel-oriented files. This proposed change would probably work well.

Chapter 12: Digital Camera

1. To the *CardFile* object, add a method which predicts the number of remaining pictures. This objects knows the sizes of recent files, so it can predict remaining shots based on the average size of recent pictures.

2. Making *Focus* a subsystem would remove four objects from the IDAR graph. There are a couple of other places that would remove only two objects.

3. I would add *ShootVideo* and *PlayVideo* objects under *Camera*, alongside *Shoot* and *Review*. *Focus* and *exposure* would need to be modified to operate on the fly.

4. Put a thread in *ImProc* to allow it to process a picture even when the camera is in compose mode. When the shutter button is depressed, *Camera* or *Shoot* must refuse to shoot if *ImProc* says that it's busy.

5. A new *Flash* object would not benefit the camera, as it would merely serve as a façade which relays calls down to *FlashTube* and *FlashCap*.

6. Combining *FlashTube* and *FlashCap* into a single *Flash* object has more merit than the prior idea. The *Flash* class would still have a small amount of source-code, but clarity might improve because the quantity of overhead-structure in the design would be smaller.

7. The IDAR graph is complex mostly due to the many hardware-centric objects scattered about, so this proposal has merit. The proposal would make the higher-level design clear, while not obscuring the low-level design. Also, the proposed *HAL* object would be trait-based with decent clarity. Overall, I think this proposal is a good one.

8. *Shoot* already commands *FlashTube*, so adding red-eye reduction would require adding a new private method inside *Shoot* that would fire the flash a few times before proceeding with the exposure. No change would be needed to the design at the object-level.

Chapter 13: Home Heating/Cooling System

1. When the acronym is expanded, the phrase becomes "liquid crystal display display", which is redundant and repeats itself.

2. The *SerialCmd* object should set the MUX before sending a command. Changing the MUX only requires one or two lines of code, and it's only done by *SerialCmd*, so there is no benefit to making it a separate object.

3. Putting *Timer* at the top would be poor design. Do you remember the *need* criterion? In this case, *Timer* could fulfill its role of "send tick messages" with no subordinates, showing that this design fails the *need* criterion.

4. Having other objects command *MainSwitches* and *Leds* directly could improve the design because it eliminates tramp coupling. But we should first weigh the fact that those other objects will now have more detailed knowledge of the rest of the system.

5. Each instance of *Room* should remember (in an instance variable) that the vent's motor is running. After five seconds, it should turn the motor off. The *oneSecTick* command can be passed down to it, giving the code the time-base it needs.

6. Two more power switches would be needed for the swamp cooler's pump and blower motors. *Comfort* would need to add a "wetting" state to its state-machine.

7. The changes needed for a burglar alarm are small, and all these changes could be implemented within the *MainPanel* object. Also, *MainPanel* would need to command *PowerSwitches* to control the (new) switch that sounds the siren.

Bibliography

[1] Kent Beck, Cynthia Andres, *Extreme Programming Explained: Embrace Change*, 2nd ed., Addison-Wesley, Boston, MA, 2004.

[2] Grady Booch, *Object Oriented Design with Applications*, Benjamin/Cummings, Redwood City, CA, 1991, pp 223-279.

[3] Timothy Boronczyk, *What's Wrong with OOP*, http://zaemis.blogspot.com/2009/06/whats-wrong-with-oop.html, 2009.

[4] Peter Coad, Edward Yourdon, *Object-Oriented Design*, Prentice-Hall, 1991, pg 134.

[5] Robert Dexter, private communication.

[6] Edsger W. Dijkstra, "The Humble Programmer", 1972 Turing Award Lecture, *Communications of the ACM*, 15(10), 1972, pp 859-866.

[7] Richard Fairley, *Software Engineering Concepts*, McGraw Hill, New York, 1985, pp 170-171.

[8] Martin Fowler, Kent Beck, John Brant, Willian Opdyke, Don Roberts, *Refactoring: Improving the Design of Existing Code*, Addison-Wesley Professional, 1999.

[9] Martin Fowler, *Inversion of Control Containers and the Dependency Injection Pattern*, http://www.martinfowler.com/articles/injection.html, Jan. 2004.

[10] Erich Gamma, Richard Helm, Ralph Johnson, and John Vlissides, *Design Patterns: Elements of Reusable Object-Oriented Software*, Addison-Wesley, Boston, MA, 1995.

[11] Matt Gatrell, Steve Counsell, *Size, Inheritance, Change and Fault-proneness in C# software*", Journal of Object Technology, Volume 9, no. 5 (September 2010), pp. 29-54, doi:10.5381/jot.2010.9.5.a2.

[12] Ibid., pg 31.

[13] Cecilia Haskins (ed), *Systems Engineering Handbook*, INCOSE-TP-2003-002-03.2, January 2010, pg 10.

[14] Ronald S. Hansell, *Study of Collector-Distributor Roads*, Publication FHWA/IN/JHRP-75/01. Joint Highway Research Project, Indiana Department of Transportation and Purdue University, West Lafayette, Indiana, 1975. doi: 10.5703/1288284313889.

[15] Ronald E. Jeffries, *You're NOT gonna need it!*, http://www.xprogramming.com/Practices/PracNotNeed.html, 1997.

[16] Do-While Jones (R. David Pogge), *The Story Behind the Breakfast Food Cooker*, http://www.scienceagainstevolution.info/dwj/toaster.htm

[17] Jean Labrosse, *Adopting C programming conventions*,
      http://www.eetimes.com/design/embedded/4215492/Adopting-C-
      programming-conventions, April, 2011.

[18] Susan Lammers, *Programmers at Work: Interviews with 19 Programmers Who
      Shaped the Computer Industry*, Tempus Books, 1989.

[19] Robert C. Martin, *Agile Software Development, Principles, Patterns, and
      Practices*, Prentice-Hall, 2002.

[20] Meilir Page-Jones, *Fundamentals of Object-Oriented Design in UML*,
      Addison-Wesley Professional, Boston, MA, 1999.

[21] Ibid., pg 227.

[22] Meilir Page-Jones, *The Practical Guide to Structured Systems Design*, 2nd ed.,
      Yourdon Press, 1988, pg 70.

[23] Ibid., pg 101.

[24] Ibid., pg 104.

[25] Ira Pohl, *Object-Oriented Programming Using C++*, 2nd ed., Addison-Wesley,
      Boston, MA, 1997, pg 391.

[26] Arthur J. Riel, *Object-Oriented Design Heuristics*, Addison-Wesley, Boston, MA,
      1996, pg 32.

[27] James Rumbaugh, Ivar Jacobson, and Grady Booch, *Unified Modeling Language
      Reference Manual*, 2nd ed., Addison-Wesley, Boston, MA, 2004.

[28] Charles M. Schulz, *It Was a Dark and Stormy Night, Snoopy*, Random House
      Publishing Group, New York, 2004.

[29] Robert C. Seacord, *Secure Coding in C and C++*, 2nd ed., Addison-Wesley, Boston,
      MA, 2013.

[30] Ian Sommerville, *Software Engineering*, 8th ed., Pearson Education Limited,
      Essex, England, 2007.

[31] Kim J. Vicente, *Cognitive Work Analysis*, Lawrence Erlbaum Associates, Mahwah,
      NJ, 1999, pp 163-177.

[32] David West, *Object Thinking*, Microsoft Press, Redmond, WA, 2004.

[33] Rebecca Wirfs-Brock and Alan McKean, *Object Design: Roles, Responsibilities,
      and Collaborations*, Addison-Wesley, Boston, MA, 2003, pp 109-147.

[34] Ibid., pg 150.

[35] Ibid., pg 179.

[36] Edward Yourdon and Larry L. Constantine, *Structured Design*, Prentice-Hall,
      1979, pp 25-28.

[37] Ibid., pp 171-174.

Index

www.ingramcontent.com/pod-product-compliance
Lightning Source LLC
Chambersburg PA
CBHW071401050326
40689CB00010B/1710